Getting Started with Tableau 2018.x

Get up and running with the new features of Tableau 2018 for impactful data visualization

Tristan Guillevin

BIRMINGHAM - MUMBAI

Getting Started with Tableau 2018.x

Commissioning Editor: Amey Varangaonkar
Acquisition Editor: Divya Poojari
Content Development Editor: Snehal Kolte
Technical Editor: Sayli Nikalje
Copy Editor: Safis Editing
Project Coordinator: Manthan Patel
Proofreader: Safis Editing
Indexer: Aishwarya Gangawane
Graphics: Jisha Chirayil
Production Coordinator: Shantanu Zagade

First published: September 2018

Production reference: 1280918

Published by Packt Publishing Ltd.
Livery Place
35 Livery Street
Birmingham
B3 2PB, UK.

ISBN 978-1-78883-868-9

`www.packt.com`

mapt.io

Mapt is an online digital library that gives you full access to over 5,000 books and videos, as well as industry leading tools to help you plan your personal development and advance your career. For more information, please visit our website.

Why subscribe?

- Spend less time learning and more time coding with practical eBooks and Videos from over 4,000 industry professionals
- Improve your learning with Skill Plans built especially for you
- Get a free eBook or video every month
- Mapt is fully searchable
- Copy and paste, print, and bookmark content

Packt.com

Did you know that Packt offers eBook versions of every book published, with PDF and ePub files available? You can upgrade to the eBook version at www.packt.com and as a print book customer, you are entitled to a discount on the eBook copy. Get in touch with us at customercare@packtpub.com for more details.

At www.packt.com, you can also read a collection of free technical articles, sign up for a range of free newsletters, and receive exclusive discounts and offers on Packt books and eBooks.

Contributors

About the author

Tristan Guillevin is a true data lover who likes to share his passion. He graduated from engineering school in 2015. During these years, he went to Burkina Faso to teach computer science in schools around the country. The will to share and help people never left him since then. He started his professional life as a consultant at Actinvision, where he discovered Tableau. Soon, data visualization became a passion that has taken him around the world. In 2017, he won the Iron Viz (the ultimate data visualization battle organized by Tableau every year) in Las Vegas. Since his winning, he helps people with Tableau by making webinars, conferences, blog articles, and finally, this book! He's currently working at Ogury as a business analyst.

First, I'd like to thanks my colleagues at Actinvision, Ogury and my friend, Maxime Baux, with whom I can share my passion. Of course, I would have never learned so much without the Tableau Community and amazing people like Eva Murray, Chloe Tseng, Jonni Walker, and Jade Le Van. Of course, a special thanks to Ivett Kovács and Dilyana Bossenz for reviewing this book. Finally, a huge thanks to my family and my love, Laura, for their daily support.

About the reviewers

Ivett Kovács was always very comfortable with data—after majoring in statistics, she started working as a data analyst. She was one of the first Hungarian power users of Tableau Desktop, 2012, and has been mastering Tableau ever since. Currently, she is Starschema's senior data visualization expert, leading a team of 10+ dataviz developers.

She is not only Tableau certified, but has also been a Tableau Ambassador since 2017. She is also a featured volunteer with Viz for Social Good. She has been developing several Tableau dashboards on various social topics—the refugee crisis and gender inequality in tech companies and political institutions. Ivett has been writing a book for Packt Publishing, *Tableau 2018.x Projects*.

Dilyana Bossenz works as a data analyst. Her professional focus is on data visualization and data analysis. She has a master's degree in business administration. She discovered her passion for data in 2014 at a workshop at Google when she was still a student. After that, she wrote a master's thesis about big data. She gained her first experience in Tableau as a four years intern in business intelligence. She is co-organizer of Tableau User Group and local chapter leader for Viz for Social Good in Berlin. In February 2018, she was recognized as a Tableau Feature Author.

Packt is searching for authors like you

If you're interested in becoming an author for Packt, please visit `authors.packtpub.com` and apply today. We have worked with thousands of developers and tech professionals, just like you, to help them share their insight with the global tech community. You can make a general application, apply for a specific hot topic that we are recruiting an author for, or submit your own idea.

Table of Contents

Preface

Tableau is one of the leading business intelligence tools used worldwide, across organizations of all scale. In its latest release, Tableau 2018 promises richer and more useful features related to visual analytics, reporting, dashboarding, and a host of other data visualization aspects. *Getting Started with Tableau 2018.x* will get you up and running with these features.

If you're familiar with Tableau, the book starts with the new functionalities of Tableau 2018, along with concrete examples of how to use them. However, if you're new to Tableau, don't worry! The rest of the book will guide you through each major aspect of Tableau with examples. You'll learn how to connect to data, build a data source, visualize your data, build a dashboard, and share it online. In the final chapters, you'll also learn advanced techniques such as creating a cross-database join and data blending.

By the end of the book, you will have a firm understanding of how to effectively use Tableau to create quick, cost-effective, and business-efficient **business intelligence** (**BI**) solutions.

Disclaimer

The features explained in the book are based on the Beta version of Tableau 2018.3, this is not the final version of Tableau 2018.3.

Who this book is for

If you're a beginner or an existing BI professional looking to get the most out of Tableau 2018's latest features, this book is for you. You'll also find this book useful if you're an aspiring data analyst who wants to learn the capabilities of Tableau to answer business-specific questions. No prior knowledge or experience with Tableau is necessary.

What this book covers

`Chapter 1`, *Catching Up with Tableau 2018*, details of every new feature of the different Tableau 2018 versions. You'll learn how to use them with clear explanations, examples, and tutorials. This chapter is the best way to catch up with the new releases if you already have some Tableau knowledge. Beginners should start with `Chapter 2`, *The Tableau Core.*

`Chapter 2`, *The Tableau Core*, explains the basics that every Tableau users should know. It contains an overview of the different products, a description of Tableau's workspaces, wordings, and clear explanations of Tableau's most crucial concepts, such as Dimension, Measure, Discrete, Continuous, Live, and Extract.

`Chapter 3`, *A First Dashboard and Exploration*, is your first real experience with Tableau and is designed as a guided tutorial. In just one chapter you'll connect to data, build three visualizations, an interactive dashboard, and answer business questions with the power of Tableau's data exploration capabilities.

`Chapter 4`, *Connect to Data and Simple Transformations*, focuses on data connections, starting with general rules when connecting to files and servers. This chapter also goes into detail about essential features such as Joins, Unions, and Transformations (Pivot, Split, and more).

`Chapter 5`, *Build an Efficient Data Source*, helps you build the best data source for your analysis. Having a customized and well-organized data source is crucial in Tableau. You'll learn the different elements that compose a data source, how to refresh and deals with the changes, and change the default format. This chapter also focuses on creating Groups, Hierarchies, Sets, and Bins.

`Chapter 6`, *Design Insightful Visualizations - Part 1*, teaches you the different ways of building visualizations in Tableau with double-clicks, the Show Me menu, or simple drag and drops. You'll also see, in this first part, a description of the different Mark Types and properties.

`Chapter 7`, *Design Insightful Visualizations - Part 2*, focuses first on building visualizations with multiple measures thanks to Dual Axis, or Measure Name and Measure Values. Filters, Quick-Filters, Pages, and an overview of the different options available complete the global vision of what you can do when creating a visualization.

`Chapter 8`, *Create Powerful Dashboards and Stories*, is a key chapter in which you'll learn the basics about building dashboards in Tableau with an overview of the different objects available and advice about which layout to use. You'll also see how to add interactivity with the different Actions, and how to tell compelling stories with the Story points.

`Chapter 9`, *Publish and Interact in Tableau Server*, is the culmination of what you've learned in the previous chapters. This chapter focuses on Tableau Server/Online, how to publish your dashboards and Data Sources online, how to interact with published content, and how to build device-specific layouts.

`Chapter 10`, *An Introduction to Calculations*, is the first advanced chapter where you'll expand Tableau's capabilities by creating new calculated fields with powerful formulas. After describing the basics of calculation, you'll understand how to use advanced formulas such as Table Calculation and Level Of Detail.

`Chapter 11`, *Analytics and Parameters*, focuses on two significant aspects of Tableau that combine well. The first part, Analytics, describes how to add Reference Lines, Forecast, Clusters, Trend Lines, Totals, and more. The second part explains how to create and use parameters to add more interactivity to your analysis. Finally, you'll create a real-life business usage combining analytics features, parameters, and calculations.

`Chapter 12`, *Advanced Data Connections*, presents three major features: cross-database Join and data-blending to create analyses that combine multiple connection types, and Wildcard Unions to build automatic unions based on multiple files. This chapter will help you tackle data connection challenges.

`Chapter 13`, *Dealing with Security*, is the last technical chapter of this book and focuses on three ways to secure your data: permissions on Tableau Server, user filters on Tableau Desktop, and row-level data security in your data.

`Chapter 14`, *How to Keep Growing Your Skills*, is a non-technical but essential chapter. You'll discover many ways of learning new things and growing your Tableau skills thanks to community projects. The chapter is also a tribute to the Tableau community, presenting many ways to be part of that big family, which shares a passion for data visualization with Tableau.

To get the most out of this book

No prerequisites is necessary. Tableau is designed to be simple to use for any user who wanted to start using it no matter it's background. This book starts from the very beginning and will teach you all major concepts.

Download the example files

You can download the example code files for this book from your account at `www.packt.com`. If you purchased this book elsewhere, you can visit `www.packt.com/support` and register to have the files emailed directly to you.

You can download the code files by following these steps:

1. Log in or register at `www.packt.com`.
2. Select the **SUPPORT** tab.
3. Click on **Code Downloads & Errata**.
4. Enter the name of the book in the **Search** box and follow the onscreen instructions.

Once the file is downloaded, please make sure that you unzip or extract the folder using the latest version of:

- WinRAR/7-Zip for Windows
- Zipeg/iZip/UnRarX for Mac
- 7-Zip/PeaZip for Linux

The code bundle for the book is also hosted on GitHub at `https://github.com/PacktPublishing/Getting-Started-with-Tableau-2018.x`. In case there's an update to the code, it will be updated on the existing GitHub repository.

We also have other code bundles from our rich catalog of books and videos available at `https://github.com/PacktPublishing/`. Check them out!

Download the color images

We also provide a PDF file that has color images of the screenshots/diagrams used in this book. You can download it here: `https://www.packtpub.com/sites/default/files/downloads/9781788838689_ColorImages.pdf`.

Conventions used

There are a number of text conventions used throughout this book.

`CodeInText`: Indicates code words in text, database table names, folder names, filenames, file extensions, pathnames, dummy URLs, user input, and Twitter handles. Here is an example: "This file contains the an `Orders` sheet, with approximately 10,000 rows and another sheet, `User Access`, with 6,000 rows."

Bold: Indicates a new term, an important word, or words that you see onscreen. For example, words in menus or dialog boxes appear in the text like this. Here is an example: "When you open Tableau, on the left, in the **Connect** area, click on **Microsoft Excel**."

Warnings or important notes appear like this.

Tips and tricks appear like this.

Get in touch

Feedback from our readers is always welcome.

General feedback: If you have questions about any aspect of this book, mention the book title in the subject of your message and email us at `customercare@packtpub.com`.

Errata: Although we have taken every care to ensure the accuracy of our content, mistakes do happen. If you have found a mistake in this book, we would be grateful if you would report this to us. Please visit `www.packt.com/submit-errata`, selecting your book, clicking on the Errata Submission Form link, and entering the details.

Piracy: If you come across any illegal copies of our works in any form on the Internet, we would be grateful if you would provide us with the location address or website name. Please contact us at `copyright@packt.com` with a link to the material.

If you are interested in becoming an author: If there is a topic that you have expertise in and you are interested in either writing or contributing to a book, please visit `authors.packtpub.com`.

Reviews

Please leave a review. Once you have read and used this book, why not leave a review on the site that you purchased it from? Potential readers can then see and use your unbiased opinion to make purchase decisions, we at Packt can understand what you think about our products, and our authors can see your feedback on their book. Thank you!

For more information about Packt, please visit `packt.com`.

1
Catching Up with Tableau 2018

Thank you for purchasing *Getting Started with Tableau 2018*. As its title suggests, this book aims to provide you with explanations, advice, tips, and the best practices to start (or continue) a journey through Tableau, using the most recent features. You'll always find clear descriptions, reproducible examples, and tutorials. Whether you already know how to use Tableau and want to get familiar with its latest features, or you've never used the tool and want to learn from the beginning, this book is for you, and I hope you enjoy it.

If you are a Tableau user looking for information about the new features and how to use them, you are in the right place. If you are new to Tableau, start with `Chapter 2`, *The Tableau Core,* to learn about the basics and advanced features of Tableau. Throughout this book, many new features will be explained. Having finished all of the chapters, you can come back here to learn about the newest features, in detail.

In this first chapter, we'll cover the new features in Tableau's 2018 releases (Tableau 2018.1, 2018.2, and 2018.3).

With the 2018.1 version, Tableau has changed the version numeration. All versions now start with the year, then the release number during that year. For example, Tableau 2018.3 is the third major release of 2018.

This chapter will be divided into two parts, as follows:

- Tableau Desktop
- Tableau Server

For each part, each major feature has its proper section. Next to the name of the feature, between brackets, the version that introduced the new feature is specified. For example, the section spatial Join (2018.2) covers the feature spatial Join, added in version 2018.2.

This book focuses on data visualization with Tableau Desktop and Tableau Server/Online. The new product that allows you to clean and prepare your data, Tableau Prep, is not covered, as it fulfills a different need. Learn more about Tableau Prep at `https://www.tableau.com/products/prep`.

Let's start with Tableau Desktop; get ready to discover many great new features!

Tableau Desktop

This first section, covering Tableau Desktop, is divided into three parts, as follows:

- **Data source improvements**: All of the new ways to connect your data and increase performance
- **Visualization improvements**: All of the things that you can do on a Worksheet, to create better visualizations
- **Dashboard improvements**: All of the options and new features to help you create better Dashboards

To understand and reproduce the examples provided in this chapter, you need to know how to connect to data, build a Data Source, and create Worksheets and Dashboards.

Data Source improvements

In this section of the book, we'll focus on two major improvements: the normalized extract and the spatial join.

Normalized extract (2018.3)

Previously, when creating an extract, Tableau always generated a single table. This was sometimes problematic, especially when a Join duplicated the number of lines. Now, when you Join multiple tables, you can choose the schema, creating either a **Single Table** or **Multiple Tables**:

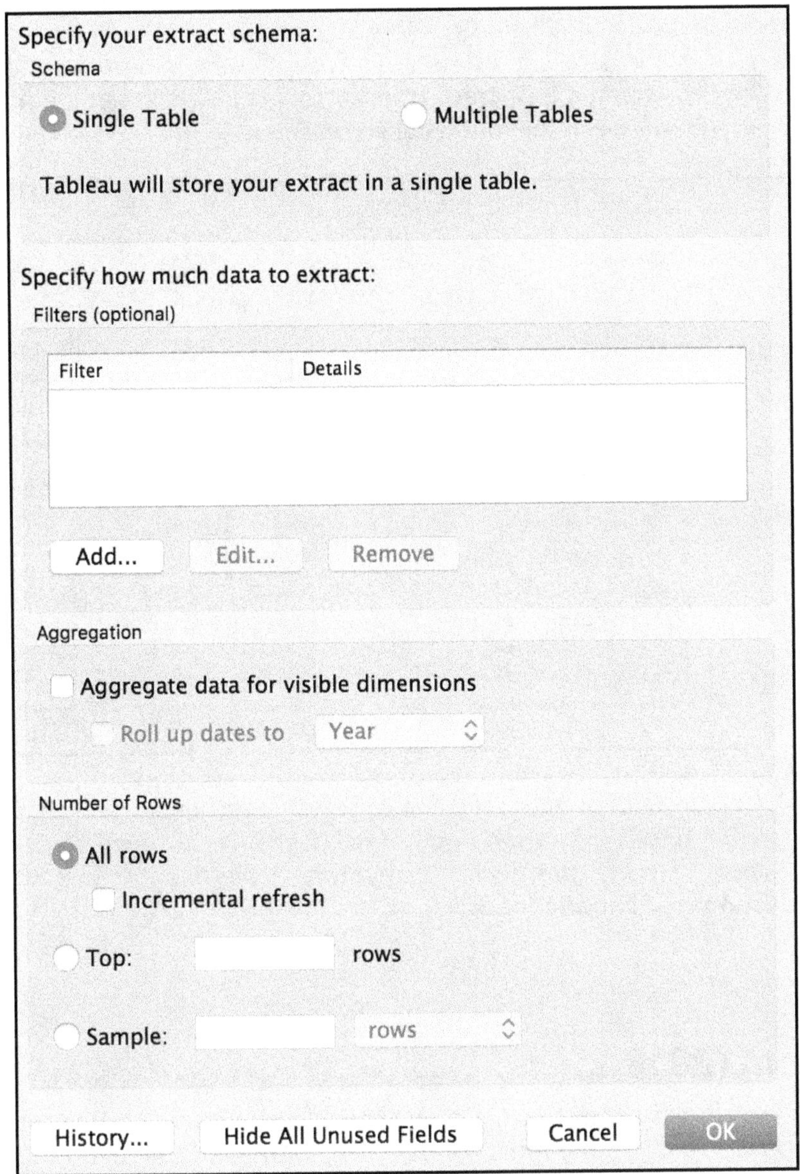

For example, you can download the Excel file `Multiple Table Storage Test` from the *Chapter 1* section of my website, `book.ladataviz.com` (or, browse to `https://ladataviz.com/wp-content/uploads/2018/09/Multiple-Table-Storage-Test.xlsx`). This file contains the an `Orders` sheet, with approximately 10,000 rows and another sheet, `User Access`, with 6,000 rows.

Individually, those tables are small, and creating an extract only takes a few seconds. When you Join the two tables, the data is duplicated. The result of the Join produces more than 11 million rows. When you created an extract, prior to Tableau 2018.3, the 11 million rows had to be retrieved, as you can see in the following screenshot:

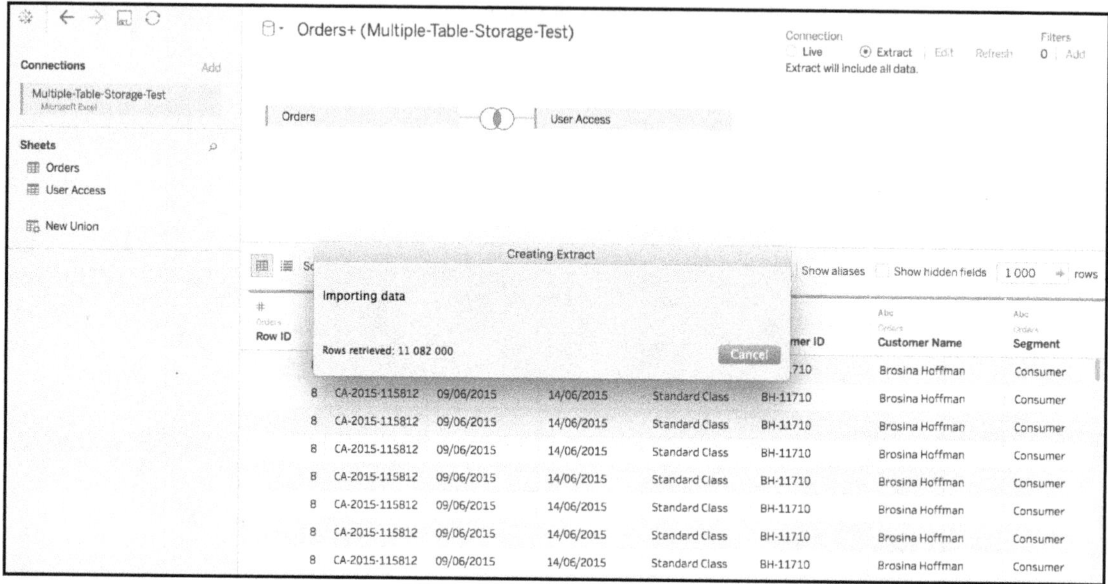

Thanks to Tableau 2018.3, if you select the **Multiple Tables** schema when creating an extract, the extraction time is very short because the two tables are generated separately, prior to being joined. The only drawback is that you can't use all of the Extract options (**Filters**, **Aggregation**, and **Number of rows**).

The next new feature is also related to Joins.

Spatial join (2018.2)

A new type of Join, called an **Intersect**, is now available, and it was created especially for spatial files. You can find it in the **Join** configuration, highlighted as follows:

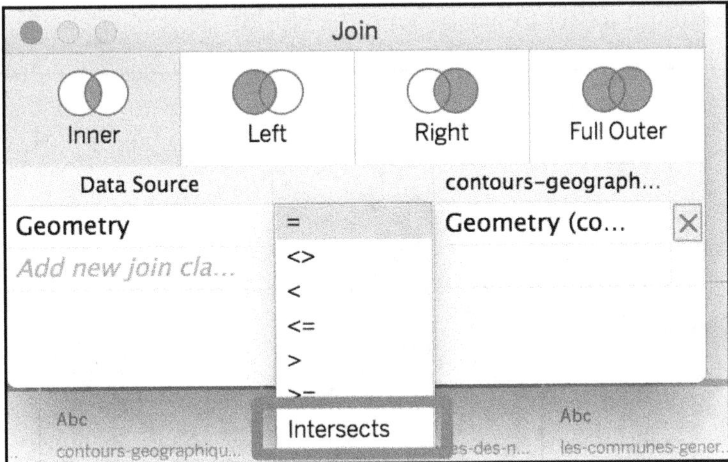

Intersects are useful when the only common field between the two tables is the spatial one. Tableau joins the data when there is a spatial intersection between a polygon and a point.

For example, let's look at how to join the two following shapefiles. The first one contains the polygons of the French regions:

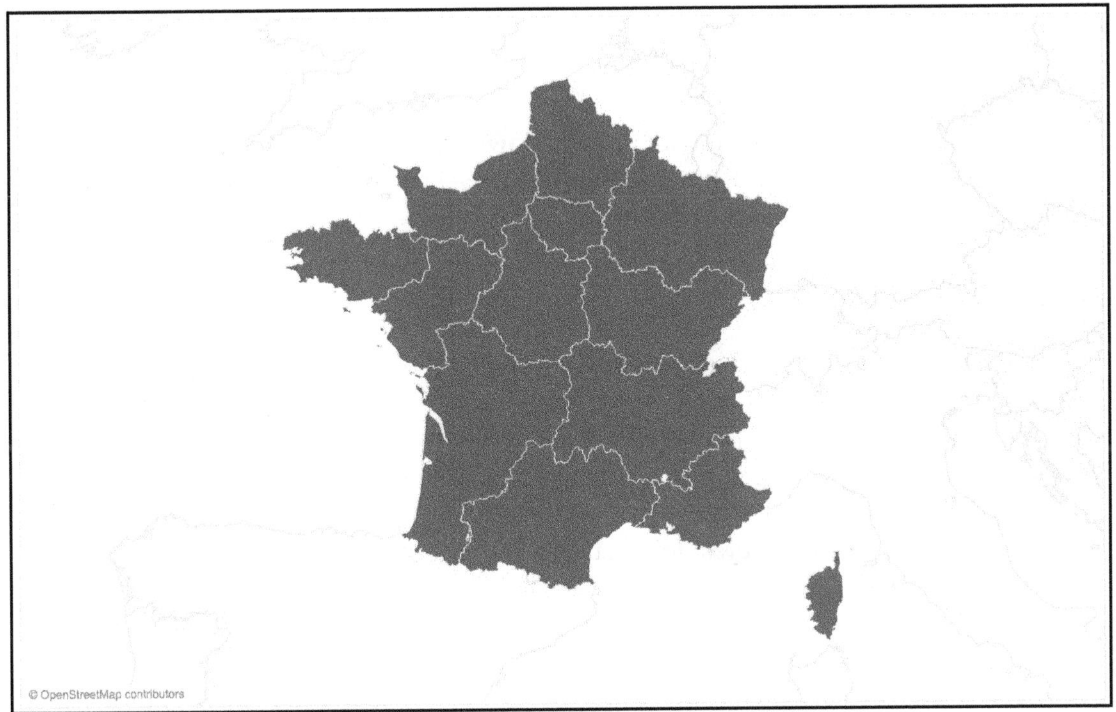

The second one contains a list of ports around the world:

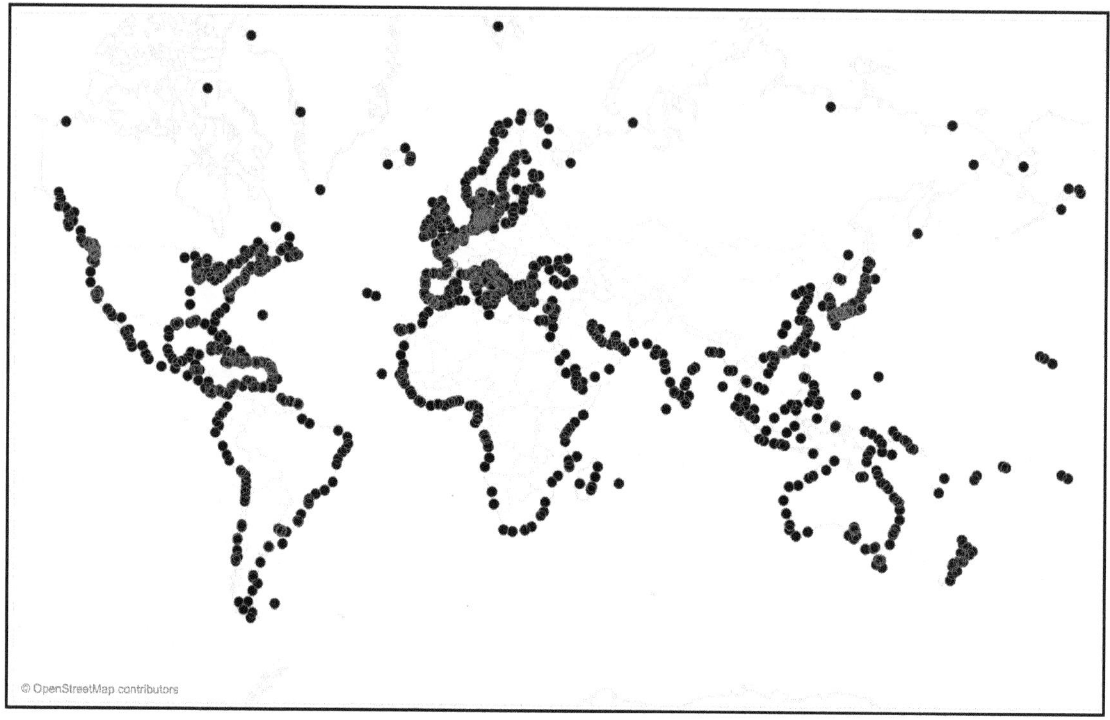

To recreate the example, you can download the ZIP file `Spatial Join` from the *Chapter 1* section of my website, `book.ladataviz.com` (or, browse to `https://ladataviz.com/wp-content/uploads/2018/09/Spatial-Join.zip`).

Let's create a spatial Join between the two spatial files, as follows:

1. Open Tableau and connect to the first spatial file, `contours-geographiques-des-nouvelles-regions-metropole.shp`.
2. Add a second spatial connection in the same Data Source (see `Chapter 12`, *Advanced Data Connections*, if you don't know how to create cross-database Joins), and choose the `ne_10m_ports.shp` file.
3. Choose an **Inner** interest Join between the two tables, shown as follows:

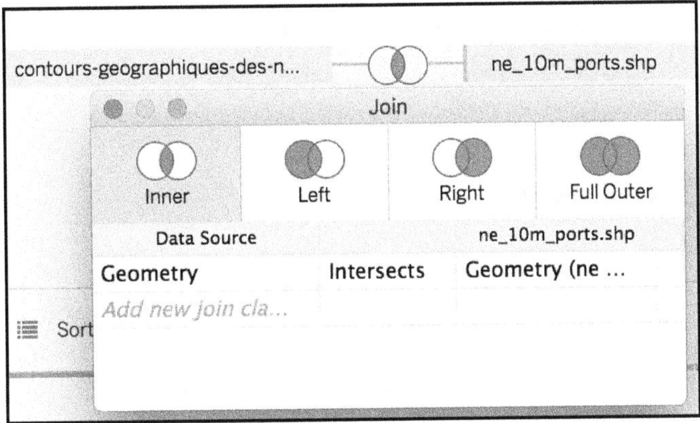

4. You can test your Data Source; the remaining French regions are the ones with ports, and the remaining ports are only French ones. If you create a Dual Axis map, you can show both the regions and the ports on the same map, as follows:

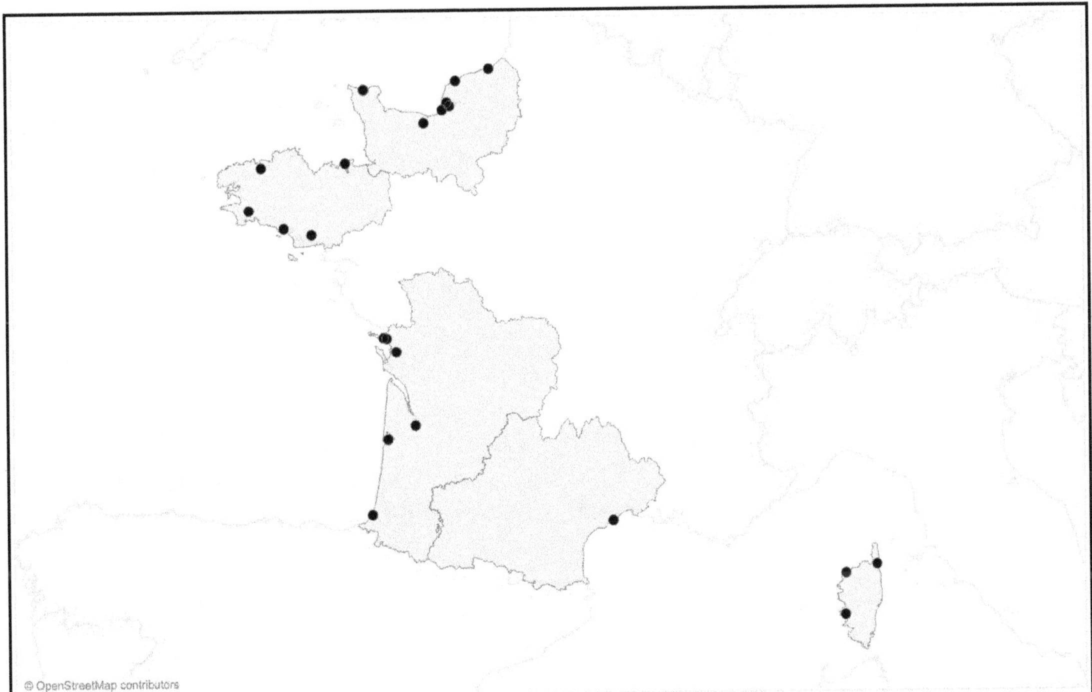

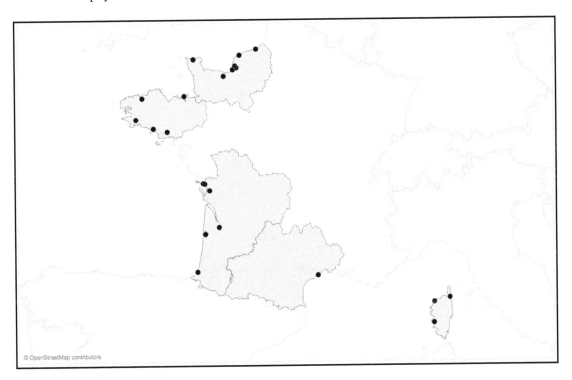

This is surely a great advancement for using spatial files in Tableau. Let's finish this section by looking at other Data Source improvements.

Other Data Source improvements

Some other Data Source improvements are as follows:

- From Tableau 2018.1, Tableau can recognize spatial columns in SQL Server and use them for mapping. You can also use Custom SQL to write an advanced analysis using your spatial fields.
- Cross-database Joins and MDX queries have improved in performance since Tableau 2018.2.

Now, let's take a look at visualization improvements.

Visualization improvements

Many new features are available when speaking about visualizations. With the new versions of Tableau, you can use a new type of Marks, create Dual Axis mapping, step lines, jump lines, save and reuse your clusters, and much more. Let's start with the new Density Mark.

Density Mark (2018.3)

Density is the newest Marks type, introduced in Tableau 2018.3 and represented with the following icon: Density

This new mark fills a gap: to show the Density of Marks. The superposition of multiple Marks determines the color intensity. It's a straightforward Marks type; you can use it in various cases, as long as you have many Marks overlapping.

In the following example, you can see that the concentration of customers by **Sales** and **Quantity**:

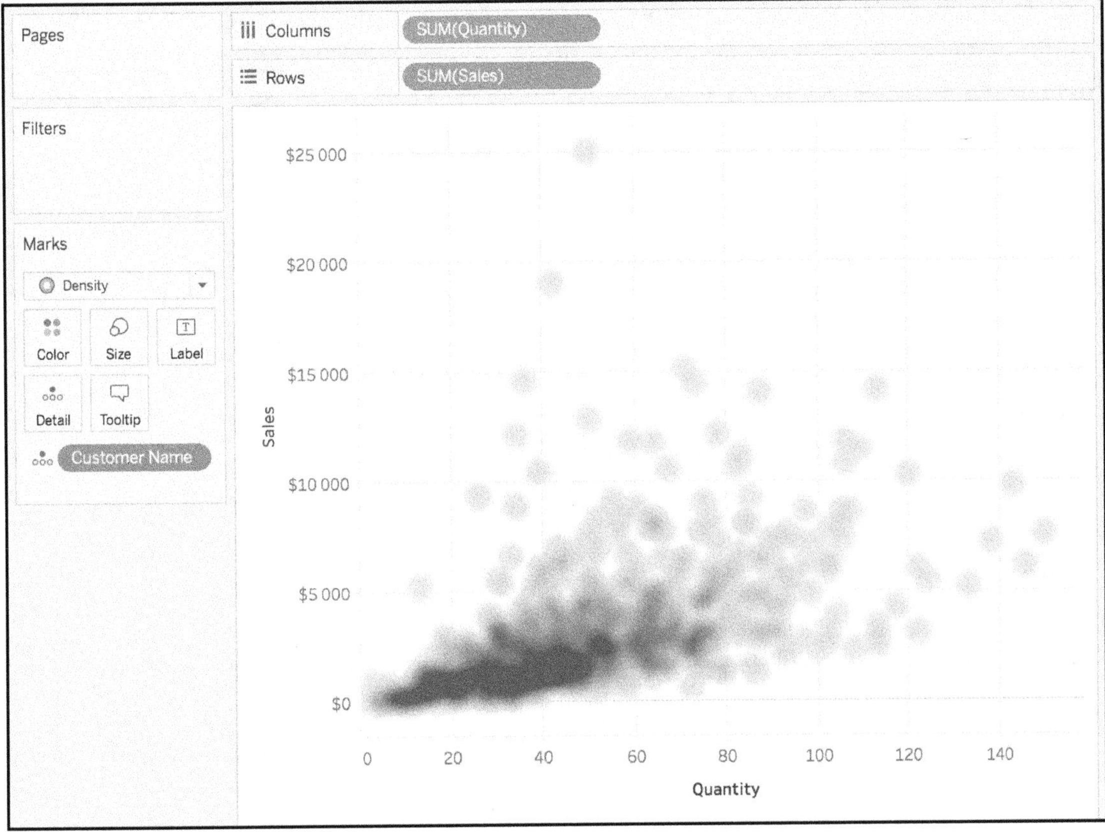

The most important property for the Density Mark is the color. Thanks to the intensity of the color, you can see the **Density** of the Marks. To deal with this particularity, there is a new option when you click on the **Color** property: **Intensity**. Changing the intensity of the color tells different stories. In the following screenshot, the **Intensity** is set to `90%`:

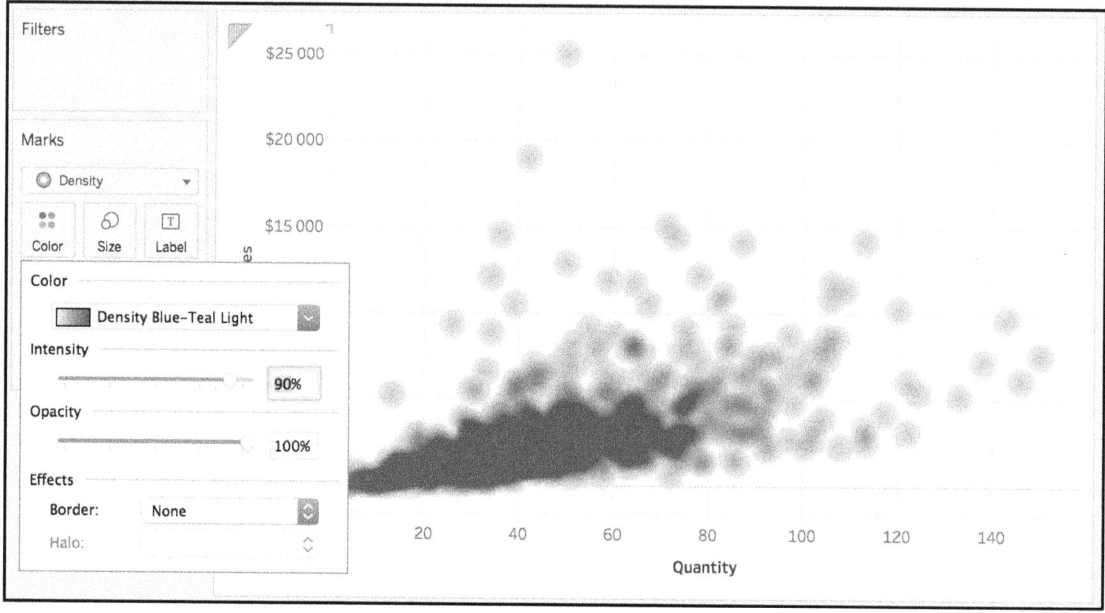

In the following screenshot, the **Intensity** is set to `40%`:

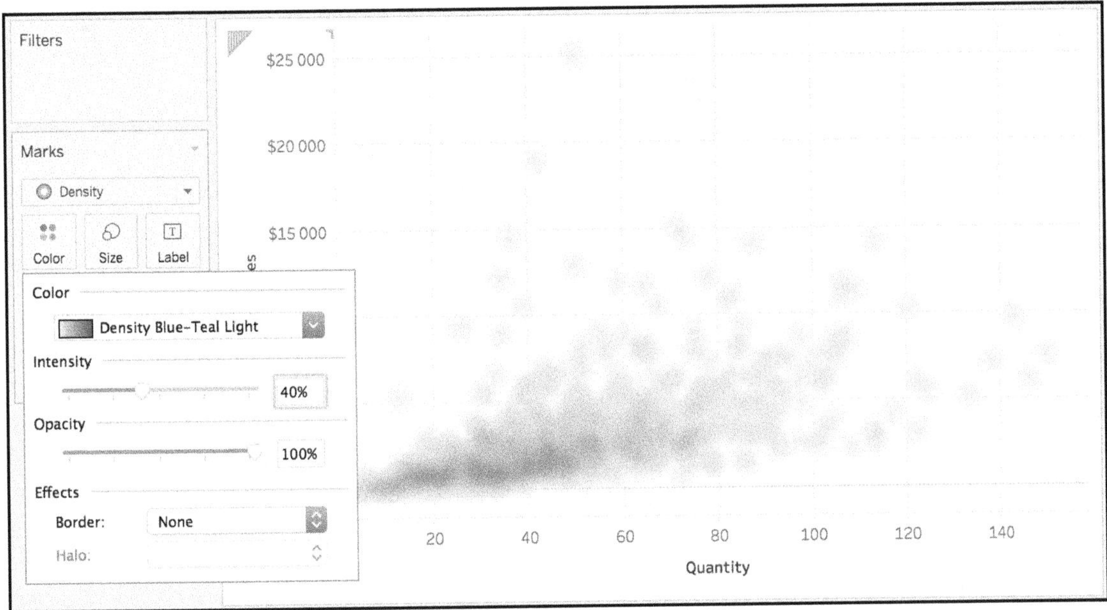

Tableau has also added new color palettes, specially designed for the Density Mark. You'll find palettes for bright and dark backgrounds. Currently, the only drawback is the impossibility to open the **Edit Color** menu and select a color on your screen or enter a color code. You can, however, use your custom palette, specified in the `Preference.tps` file of your Tableau Repository.

Step and jump lines (2018.1)

Since version 2018.1, when you use the Line Marks type, a click on the **Path** button has opened a menu where you can select the **Line Type**: **Linear**, **Step**, or **Jump**. The following screenshot shows an example of a step line:

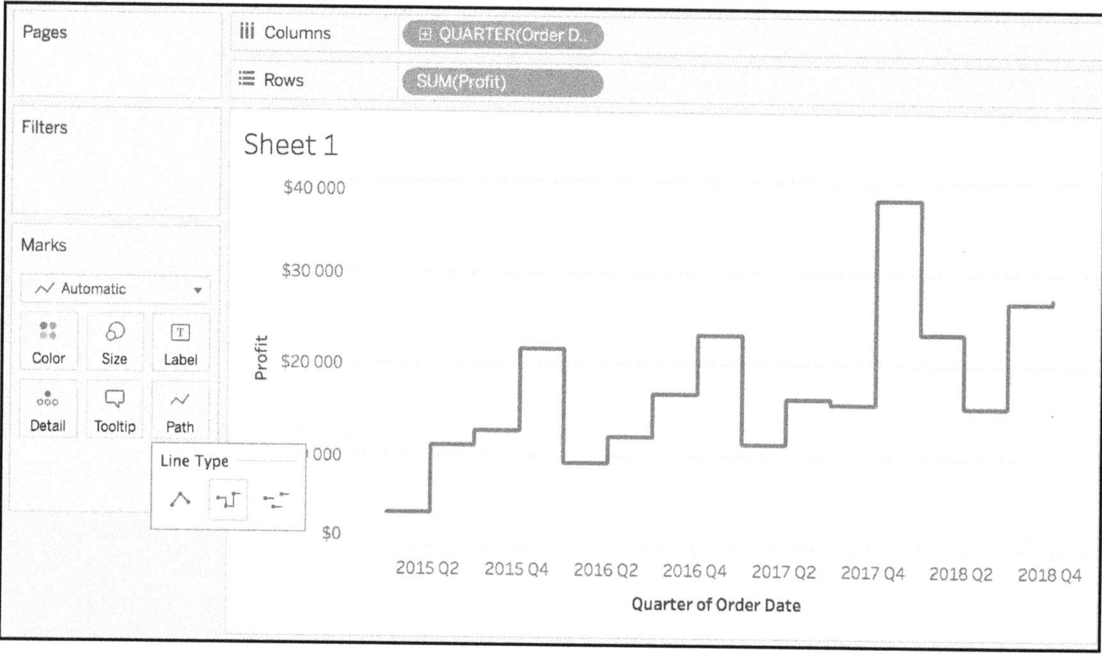

Although it's not the most spectacular new feature, it's nevertheless a great addition, simplifying a complicated procedure to build the same visualization.

Worksheet transparency (2018.3)

A long-awaited feature is the Worksheet transparency. It is a great addition, allowing you to build better visualizations; but it's also an open door to terrible practices and designs.

Data is the most crucial element in data visualization—not the design. The design is important, as it's a vector of success for your Dashboards, but it's not the primary concern. Please, always focus on the clarity of the data, and keep in mind the Data-Ink Ratio introduced by Edward Tufte: `https://infovis-wiki.net/wiki/Data-Ink_Ratio`.

To make the background of a Worksheet transparent, follow these steps:

1. Click on **Format...** in the Worksheet options, as highlighted in the following screenshot:

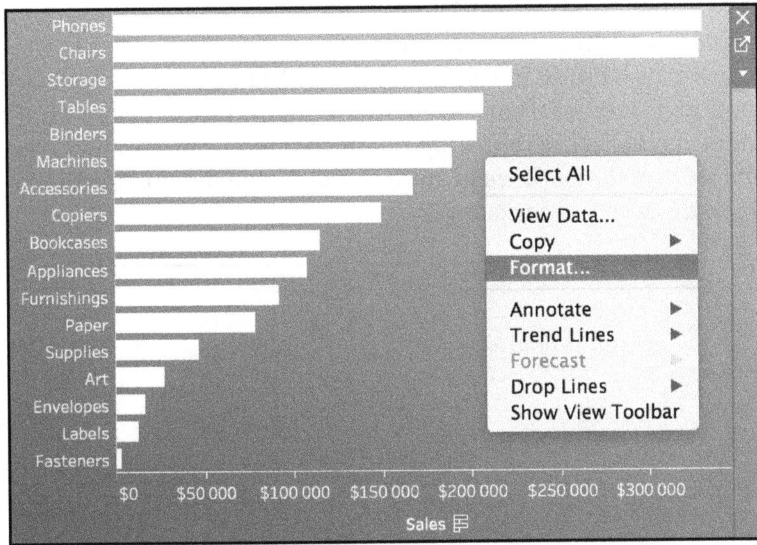

2. Click on the third icon, **Shading**, to modify the shading format.
3. Select **None** in the **Default** Worksheet shading, highlighted as follows:

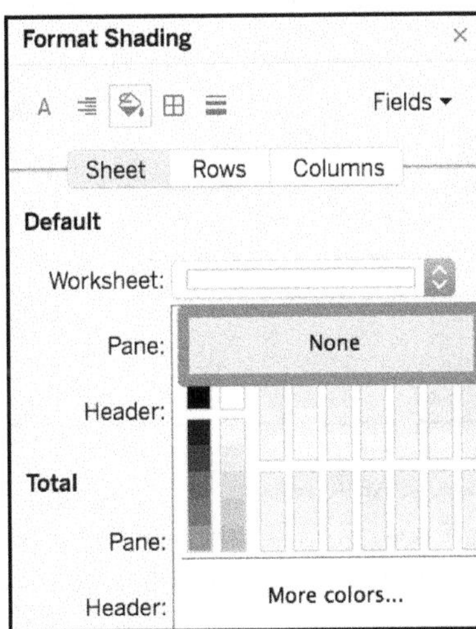

Use this new feature with caution! The next new feature is the ability to create Dual Axis, with different types of coordinates.

Dual Axis mapping (2018.1)

Before Tableau 2018.1, you could already build a Dual Axis map. To do so, duplicate the longitude in columns, or latitude in rows, and select **Dual Axis** in the pill option. Thanks to the **Dual Axis** option, it is possible to have two different Mark types and a different level of detail in each Marks layer. In the following screenshot, you can see a Dual Axis map, with a filled map for the state with the **Sales** in color in the first layer, and circles for each city, colored in black, in the second Marks layer:

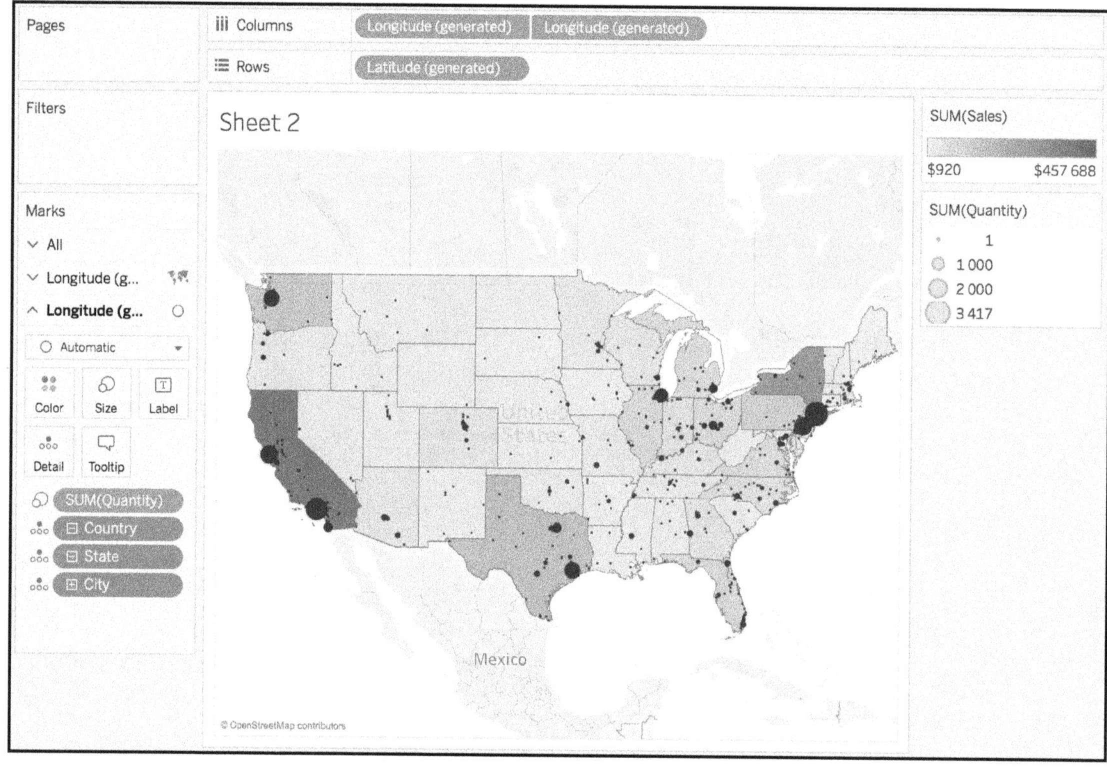

Unfortunately, in previous versions of Tableau, it was impossible to create a Dual Axis map by combining Tableau-generated coordinates and custom coordinates in your data. Since Tableau 2018.1, it's been possible. Let's look at how to do it.

To reproduce the example, download the `Orders without City` file from my website, `book.ladataviz.com`, or browse to `https://ladataviz.com/wp-content/uploads/2018/09/Orders-without-City.xlsx`.

In the `Orders without City` file, the cities have been removed and replaced by their latitude and longitude, in two different columns: `Latitude City` and `Longitude City`. The goal is to rebuild the preceding example with this new file. Do as follows:

1. Open Tableau and connect to the `Orders without City` file.
2. Right-click on the **Latitude City** field and select **Convert to Dimension**. Repeat the same for **Longitude City**.
3. Double-click on **State** to create a map, and put **Sales** in color.
4. Add **Latitude (generated)** next to the existing **Latitude (generated)** pill.
5. Right-click on the second **Latitude (generated)** pill and click on **Dual Axis**.
6. On the second Marks layer, change the **Type** to **Circle**, add **Latitude City** and **Longitude City** in **Detail**, change the **Quantity** from **Color** to **Size**, and, finally, change the color of the **Marks** to black. The final result is as follows:

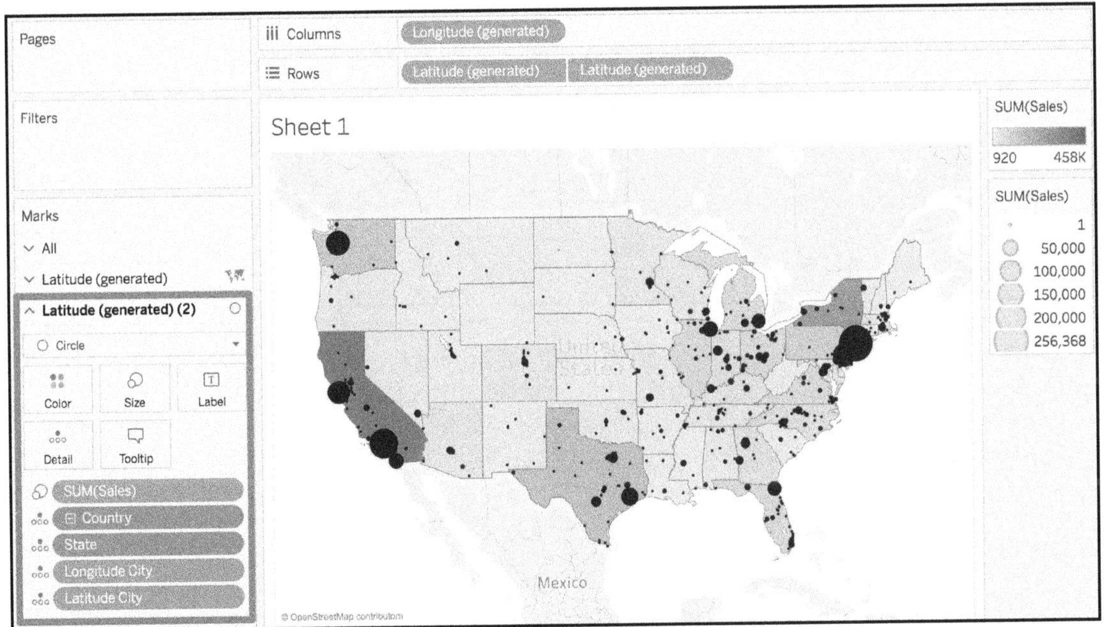

As you can see, since Tableau 2018.1, you can combine generated coordinates with custom ones.

The next enhancement was one of the longest-standing requests from the community: the nested sort.

Nested sort (2018.2)

Sorting a measure across two dimensions was inexplicably difficult prior to Tableau 2018.2. If you tried to sort the categories by Sales for each dimension, you would see the following:

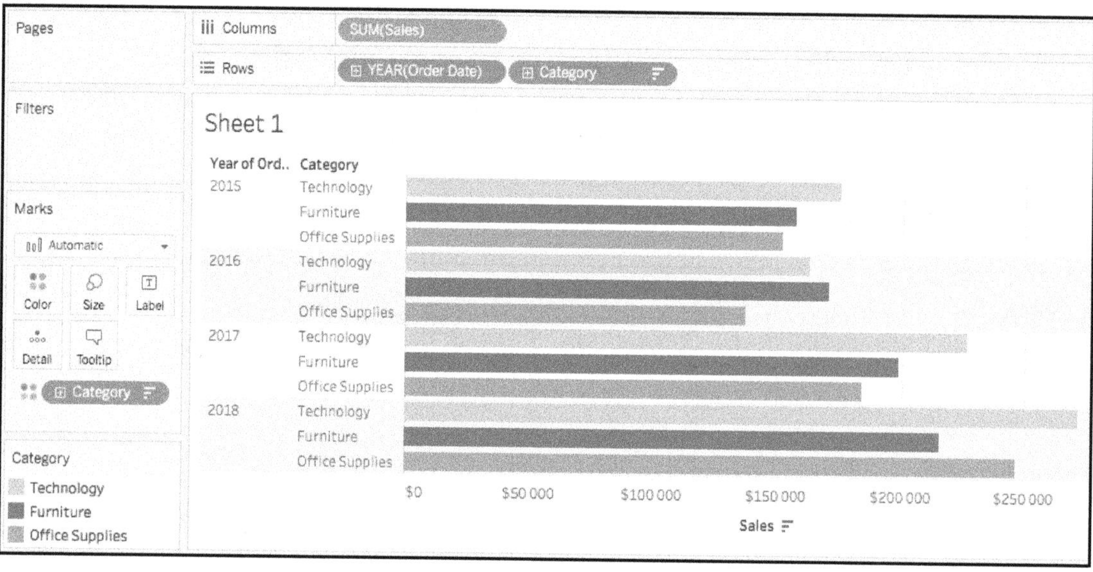

As you can see, the categories were sorted without taking the years into account (making it difficult to rank the categories in *2016* or *2018*, for example). It was possible to get the desired sort with a hidden combined field or some table calculations, but everyone agrees that it was unnecessarily complicated.

From Tableau 2018.2, if you click on the **Sort** button on the axis, Tableau creates a nested sort, displaying the best **Category** per year as follows:

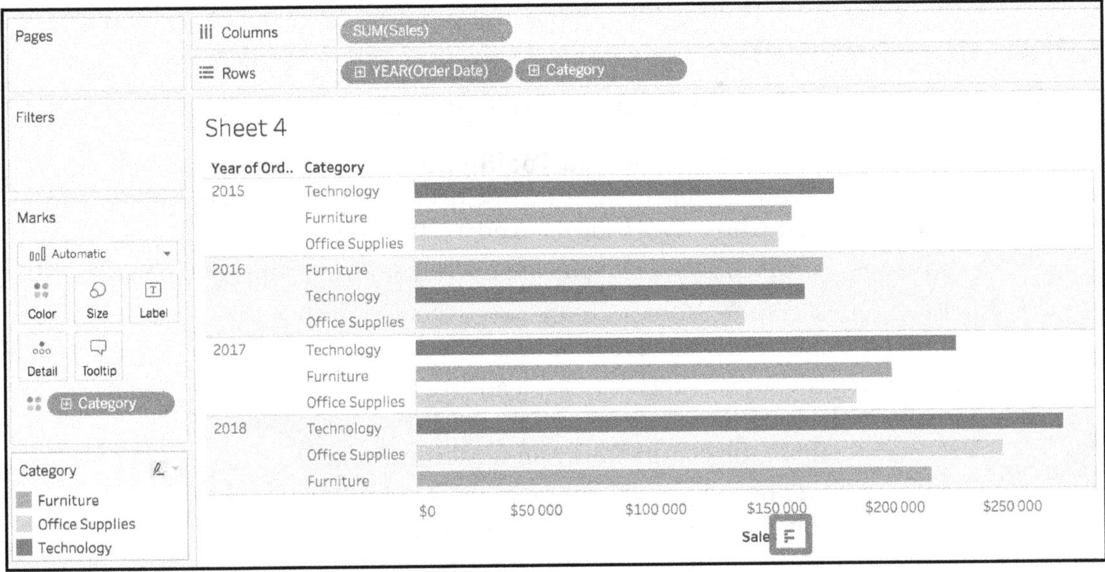

If you still want to use the previous method of sorting, you can use the sorting icon in the toolbar.

This small enhancement makes the product a lot simpler to use. The next feature is quite similar, with a simple addition having a tremendous positive impact.

Hierarchy filtering (2018.1)

If you display the **Quick Filter** of a field that is part of a hierarchy, a new option is now available: **All Values in Hierarchy**. This new option is applied by default.

With this option, the **Quick Filter** only shows the possible values, considering the filtered parent value of the hierarchy. It produces the same result as the **Only relevant values** option, but automatically, and with better performance.

Let's finish by looking at a list of other small enhancements that will make your life easier (when using Tableau, of course).

Other improvements

The following is a list of other small visualization improvements:

- Tableau 10.5 introduced the **Viz In Tooltip** feature. Unfortunately, in previous versions, it was impossible to hide a worksheet that was only used in a tooltip. You can now hide those Worksheets in every Tableau 2018 version.
- From Tableau 2018.1, saved clusters are no longer just groups, but are a special field with this icon: You can reuse saved clusters, and, with a right-click, you can refit the clusters to take the new data into account.
- You can revert your workbook to Tableau 10.2 by using the option **Export as Version** in the top **File** menu. From Tableau 2018.2, you also get clear information about the compatibility and lost functions.
- When you hover over a grayed option in the **Analytics** pane, Tableau now gives you information about why you can't use that option.
- Tableau now displays the link to the *Driver Installation* page in the **Connection** menu, for a specific connection.
- You can display negative values on a logarithmic axis, from Tableau 2018.2.
- Dates can be represented in ISO 8601 format, from Tableau 2018.2.
- Geocoding has been improved in the 2018.2 version, with Japanese municipalities, wards, seven-digit postal codes, and 2018 Pennsylvania Congressional Districts.
- Cross-database Joins and multi-dimensional expression queries for cubes have improved performance since Tableau 2018.2.
- In Tableau 2018.3, you can connect to the ESRI Geodatabase, KML, and the TopoJSON file.

Now, we'll look at the new features available for Dashboards.

Dashboard improvements

This year, two new Dashboard items, two new actions, the Grid, and the automatic Mobile layout were released by Tableau.

Let's start with the extensions, which are likely the most important new feature in this book.

Extensions (2018.2)

If you have been a Tableau user for a long time, I'm sure that you have dreamed about one of the following features: dynamic parameters, an automatic date updater, export to CSV buttons, an automatic radar chart or Sankey diagram, and more. Thanks to the extensions, all of these features are now available! And the best part is: this is just the beginning.

Extensions provide the ability to interact with other applications or services, directly inside Tableau, without leaving your Dashboard. You can also use them to expand Tableau's limits. The extensions are supported on Tableau Desktop and Tableau Server.

You can add new extensions from the **Dashboard** pane, on the left-hand side, as follows:

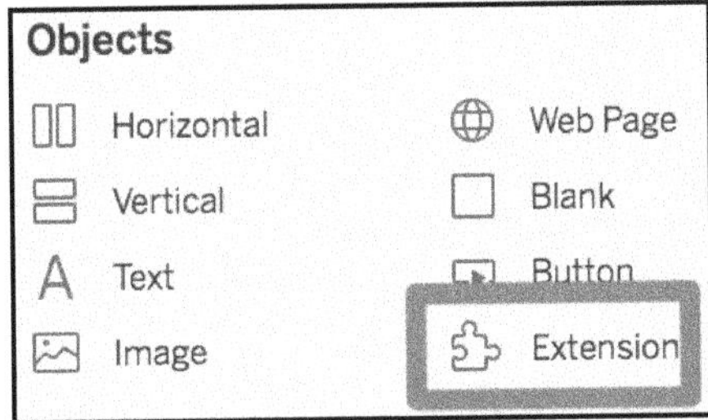

When you add an **Extension** object, Tableau opens a new window, where you have to select a `.TREX` file. You can either download existing `.TREX` files in the **Extension Gallery**, or create your own.

The **Extension Gallery** is available at `https://extensiongallery.tableau.com`. From here, you can find and download many extensions, developed by Tableau and their partners. One example is the **Data-Driven Parameters** extension page, with the **Download** button highlighted, as follows:

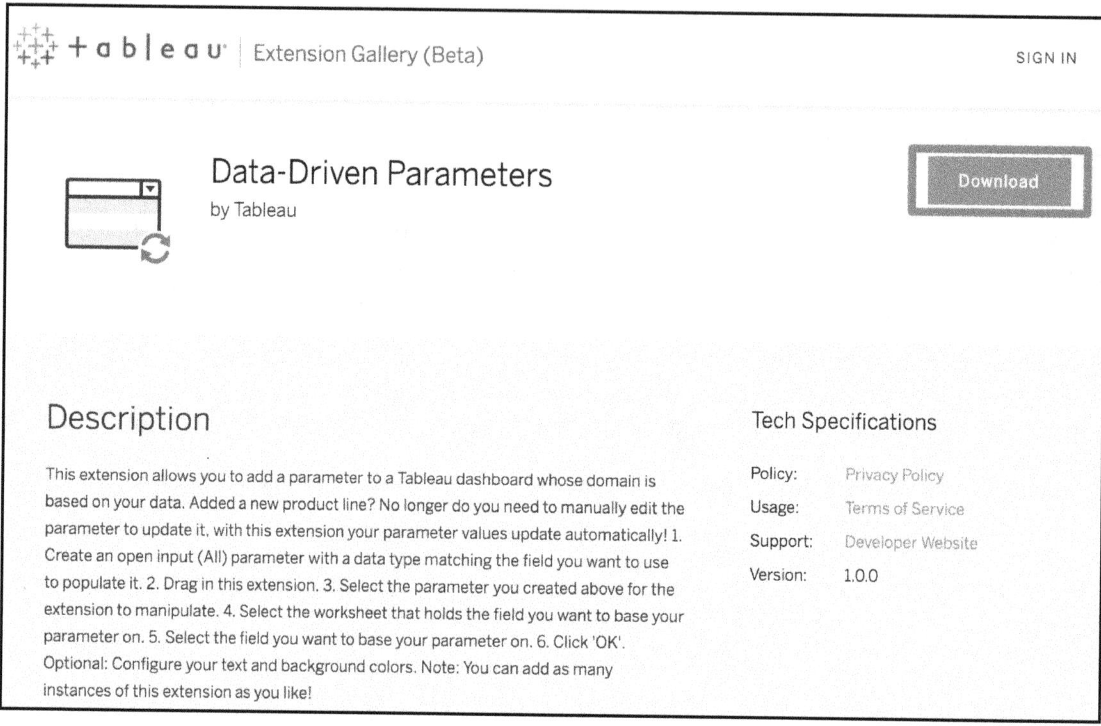

When you add an extension, Tableau opens a warning, asking you to allow and trust the extension. Then, you'll likely have to configure the extension. As every extension is different, each configuration window is different. The following is an example of the **Data-Driven Parameter Configuration** window, where you have to select a parameter, a worksheet, and a field:

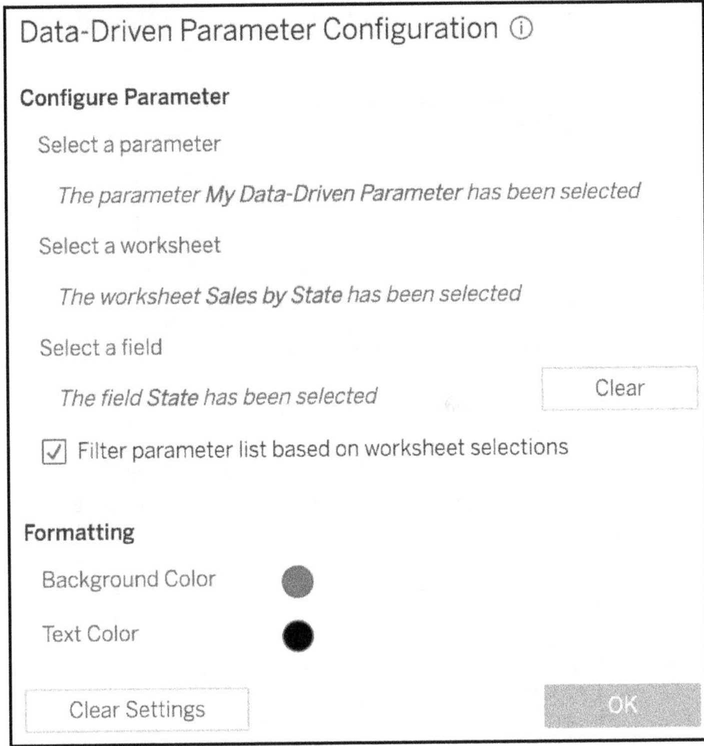

Using the Extensions API, you can also develop new extensions in Node.js to create new interactions with your applications. Unfortunately, you will not learn how to code in Node.js in this book. However, if you want to learn how to build your own extensions, you'll find tutorials, samples, and clear explanations in the Tableau Extensions GitHub page, at `https://tableau.github.io/extensions-api`.

As you can see, the possibilities are infinite. Tableau will frequently update the Extension Gallery, offering new ways to work with Tableau.

The next feature is also a new Dashboard object!

Dashboard navigation button (2018.3)

Have you ever created a navigation button in Tableau, to change from one Dashboard to another? It was one of those unnecessarily complicated processes: you had to add a Worksheet with a custom shape on a Dashboard, and add an action to another Dashboard: complicated, long, and now, obsolete.

Since Tableau 2018.3, the **Button** object is available on the Dashboard pane, as highlighted in the following screenshot:

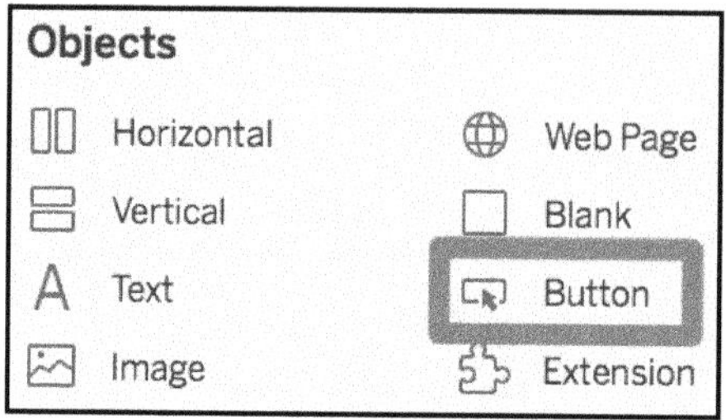

You can add a Button to your Dashboard as follows:

1. Drag and drop the **Button** object to wherever you please.
2. When you add a Button, Tableau will display it, and you can then configure it with a right-click, as follows:

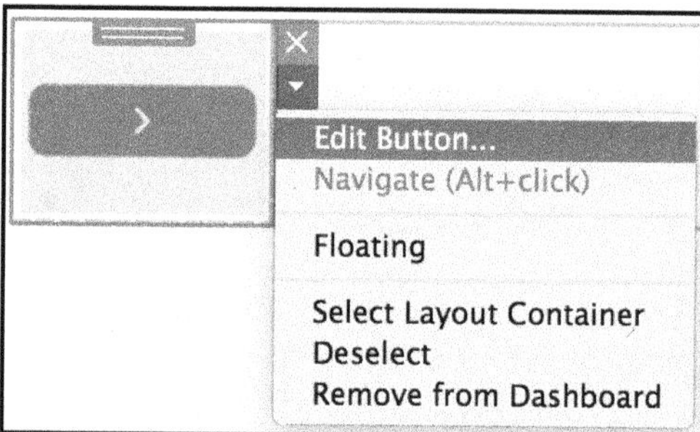

3. On the configuration window, you will have to specify a target sheet (a Worksheet, Dashboard, or Story), and you can change the image and add a tooltip. The following is an example of a button that redirects to the **Product Dashboard**, with a personalized image and a tooltip:

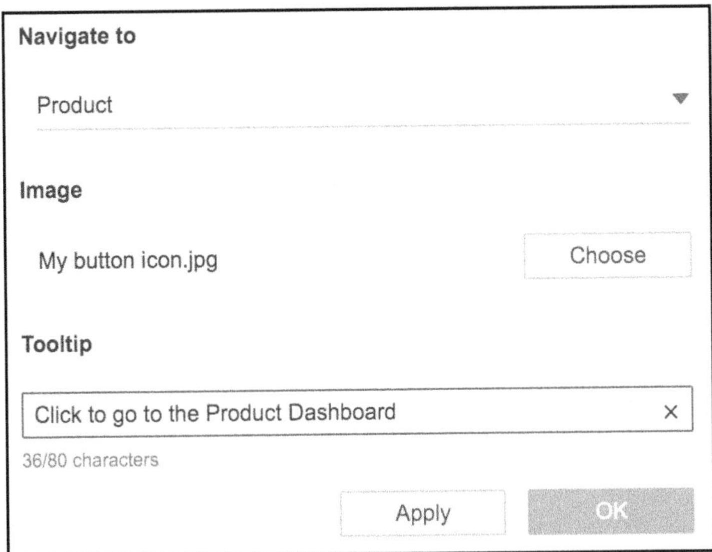

4. Finally, without having to use shapes and actions, you can add navigation buttons to your Dashboard, as highlighted in the following screenshot:

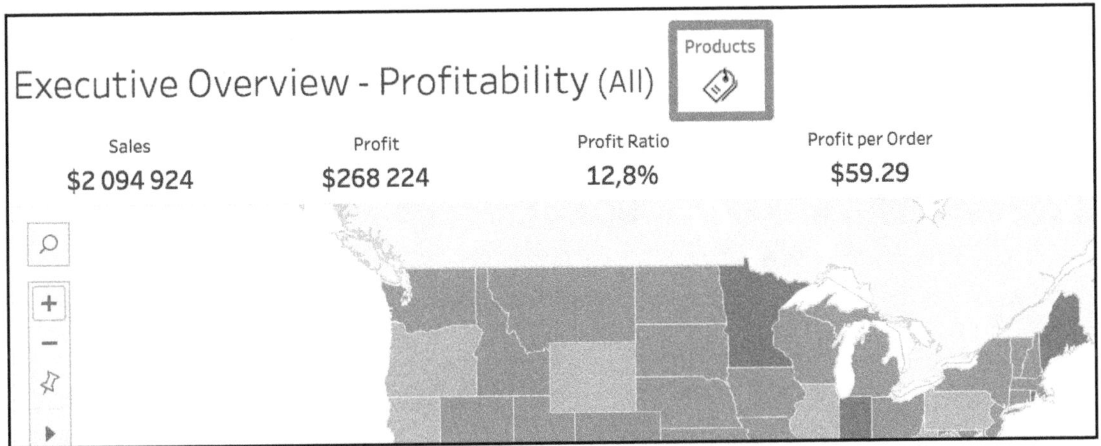

In 2018, Tableau added two new Dashboard objects, and also two new actions. Let's start with the first one, which is really close to the **Button** object.

Navigation action (2018.3)

In Tableau 2018.3, when you add an **Action**, you will find the **Go to Sheet...** action, highlighted as follows:

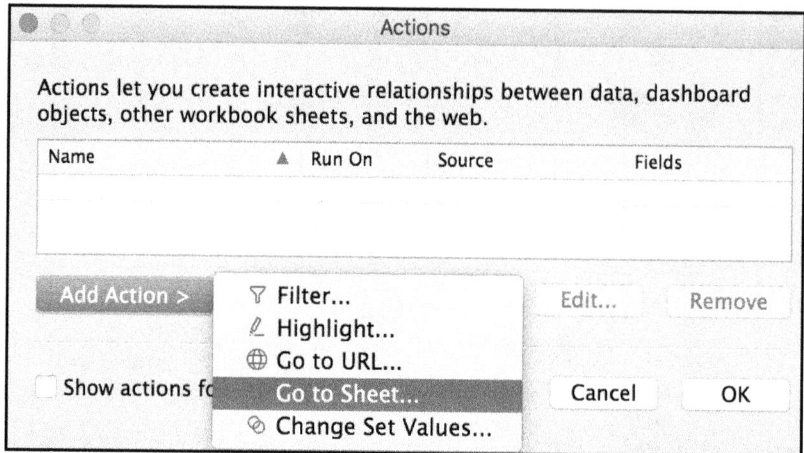

This action is straightforward: from one or multiple source Worksheets, you can navigate to a **Target Sheet** (Worksheet, Dashboard, or Story). The following screenshot shows the configuration window, when you add a **Go to Sheet...** action:

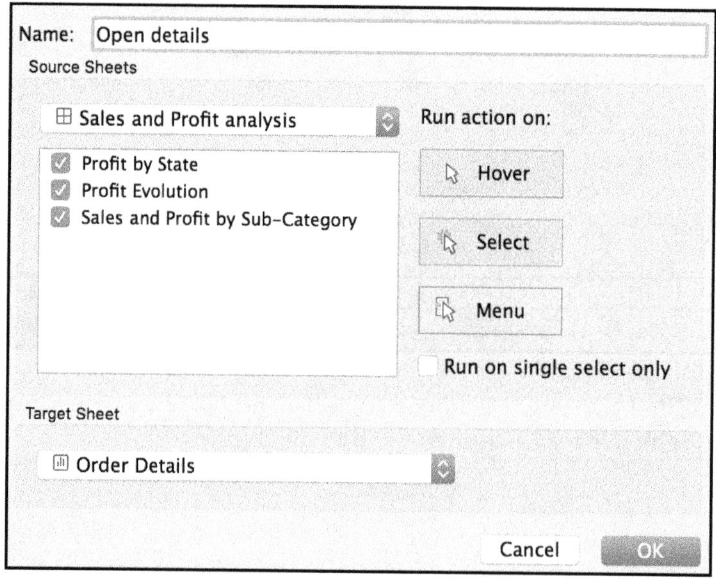

In this configuration window, you can specify the following:

- The **Name** of the action
- The **Source Sheets**
- The trigger (**Hover**, **Select**, or **Menu**)
- The **Target Sheet** (Worksheet, Dashboard, or Story)

This action is quite similar to the **Button** object, as both allow you to navigate between your sheets. The difference, however, is crucial: one is a configurable Dashboard object, while the other is an action based on a sheet and a trigger.

The second new action allows you to create new ways to interact with your Worksheets.

The Change Set Values action (2018.3)

The **Change Set Values** action allows you to visually select the values to put in a set. From one or multiple source Worksheets, you can update the values of a set in your Data Source to impact other visualization in your Workbook.

When you create a **Change Set Values** action, a configuration window will open, where you can specify the following:

- The **Name** of the action
- The **Source Sheets**
- The trigger (**Hover**, **Select**, or **Menu**)
- The **set**—you have to specify the Data Source and the set

As for the action filter, you can dictate the behavior when clearing the action. There are three different behaviors, as follows:

- **Keep set value**: When you clear the selection, the current values of the set stay as selected.
- **Add all values to set**: When you clear the selection, all of the values will be in the set.
- **Remove all values from set**: When you clear the selection, all of the values will be out of the set.

Let's go through a guided tutorial, using **Sample-Superstore**, to see how to configure and use this new action:

1. Create a first Worksheet, `Sales by State` a map of **State** with **Sales** in color, as shown in the following screenshot:

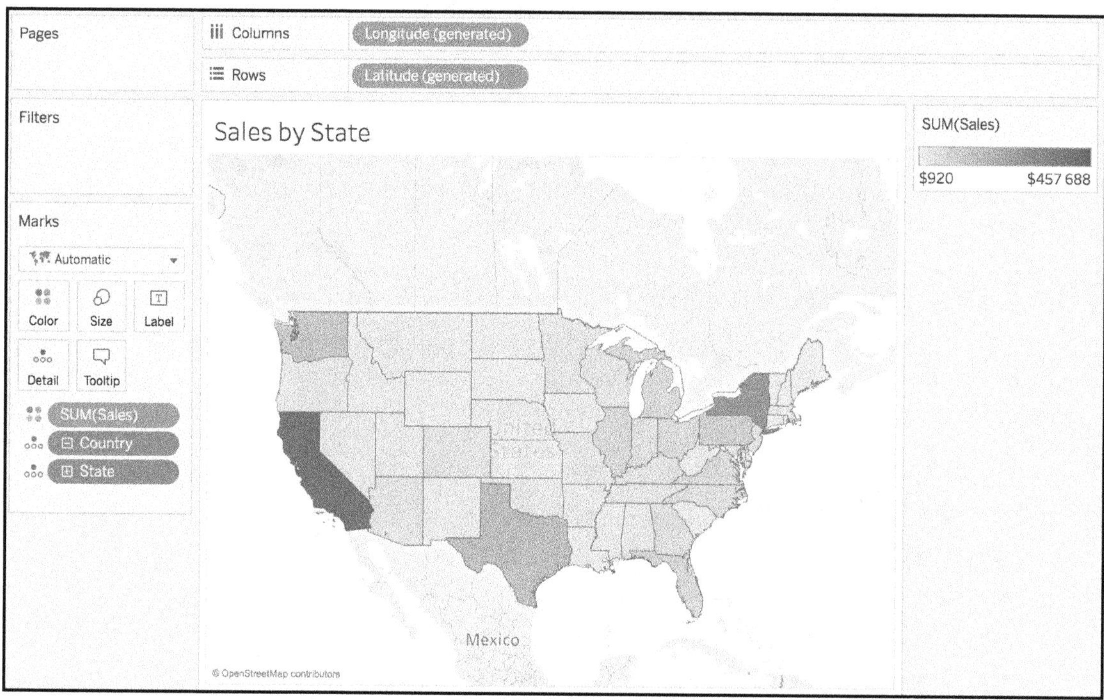

2. Create a set, `State Set`, based on **State** (right-click on the **State** field and go to **Create**, then **Set**). On the **Edit Set** window, select **Use all**, as follows:

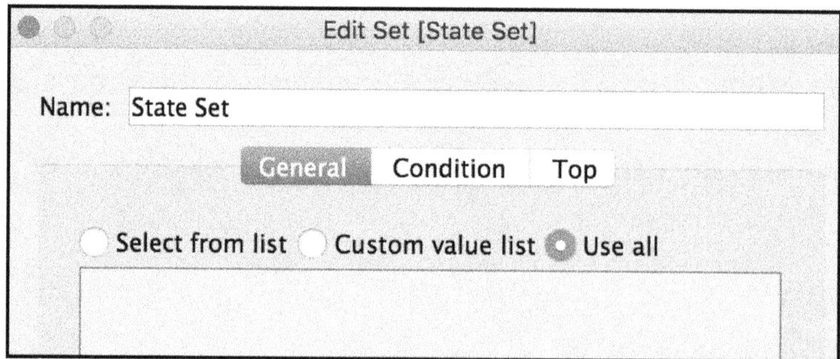

3. Create a second Worksheet, `Sales by Sub-Category`, with **Sales** in **Columns**, **Sub-Category** in **Rows**, and the new **State Set** in **Color**. The following screenshot shows what your Worksheet should look like:

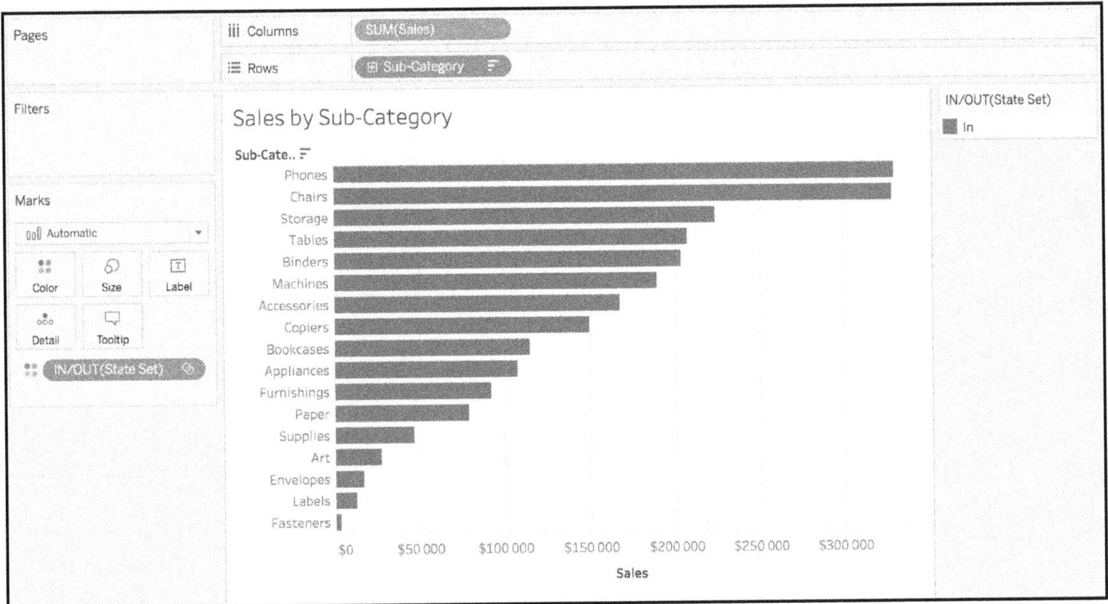

4. Create a Dashboard. First, add **Sales by State**, then add **Sales by Sub-Category** to the right. Add an action and choose **Change Set Values**. We want to update **State Set** when we click on a state on the map. When we clear the selection, all of the values will be **In** the set. The following screenshot illustrates the required configuration:

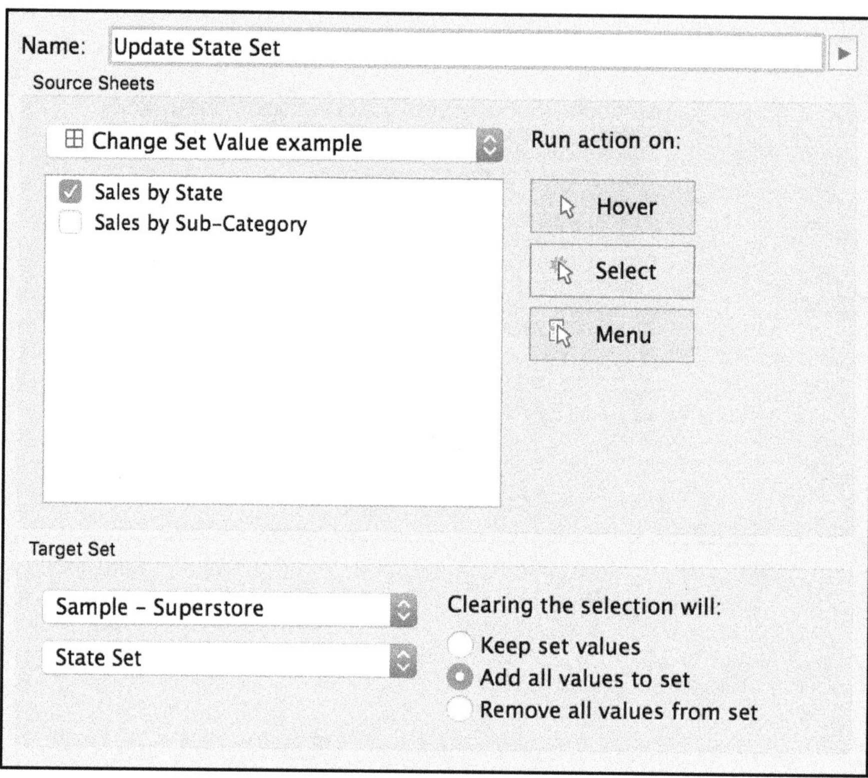

5. Let's test our action! When you select one or multiple states on the map, you should see the portion of sales coming from the selected state(s) on the right. In the following screenshot, you can see the portion of Sales coming from the state of California:

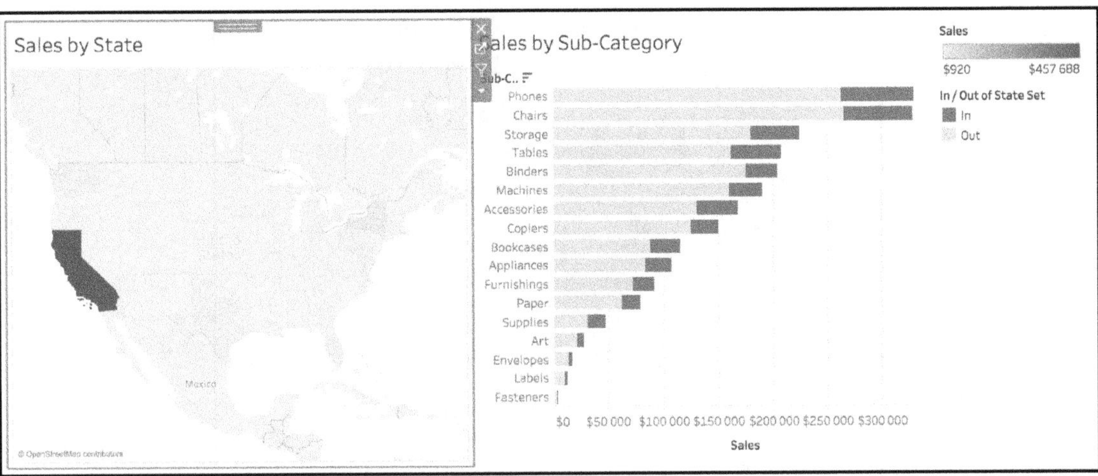

The ability to visually select the values of a set will surely provide great opportunities.

The next feature will be a great time saver if you have to create Mobile layouts.

Automatic Mobile layouts (2018.2)

From Tableau 2018.2, when you add a Phone or Tablet layout, Tableau automatically rearranges the Dashboard layout, making it ready to use. In the previous versions, you had to reorder it yourself.

Consider the automatic Phone layout created by Tableau before 2018.2, as shown in the following screenshot:

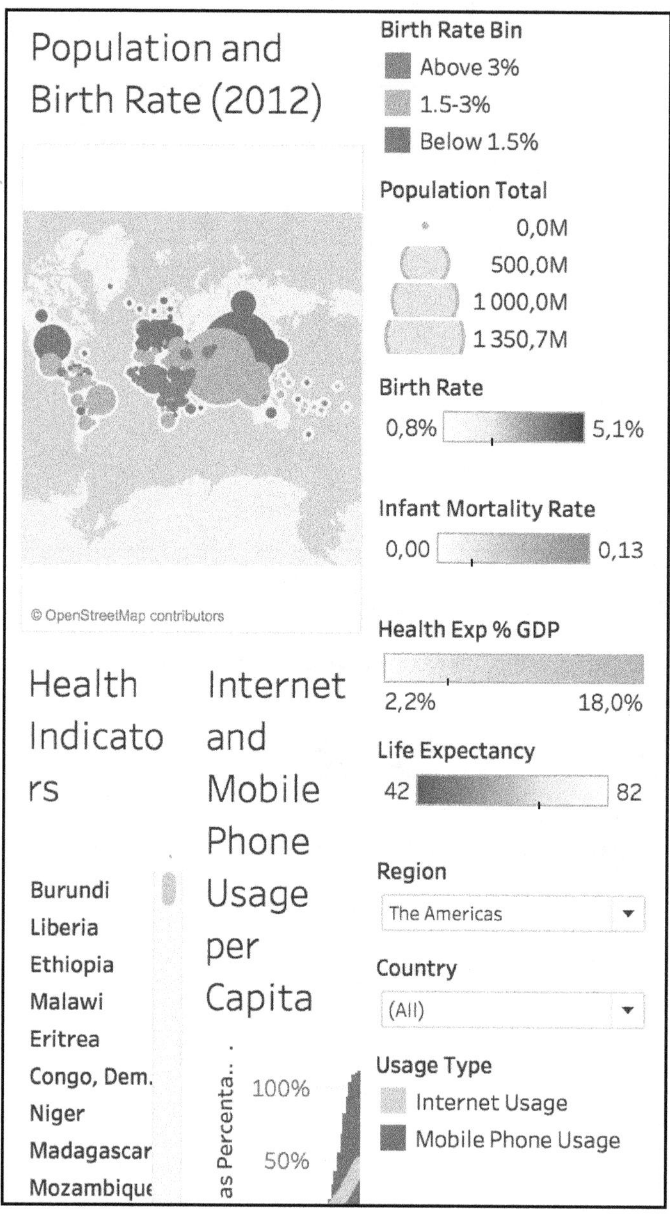

The following is the same layout, automatically built by Tableau in 2018.2:

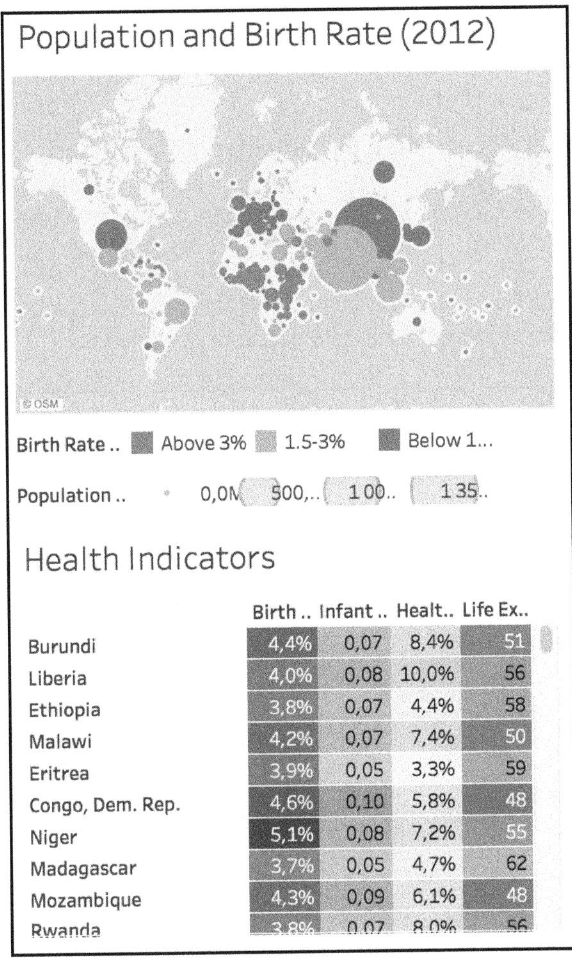

Population and Birth Rate (2012)
© OSM
Birth Rate .. Above 3% 1.5-3% Below 1...
Population .. 0,0M 500,.. 1 00.. 1 35..
Health Indicators
Birth .. Infant .. Healt.. Life Ex..
Burundi 4,4% 0,07 8,4% 51
Liberia 4,0% 0,08 10,0% 56
Ethiopia 3,8% 0,07 4,4% 58
Malawi 4,2% 0,07 7,4% 50
Eritrea 3,9% 0,05 3,3% 59
Congo, Dem. Rep. 4,6% 0,10 5,8% 48
Niger 5,1% 0,08 7,2% 55
Madagascar 3,7% 0,05 4,7% 62
Mozambique 4,3% 0,09 6,1% 48
Rwanda

If you decide to change something inside of your custom layout, you can use the **Rearrange layout** option. It will automatically reorder the items and change the sizes. The option is available when you click on the three dots (**...**) next to a layout, highlighted as follows:

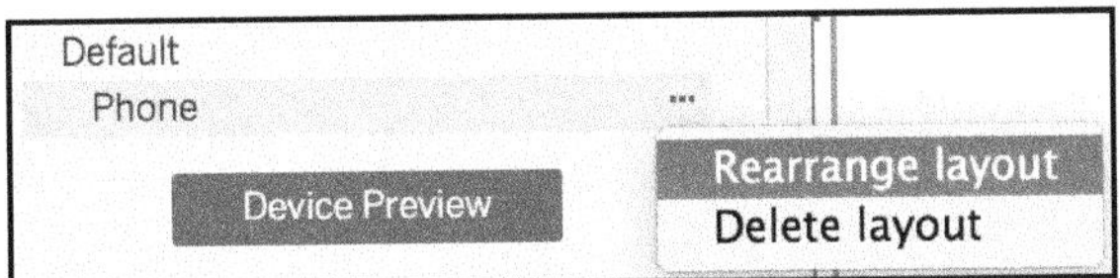

This feature doesn't allow you to create new things, but it'll save you a lot of time. The next feature is similar.

Grids (2018.2)

Whether you are working with floating or container layouts, the goal is the same: to have a nice-looking Dashboard. With Grids, Tableau makes it easier for you to achieve this. You can show or hide the Grid from the Dashboard menu, or by pressing the *G* key on your keyboard.

From the Dashboard menu, you can also open the **Grid** option and choose its size in pixels. The following screenshot shows an example of a ten-pixel grid:

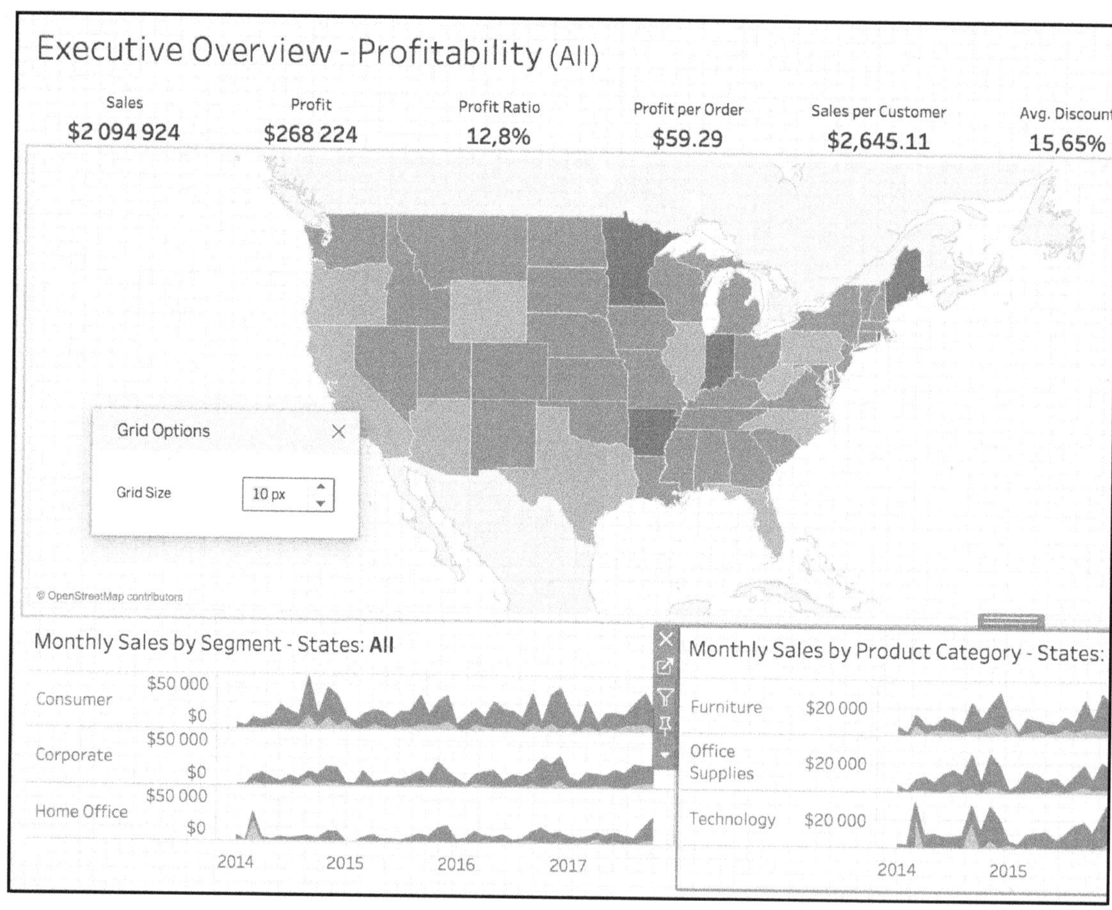

The Grid comes with another great enhancement: you can move the floating items, pixel by pixel, with the keyboard arrows. Achieving great designs has never been simpler!

This ends the section about Tableau Desktop. As always, Tableau has improved both Tableau Desktop and Tableau Server. Now, let's look at all of the new features available in Tableau Server and Tableau Online.

Tableau Server/Online

This second section, about Tableau Server, is also divided into three parts, as follows:

- **Interacting**: The new features available when you open a published Workbook
- **Web authoring**: The new features available when you create a new Workbook online
- **Administration**: The changes and enhancements involved in administrating a Tableau Server

To reproduce the examples presented in this chapter, you will have to know how to connect to Tableau Server, open published Workbooks, and create new Workbooks online.

Interacting

The major change comes in Tableau 2018.3 with the new browsing experience: mixed content. However, there are other nice new features when interacting with a view like the preview for Mobile layout and the ability to tag people in the comments.

Mixed content (2018.3)

From version 2018.3, Tableau Server has two ways to display the content. The new default way is called **mixed content**, and it shows different types of content in the same place.

Before Tableau Server 2018.3, the different types of content were separated into different tabs, and you had to select a specific tab to see its content. In the following screenshot, you can see an example of a project called **Sales**:

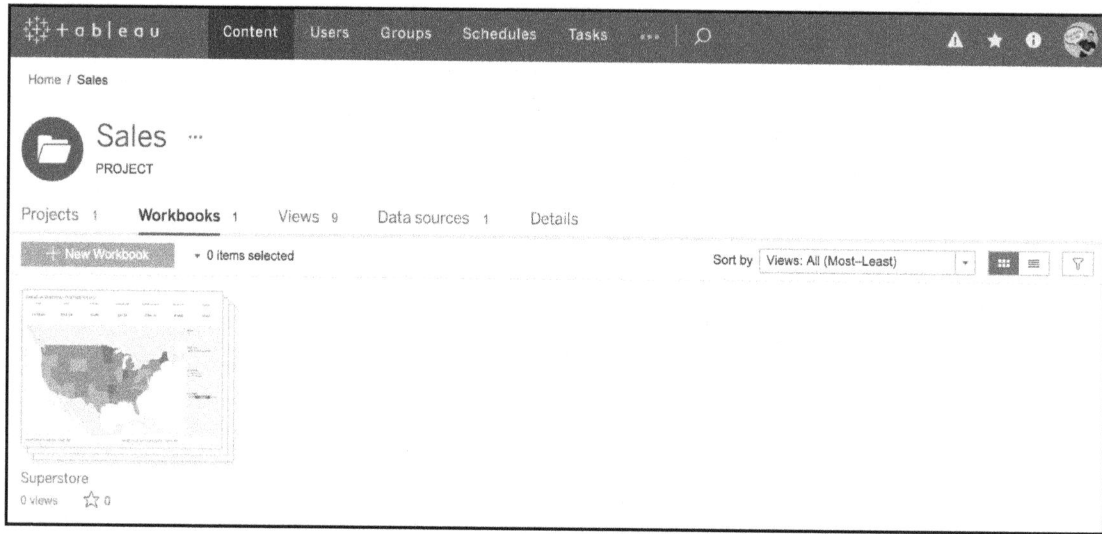

As you can see in the preceding screenshot, each tab contains a different type of content. In the following screenshot, you can see the same sales project with the sub-project (**Sales Projection**), one Workbook, and one Data Source, all displayed in the same place:

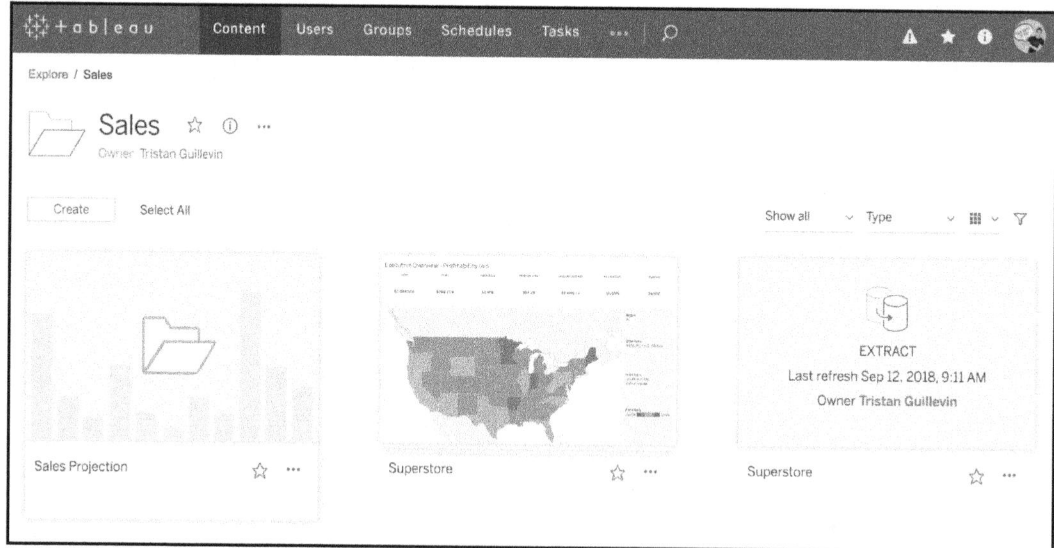

This new browsing method is simpler, and it keeps all of the same functionalities. If you prefer to keep the traditional browsing experience, you can deactivate the option in the **Settings** of Tableau Server, as follows:

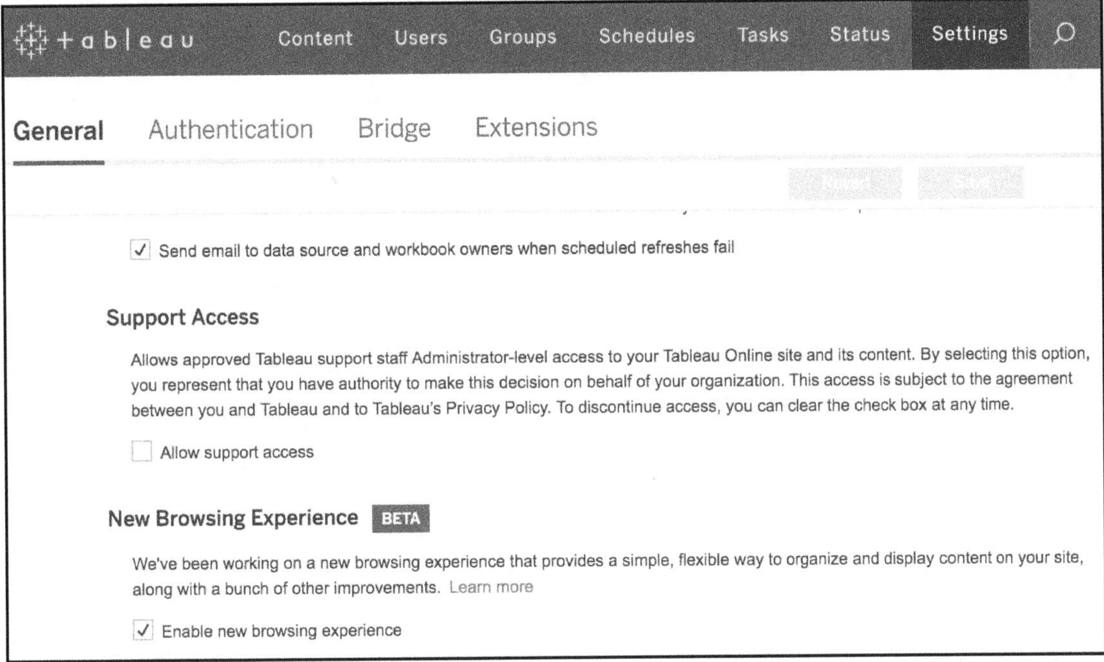

In Tableau Desktop 2018.2, the Automatic Mobile layout feature allows you to build great Phone and Tablet layouts more efficiently. With the next feature, you'll be able to test them online in seconds.

Mobile preview (2018.3)

From Tableau 2018.3, you can preview the different layouts in Tableau Server. Above the toolbar, when you open a **View**, a new button, **Preview Device Layouts**, is now available, as follows:

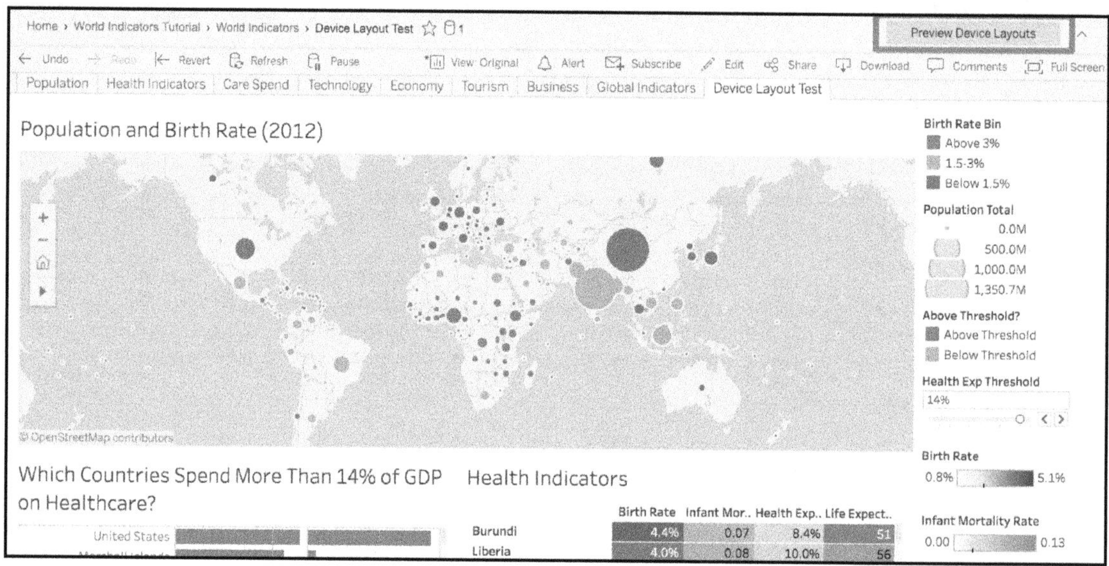

When you click on the button, Tableau opens the preview mode, where you can select **Laptop**, **Tablet**, or **Phone**, to see how your Dashboard renders. For example, if you preview the preceding Dashboard, you can see the Phone layout, as follows:

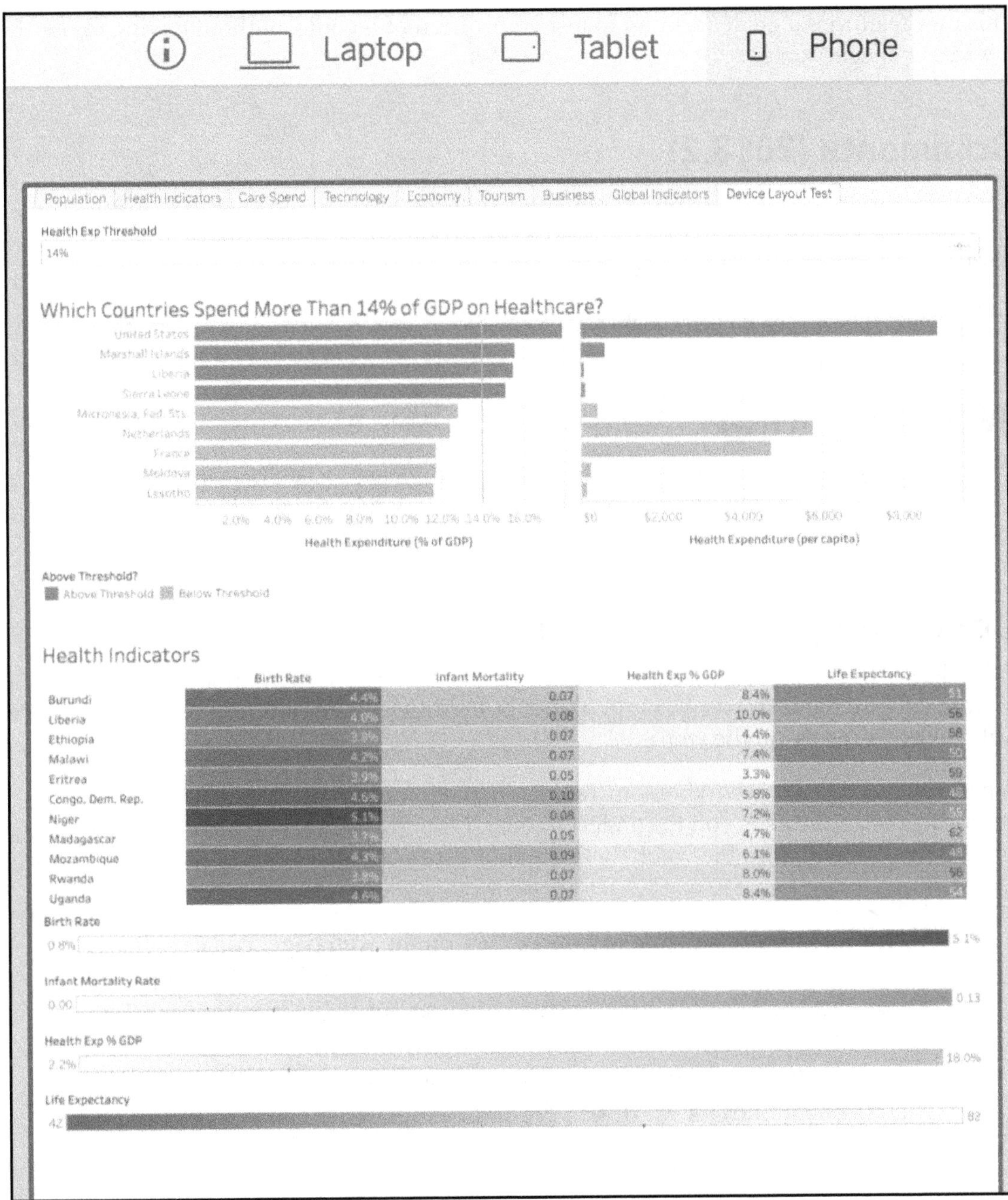
Laptop
Tablet
Phone
Population
Health Indicators
Care Spend
Technology
Economy
Tourism
Business
Global Indicators
Device Layout Test
Health Exp Threshold
14%
Which Countries Spend More Than 14% of GDP on Healthcare?
United States
Marshall Islands
Liberia
Sierra Leone
Micronesia, Fed. Sts.
Netherlands
France
Moldova
Lesotho
2.0% 4.0% 6.0% 8.0% 10.0% 12.0% 14.0% 16.0%
Health Expenditure (% of GDP)
$0 $2,000 $4,000 $6,000 $8,000
Health Expenditure (per capita)
Above Threshold?
Above Threshold
Below Threshold
Health Indicators
Birth Rate
Infant Mortality
Health Exp % GDP
Life Expectancy
Burundi
Liberia
Ethiopia
Malawi
Eritrea
Congo, Dem. Rep.
Niger
Madagascar
Mozambique
Rwanda
Uganda
Birth Rate
0.8%
5.1%
Infant Mortality Rate
0.00
0.13
Health Exp % GDP
2.2%
18.0%
Life Expectancy
42
82

Phone layout view

This new feature is a great addition to test your different layouts, without having to use the devices or special tools.

Comments (2018.2)

From Tableau Server 2018.3, you can mention Tableau Server/Online users by using the `@` symbol in the comments. They will be notified by email, making it easier to follow the discussions and answer questions.

Let's move on to the web authoring improvements.

Web authoring

Web authoring is getting better and better with each release of Tableau Server. Tableau Server 2018.1 added a significant new feature: the ability to connect to data directly from the web.

Connecting to data (2018.1)

In Tableau 2018.1, Tableau changed its Tableau License model, with three new roles: creator, explorer, and viewer. A particularity of the creator role is the ability to create a new Data Source, directly on the web.

When you create a new Workbook in Tableau Server, Tableau opens the web authoring mode and asks you to connect to data. From this page, you can connect to files and servers directly from the web! There are four types of data connections available, as follows:

- **File**: Drag and drop an Excel file or CSV on the web page; you can choose the sheets and build a new Data Source, just like in Tableau Desktop.
- **Connectors**: A list of server-hosted databases available directly from Tableau Server.
- **On this site**: Use an existing, published Data Source.
- **Dashboard Starters**: Start with pre-built templates of cloud-based systems.

Users that don't have a creator license can always use published Data Sources to create new analyses, but they can't connect to new data from files or servers.

You can also add a new Data Source to an existing workbook in the web authoring, just like in Tableau Desktop.

Other web authoring improvements

As you know, the web authoring mode of Tableau Server does not yet include all of the functionalities of Tableau Desktop. However, each new version adds a list of new capabilities, getting closer and closer to Tableau Desktop. The following are some of the important missing functionalities, which are now available online:

- Adding, removing, and editing annotations
- Updating axes and resizing headers
- Using **Show Me** from a Dashboard
- Finding fields in your Data Source by using the search button
- Adding images to a Dashboard
- Connecting to Google BigQuery and opening files from Dropbox and OneDrive
- Creating Joins, cross-database Joins, Unions, and Pivots

You can find all of the differences between Tableau Desktop and Tableau Server/Online at `https://public.tableau.com/views/TableauDesktopvTableauWebEditing/DesktopvsWebEdit`, created by Andrew Pick.

From Tableau Server 2018.1, the toolbar used to interact with a view is WCAG 2.0 AA compliant. Thanks to this improvement, the experience of using Tableau Online has been better for people that use screen readers, keyboards in braille, or keyboards only.

The time when saving a workbook online was also optimized in Tableau Server 2018.3. Of course, many of the new features of the latest Tableau Desktop version, such as extensions, buttons, and the Density Mark, are also included in the web authoring mode.

In the last section, we'll focus on the improvements for Tableau Server administrators.

Administration

The major change for administrators is the new Tableau Service Manager, but you'll find many other enhancements.

Tableau Service Manager (2018.2)

The first version of **Tableau Service Manager** (**TSM**) was introduced in Tableau Server 10.5, on Linux, with the TSM **command-line interface** (**CLI**). Now, with Tableau Server 2018.2, the TSM is available for both Windows and Linux, and contains three major components, as follows:

- A TSM CLI that replaces the previous `tabadmin` commands.

If you migrate from Tabadmin to the TSM CLI, the corresponding commands are available at `https://onlinehelp.tableau.com/current/server/en-us/tabadmin_to_tsm_cli.htm`.

- A Tableau Service Manager API (currently in alpha) that allows you to perform administrative tasks through an API.

You can find the documentation of the API at `https://onlinehelp.tableau.com/v0.0/api/tsm_api/en-us/index.htm#get-started`.

- A web UI interface that allows Tableau Server administrators to configure and manage the server directly from the web, without having to connect to the machine to open the configuration.

The most interesting feature is undoubtedly the web interface. You can access the administrative Tableau Server web page by using a URL, as if you were logging in to Tableau Server. From the web page, you can directly stop and start Tableau Server. The administration web page contains three tabs, as follows:

- **Status**: Check the current state of your Tableau Server.
- **Maintenance**: Generate, download, and analyze the log files, as well as other maintenance tasks.
- **Configuration**: Modify the topology of the server (the number of processes and nodes), the security, the user identity access, the notifications, and the licensing.

In short, all of the actions that require the administrators to connect to the machine where the server is installed to perform administrative tasks can now be done from the web, or by using the API. This improvement will surely make life easier for all administrators and DevOps teams!

To finish, let's review some other administrative improvements.

Other administrative improvements

The following is a list of other improvements for admins:

- Tableau Bridge handles load-balanced live connections across multiple pooled clients.
- Two new backgrounder API functions are available: the GetJobList API (pulls the list of all jobs) and the CancelJob API (reclaims the resources of running and pending jobs).
- Tableau Online users are notified by email when they are added to a Tableau Online site.
- New admin Data Sources are available online, to create administrative views.
- You can activate **System for Cross-Domain Identity Provider** (**SCMI**) to manage the Tableau Server users with an external identity provider, such as Okta or OneLogin.

Summary

With version 10.5, Tableau introduced a new data engine, Hyper, and included a long-awaited feature, the Viz in Tooltip. The 2018 releases have nothing to be ashamed of, in comparison! Every release brings a lot of new features and improvements.

In Tableau Desktop, with the multiple table schema and the spatial Join, you can create better Data Sources with improved performances. Visualizing the data has also improved considerably, with the new Density Marks type, step and jump lines, Worksheet transparency, and many more improvements for Dual Axis map, hierarchy filters, and nested sorts.

The most notable new features concern Dashboards. The ability to download and add extensions developed by Tableau and their partners from the Extension Gallery provides tons of new uses for Tableau. A few of the Tableau user dreams have already come true, thanks to the extensions. Also, you can develop your extensions to create the interactions that meet your needs. That's just one new feature! The navigation button and action, the update set value action, the automatic Mobile layout, and the grid, are some of the other features that will have huge impacts on building a Dashboard.

Tableau Server was not left out! A new browsing experience, a Mobile layout preview, and improved comments are now available when you interact with Tableau Server. Administrators also have some great new ways to perform their work, with the TSM allowing them to manage the server from a web page. However, the biggest change has come with the 2018.1 version and the ability to connect to data directly from a browser.

2018 was a great year for Tableau users and the Tableau community. This first chapter, which described the new features, is now over. If you learned how to use Tableau with this book, I hope that this chapter has provided you with a greater desire to use Tableau. If you started with this chapter, you must already know about Tableau. However, I'm sure this book has more to teach you (and that's surely why you purchased it), so don't hesitate to continue reading: read the tips, try the tutorials, and learn more about Tableau Desktop, Tableau Server, and the Tableau community.

2
The Tableau Core

New to Tableau? This is the first chapter you should read. Tableau is an easy tool, and you can even start using it without any training. However, using it the wrong way or without knowing the basics is a big mistake. People who are unhappy with Tableau, or who find it difficult to use, don't have the necessary knowledge to have a great start.

To begin, we'll go through all the things that every Tableau user should know. The following topics will be covered in this chapter:

- The different Tableau products
- Speaking Tableau
- Dimensions and Measures
- Blue and green—Discrete and Continuous
- The toolbar options
- Live or Extract

By the end of this chapter, you'll have all the knowledge to start your Tableau journey in the best possible way.

The different Tableau products

There are seven Tableau products:

- **Tableau Desktop** is the product. It is a software to install on your computer. It is the core tool to connect to the data, build a Data Source, and create visualizations and a dashboard. This book focuses on Tableau Desktop.
- **Tableau Server** is an online tool for sharing your work in a business environment. You need this tool to secure your data. Tableau Server is accessible with a simple browser. Your company hosts the server.

- **Tableau Online** is the same as Tableau Server but hosted by Tableau. They do the updates and maintenance, but you lose some personalization features.
- **Tableau Reader** is a software to install on your computer that can read Tableau Desktop files. With Tableau Reader, you are not able to modify the visualization, but you can read it and keep all the interactivity, making it a better export than a PDF or a picture.
- **Tableau Public** is a free software with almost the same capabilities as Tableau Desktop, but you can only save your work online in a public environment, and not all connectors are available. Of course, it's not the best if you don't want to share your data with the world, but it's a great place to find inspiration and share public visualizations.
- **Tableau Mobile** is an application that you can install on your smartphone or tablet. You can connect to a server and visualize your Dashboard directly with the app.
- **Tableau Prep** is a new software that is very different from the others. It is not a data visualization tool but a data preparation tool. We'll not speak about Tableau Prep in this book, but know that it exists, and it is a great solution for cleaning your data.

Like every tool, Tableau has its wording. Let's learn how to speak Tableau.

Speaking Tableau

Rather than a big list of all the terms, let's go through the basic Tableau usage.

When you open Tableau, you start working on a Workbook. After you're done working, you save your work in that Workbook (a `.twb` or `.twbx` file). You can open multiple instances of Tableau, each of them being a different Workbook.

The first page when creating a Workbook is the start page. Here, you can **Connect** to data and open recent Workbooks. Here is the start page:

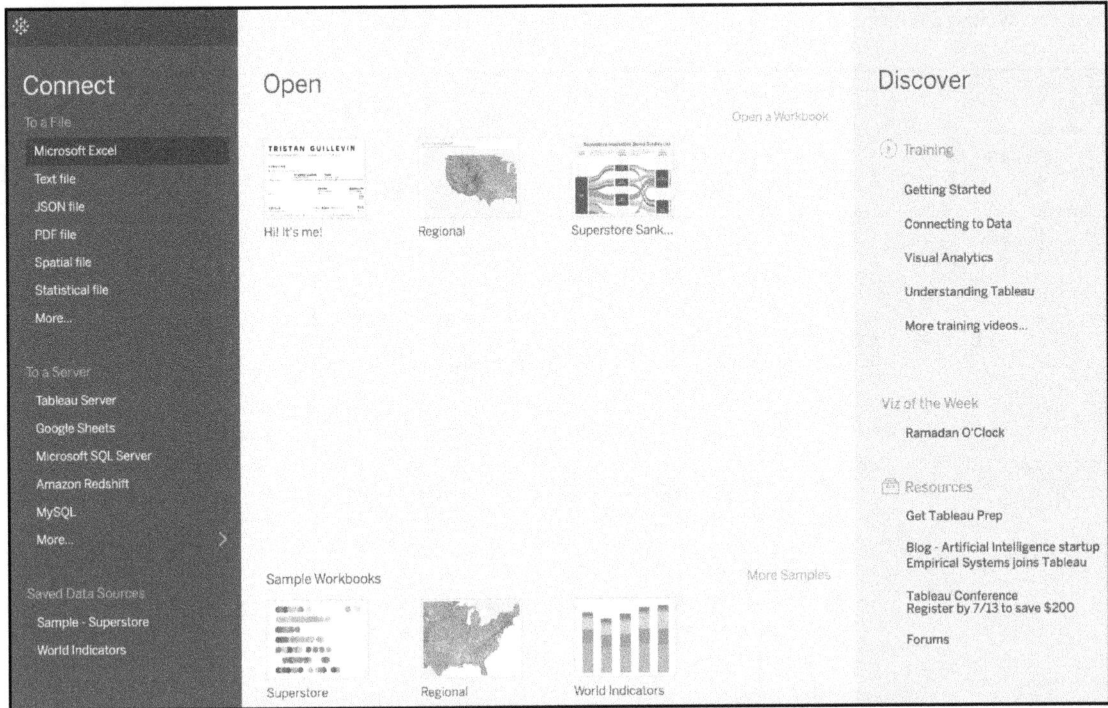

After connecting to a File or a Server, Tableau opens the Data Source workplace. On this page, you can create the Data Source by choosing the tables you want to use and creating Joins, Unions, or other transformations. The following screenshot illustrates the Data Source workplace:

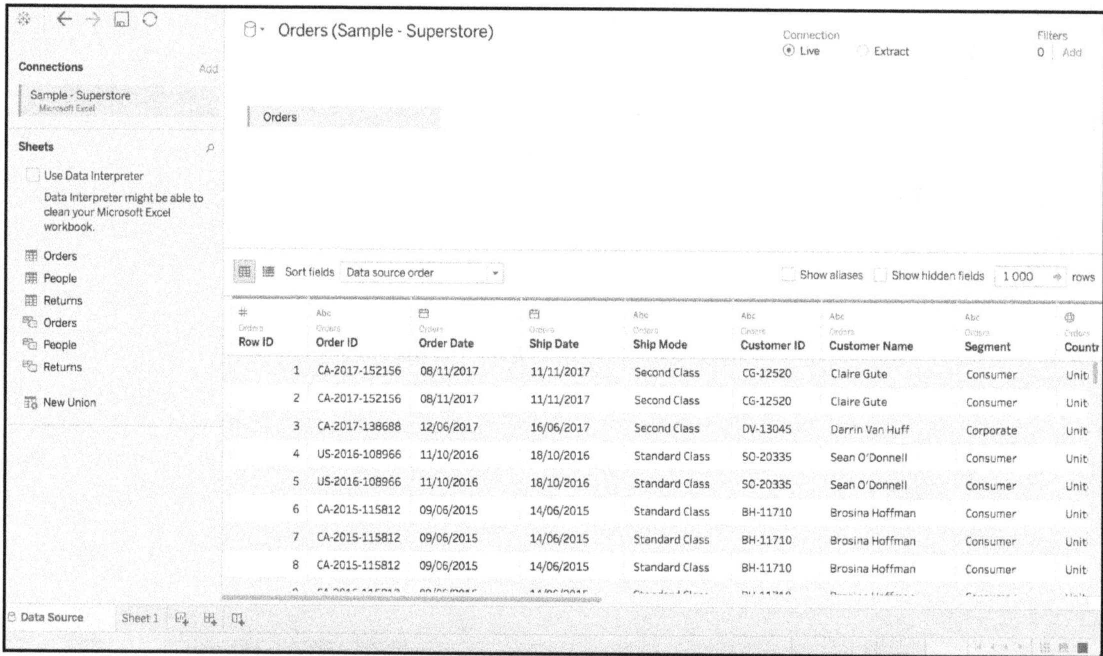

Once your Data Source is done, you can start working on a Worksheet. **Sheet 1** is your first Worksheet. On the left you can see your Data Source with all the fields, split between four elements: **Measures**, **Dimensions**, **Sets**, and **Parameters**. Each field has a data type (Text, Number, Boolean, and so on). You can create new fields, such as Groups, Bins, Hierarchies, or Calculated Fields.

The big blank part is the View. It is here that your visualization is displayed. Around the View, you can see different shelves (**Rows**, **Columns**, **Pages**, **Filters**, and **Marks**). To create a visualization, you have to put fields on those shelves. Once a field is on a shelf, it is called a **pill**. Pills can be green if Continuous or blue if Discrete. In your visualization, every distinct element you can select is called a **mark**. The next screenshot displays the Worksheet workplace:

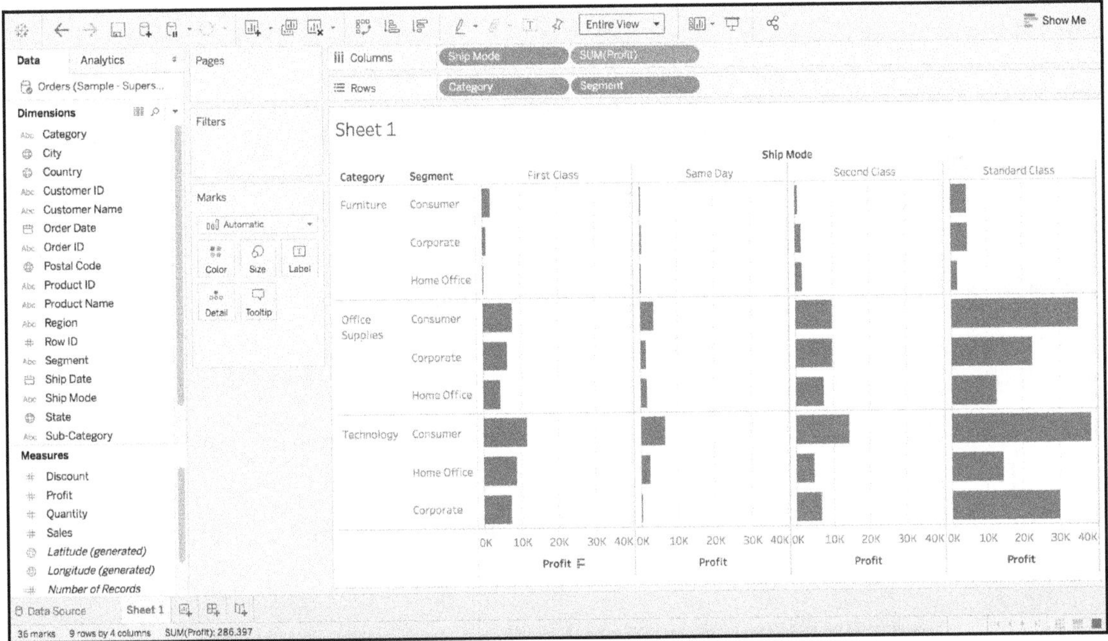

In Tableau, one Worksheet is one idea, one way of answering a question, and one visualization. You can create as many Worksheets as you want to find the best way to represent your data. Once you have enough Worksheets to answer all your questions, you create a Dashboard. A Dashboard is a combination of multiple Worksheets and objects. You can add actions for interactivity between the different Worksheets and other objects, such as text and image to add context.

If you want to tell a story with your data, you can create a Story. The goal of the Story is to prepare a succession of Story points (each of them could be a Dashboard or a Worksheet). On each Story point, you can add a caption, annotate the visualization, and put some filters that the Story point will remember. So, when presenting or sharing your Story, every interaction or explanation is already done.

You can breathe now! I understand if you think that there are too many words. Don't worry; you don't have to remember all of them now. Each chapter of this book focuses on a specific part of Tableau, and you'll have plenty of time to get familiar with these words with real examples. However, two words need a particular explanation: Dimension and Measure.

Dimension and Measure

When you create a data source, the fields are split between Dimensions and Measures. The *Measure* is what you want to analyze, and the *Dimension* is the angle of analysis.

By default, numbers are Measures, and the other data types (Text, Date, Geographical Role) are Dimensions, but that's not always the case. Any data type can be either a Dimension or a Measure.

A Dimension contains qualitative information. It always splits the Marks and is never aggregated.

A Measure is, by default, aggregated, contains quantitative information, and is almost always numeric.

You can easily see whether a field is aggregated or not by looking at its corresponding pill when you use it in a shelf. If it is aggregated, the name of the field is in brackets, with the name of the aggregation at the beginning (for example, **SUM(Profit)**).

As you can see, it's hard to give an exact rule to discern Measure and Dimension. It's more a concept to understand and a useful way to arrange the fields. Yes, you could have believed that *Dimensions* are blue and *Measures* are green. It is an easy mistake to make when you start using Tableau.

Curious to know the real difference between the blue and green fields? Everything is explained in the next topic.

Blue and green – Discrete and Continuous

A field or pill in blue is *Discrete*. A field or pill in green is *Continuous*. Dimensions and Measures can be either Continuous or Discrete.

A Discrete field displays each distinct value. Any data types can be expressed in a discrete way. In the View, a Discrete field placed in Rows or Columns is represented with headers. Here is an example of a Discrete Dimension and a Discrete Measure, as you can see both have clickable and distinct headers:

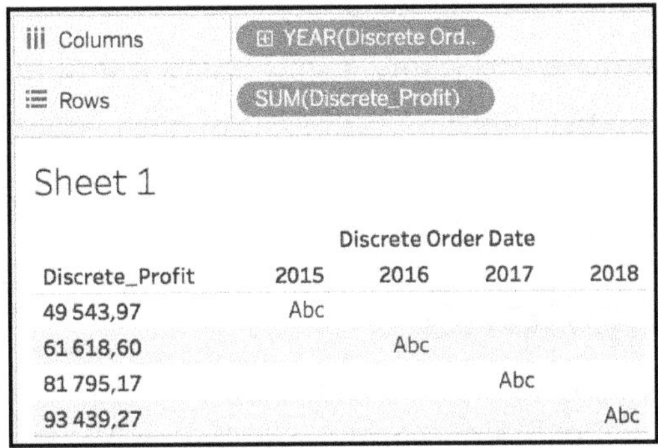

A Continuous field represents values from an infinite set. Only numbers and dates can be continuous. In the View, Continuous fields are represented on an axis. Here is an example of a Continuous Dimension and a Continuous Measure, as you can see, both are displayed on an axis:

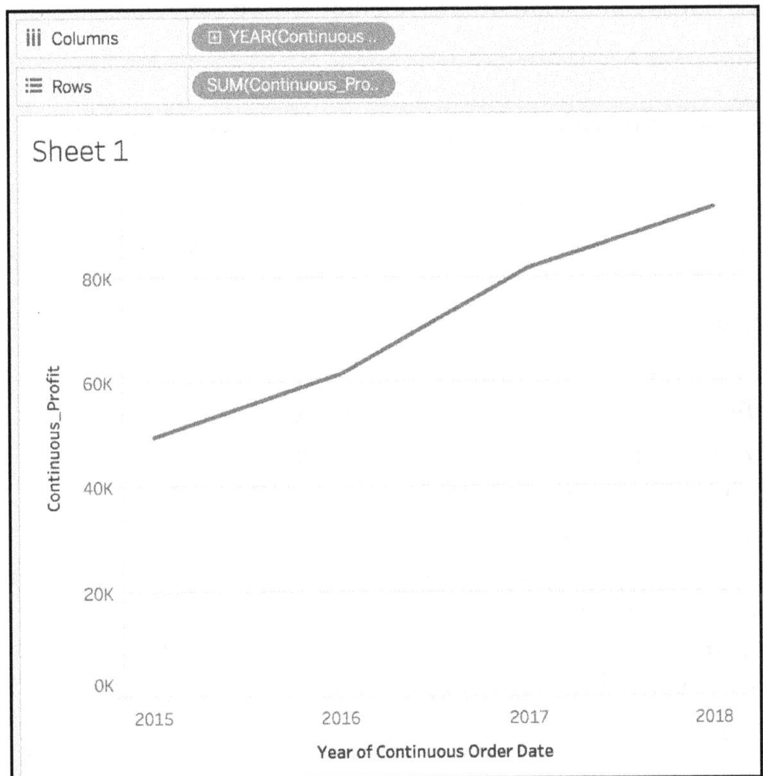

It is crucial to understand these differences. It may sound a bit abstract, but it'll help you when you start building visualizations. Talking about visualizations, there is a bar that you constantly see when using Tableau: *the toolbar*. Let's see the different options available with a single click.

The toolbar options

Whether you are working on a Worksheet, Dashboard, or Story, you can always see the toolbar on top. Let's review the different options it offers while knowing that a lot of specific words will be explained in other chapters:

- **Tableau icon** : Opens the start page (you don't lose your work).
- **Undo** ←: Reverses your action. The great thing is that you can undo an unlimited number of times, starting back from the very beginning if you want!
- **Redo** →: Useful if you undo a bit too much. You can redo the most recent undone action.
- **Save** : Saves your Workbook on your computer.
- **Add a new Data Source** : Opens the menu to choose a new connection to a file or a server.
- **Auto update Pause** /**Play** : Interrupts all the queries to the connection. If you try to build a visualization, everything will be grayed out until you hit play again. It's useful when the query is very long.
- **Refresh** : Executes a query to refresh the data.
- **New Worksheet** : Opens a new blank Worksheet.
- **Duplicate Worksheet** : Creates a copy of the current Worksheet.
- **Clear** : Removes the pills and formatting in the Worksheet. You can use the arrow to clear only specific parts.
- **Swap** : Replaces the pills in Rows with those in the Columns and vice versa.
- **Sort ascending** : Automatically sorts the selected Dimension from the lowest value to the highest value.
- **Sort descending** : Automatically sorts the selected Dimension from the highest value to the lowest value.

- **Highlight** : Enables or disables highlights in the Worksheet or Workbook.
- **Group** : A shortcut to create Groups.
- **Show Labels** : A shortcut to display the Labels.
- **Fix axis** : By default, the axis range is automatic. With this option, you can fix the axis at its current state.
- **Fit** Standard : Defines how the Worksheet should fit on the screen. For *Standard*, the size of the cells defines the size of the visualization. The other fitting options force the View to fit the width, the height, or both.
- **Show/Hide Cards** : Opens a menu where you can decide which elements to show in the current Worksheet.
- **Presentation mode** : Turns Tableau fullscreen for your presentation.
- **Share** : Opens a new window to publish the Workbook on a Tableau Server/Online or Tableau Public.
- **Show me** Show Me: Lets you, at any time, change the visualization in the Worksheet.

Before we finish this chapter, it's important to understand one last fundamental element of Tableau: the difference between a Live connection and an Extract.

Live or Extract

When you connect to a file or a server, on the *Data Source* workplace, at the top right, you have the option to use the Data Source **Live** or **Extract**, as you can see in the following screenshot:

There is a big difference between the two options, so let's see them in detail.

Live

A Live connection creates a direct link between the Tableau Data Source and the database (server or file). It means that, if the data changes, you see the impact in Tableau directly after refreshing the Data Source, or when you reopen the Workbook.

The problem with a Live connection is that you are dependent on the performance of the database. Large text files, big Excel files, or an unoptimized database can be very slow to analyze in Tableau. Also, if you are connected to an online database, you are dependent on the internet connection, and you won't be able to work offline.

For these reasons, I advise you to always work with an Extract.

Extract

When you create an Extract, Tableau copies your database into a Hyper file (since Tableau 10.5) on your computer. Then, the Data Source is no longer linked to the database but to the Hyper file.

The first advantage of the Extract is that it's optimized for Tableau, meaning that no matter the speed of your initial connection, you will have excellent performance. Keep that in mind. If you think that your Dashboard is slow, the first thing to check is whether you are using an Extract. You are also able to work offline because the Extract is a local copy of your database.

Unlike a Live connection, you don't observe instantly the changes in the database. To see the changes, you need to refresh the Extract. When you update it, Tableau connects again to the database and creates a new copy of the data into the Hyper file.

The only problem you may encounter is when you try to create an Extract from a huge database. As Tableau needs to copy the data, it could take a long time to retrieve all the rows. To deal with that, you can click on **Edit**, next to the **Extract** option, add some **Filters**, and aggregate the data or indicate the number of rows to retrieve. Usually, you don't need to do that, but keep in mind that it exists.

You can see in the following screenshot the options when editing an **Extract**:

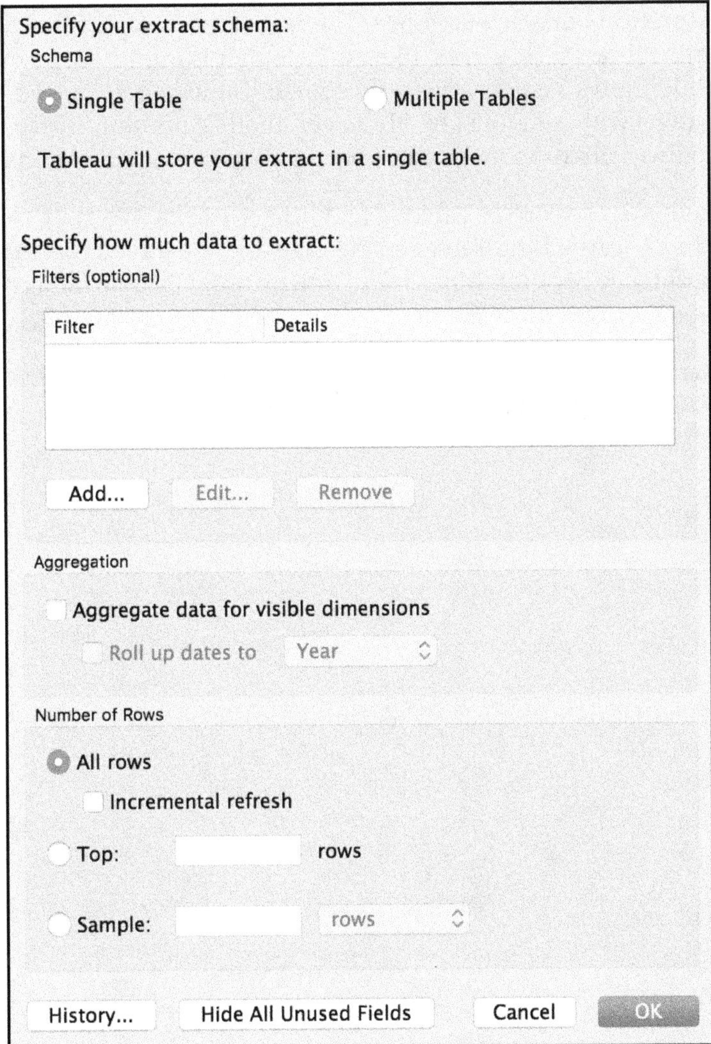

Since Tableau 2018.3, you can specify the schema used for the extract. If you create a data source combining **Multiple Tables**, it could be better to use the **Multiple Tables** schema for better performance. This topic is covered in detail the `Chapter 1`, *Catch up with Tableau 2018*.

There are pros and cons of using either the Live or Extract Data Source. In the end, the choice is yours, but now you can make the best decision.

Summary

This chapter is theoretical but also necessary. The rest of the book is filled with concrete examples based on real cases. However, like every tool, it is important to understand the core principle to build great visualizations. Of course, Tableau is easy, and you can start creating visualizations without any help. However, there is nothing worse than starting with bad habits, only to discover that you've been doing it wrong the whole time.

What we saw together is the core of Tableau and how it works. We got a clear overview of the different products, learned the Tableau language and the toolbar options, and understood the difference between Measures, Dimensions, Discrete fields, Continuous fields, a Live connection, and an Extract.

How about we start using Tableau now? Isn't that why you bought this book? The next chapter is all about showing you how to build great things.

3
A First Dashboard and Exploration

This chapter is your first concrete introduction to Tableau. Together, we'll connect to data, create three visualizations, and assemble them in what will be your first Dashboard. Then, we'll use Tableau as a data exploration tool and answer business questions by using only the power of data visualization.

The following are the topics covered in this chapter:

- Connecting to data
- Creating a first set of visualizations
- Building your first Dashboard
- Using Tableau for data exploration

A few things before we start. Be not afraid. Two buttons on the toolbar will always save you:

- ←: This lets you undo any actions, and, good news, it's unlimited. So if you make a mistake, use it!
- : This lets you start from the beginning. It removes everything in the Worksheet or Dashboard. Start fresh start if you feel stuck somewhere!

Are you ready? Then double-click on the Tableau icon and let's get started.

Connect to data

For this first guided tutorial, we are using the Tableau iconic dataset: **Sample-Superstore**. This dataset is an Excel file about supermarket sales in the United States, contained in your Tableau repository folder. It's easy to understand and use. The Excel file is composed of three sheets: **Orders**, **People**, and **Returns**.

When you open Tableau, on the left, in the **Connect** area, click on **Microsoft Excel**:

- If you're a Mac user, navigate to **Documents** | **My Tableau Repository** | **Data Source** | **[Your Tableau Version]** | **en_US-US** and open the file named `Sample - Superstore.xls`
- If you're a Windows user, go to **My Documents** | **My Tableau Repository** | **Data Source** | **[Your Tableau Version]** | **en_US-US** and open the file named `Sample - Superstore.xls`

If you can't find the file, you can download it from the *Chapter 3 : A First Dashboard and Exploration* section on my website: `book.ladataviz.com` or by using this direct link: `https://ladataviz.com/wp-content/uploads/2018/09/Sample-Superstore.xlsx`. Then, select the downloaded file when connecting from Tableau.

After selecting the file, you are in the **Data Source** workplace. In the top-left, you can see the name of the `Sample -Superstore` file and, underneath it, you can see the three sheets in the Excel file: **Orders**, **People**, and **Returns**.

For this example, we only use **Orders**, so follow Tableau's invitation and drag the **Orders** table into the middle of the page:

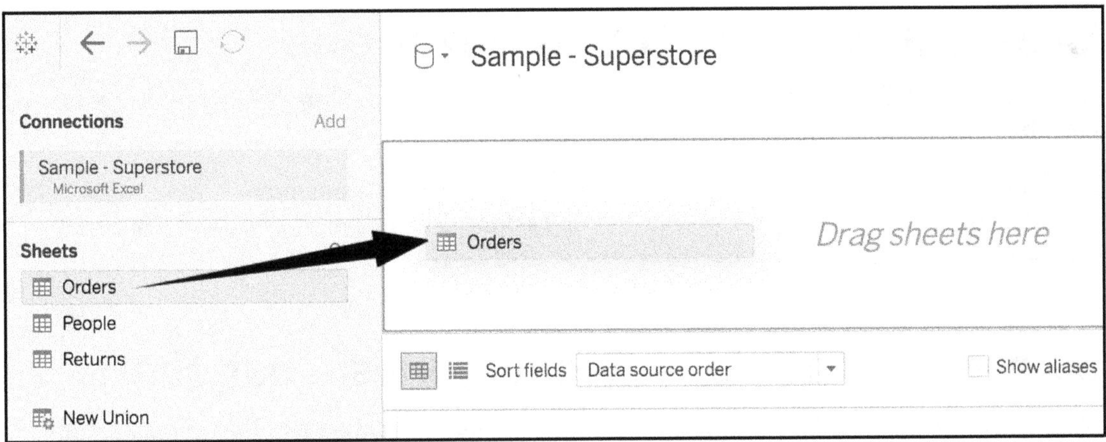

Once it's done, Tableau gives you a snapshot of the first 1,000 rows. You can also see that, preceding each column name, an icon indicates the data type defined by Tableau:

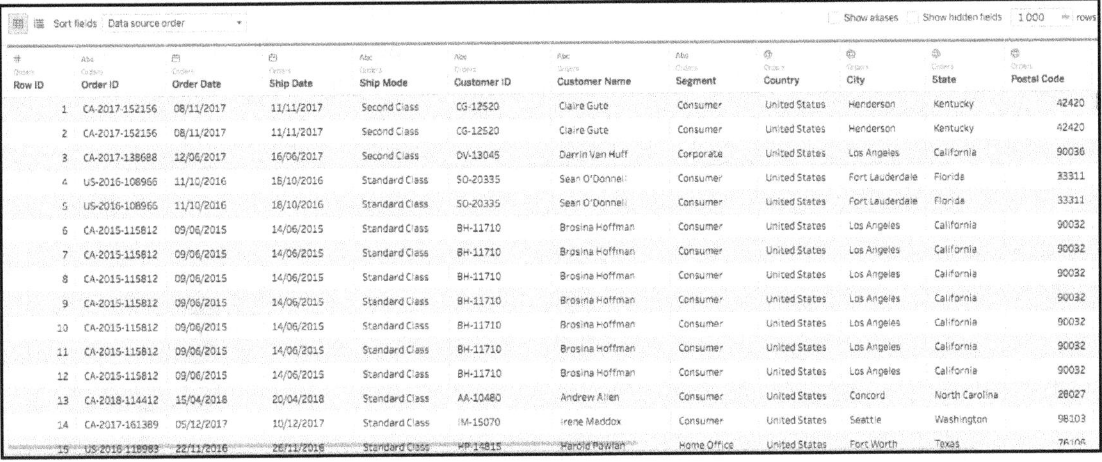

Row ID	Order ID	Order Date	Ship Date	Ship Mode	Customer ID	Customer Name	Segment	Country	City	State	Postal Code
1	CA-2017-152156	08/11/2017	11/11/2017	Second Class	CG-12520	Claire Gute	Consumer	United States	Henderson	Kentucky	42420
2	CA-2017-152156	08/11/2017	11/11/2017	Second Class	CG-12520	Claire Gute	Consumer	United States	Henderson	Kentucky	42420
3	CA-2017-138688	12/06/2017	16/06/2017	Second Class	DV-13045	Darrin Van Huff	Corporate	United States	Los Angeles	California	90036
4	US-2016-108966	11/10/2016	18/10/2016	Standard Class	SO-20335	Sean O'Donnell	Consumer	United States	Fort Lauderdale	Florida	33311
5	US-2016-108966	11/10/2016	18/10/2016	Standard Class	SO-20335	Sean O'Donnell	Consumer	United States	Fort Lauderdale	Florida	33311
6	CA-2015-115812	09/06/2015	14/06/2015	Standard Class	BH-11710	Brosina Hoffman	Consumer	United States	Los Angeles	California	90032
7	CA-2015-115812	09/06/2015	14/06/2015	Standard Class	BH-11710	Brosina Hoffman	Consumer	United States	Los Angeles	California	90032
8	CA-2015-115812	09/06/2015	14/06/2015	Standard Class	BH-11710	Brosina Hoffman	Consumer	United States	Los Angeles	California	90032
9	CA-2015-115812	09/06/2015	14/06/2015	Standard Class	BH-11710	Brosina Hoffman	Consumer	United States	Los Angeles	California	90032
10	CA-2015-115812	09/06/2015	14/06/2015	Standard Class	BH-11710	Brosina Hoffman	Consumer	United States	Los Angeles	California	90032
11	CA-2015-115812	09/06/2015	14/06/2015	Standard Class	BH-11710	Brosina Hoffman	Consumer	United States	Los Angeles	California	90032
12	CA-2015-115812	09/06/2015	14/06/2015	Standard Class	BH-11710	Brosina Hoffman	Consumer	United States	Los Angeles	California	90032
13	CA-2018-114412	15/04/2018	20/04/2018	Standard Class	AA-10480	Andrew Allen	Consumer	United States	Concord	North Carolina	28027
14	CA-2017-161389	05/12/2017	10/12/2017	Standard Class	IM-15070	Irene Maddox	Consumer	United States	Seattle	Washington	98103
15	US-2016-118983	22/11/2016	26/11/2016	Standard Class	HP-14815	Harold Pawlan	Home Office	United States	Fort Worth	Texas	76106

Bravo! You've built your first Data Source. In the next chapters, we'll see in detail the meaning of each data type and the other options when connecting to data. For the moment, keep everything as it is and, at the bottom of the page, click on **Sheet 1**.

Create a first set of visualizations

After clicking on **Sheet 1**, you enter the Worksheet workplace. Here is where you create visualizations. One Worksheet answers one question.

You can also see that your data source is divided between **Dimensions** and **Measures** (please refer to `Chapter 2`, *The Tableau Core*, in the *Measure and Dimension* section). Let's create our first visualization.

Sales and profit by sub-categories – bar chart

The first question we'll answer is: what are the product sub-categories that generate the most sales and profits? Let's find out how to do that:

1. Double-click on **Sales** in the **Data Source**. You should now see one bar. If you put the mouse over the bar, you should read **Sales: 2,297,201**. As a measure is always aggregated, here you can see the sum of all the sales.
2. On the **Data Source**, double-click on **Sub-Category**. The sub-categories now split the bar. A quick look can tell you that **Chairs** and **Phones** are the best-selling products:

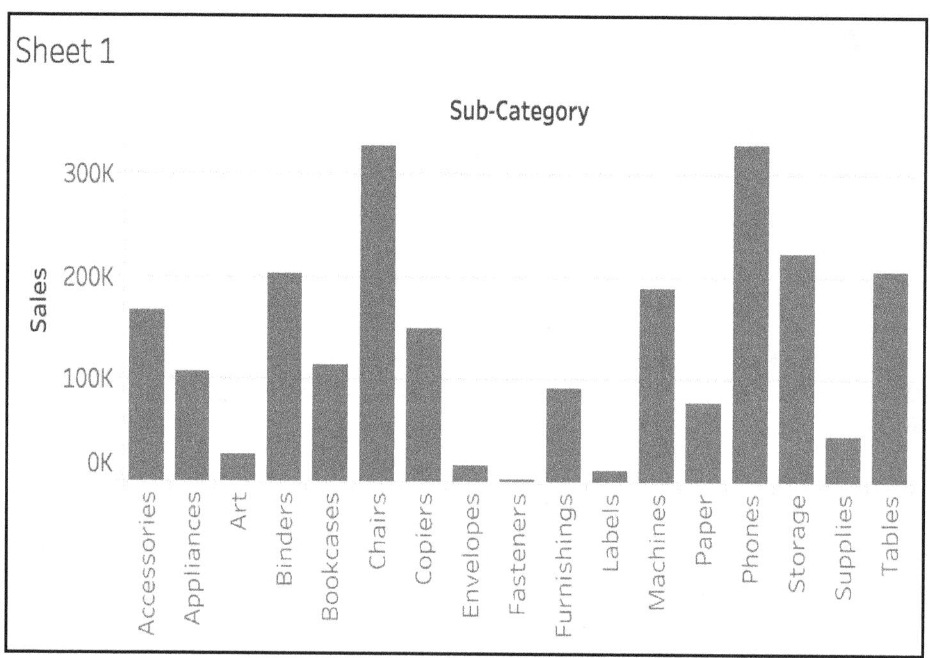

3. On the toolbar, click on the Swap icon: .This way it's easier to read the sub-categories. We can do even better by clicking on the descending Sort icon to show this:

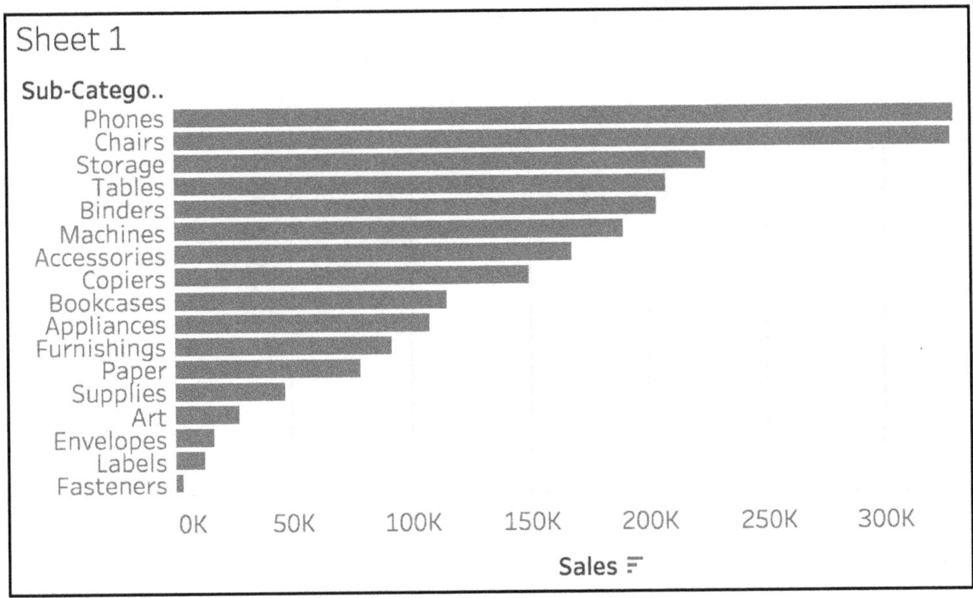

Now the sub-categories are sorted, and it's effortless to answer questions such as *What are the top three sub-categories?*, *What are the bottom three sub-categories?*, and *How do tables perform compared to bookcases?*

4. Sales often come with Profits. In Tableau, it's straightforward to use pre-attentive attributes (Color, Size, Shape, and so on) to add secondary information. Here, simply drag and drop **Profit** in **Color**:

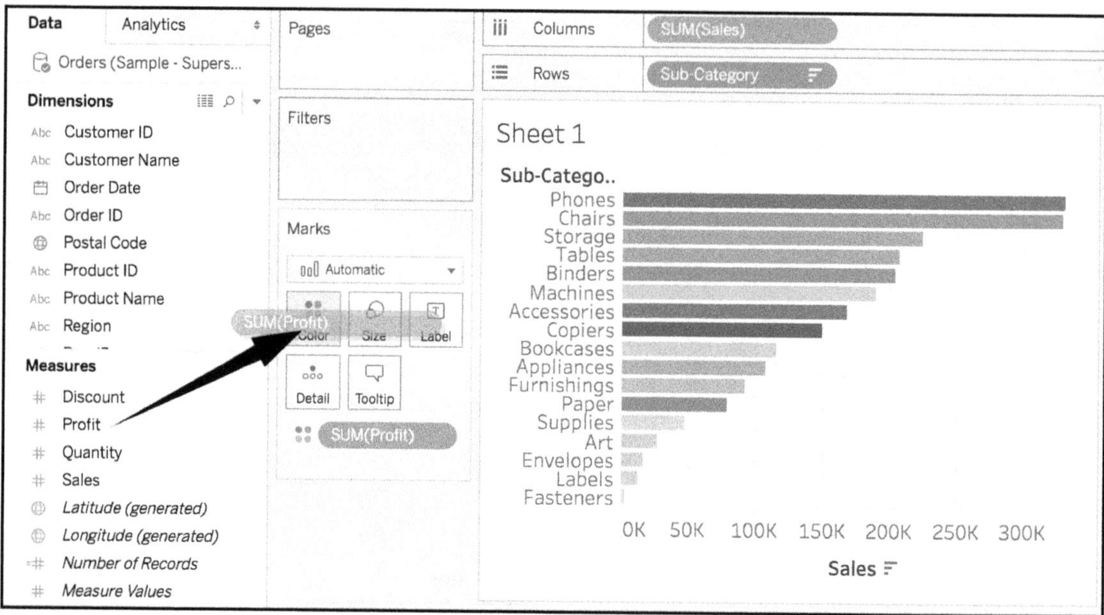

Tableau automatically uses a diverging color palette: orange for negative values and blue for positive. Now we can also see that **Tables**, **Bookcases**, and **Supplies** lose the company money.

Tableau's default color choice is adapted for colorblind people. People usually use red and green for negative and positive values. In data visualization, it's the wrong color choice because colorblind people can't see the difference. If the only way to understand something is by its color, be sure that everyone can see the difference.

5. Double-click on **Sheet 1**, at the very bottom, next to the **Data Source** tab, and rename the Worksheet `Sales and Profit by Sub-Category`. It's crucial to give a name to each of your Worksheets in Tableau.

A few clicks and one drag and drop later, you just created your first visualization in Tableau, congratulations! Ready for the next one?

Profit evolution – line chart

Let's see now how the profit evolves. Do you have bad memories about how other tools deal with dates? Tableau will change your mind! To build this new analysis, we need to create a new Worksheet. In Tableau, there is always more than one way to do something. To create a new Worksheet, you have at least three ways by clicking on one of these buttons:

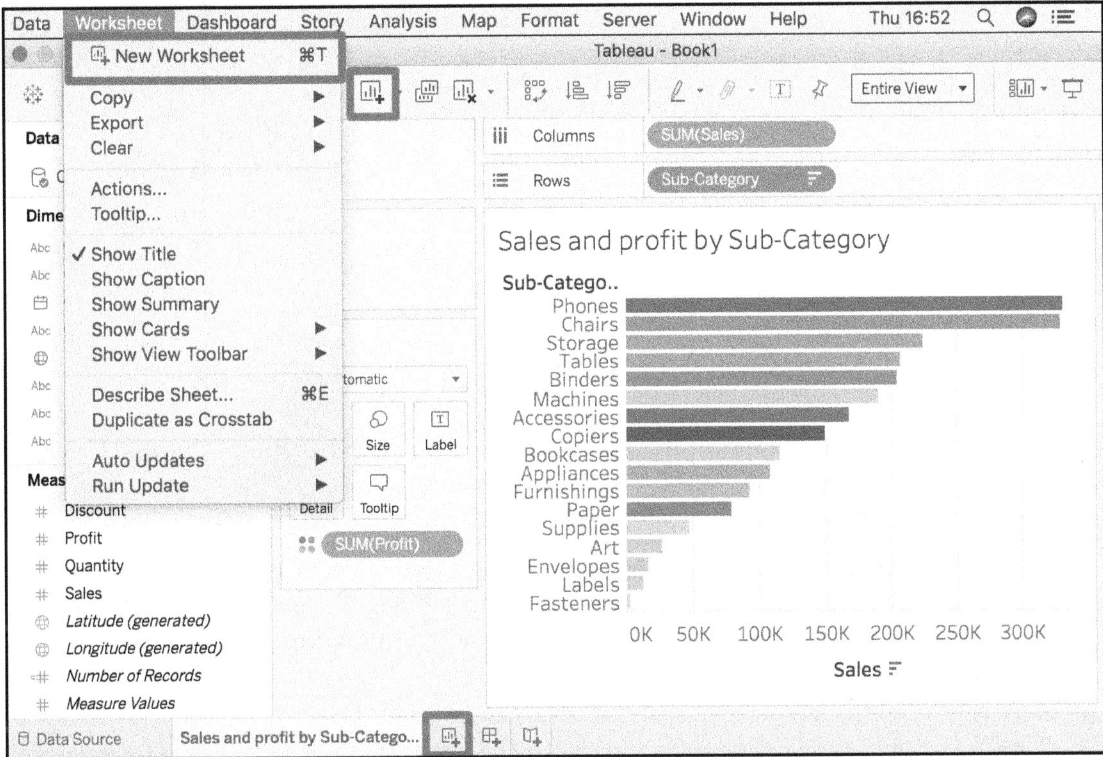

On your new **Sheet 2**, execute the following steps:

1. Double-click on **Profit**.
2. Double-click on **Order date**. Tableau automatically transforms the bar into a line:

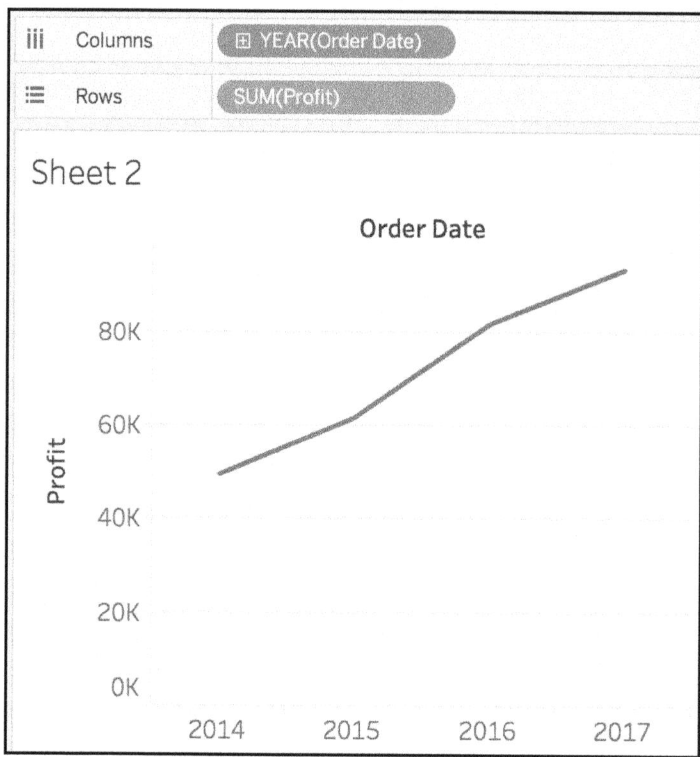

You see a line because, depending on the data type you use, Tableau selects the best way to visualize it. Of course, that can be changed, and it's part of the next chapters. Here, you can see the year-by-year evolution. Profit is growing, that's great! But what if we want more details?

3. Right-click on **YEAR (Order Date)** in **Columns** and select the second instance of **Quarter**, where it's written **Q2 2015**:

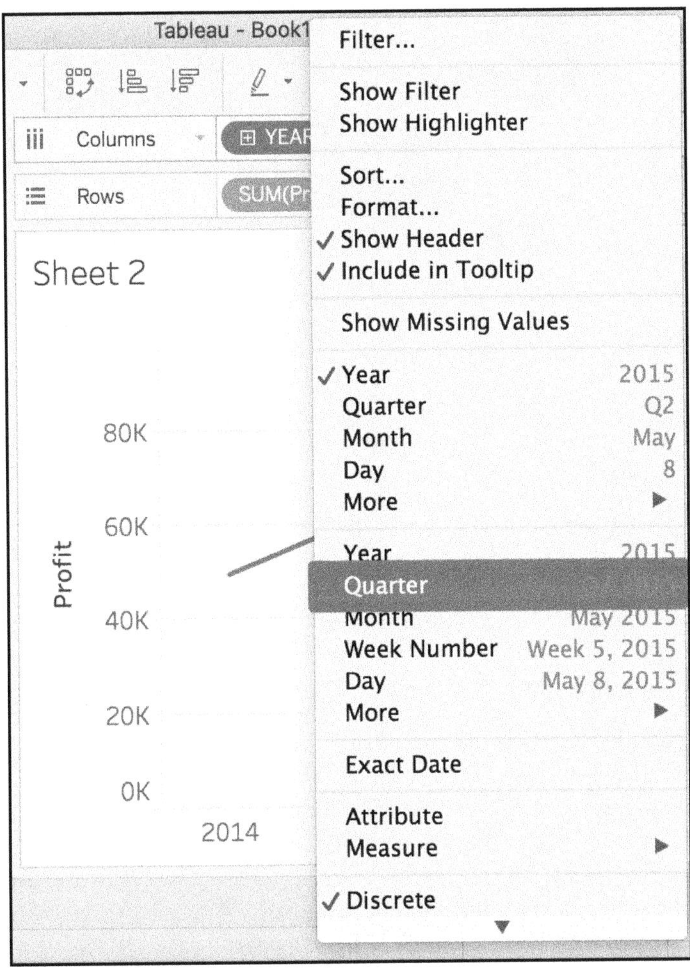

4. You can now see the quarterly evolution of the profit and discover that the fourth quarter is always the best:

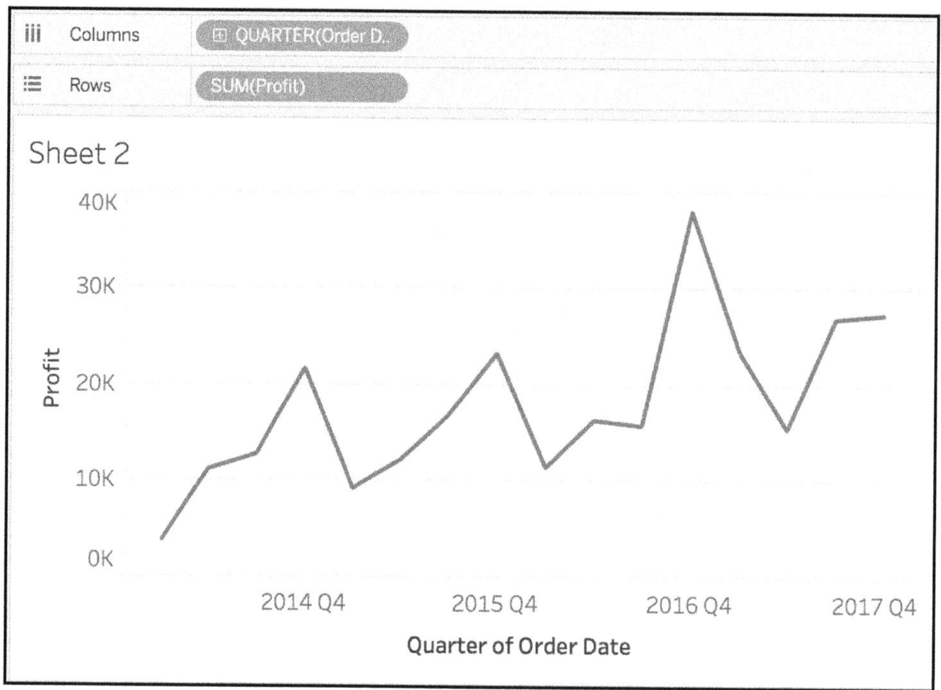

For each **Date** field, Tableau generates all the hierarchy: Year, Month, Quarter, Day Name, Week, Week Number, and other. The Date part on top is discrete and doesn't include the Year. For example, the Discrete Quarter only shows four values: **Q1**, **Q2**, **Q3**, and **Q4**, no matter the Year. The following Date part is continuous and includes the Year. You see the evolution over time. For example, the bottom quarter shows sixteen points: four quarters per four years.

5. Rename **Sheet 2** as `Profit Evolution`. Just as we did before, double-click on the Worksheet name at the bottom. Make sure that if you change the title (on top of the visualization), it doesn't affect the name of the Worksheet.

How was that second experience? I'm sure you will love using dates in Tableau! Let's finish with my favorite: Maps!

Profit by state – filled map

Ready for the third and last visualization of this tutorial? We are going to see where the profit is generated and use Tableau mapping power:

1. Start by creating a new Worksheet.

(Hint: click on the **New Worksheet** icon, at the bottom:)

2. Double-click on **Country**. Tableau automatically puts the generated longitude and latitude in columns and rows and generates a map. As you can see, the company only sell products in the US.
3. Double-click on **State.** Each point now represents a State:

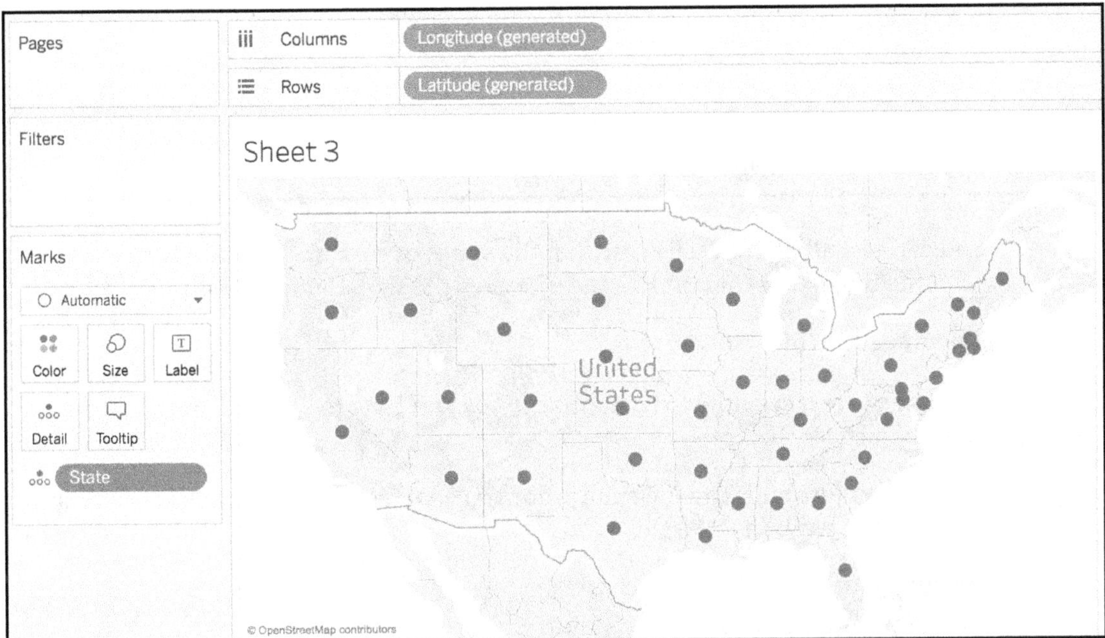

4. Drag and drop **Profit** in **Color**:

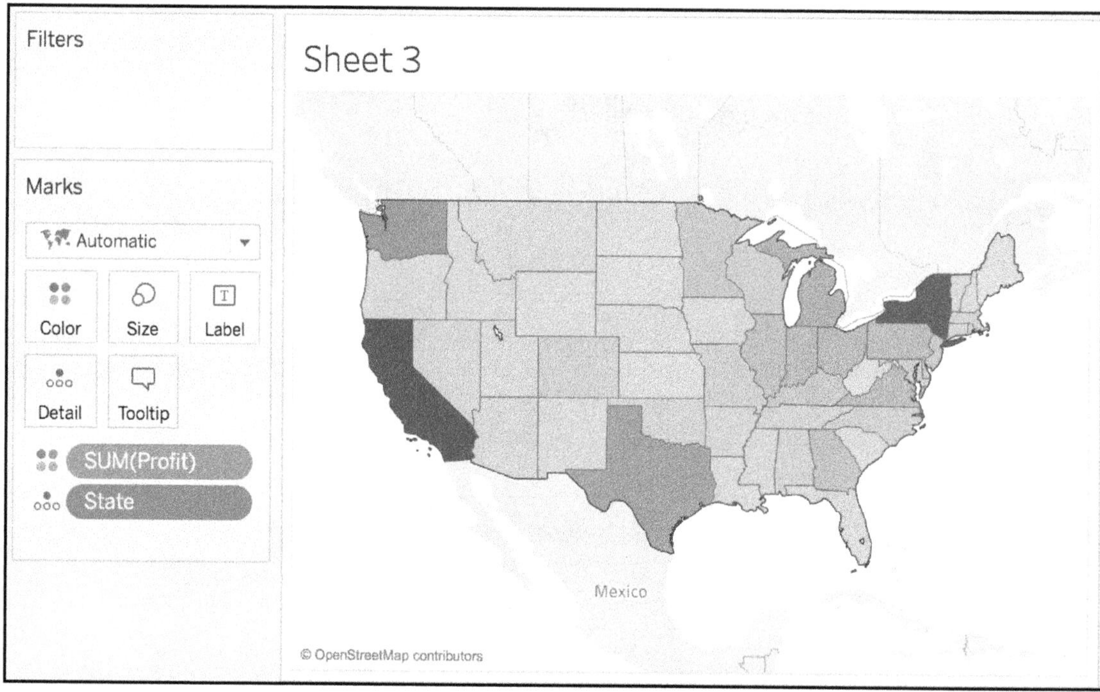

You can visually (and easily) see that the states of *New York* and *California* generate the most profit and *Texas* generates the worst money loss.

5. Rename the Worksheet `Profit by State`.

In the next chapters, we'll see how to customize maps and how to switch from a filled map (choropleth) to points.

Congratulations! You just built three visualizations to analyze your supermarket sales and profit in the following way:

- By sub-categories with a bar chart
- Over time, quarterly with a line chart
- By state, with a filled-map

It's now time to build your first Dashboard. You'll be able to make your Worksheets communicate together and enhance your analysis capabilities.

Building your first Dashboard

Creating a new Dashboard is as simple as creating a new Worksheet: choose one of the following ways (and find your new favorite one!):

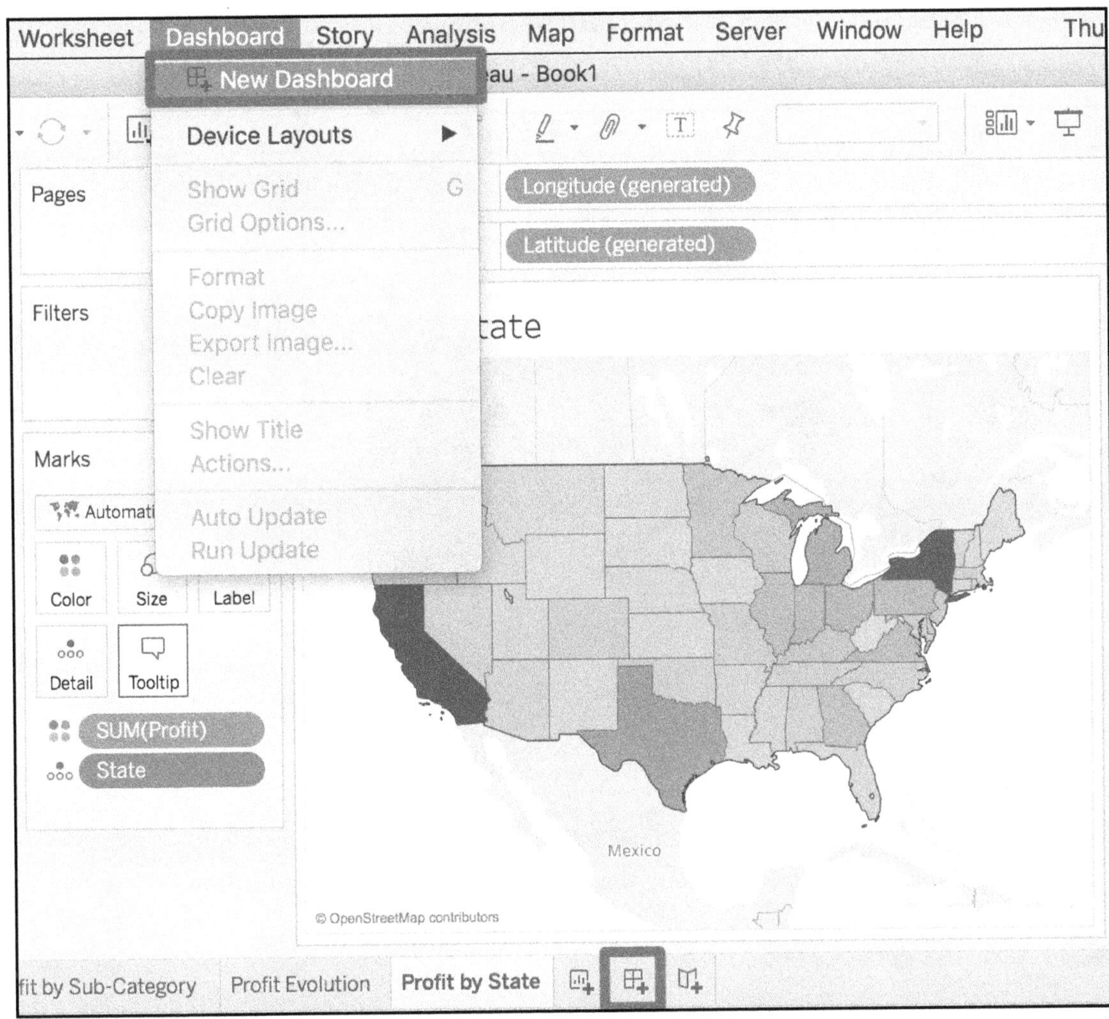

Welcome to the **Dashboard** workplace. Do you see the three Worksheets you built on the left? I hope you understand now why renaming them was very important. You don't want too have many Worksheets named Sheet 1, Sheet 2, Sheet 3, and so on. I've been there and trust me, it's a nightmare!

Assembling the Dashboard

The first step when you build a Dashboard is to assemble your Worksheets:

1. Drag and drop the **Profit by State** Worksheet where Tableau invites you to do so.
2. Drag and drop the **Sales and profit by Sub-Category** Worksheet beneath the map. The gray area helps you to see where the Worksheets are going to be:

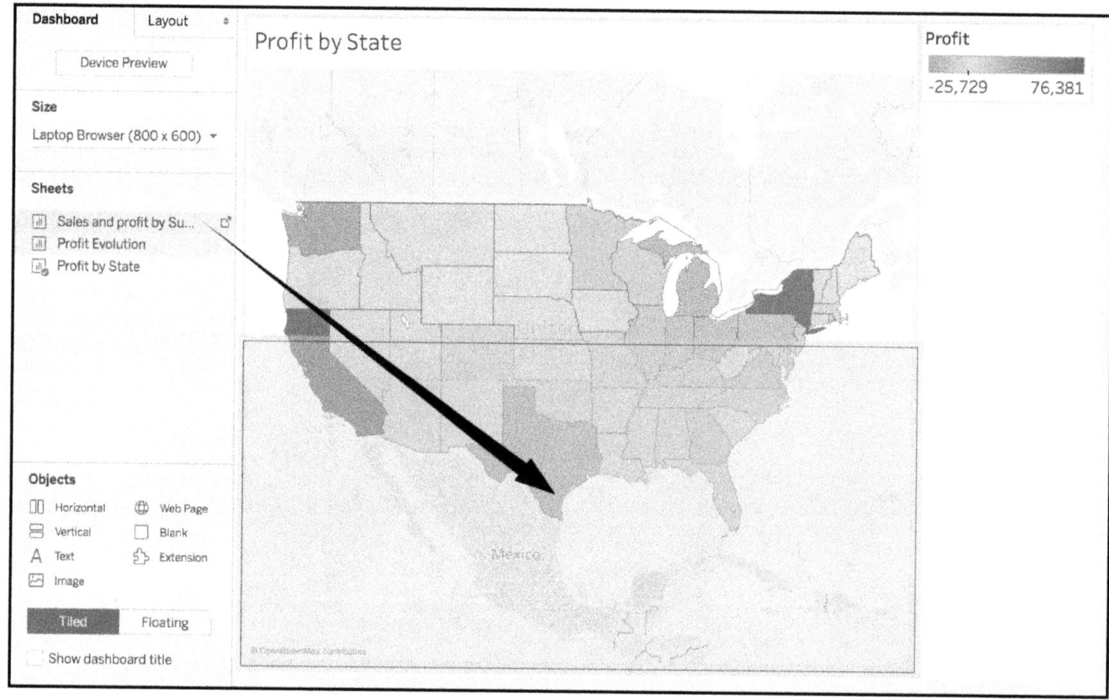

3. Drag and drop the **Profit Evolution** Worksheet on the right of **Sales and profit by Sub-Category**. Again, use the gray area to preview the location:

4. Double-click on **Dashboard 1** at the bottom and rename your Dashboard `Sales and profit analysis`, for example.
5. Click on **Show dashboard title** to show the title:

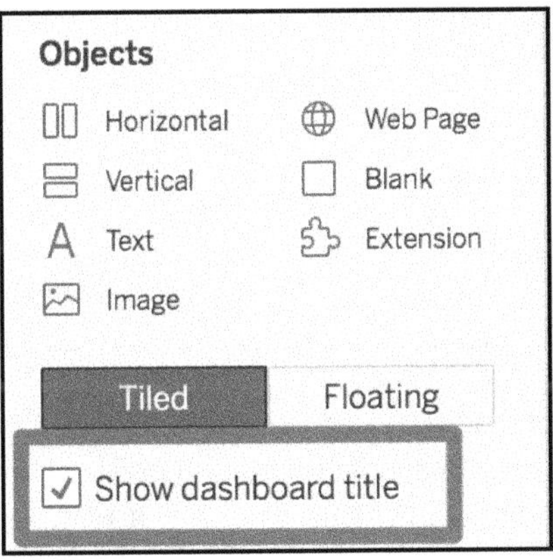

That's it! You built your first Dashboard!

Is that it? Of course not! The magic starts in the next section.

Adding interactivity to your Dashboard

Be careful; this is going to be quick:

1. Click on the **Profit by State** Worksheet to select it (there is a gray outline once it's selected).
2. Click on the funnel icon, the third one. It turns white once you've clicked on it. The icon is highlighted:

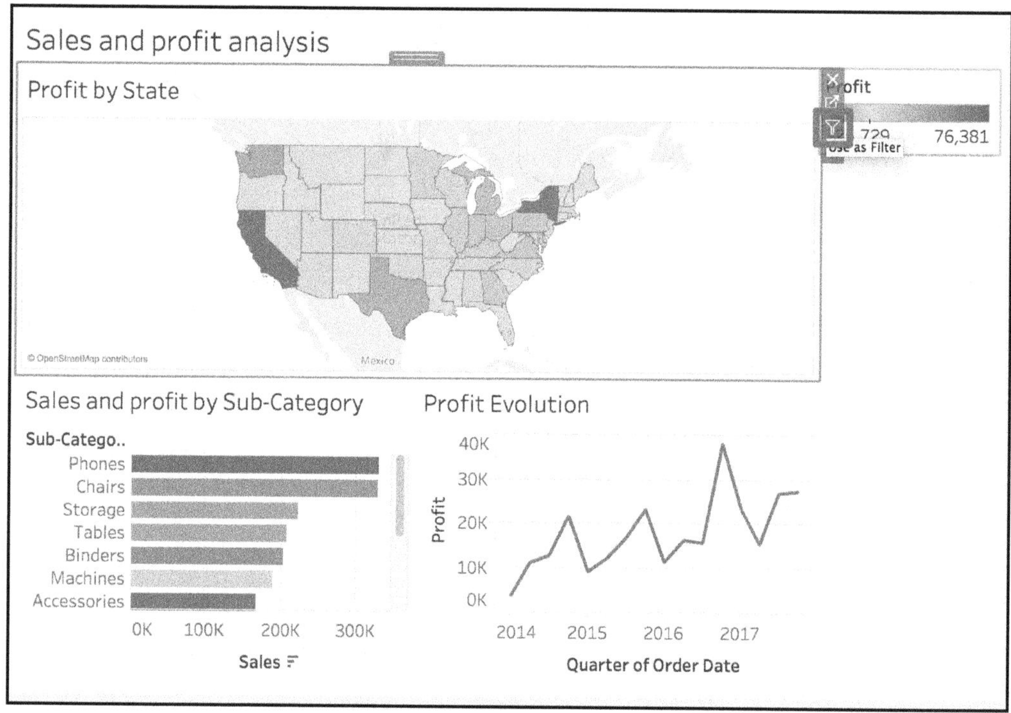

3. Click on any state on the map and be proud! You just created an interactive Dashboard that automatically filters a selected state. You can also use *Ctrl* (Windows) or *command* (Mac) to select multiple states.

Why stop there? You can do the same with **Sales and profit by Sub-Category**. Just click on the visualization, then on the funnel icon, and voilà, you can filter the Dashboard by Sub-Category.

The Dashboard tutorial is now over. I hope that you are as amazed as I was the first time someone showed me how to build a Dashboard. Don't skip the last part, where we are going to use Tableau as a data exploration tool.

Using Tableau for data exploration

Tableau can be used to answer business questions easily and visually. In the section, we'll explore our data to find insights. For this example, we use the `Sample - Superstore` dataset again. If you are starting here, please refer to the preceding *Connect to data* section. If you're continuing from the previous exercise, create a new Worksheet.

Let's start by building a scatterplot. It's a visualization that allows you to analyze two Measures at the same time:

1. Double-click on **Profit** then on **Quantity**. You should see one mark that shows the sum of sales and quantity:

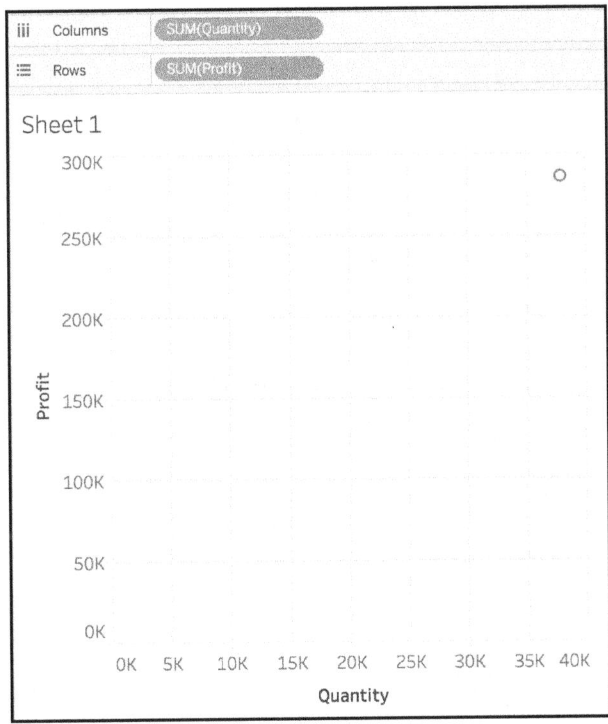

Are there unprofitable sub-categories?

2. Drag and drop **Sub-Category** to **Label**. You should see now one mark per Sub-Category with, for some, their label:

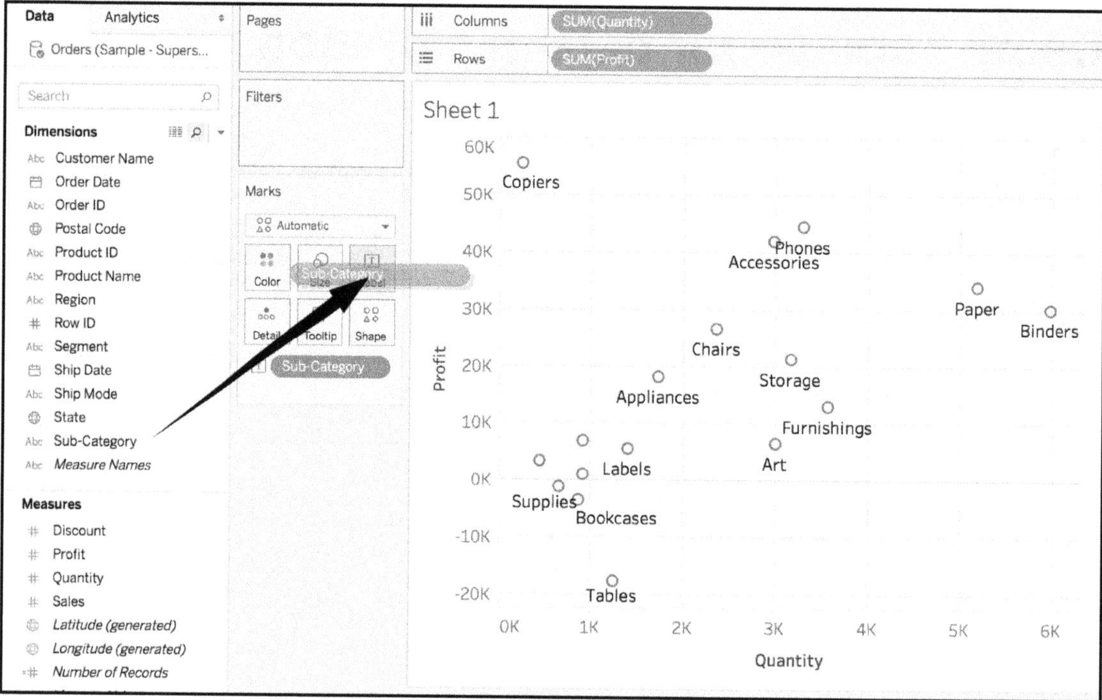

Supplies, **Bookcases**, and **Tables** are unprofitable sub-categories. Now that you have answered your first question, you have two options: be happy because that's all you wanted to know, or go deeper. Let's try the second option.

3. Select the three nonprofitable sub-categories and click on **Keep Only**:

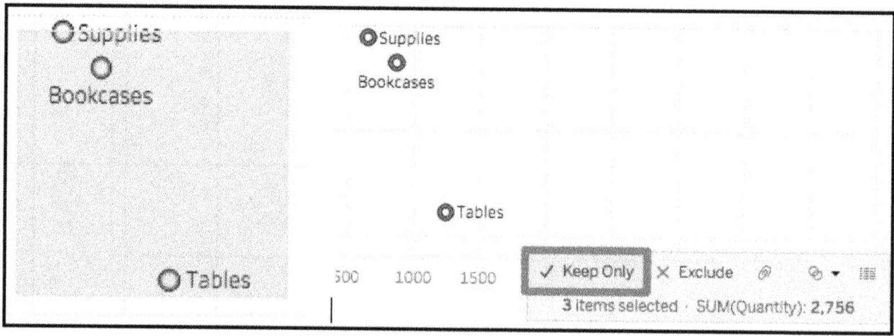

You can see that **Sub-Category** has been added to the **Filters** shelf. Let's continue with another question: *are all the States unprofitable?*

4. Drag and drop **State** over **Sub-Category**. It replaces the existing label, **Sub-Category**, with the new one, **State**:

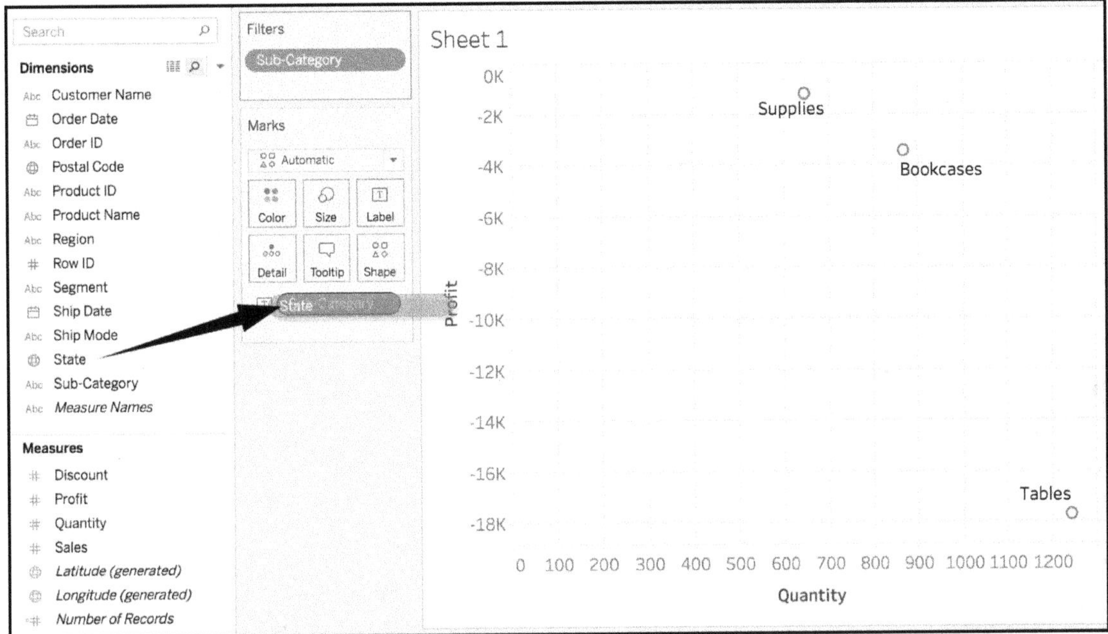

You can see that there are 11 unprofitable states. The worst one is *Pennsylvania*. Let's take a closer look at it.

5. Click on **Pennsylvania**, then on **Keep only**. **State** has been added to **Filter** and, as in the beginning, there is only one mark left.

Let's answer one last question: *are all the clients unprofitable in Pennsylvania?*

6. Drag and drop **Customer Name** over **State**:

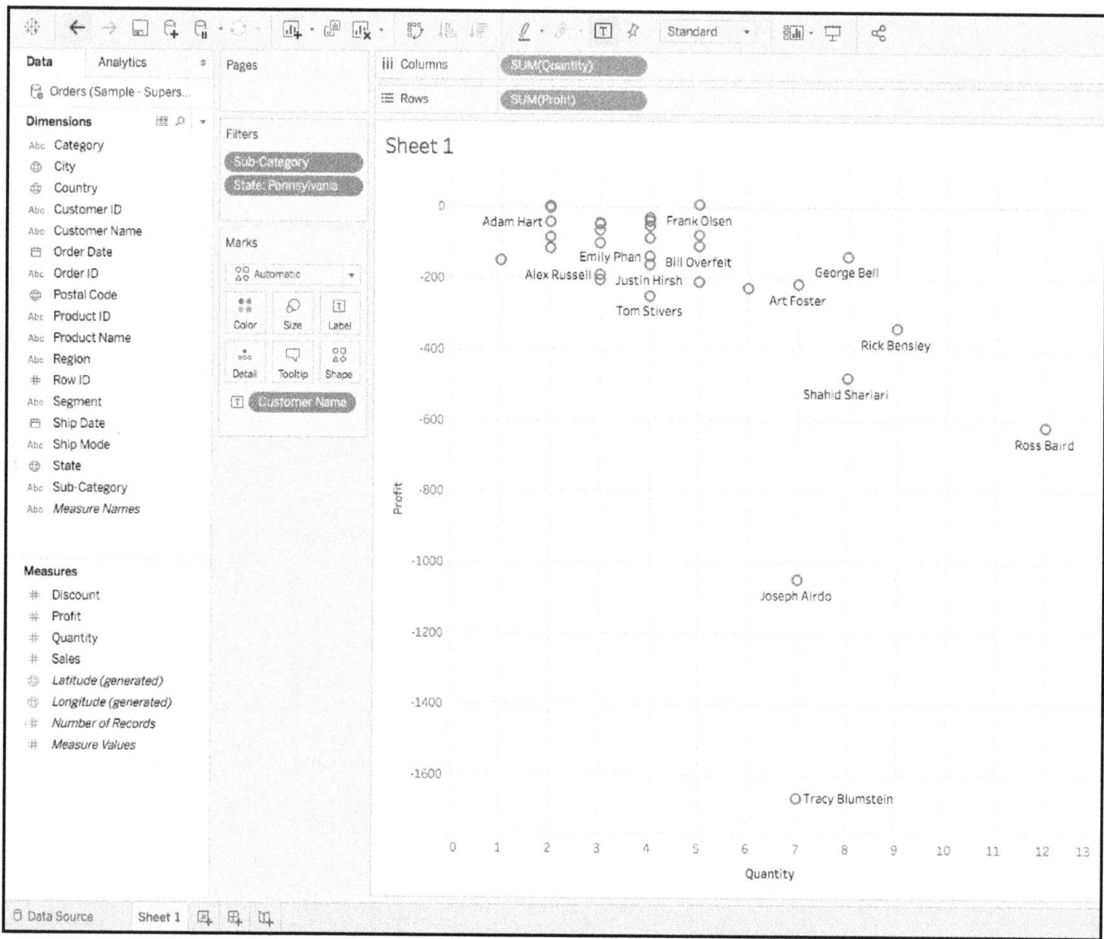

You now see all the customers who purchased a product in one the previously-selected sub-categories in *Pennsylvania*. Only two of them are profitable (with meager profits); the 30 other customers are unprofitable.

If you want to have an even more in-depth analysis, right-click somewhere on the View (but not on a mark) and click on **View Data...**:

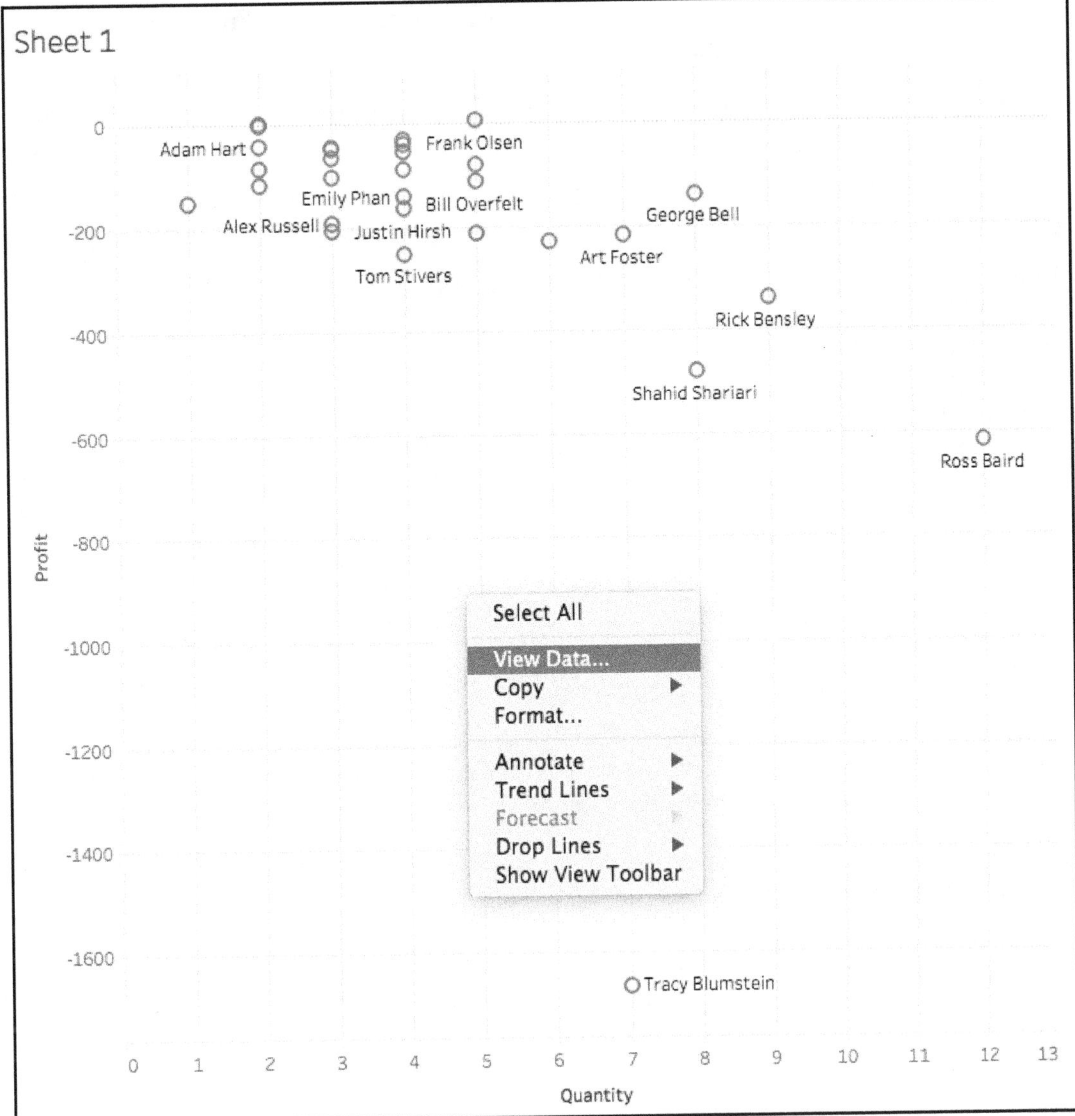

This opens a new window with the following:

- On the first tab, a `Summary` table of the visualization.
- On the second tab, the `Full Data` with all the columns and rows used by Tableau to generate the visualization:

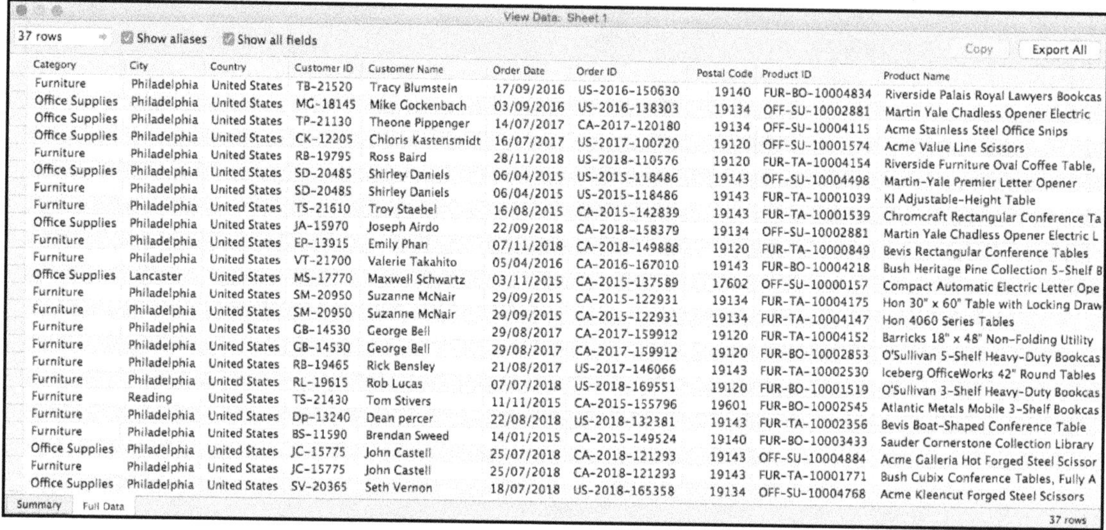

View Data: Sheet 1

37 rows | Show aliases | Show all fields | Copy | Export All

Category	City	Country	Customer ID	Customer Name	Order Date	Order ID	Postal Code	Product ID	Product Name
Furniture	Philadelphia	United States	TB-21520	Tracy Blumstein	17/09/2016	US-2016-150630	19140	FUR-BO-10004834	Riverside Palais Royal Lawyers Bookcas
Office Supplies	Philadelphia	United States	MG-18145	Mike Gockenbach	03/09/2016	US-2016-138303	19134	OFF-SU-10002881	Martin Yale Chadless Opener Electric
Office Supplies	Philadelphia	United States	TP-21130	Theone Pippenger	14/07/2017	CA-2017-120180	19134	OFF-SU-10004115	Acme Stainless Steel Office Snips
Office Supplies	Philadelphia	United States	CK-12205	Chloris Kastensmidt	16/07/2017	US-2017-100720	19120	OFF-SU-10001574	Acme Value Line Scissors
Furniture	Philadelphia	United States	RB-19795	Ross Baird	28/11/2018	US-2018-110576	19120	FUR-TA-10004154	Riverside Furniture Oval Coffee Table,
Office Supplies	Philadelphia	United States	SD-20485	Shirley Daniels	06/04/2015	US-2015-118486	19143	OFF-SU-10004498	Martin-Yale Premier Letter Opener
Furniture	Philadelphia	United States	SD-20485	Shirley Daniels	06/04/2015	US-2015-118486	19143	FUR-TA-10001039	KI Adjustable-Height Table
Furniture	Philadelphia	United States	TS-21610	Troy Staebel	16/08/2015	CA-2015-142839	19143	FUR-TA-10001539	Chromcraft Rectangular Conference Ta
Office Supplies	Philadelphia	United States	JA-15970	Joseph Airdo	22/09/2018	CA-2018-158379	19134	OFF-SU-10002881	Martin Yale Chadless Opener Electric L
Furniture	Philadelphia	United States	EP-13915	Emily Phan	07/11/2018	CA-2018-149888	19120	FUR-TA-10000849	Bevis Rectangular Conference Tables
Furniture	Philadelphia	United States	VT-21700	Valerie Takahito	05/04/2016	CA-2016-167010	19143	FUR-BO-10004218	Bush Heritage Pine Collection 5-Shelf B
Office Supplies	Lancaster	United States	MS-17770	Maxwell Schwartz	03/11/2015	CA-2015-137589	17602	OFF-SU-10000157	Compact Automatic Electric Letter Ope
Furniture	Philadelphia	United States	SM-20950	Suzanne McNair	29/09/2015	CA-2015-122931	19134	FUR-TA-10004175	Hon 30" x 60" Table with Locking Draw
Furniture	Philadelphia	United States	SM-20950	Suzanne McNair	29/09/2015	CA-2015-122931	19134	FUR-TA-10004147	Hon 4060 Series Tables
Furniture	Philadelphia	United States	GB-14530	George Bell	29/08/2017	CA-2017-159912	19120	FUR-TA-10004152	Barricks 18" x 48" Non-Folding Utility
Furniture	Philadelphia	United States	GB-14530	George Bell	29/08/2017	CA-2017-159912	19120	FUR-BO-10002853	O'Sullivan 5-Shelf Heavy-Duty Bookcas
Furniture	Philadelphia	United States	RB-19465	Rick Bensley	21/08/2017	US-2017-146066	19143	FUR-TA-10002530	Iceberg OfficeWorks 42" Round Tables
Furniture	Philadelphia	United States	RL-19615	Rob Lucas	07/07/2018	US-2018-169551	19120	FUR-BO-10001519	O'Sullivan 3-Shelf Heavy-Duty Bookcas
Furniture	Reading	United States	TS-21430	Tom Stivers	11/11/2015	CA-2015-155796	19601	FUR-BO-10002545	Atlantic Metals Mobile 3-Shelf Bookcas
Furniture	Philadelphia	United States	Dp-13240	Dean percer	22/08/2018	US-2018-132381	19143	FUR-TA-10002356	Bevis Boat-Shaped Conference Table
Furniture	Philadelphia	United States	BS-11590	Brendan Sweed	14/01/2015	CA-2015-149524	19140	FUR-BO-10003433	Sauder Cornerstone Collection Library
Office Supplies	Philadelphia	United States	JC-15775	John Castell	25/07/2018	CA-2018-121293	19143	OFF-SU-10004884	Acme Galleria Hot Forged Steel Scissor
Furniture	Philadelphia	United States	JC-15775	John Castell	25/07/2018	CA-2018-121293	19143	FUR-TA-10001771	Bush Cubix Conference Tables, Fully A
Office Supplies	Philadelphia	United States	SV-20365	Seth Vernon	18/07/2018	US-2018-165358	19134	OFF-SU-10004768	Acme Kleencut Forged Steel Scissors

Summary | Full Data | 37 rows

In the top left, you can export the data in CSV format if you want to share it.

As you can see, we were able to answer questions, and go deeper into the analysis, all by staying on one Worksheet. By using the power of Tableau to visualize data, exploration is straightforward and often looks similar to a game.

Whether to create Dashboards or to answer questions, I hope that this chapter has given you the desire to continue to discover all the great functionalities Tableau has to offer.

Summary

This chapter was your first concrete introduction to Tableau. I hope you enjoyed it! In this guided tutorial, you learned how to connect to an Excel file and create three Worksheets using a bar chart, a line chart, and a map. Then you built a Dashboard and made it interactive. Finally, you explored the data to visually answer business questions.

The introduction is now over. In the following chapters, we'll focus on specific aspects of Tableau and enter in the details. Speaking of what's next, I invite you to continue your journey with the next chapter. In it, you'll learn everything you need to know to connect to any dataset, add joins or unions, pivot your data, and much more.

4
Connect to Data and Simple Transformations

The first thing you usually do when opening Tableau is to connect to a dataset. You already had a glimpse of data connection in the previous chapter when we used an Excel file. In this chapter, you'll see the most important options that Tableau offers when connecting to data. Here are our main focuses:

- Data connection
- Join data easily
- Union your data
- Simple transformation

To harmonize all the different words among the various data providers, we'll use the following terms through the chapter:

- **Dataset** to represent any sources. It is where your data is located. It could be an Excel file, a database on a server, or a file on the cloud. The dataset is what you want to connect to Tableau.

- **Tables** to represent, no matter the connection, a sheet in Excel or a table in a database. For example, there are three tables in the following screenshot:

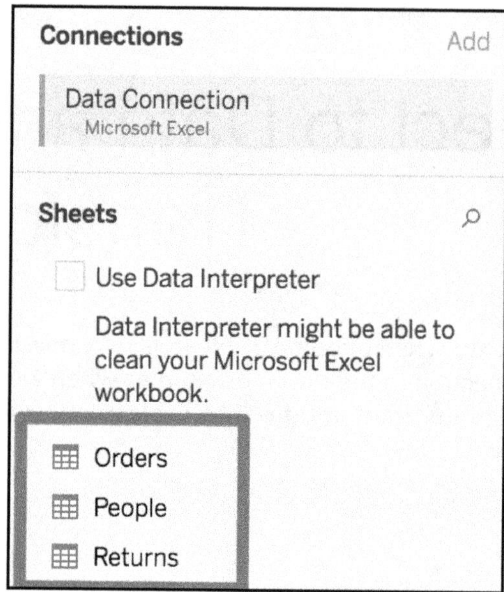

- **Data Source** to represent the result of your connection, after all the transformations.

Let's now start with some examples of data connections.

Data connection

In this section, we'll see how to connect to different datasets (file or database). Of course, with more than 50 different connectors available, it's impossible to see each in detail. You can see, in the following screenshot, all the current available connections:

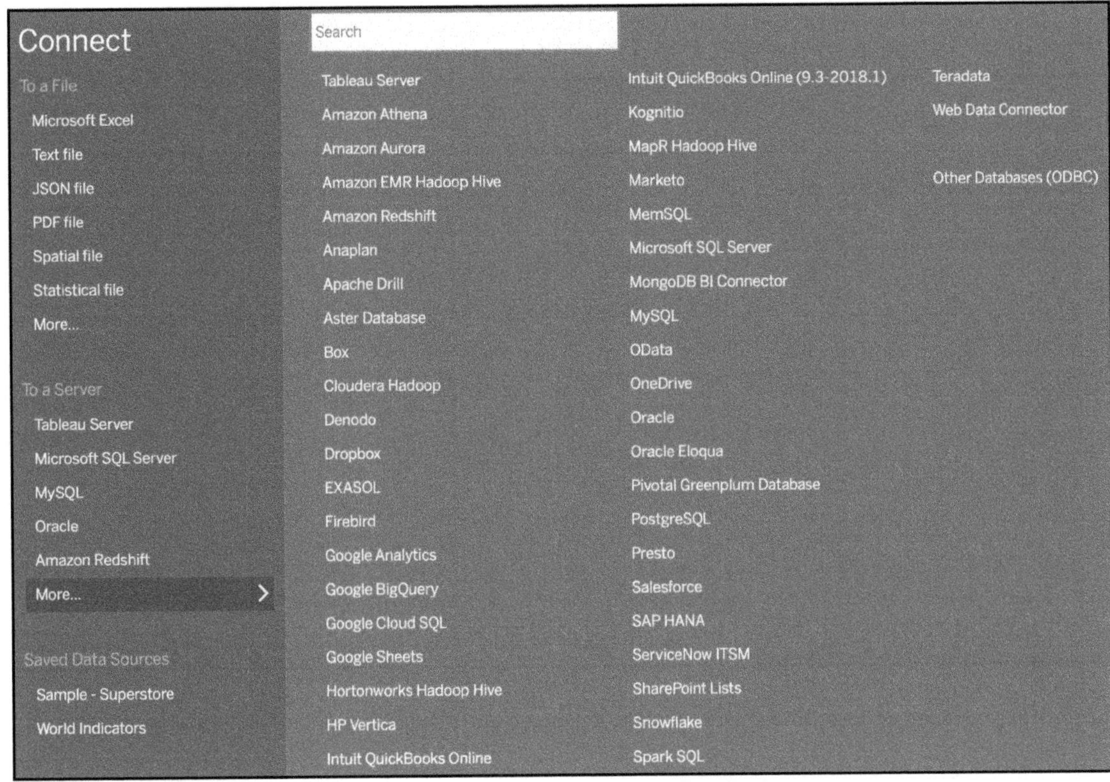

The goal when connecting to a dataset in Tableau is always the same:

1. Choose your connection (File/Server).
2. Connect by selecting the file or entering the login information.

3. Reach the **Data Source** workplace and have at least one table in the framed area:

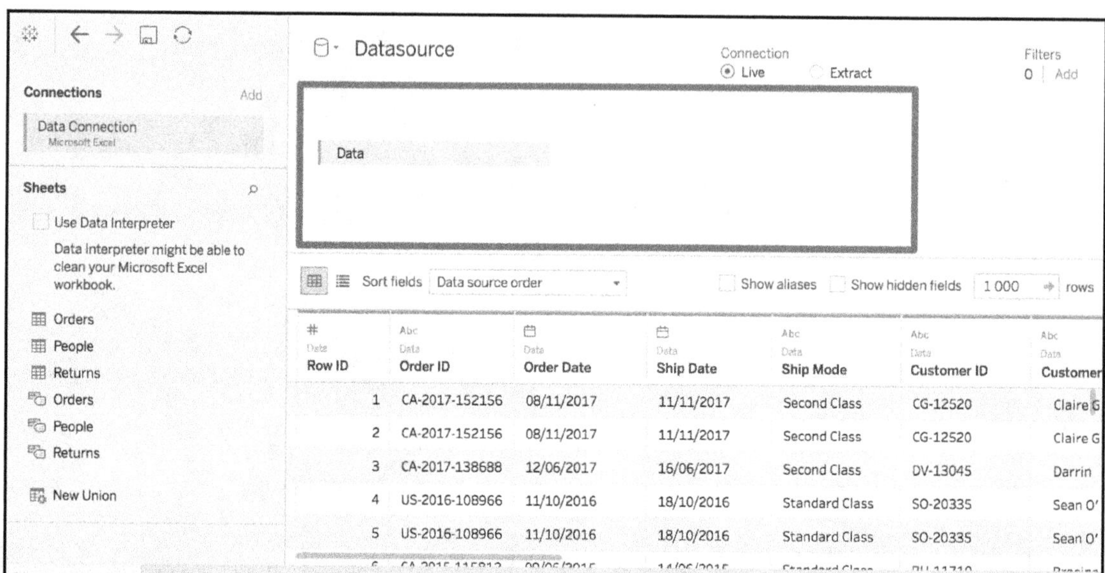

Let's start by seeing how to connect to files, then to databases, and, in the end, Spatial files.

Connecting to a file

In this section, you'll see two examples of file connections: an Excel file and then a CSV file.

Excel files

If you want to connect to an Excel file, follow these steps:

1. Click on **Microsoft Excel** in the list of available connections when you open Tableau.
2. Search for your file in your computer, double-click on it, and Tableau automatically opens the file.

3. The different tables are displayed on the left, as in the following screenshot:

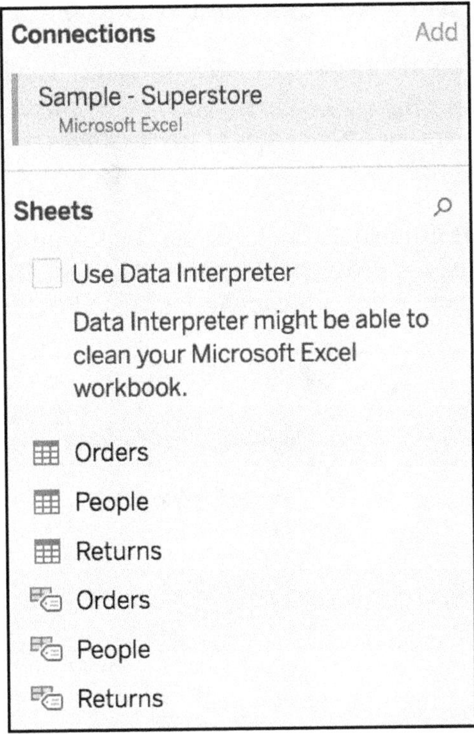

4. Drag and drop the table you want to analyze on the Data Source part, on the right.

If your file is not clean or contains, for example, a title or merged cells, try to click on **Use Data Interpreter** to clean your file.

Connecting to an Excel file is straightforward. Let's now try another type of file: a text file.

Text files

The following are the steps if you need to connect to a text file (such as a `.csv` file):

1. Click on **Text file** in the list of available connections when you open Tableau.
2. Search for your text file (`.txt`, `.csv`, and so on) and double-click on it. As there are no different tables with text files, Tableau automatically takes the unique table available in the Data Source.

Sometimes, if the field separator is not standard, the Data Source shows an error. To correct that, you can manually specify the field separator, the text qualifier, the character set, and the locale. To do so, right-click on the table and select **Text File Properties...**:

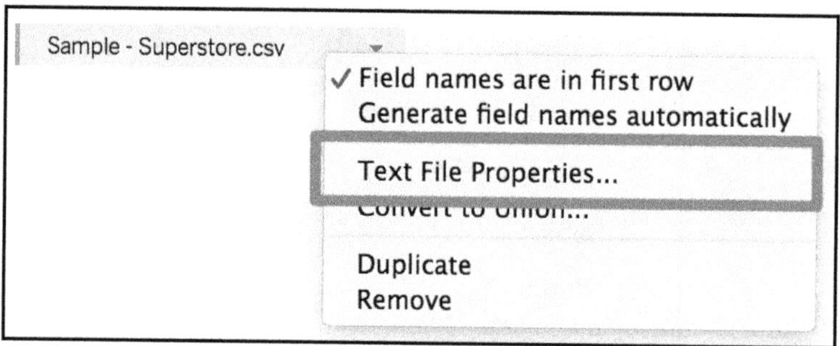

Let's now see how to connect to different servers.

Connecting to a server

In this section, you'll start by discovering a Tableau Server connection, then a database connection (SQL Server), and, finally, some pieces of advice for other types of connection.

Tableau Server/Online

If you have access to **Tableau Server** or **Tableau Online**, you can directly connect to a published Data Source. To do so, follow these steps:

1. Click on Tableau Server on the **Connect** pane.
2. Enter the URL of your server or click on **Tableau Online**:

3. Enter your username and password:

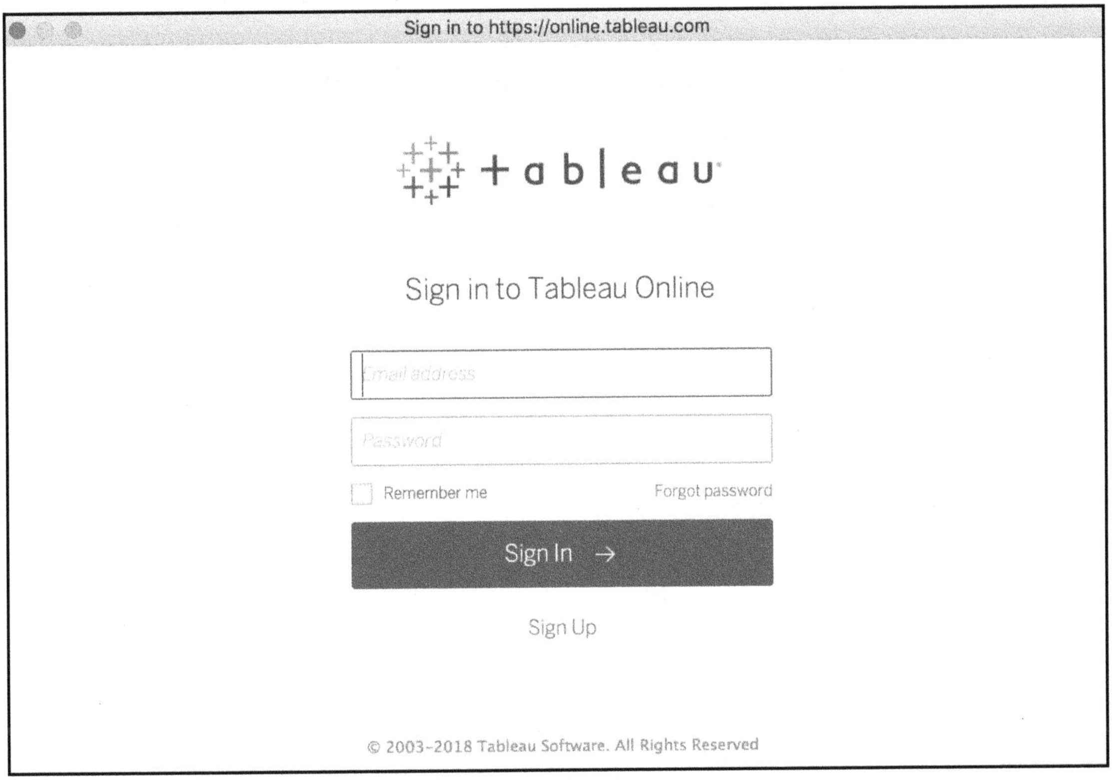

Sign in to https://online.tableau.com

tableau

Sign in to Tableau Online

Email address

Password

Remember me

Forgot password

Sign In →

Sign Up

4. Click on the Data Source you want to use.

Actually, with a Tableau Server connection, you don't have anything to do. The connection to the dataset has already been made by someone else. Let's now see how to create a new connection to a database.

Common servers (MS SQL Server, Oracle, Redshift, MySQL)

The process to connect to a server is very similar from one data provider to another.

1. **Driver installation (Optional)**: If the driver of the server is not pre-installed, you have to click on **Download and install the drivers** at the bottom of the connection page. You will be redirected to Tableau's website where you can find it and download it. The link is highlighted in the following screenshot:

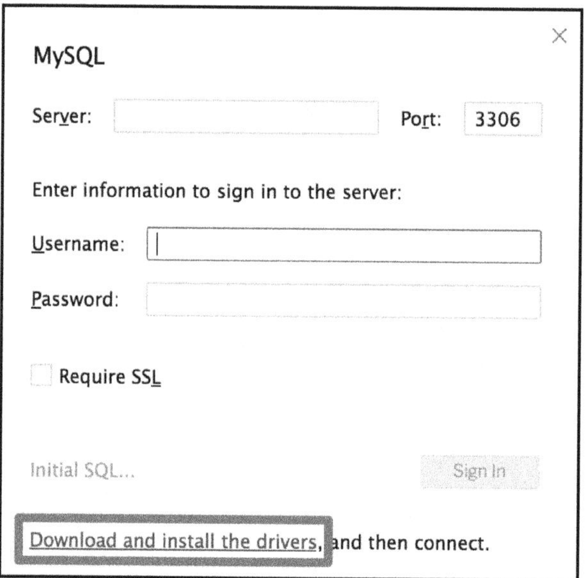

2. **Connection information**: Fill in the server address, the login, and the password, and click on **Sign In** to connect. Here's an example of an MS SQL connection:

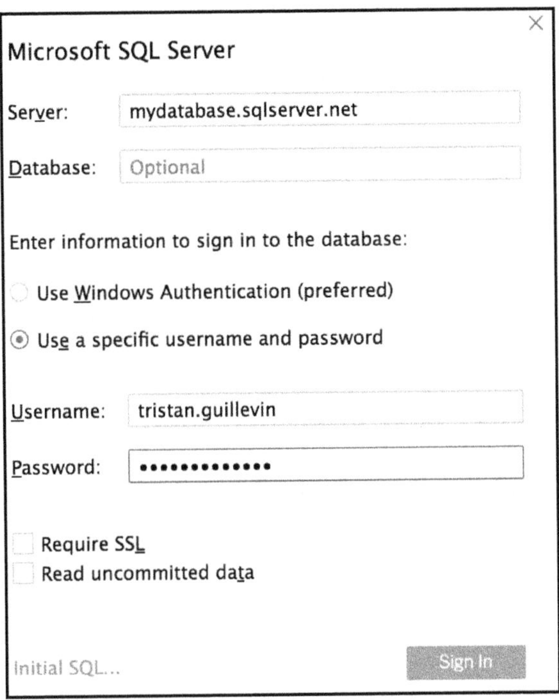

3. **Select the database and tables**: Once you are connected to the server, you may be invited to select a specific database, as in the following screenshot:

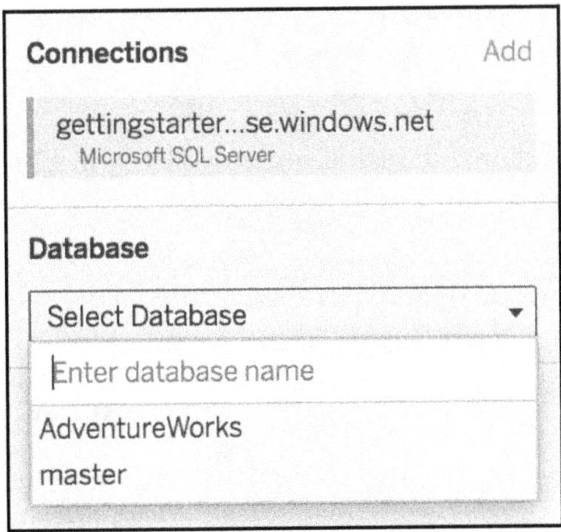

After choosing the database, you see the different tables. Here are the tables of the `AdventureWorks` database:

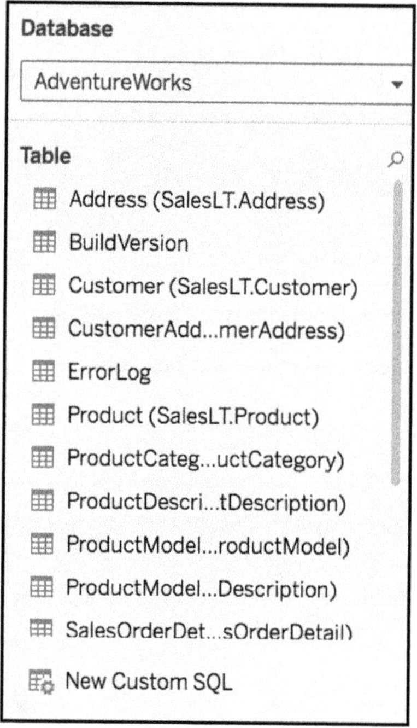

When connected to a database, you can also create a custom SQL query if you have special needs. To do so, double-click on **New Custom SQL** and write your query.

Using a Custom SQL query is slower than letting Tableau build the query with simple drag and drop.

To finish this section, here is some advice if you have to connect to different servers.

Other servers

Tableau can connect to a lot of different servers. They all have their specificities, but Tableau always keeps it simple. For example, if you want to connect to Google Drive, enter your Google account information and select the Google Sheet you want, as shown in the following screenshot:

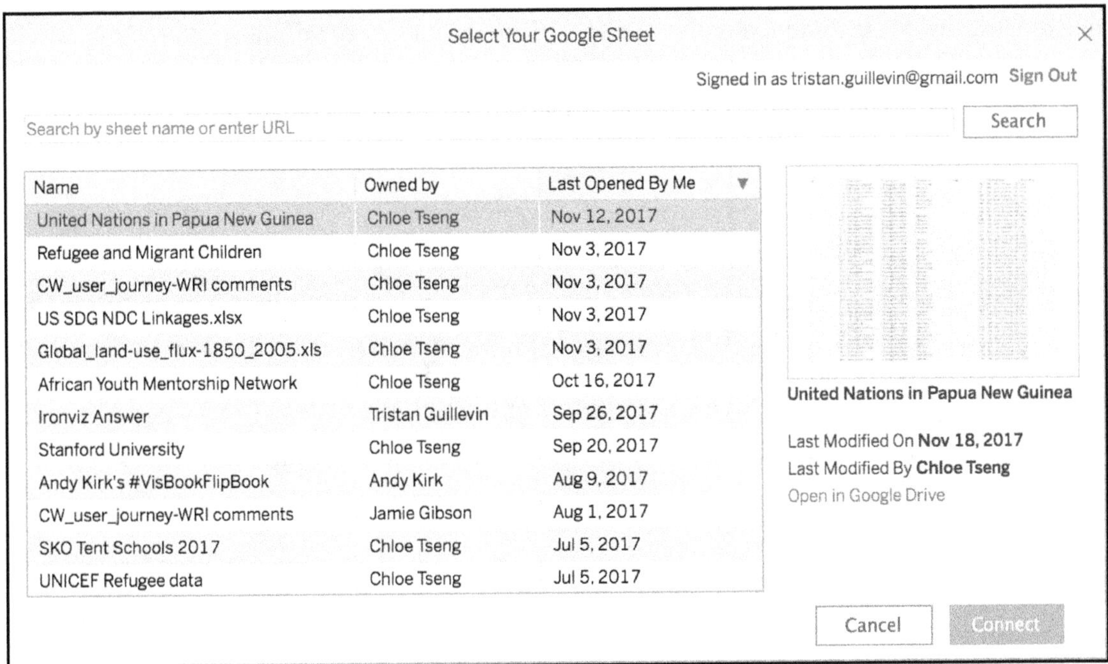

Also, don't forget to use Tableau's help! A simple search on the internet for Tableau connects to *this server*, *this server* being any data provider, and you'll find Tableau's official step-by-step guide.

Before the next section about **Joins**, let's do a quick focus on a special kind of file: the Spatial file.

Spatial files

Tableau offers the possibility to connect to Spatial files to display custom maps. You can use this feature to create maps with your specific territories or to add new interesting layers of information. The following types of file are accepted:

KML Files (*.kml)
ESRI Shapefiles (*.shp)
MapInfo Tables (*.tab)
MapInfo Interchange Formats (*.mif)
GeoJSON Files (*.geojson)
TopoJSON Files (*.json *.topojson)

When you connect to a **Spatial file**, a special field, **Geometry**, is available. You just have to double-click on that field to display your custom territories. Here's an example of what you can do with Spatial files, displaying the borders of the tectonic plates:

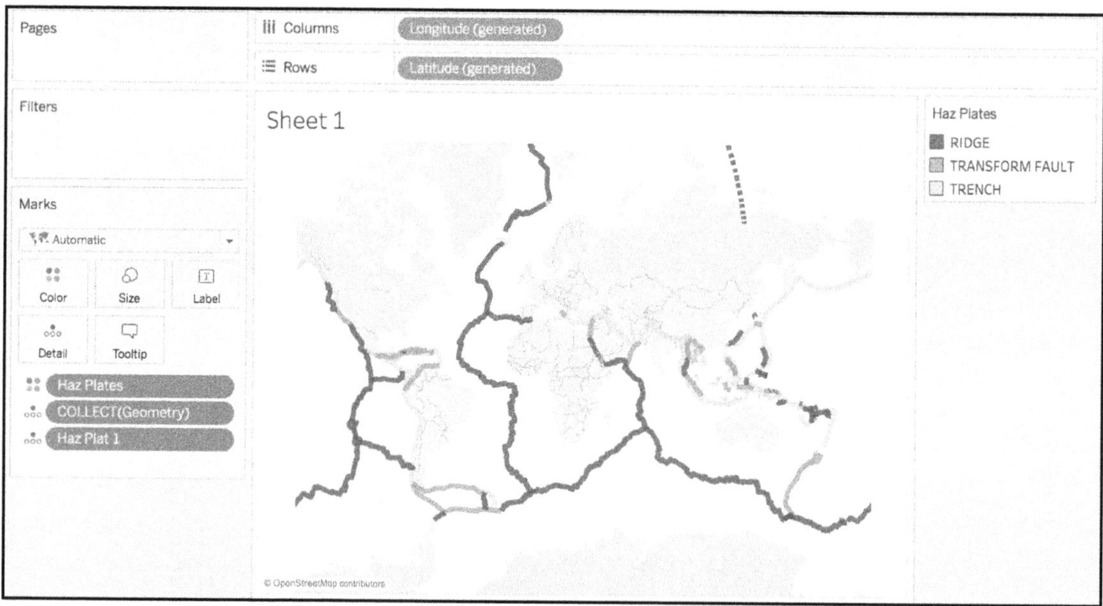

Don't hesitate to use this functionality to add roads, rivers, mountains, or special boundaries to your data.

Now that you know how to connect to different datasets, it's time to discover what you can do in the **Data Source** workplace, starting with Joins.

Join data easily

A Join creates a single Data Source with columns coming from two (or more) tables. How do Joins work? How can you create them? Are there risks? You'll learn everything in this section.

The Join principle

So far, we've only used one table. A Join is automatically created when using two or more tables. There is always a left table and a right table. In the following screenshot, you see a Join between **Orders** (the left table), and **People** (the right table):

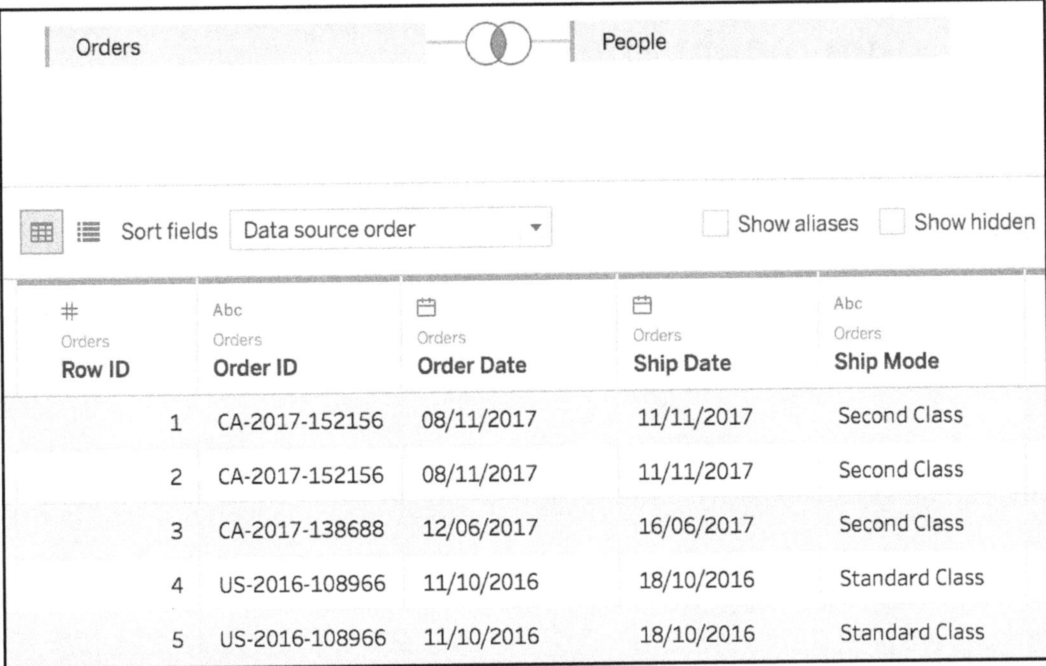

Orders Row ID	Orders Order ID	Orders Order Date	Orders Ship Date	Orders Ship Mode
1	CA-2017-152156	08/11/2017	11/11/2017	Second Class
2	CA-2017-152156	08/11/2017	11/11/2017	Second Class
3	CA-2017-138688	12/06/2017	16/06/2017	Second Class
4	US-2016-108966	11/10/2016	18/10/2016	Standard Class
5	US-2016-108966	11/10/2016	18/10/2016	Standard Class

The result of a Join is a Data Source that contains the columns from the different tables. As highlighted in the screenshot, you can see that the `Profit` column comes from the `Orders` table, and the `Person` column comes from the `People` table:

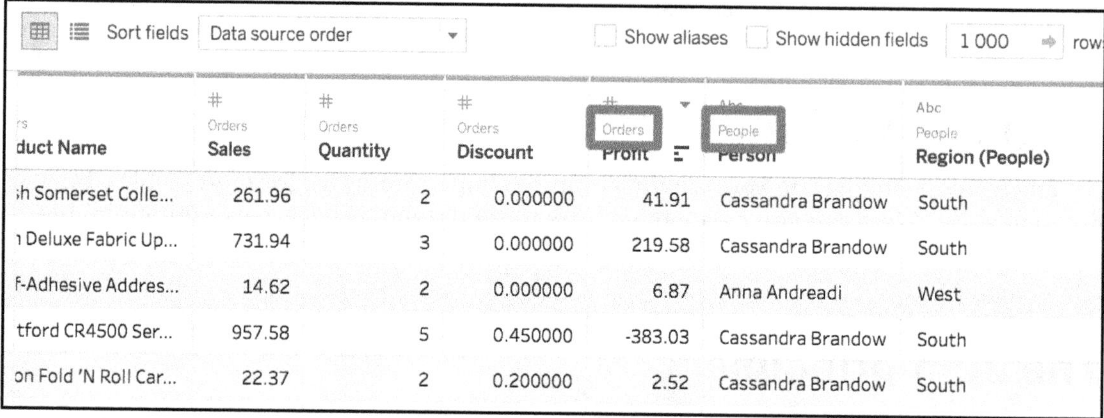

Sort fields Data source order Show aliases Show hidden fields 1 000 rows

rs duct Name	Orders Sales	Orders Quantity	Orders Discount	Orders Profit	People Person	People Region (People)
;h Somerset Colle...	261.96	2	0.000000	41.91	Cassandra Brandow	South
ı Deluxe Fabric Up...	731.94	3	0.000000	219.58	Cassandra Brandow	South
f-Adhesive Addres...	14.62	2	0.000000	6.87	Anna Andreadi	West
tford CR4500 Ser...	957.58	5	0.450000	-383.03	Cassandra Brandow	South
on Fold 'N Roll Car...	22.37	2	0.200000	2.52	Cassandra Brandow	South

There are four different types of join. Discover them in the next section.

Join requirements and types

To create a Join between two tables, you need at least one column in each table that contains the same values. These common columns create the link between the two tables. When you create a Join, Tableau automatically uses the columns that have the same name as links. If there are no columns with the same name, you have to select the common columns manually in the **Join** menu that opens when you click on the Join icon.

The following screenshot illustrates how you can choose the columns when you click on the icon:

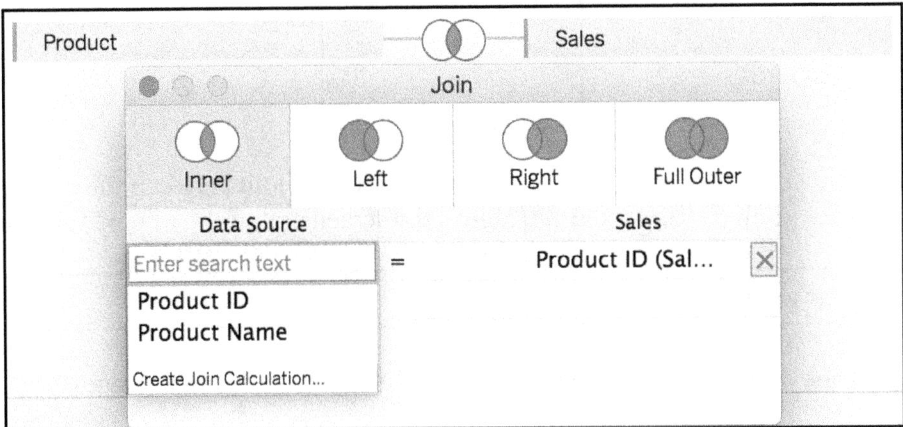

If there are no common columns, you can also create a **Join Calculation** (you'll learn how to create a calculation in `Chapter 10`, *An Introduction to Calculations*).

Sometimes, you have two columns with some values in common, but not all the values. It's up to you to decide how to deal with that by choosing the correct Join type: Inner, Left, Right, or Full Outer. To select a Join type, click on one of the four icons in the **Join** menu.

To illustrate the different Join types, I created an Excel file, `Join example`.

If you want to reproduce the example, you can download the `Join example` file from my website, `book.ladataviz.com` in the *Chapter 4: Connect To Data and Simple Transformation* section or use this direct link: `https://ladataviz.com/wp-content/uploads/2018/09/Join-example.xlsx`.

The Excel file contains two sheets. The first one is named `Left table` and contains the following data:

Common column	Value
a	100
b	200
c	300

The second sheet, named `Right table`, contains the following data:

Common column	Info
b	us
c	fr
d	es

In Tableau, connect to the `Join example` file, and create a Join between the two tables. The link is the `Common column` column. Here's the screenshot of the Join in Tableau:

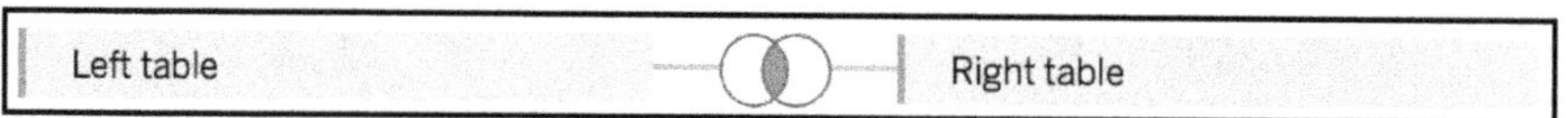

Now let's see the difference between the four different Join types in Tableau:

- **Inner Join** Inner **(default)**: Tableau keeps only the lines with common values between the two tables. In the example, those are the `b` and `c` values. The result is displayed in the following screenshot:

Left Table Value (Left Table)	Left Table Common column	Right table Common column (...	Right table Info
200	b	b	us
300	c	c	fr

- **Left Join** Left : Tableau keeps all the lines from the left table, and adds the information from the right table if the values match. If there is no match, Tableau puts `null`. In the example, Tableau keeps the `a`, `b`, and `c` values but puts `null` in the `Info` column for `c`. The result is displayed in the following screenshot:

Left Table Value (Left Table)	Left Table Common column	Right table Common column (...	Right table Info
200	b	b	us
300	c	c	fr
100	a	*null*	*null*

- **Right Join** : Tableau keeps all the lines from the right table, and adds the information from the left table if the values match. If there is no match, Tableau puts `null`. In the example, Tableau keeps the `b`, `c`, and `d` values but puts `null` in the `Value` column for `d`. The result is displayed in the following screenshot:

Left Table Value (Left Table)	Left Table Common column	Right table Common column (...	Right table Info
200	b	b	us
300	c	c	fr
null	*null*	d	es

- **Full Outer** : Tableau keeps all the lines from the two tables. If the values don't match, Tableau puts `null`. The result is displayed in the following screenshot:

Left Table Value (Left Table)	Left Table Common column	Right table Common column (...	Right table Info
200	b	b	us
300	c	c	fr
null	*null*	d	es
100	a	*null*	*null*

As you can see, Joins are very powerful. Be careful; there are some risks.

Join risks

The main risk with **Joins** is data duplication. Rather than a theoretical explanation, consider the following example.

If you want to reproduce the example, you can download the file `Data duplication example` file from my website, `book.ladataviz.com` in, the *Chapter 4: Connect To Data and Simple Transformation* section, or use this direct link: `https://ladataviz.com/wp-content/uploads/2018/09/Data-duplication-example.xlsx`.

The `Data duplication example` Excel file contains two sheets: **Sales** and **Product**. Sales contains the following data:

Product ID	Sales
1	100
2	100
3	100

The total volume of sales is `300`.

Product contains the following data:

Product ID	Product Name
1	Shield
2	Bow
3	Fire arrow
3	Ice arrow

Now let's join the two tables and see what happens. Here's the result in Tableau:

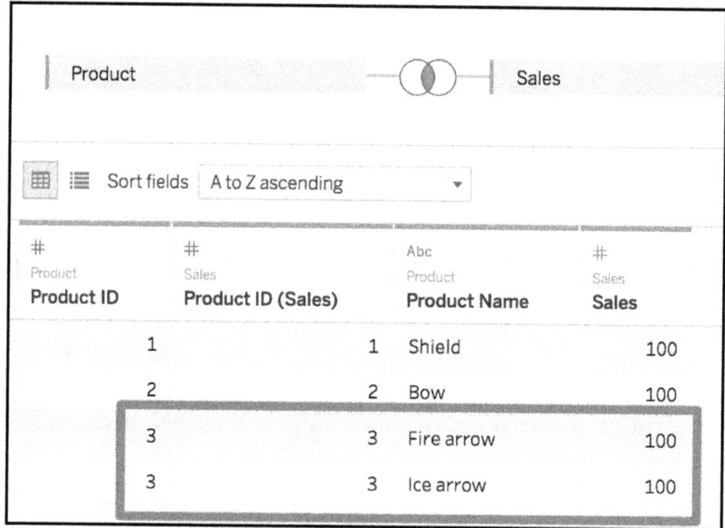

# Product Product ID	# Sales Product ID (Sales)	Abc Product Product Name	# Sales Sales
1	1	Shield	100
2	2	Bow	100
3	3	Fire arrow	100
3	3	Ice arrow	100

As you can see, the product number `3` is duplicated. The reason for that duplication is because there are two product names with the same `Product ID`. The volume of sales here is `400`, which is wrong.

When you Join two or more tables, always be sure that the values you want to analyze won't be duplicated. There are three solutions to deal with data duplication:

- **The easiest**: Clean the file to remove the duplication. In the example, it means changing the ID of a product to `4`.
- **Use data blending**: Explained in `Chapter 12`, *Advanced Data Connection*.
- **Use level-of-detail calculation functions**: Explained in `Chapter 10`, *An Introduction to Calculations*.

To finish this section, let's create a Join together, step by step.

Hands-on – a first simple Join

Enough for the theory, let's create a simple Join between the **Orders** and **People** tables from `Sample - Superstore`. Before we start, let's see what those tables contain:

- **Orders** is the main table (the left one). We already used it in `Chapter 3`, *A First Dashboard and Exploration*, and it contains the profit.
- **People** is a table that contains only four lines and two columns. It associates a region with a person.

Our goal is to create a Data Source that allows us to look at the profit (which exists only in the `Orders` table) by person (which exists only in the `People` table).

Open Tableau and follow these instructions:

1. Connect to the `Sample-Superstore` Excel file in your Tableau repository (use the *Connecting to data* section from `Chapter 3`, *A First Dashboard and Exploration*, if you don't remember the file's location).
2. In the **Data Source** workspace, drag and drop the `Orders` table.

3. Drag and drop the **People** table next to **Orders**, as in the following screenshot:

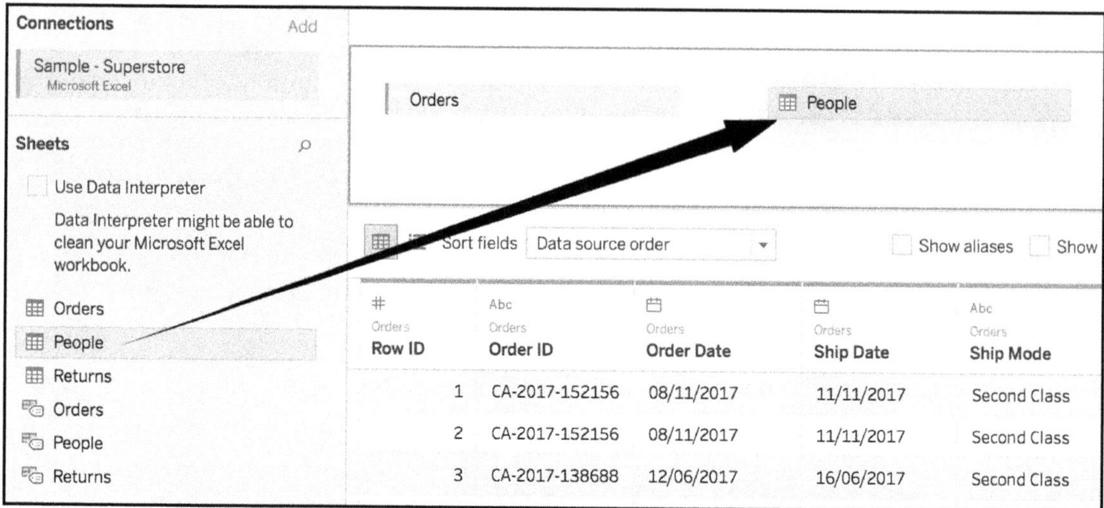

4. Tableau automatically creates a Join between the two tables with **Region** as the link, as shown in the following screenshot:

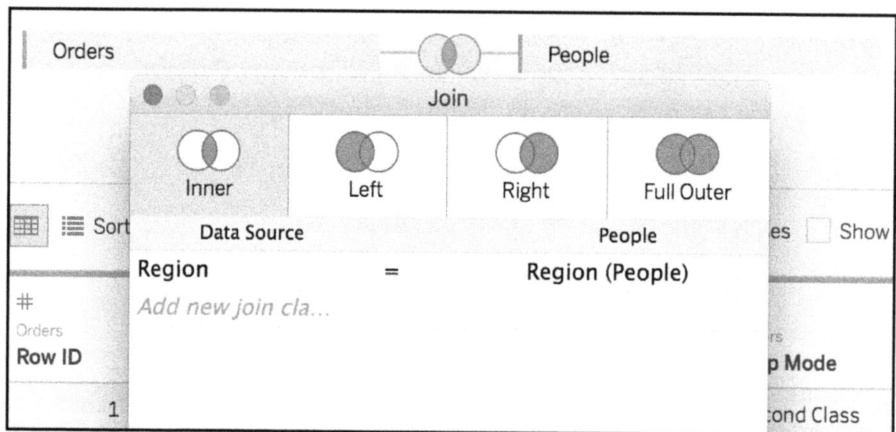

5. On the preview, you can see, on the right, the two new columns from the `Person` table:

# Orders **Discount**	# Orders **Profit**	Abc People **Person**	Abc People **Region (People)**
0.000000	41.91	Cassandra Brandow	South
0.000000	219.58	Cassandra Brandow	South
0.000000	6.87	Anna Andreadi	West
0.450000	-383.03	Cassandra Brandow	South
0.200000	2.52	Cassandra Brandow	South
0.000000	14.17	Anna Andreadi	West

6. The Data Source is ready. You can test it on a Worksheet and display the profit by person as we wanted.

This is a first and simple example. You can build more complex Joins by adding more tables. In the following screenshot, we also added the `Returns` table:

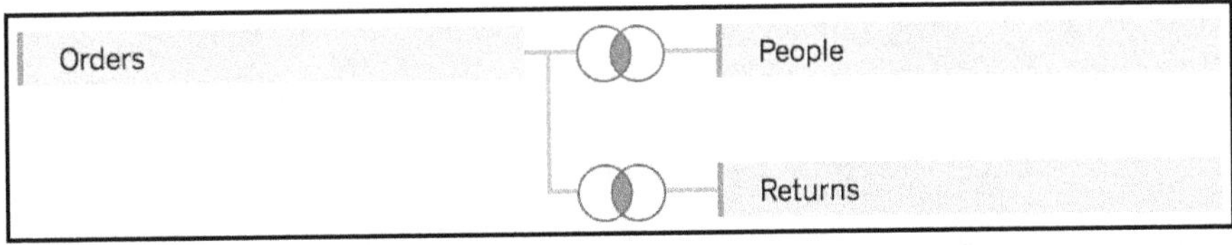

Be careful when multiplying the Joins; it has an impact on performance.

After Joins, the next interesting feature is Unions.

Union your data

If a Join adds columns, a Union adds lines.

Unions are useful when you have two (or more) tables with an identical structure that you want to combine to create a unique Data Source.

The typical use case is when you receive an Excel file with one sheet per year, and you need to compare those years. To do that, you need to combine those different sheets into a single Data Source. You can, of course, spend some time copying and pasting the data into a new, big Excel file, but with Tableau and Unions, you can combine them in a few clicks.

To create useful Unions, the different tables must contain the same column names. Otherwise, Tableau will not consider them identical and will create new columns.

Let's start with an example.

A Union example

For this example, I created an Excel file with two sheets to Union.

If you want to reproduce the example, you can download the `Union example` file from my website, `book.ladataviz.com`, in the section *Chapter 4: Connect To Data and Simple Transformation* section, or use this direct link: `https://ladataviz.com/wp-content/uploads/2018/09/Union-example.xlsx`.

The `Union example` Excel file contains two sheets:

- One named `2017`, which contains the data shown in the following screenshot:

Value	Country
310	United States
120	France
100	Spain

- One named `2018`, with the data shown in the following screenshot:

Value	Country
130	United States
60	France
940	Spain

As you can see, the two sheets have the same column name. In Tableau, after connecting to the Excel file, there are two ways of making a Union:

- **The first way**: Drag and drop the `2017` table, then drag and drop the second table, `2018`, just beneath the first one, where it says **Drag table to union**:

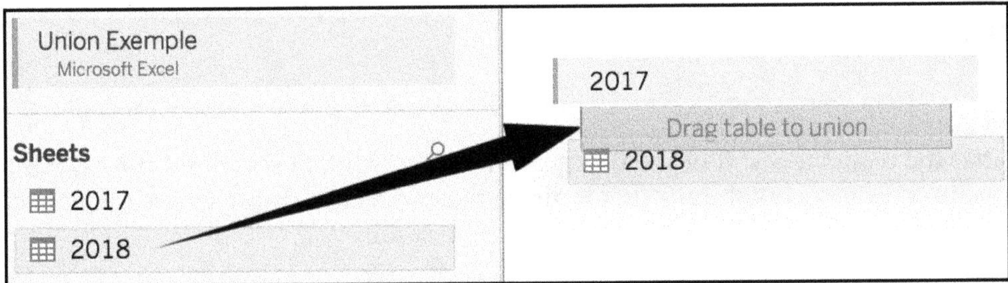

- **The second way**: Drag an drop **New Union**, as shown in the following screenshot:

It opens a new window where you can drag and drop the two tables to Union them:

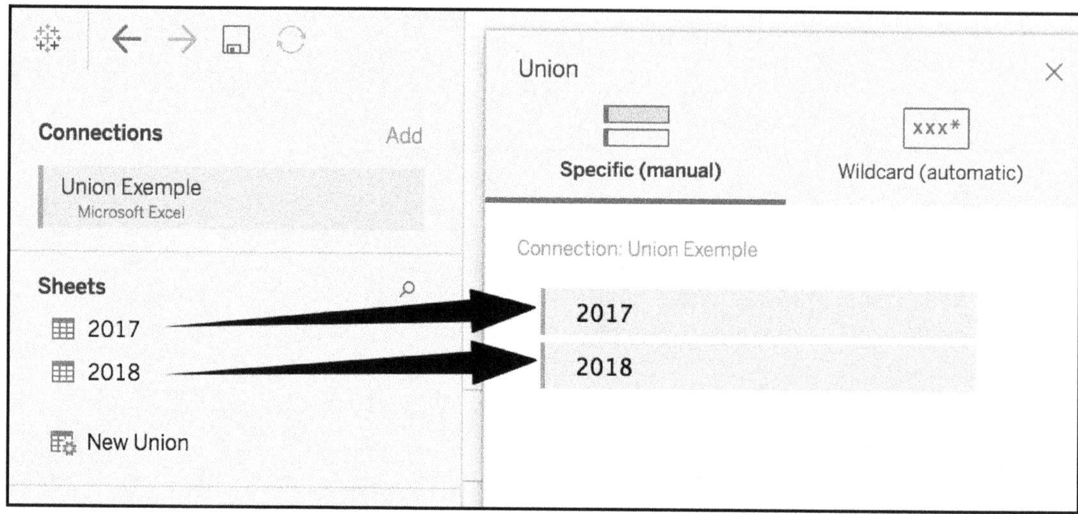

No matter the way, the result of the Union is a Data Source that combines the two tables. Tableau also creates new columns that indicate the name of the table where the data comes from. The following screenshot shows you the final result:

Union Value	Union Country	Union Sheet	Union Table Name
310	United States	2017	2017
120	France	2017	2017
100	Spain	2017	2017
130	United States	2018	2018
60	France	2018	2018
940	Spain	2018	2018

To end this chapter about data connections, let's see some of the transformations you can apply to the Data Source.

Simple transformations

Tableau is not a data-preparation tool. It's always better to have a clean file to start with. However, Tableau offers some simple transformation tools. When you connect to a dataset, you can, for example, use the Data Interpreter, split a column into multiple columns, or pivot your data. Let's see a case for these transformations.

For this section, I created a dataset to clean in Excel, as illustrated here:

	Year			
Country and City	2015	2016	2017	2018
Kenya/Nairobi	74271	13190	40746	22826
Brazil/Rio	52579	17388	30067	1849
United States/Denver	21691	7765	44720	3394
Germany/Berlin	47946	43622	19961	2537
Japan/Tokyo	5072	49598	29861	33979
Finland/Helsinki	59153	80023	61742	65594
Russia/Moscow	22697	38769	21267	12695
Norway/Oslo	61135	20984	42127	28246

If you want to reproduce the example, you can download the `Dataset to clean` file from my website, `book.ladataviz.com` section in the *Chapter 4: Connect To Data and Simple Transformation* section, or use this direct link: `https://ladataviz.com/wp-content/uploads/2018/09/Dataset-to-clean.xlsx`.

Three things are problematic with this dataset:

- There is a column header for the years
- The countries and the cities are in the same column
- Each year is in a different column, preventing the creation of a simple line chart

Now, let's fix the first problem of this dataset with the Data Interpreter!

Data Interpreter

Let's start by connecting to the `Dataset to clean` file in Tableau:

1. Open Tableau, select Microsoft Excel in the list of connectors, and select the `Dataset to clean` Excel file.
2. Tableau automatically puts the unique sheet, **Sales**, in the **Data Source** pane, but as you can see in the preview, the connection needs cleansing:

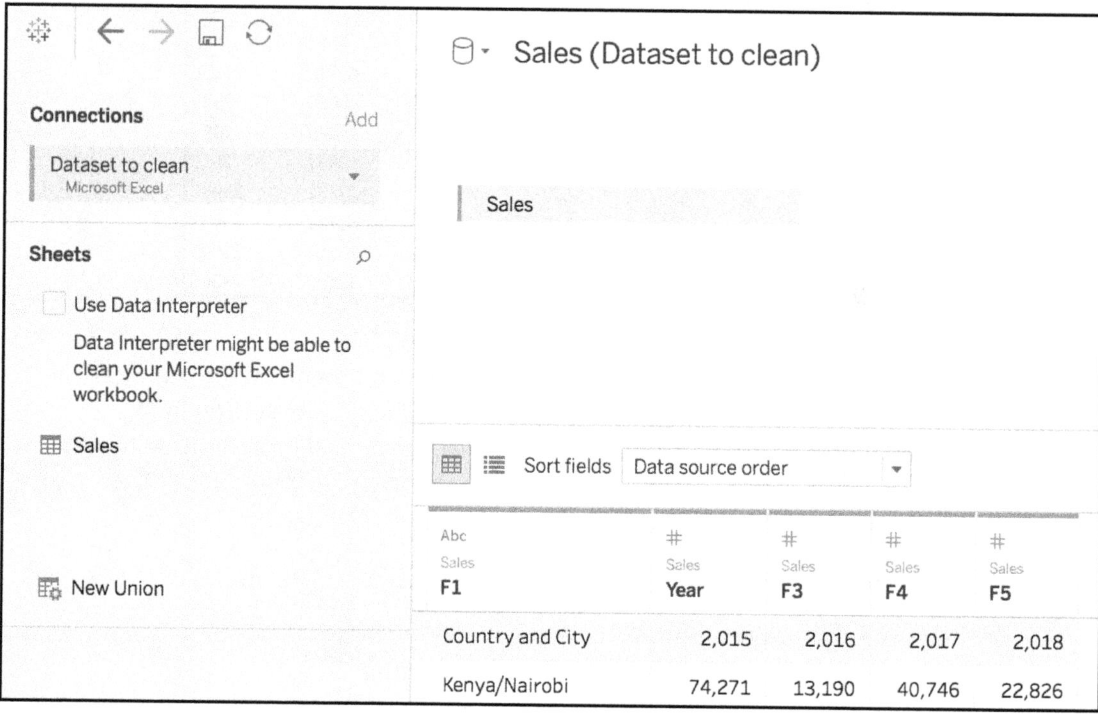

3. To clean the file, click on **Use Data Interpreter**, underneath **Sheets**.

As you can see in the following screenshot, it's already much better:

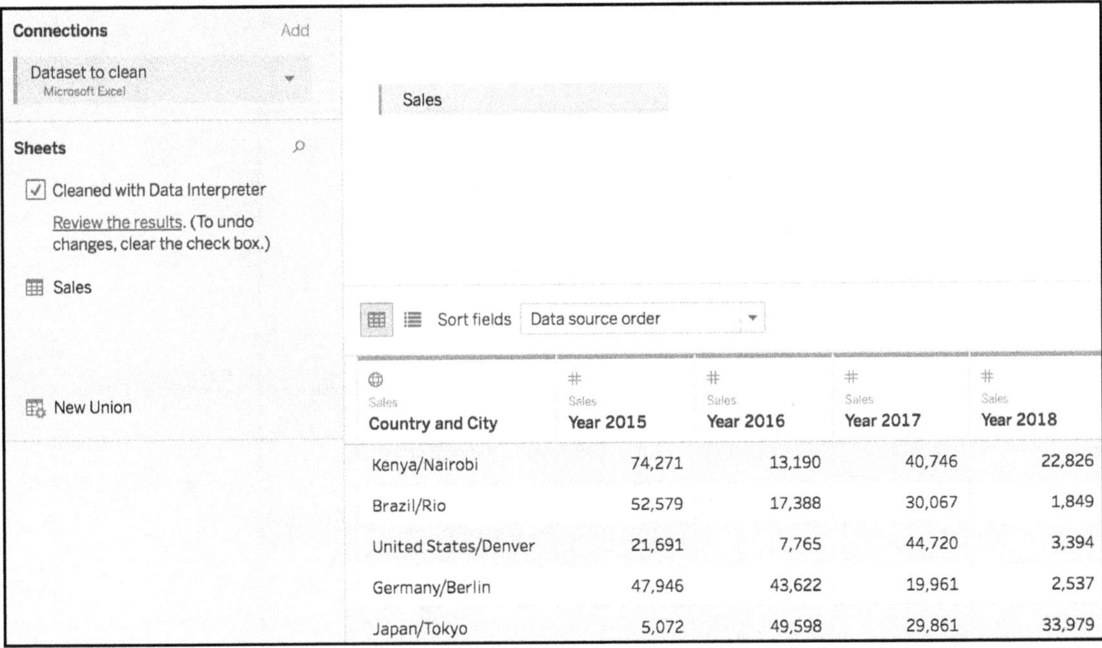

However, we still need to split the `Country and City` column and pivot the years.

Splitting a column

The second goal is to split the `Country and City` column into two columns:

1. Right-click on the `Country and City` column and click on **Split**, as shown highlighted in the following screenshot:

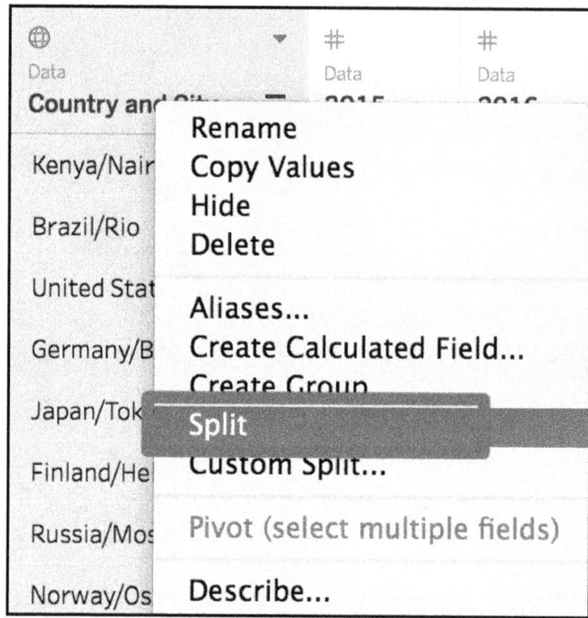

2. Tableau automatically recognizes that there is a common character and uses it to split the column into two new ones: `Country and City—Split 1`, and `Country and City—Split 2`.
3. Right-click on the new columns and select rename. Rename the first one `Country`, and the second one `City`.

The result is displayed in the following table:

Sales Country and City	Calculation Country	Calculation City
Kenya/Nairobi	Kenya	Nairobi
Brazil/Rio	Brazil	Rio
United States/Denver	United States	Denver
Germany/Berlin	Germany	Berlin
Japan/Tokyo	Japan	Tokyo

If Tableau cannot find a character for the split, or if Tableau chooses the wrong one, you can use a **Custom Split** to have advanced options. Selecting **Custom Split...** opens the following window:

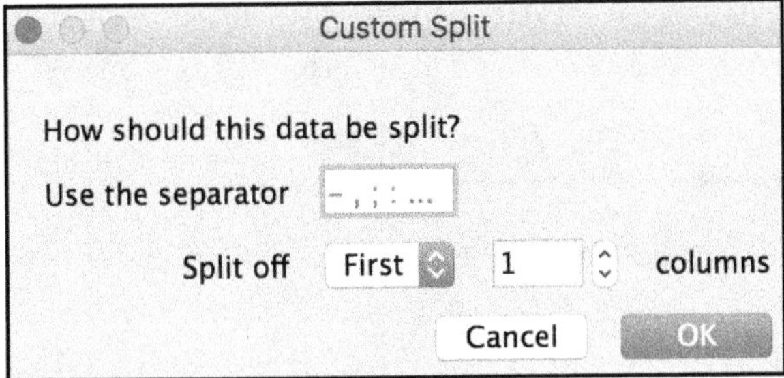

That's two problems fixed! Let's finish with the pivot.

Pivot

Pivot consists of transforming columns into lines. In this example, we want to pivot the four columns with the different years into two columns: one for the name of the year and one for the value.

To do that, follow these steps:

1. Select all the years' columns to pivot (click on them while pressing *Ctrl* (Windows) or *command* (macOS)).
2. Right-click on the last selected one and select **Pivot**, as highlighted here:

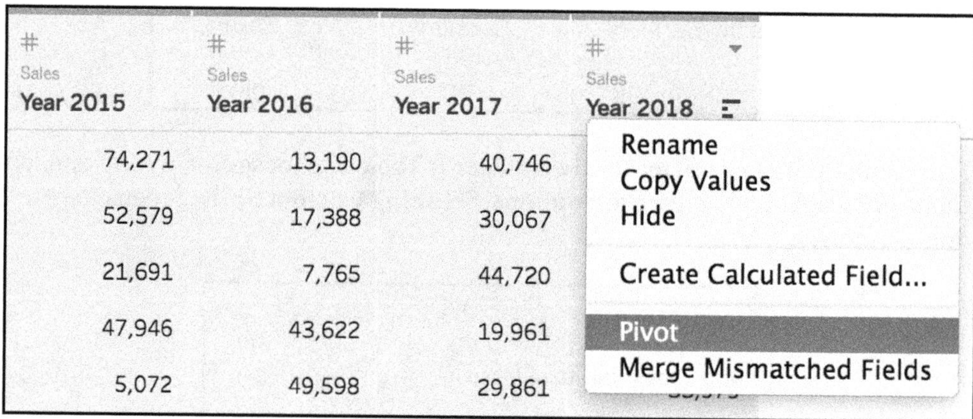

The result of the pivot is two columns:

- **One Dimension**: `Pivot Field Names`
- **One Measure**: `Pivot Field Values`

You can rename them to `Year` and `Values`, respectively.

The transformations are complete. You have a clean and simple Data Source. Here's the result:

Abc Pivot **Year**	# Pivot **Value**	Sales **Country and City**	Calculation **Country**	Calculation **City**
Year 2015	74,271	Kenya/Nairobi	Kenya	Nairobi
Year 2015	52,579	Brazil/Rio	Brazil	Rio
Year 2015	21,691	United States/Denver	United States	Denver
Year 2015	47,946	Germany/Berlin	Germany	Berlin
Year 2015	5,072	Japan/Tokyo	Japan	Tokyo
Year 2015	59,153	Finland/Helsinki	Finland	Helsinki
Year 2015	22,697	Russia/Moscow	Russia	Moscow

As you can see, you can even use Tableau to clean your data very quickly!

Summary

We have finished our first chapter about data connections. We saw how to connect to different sorts of datasets and use some features, such as Join, Union, and some data transformation. Later in the book, you'll learn other useful and powerful data transformation features.

After connecting to the data, you have a Data Source. You can directly use it to create visualizations, but I advise you to spend some time customizing and preparing your Data Source. There are many ways to enhance it and create something shareable, easy to understand, and compelling for your analysis.

In the next chapter, we'll learn how to build an efficient Data Source.

5
Build an Efficient Data Source

The **Data Source** is a crucial part of Tableau. Of course, the purpose of the tool is to visualize data, but without Data Source, there's no visualization. The Data Source is the engine of Tableau. It affects the performance, the quality of the analysis, the speed, and more. Also, like any engine, it's necessary to spend some time taking care of it.

In this chapter, you'll learn how to build the best possible engine for your analysis. We will cover the following topics:

- Understanding the Data Source
- Refreshing a Data Source and dealing with changes
- Field customization and default properties
- Hierarchies
- Groups, Sets, and Bins

Let's start with a clear explanation of what a Data Source is.

Understanding the Data Source

The Data Source is the final result of all the actions (Join, Union, Split, Pivot, and more) when connecting to a dataset, and all the customization you can apply afterward (Hide, Rename, Add Aliases, and so on). The goal for your Data Source is to be as performant, simple, and easy to understand as possible.

A Data Source can be a **Live** connection, an **Extract**, or published on **Tableau Server**. But no matter the type of connection, you will always find the same elements.

Data Sources elements

Four different elements comprise the Data Source:

- Dimensions
- Measures
- Sets
- Parameters

Dimensions and Measures are mandatory in Tableau. You'll always find them. They have at least one field, and that field has a data type.

It's essential to understand the difference between Dimensions and Measures. Everything is explained in `Chapter 2`, *The Tableau Core*.

Sets and parameters are your creation. A Data Source can have no sets and no parameters. Sets are explained in the section *Groups, Sets, and Bins*, and there is a focus on parameters in `Chapter 11`, *Analytics and Parameters*.

Let's continue with an overview of the different data types.

Data types

Each field has a data type. There are seven data types in Tableau:

- Text Abc (also called string)
- Number, decimal, or whole # (they share the same icon)
- Date
- Date and Time
- Boolean T|F (true or false)
- Geographic values

When you connect to a dataset, Tableau automatically chooses a type for each column of the dataset. However, as with almost everything in Tableau, you can customize it. To change the data type, you can either click on the icon, or right-click on the field and use **Change Data Type**, as in the following screenshot:

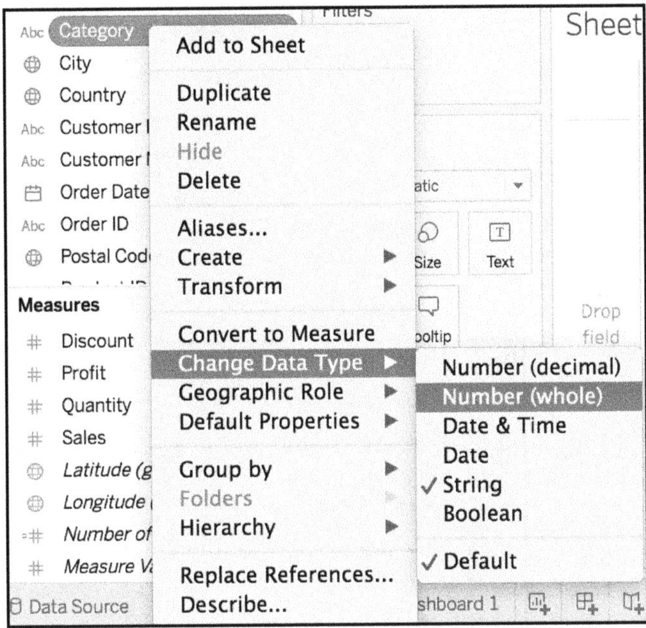

The different fields in your Data Source come from the dataset. Did you notice that some Measures and Dimensions are not from your dataset? Continue reading to learn more about the generated information.

Generated information

Every data source can have up to five generated pieces of information:

- **Number of records**: You can use it to find out how many lines are in your Data Source.
- **Latitude (generated) and Longitude (generated)**: You'll find this information if you have a **Geographical** field in your Data Source. They are used to create maps.
- **Measure Names and Measure Values**: The first one contains the name of each Measure, the second one contains the values of each Measure. They have to be combined and you can use them to display multiple Measures at the same time (this is a focus of `Chapter 7`, *Design Insightful Visualizations - Part 2*).

Now that you have a clear view of what exists in your Data Source, let's see the options to customize it.

Data Source options

All the Data Source options are available with a right-click on its name on the top left. You can also access them by clicking on **Data** in the top menu. In the following screenshot, you can see the full list of options:

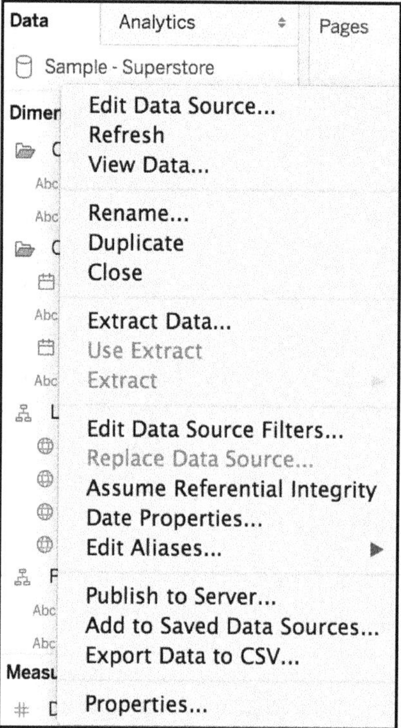

Here's a quick description of the most important options:

- **Edit Data Source...**: Takes you to the **Data Source** page where you can change your connection, add new tables, or do some transformations.
- **Refresh**: Refreshes your data if you are using a live connection.
- **View Data**: Opens a window where you can see your raw data, copy it, or export in a `.csv` file. Here's the **View Data** window:

View Data: Datasource

9 994 rows ☑ Show aliases Copy Export All

Category	City	Country	Customer ID	Customer Name	New Region	Order Date
Furniture	Henderson	United States	CG-12520	Claire Gute	South	08/11/2017
Furniture	Henderson	United States	CG-12520	Claire Gute	South	08/11/2017
Office Supplies	Los Angeles	United States	DV-13045	Darrin Van Huff	West	12/06/2017
Furniture	Fort Lauderdale	United States	SO-20335	Sean O'Donnell	South	11/10/2016
Office Supplies	Fort Lauderdale	United States	SO-20335	Sean O'Donnell	South	11/10/2016
Furniture	Los Angeles	United States	BH-11710	Brosina Hoffman	West	09/06/2015
Office Supplies	Los Angeles	United States	BH-11710	Brosina Hoffman	West	09/06/2015
Technology	Los Angeles	United States	BH-11710	Brosina Hoffman	West	09/06/2015
Office Supplies	Los Angeles	United States	BH-11710	Brosina Hoffman	West	09/06/2015
Office Supplies	Los Angeles	United States	BH-11710	Brosina Hoffman	West	09/06/2015
Furniture	Los Angeles	United States	BH-11710	Brosina Hoffman	West	09/06/2015
Technology	Los Angeles	United States	BH-11710	Brosina Hoffman	West	09/06/2015
Office Supplies	Concord	United States	AA-10480	Andrew Allen	South	15/04/2018
Office Supplies	Seattle	United States	IM-15070	Irene Maddox	West	05/12/2017
Office Supplies	Fort Worth	United States	HP-14815	Harold Pawlan	Central	22/11/2016
Office Supplies	Fort Worth	United States	HP-14815	Harold Pawlan	Central	22/11/2016
Office Supplies	Madison	United States	PK-19075	Pete Kriz	Central	11/11/2015
Office Supplies	West Jordan	United States	AG-10270	Alejandro Grove	West	13/05/2015

- **Close**: Removes your Data Source. It also removes all the Worksheets with a visualization based on that Data Source.
- **Extract Data**: Opens a new window where you can configure the Extract and create it.
- **Extract...**: Submenu is available when you are using an Extract and allows you to refresh it, append data from a file or show the history.
- **Edit Data Source Filters**: Opens a new window where you can add some filters (detailed in `Chapter 7`, *Design Insightful Visualizations - Part 2*).

You can also add a **Data Source filter** in the **Data Source** page, on the top-right, next to the menu where you select **Live** or **Extract**.

- **Replace Data Source**: Opens a menu where you can select the **Current** and the **Replacement** Data Source. All the Worksheets that use the current source will use the replacement one.
- **Date Properties**: Allows you to change three options: the week's starting day, the fiscal year start, and the default date format.
- **Edit Aliases**: Allows you to add an Alias to the values of a Dimension.

- **Add to Saved Data Source**: Allows you to export the Data Source as a file for further usage.
- **Export Data to CSV**: Exports the data in a CSV file. Be careful; if you have a large Data Source, the export can be very long.

The list is long, but you don't have to remember all of the options. Keep in mind that if you want to do something related to your Data Source, it's probably one right-click away.

In the next section, we'll see in detail how to refresh your data and deal with the changes.

Refresh a Data Source and deal with changes

Data lives and changes. Any analysis tool, such as Tableau, needs to allow users to refresh data and deal with changes as easily as possible.

In this section, we won't talk about the published Data Source on Tableau Server. The way to refresh or modifying a published Data Source is different and explained in `Chapter 9`, *Publish and Interact in Tableau Server*.

The following section describes how to refresh a Data Source.

How to refresh a Data Source

Refreshing a Data Source is simple for both Live and Extract Data Sources.

For a Live connection, right-click on the Data Source and click on **Refresh**. That's it.

For an Extract, clicking on Refresh won't work because the data in the extract file (`.hyper`) hasn't changed. Remember that when you create an Extract, you create a copy of your dataset in a Hyper file. Even if the data changes in the dataset, the data in the Hyper doesn't. To refresh an Extract, you need to refresh the Hyper file. To do so, right-click on the Data Source name, go to **Extract**, and then **Refresh**, as in the following screenshot:

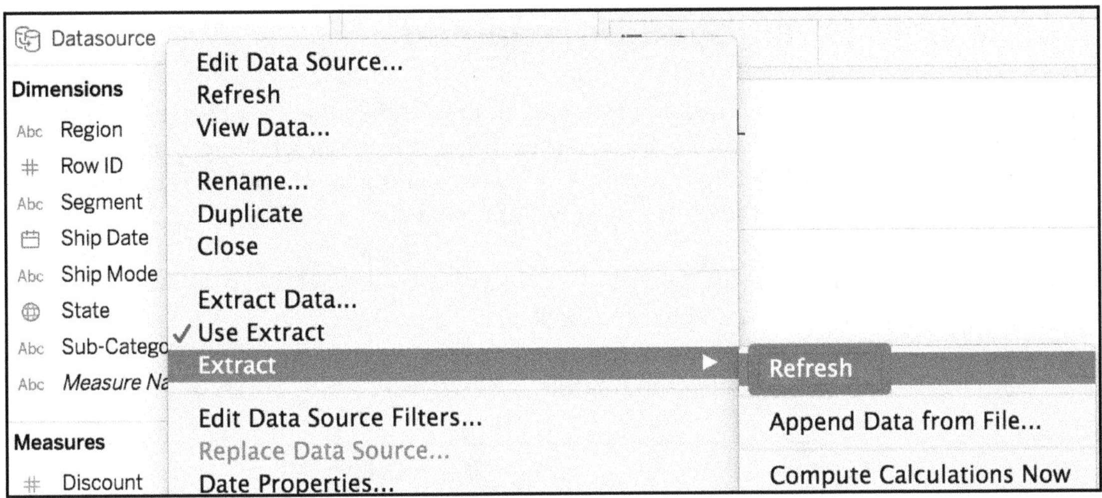

When refreshing an Extract, Tableau warns you that the data will change. If you click on **Yes** to continue, Tableau establishes a new connection to the dataset and imports the data again. At the end of the extraction, your Extract is refreshed.

What if there were some modifications in the dataset between two refreshes?

Deal with changes

Again, Tableau is here to help you if there are changes in the dataset. Not all changes cause a problem.

Trivial cases

There are two trivial cases:

- **A new column is added to the dataset**: If there is a new column in the dataset, you'll see a new field in the Data Source. You don't have to do anything.
- **An unused Field is removed or renamed**: If there is an unused field in your Data Source that is deleted or renamed from the dataset, you won't even notice it. It'll simply be suppressed on renamed in the Data Source.

The last case, when a field that you use in Tableau is deleted or renamed in the dataset, is a bit more problematic.

A used field is removed or renamed

If a field used in Tableau is removed or renamed in the dataset, there will be an exclamation point next to it when you refresh the Data Source. If the column is removed, you can't do anything except put it back. More often, the column is just renamed and, in Tableau, you can replace the references to the old column with the new one.

Let me illustrate the process with the `Sample-Superstore` dataset. Let's say that the `Region` column was renamed `New Region`:

1. In a Workbook, I display the **Region** in Rows:

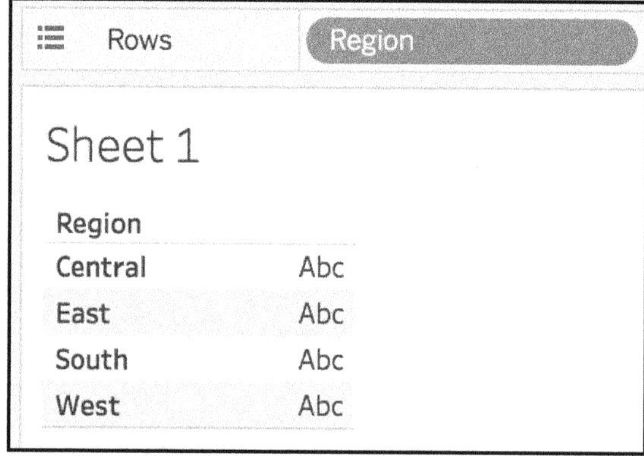

2. I refresh the Data Source—the **Region** pill turns red, and in the **Data** pane, there is an exclamation mark next to the **Region** field:

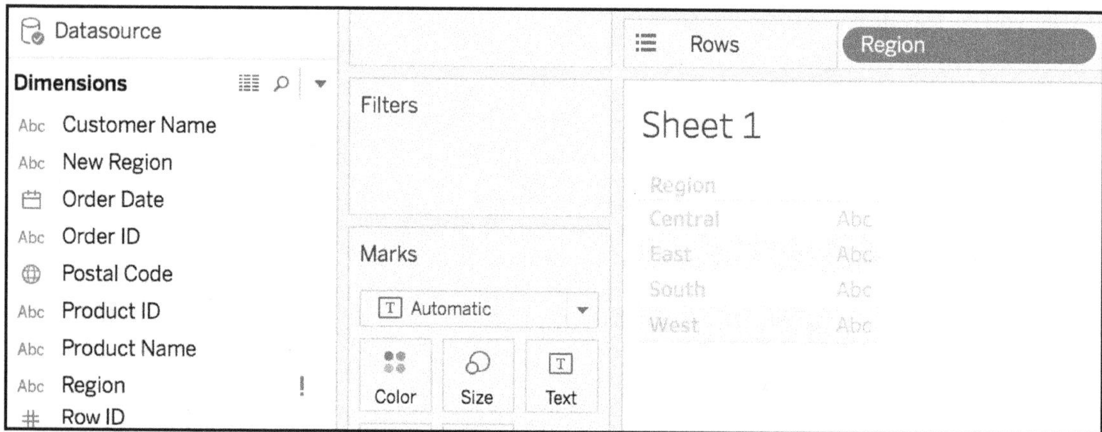

3. To correct the error, I right-click on the **Region** field and select **Replace References...**:

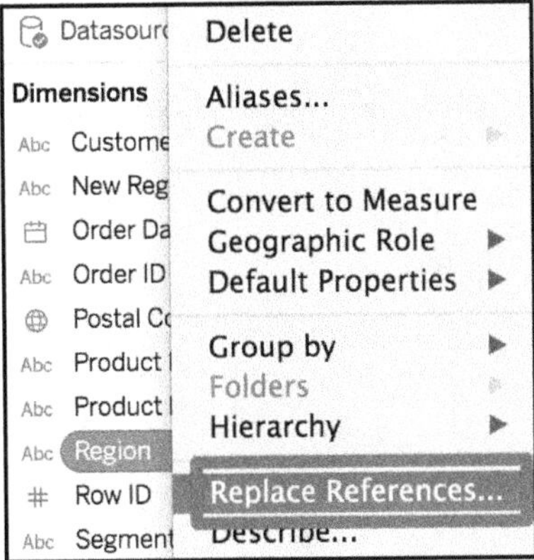

4. Select the new field that replaces the old one. In this example, it's **New Region**.
5. The old field, `Region`, is removed from the Data Source and, in the Worksheets, the pill is now using `New Region`. You can see the result in the following screenshot:

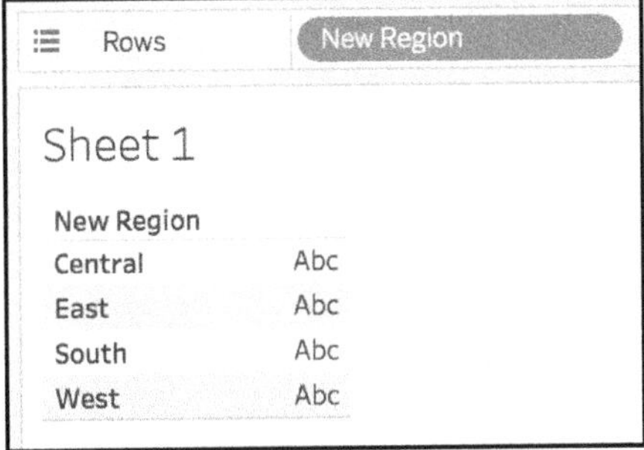

Easy, isn't it? Now that you have a clear view of how to use and refresh your Data Source, it's time to see how to customize it.

Field customization and default properties

Customizing the Data Source is the best way to make it easier to use and share. Let's see the different options you have to transform a raw Data Source into a better one.

You can reproduce all the examples with the `Sample-Superstore` dataset.

First, let's do a tour of the different field options, and then focus on the default properties.

Field customization and options

All the field options are available with a right-click on any field. Here's the list of all the options:

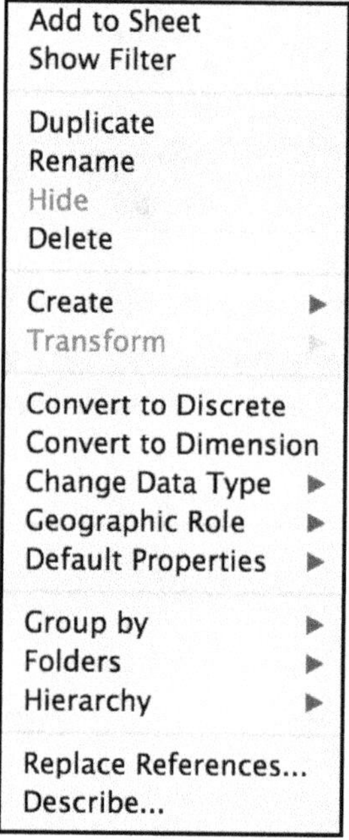

There are some straightforward options, so let's see a short description for those that aren't trivial:

- **Show filter**: Only appears if you have something in the Worksheet. We'll see this option in `Chapter 7`, *Design Insightful Visualizations - Part 2*.
- **Hide**: Hides the field but doesn't suppress it. It's a great way to clean your Data Source if there are many fields that you won't use. The option is only available if the field is never used. You can show the hidden field by clicking on the arrow next to **Dimension** and selecting **Show Hidden Fields**:

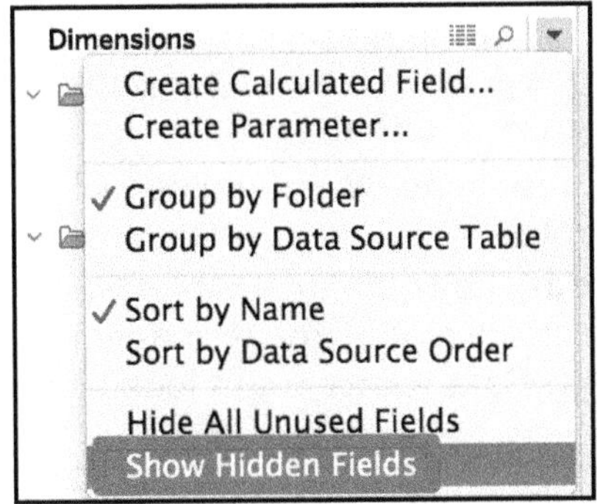

- **Delete**: Suppresses custom fields (Bins, Sets, Parameters, Calculated Fields, and others) from the Data Source.
- **Aliases...**: Allows you to rename the values of a Dimension. It opens a new window with the list of the values. For example, you can add Aliases to Ship Mode:

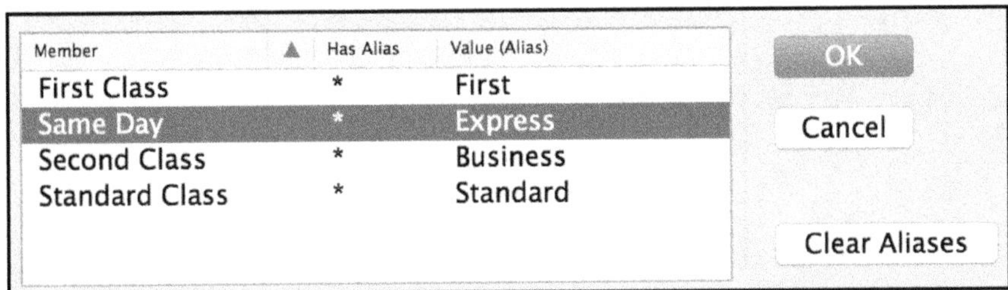

- **Create**: Opens a sub-menu where you can create new Fields. Groups, Bins, and Set are explained in the *Groups, Sets, and Bins* section of this chapter, Calculated Fields are detailed in `Chapter 10`, *An Introduction to Calculations*, and Parameters are the focus of `Chapter 11`, *Analytics and Parameters*.
- **Convert to Discrete or Convert to Continuous**: Only applies to Numbers and allows you to switch from a Continuous field to a Discrete field or vice versa.
- **Convert to Dimension or Convert to Measure**: Allows you to switch from a Measure to a Dimension or vice versa. If you try to convert anything other than a Number from a Dimension to a Measure, an aggregation is automatically applied. For example, if you Convert the **Customer ID** field to a Measure, the **Count Distinct** aggregation is automatically applied:

Abc Customer ID (Count (Distinct))

- **Geographical role**: The geographical role is available on a text dimension and allows you to specify a geographical role (Country, State, Region, or Other) if Tableau didn't recognize it automatically.
- **Group by**: Opens a sub-menu where you can select **Folder** or **Data Source Table**. It affects the way Tableau organizes the Dimension and Measure. With **Data Source Table**, fields are linked to their tables. With **Folder**, all the fields are mixed, and you can create folders to group them. The following screenshot is an example of what your Data Source could look like with folders:

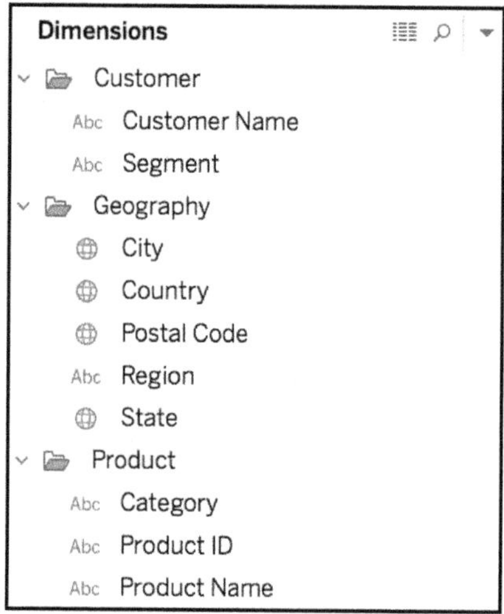

- Hierarchy is the topic of the next section.

Again, you don't have to remember everything. Keep in mind that if you want to change or customize something related to a field, you'll surely find it with a simple right-click.

The last option we have to see in detail is default properties.

Default properties

With this option, you can define default properties for your fields. The properties are a bit different between Measures and Dimensions:

- **Comments** and **Color** exist for both
- **Number format**, **Aggregation**, and **Total Use** exist only for Measures
- **Shape**, **Sort**, and **Clear Sort** exist only for Dimensions

Let's see an example of each default property.

Comment

Comment adds a comment to a field that appears when you hover over it. Here's an example:

1. Right-click on **Ship Mode**, go to **Default Properties**, and then **Comment...**.
2. A new window opens where you can write some text. Write a comment and then click on **OK**.
3. Hover over **Ship Mode** and you'll see your comments:

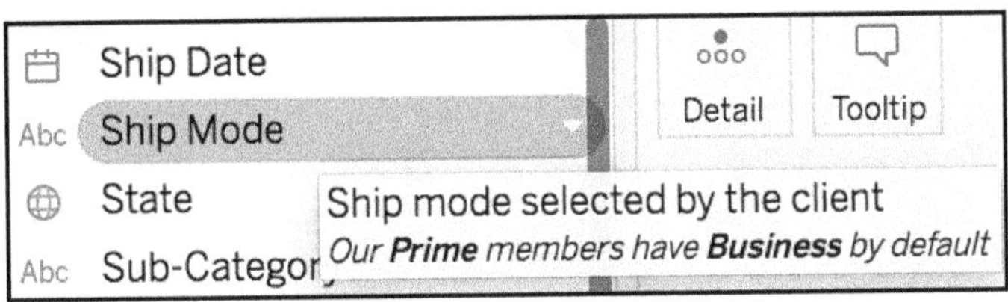

This option is quite handy if anyone other than you is going to use the Data Source. They'll be able to see the comment and have a better understanding of the field.

Let's continue with the second common default property: **Color...**.

Color

Color is really important in data visualizations. With this default property, you can predefine the color of the field when it's used in the Color Marks property. Here's an example of how it works:

1. Right-click on **Ship Mode**, go to **Default Properties**, and then **Color...**.
2. A new window opens where you can assign a color to the different values.

3. Assign a color of your choice to each item by first clicking on the value on the left, then on the color of your choice on the right. Here's an example of color assignments:

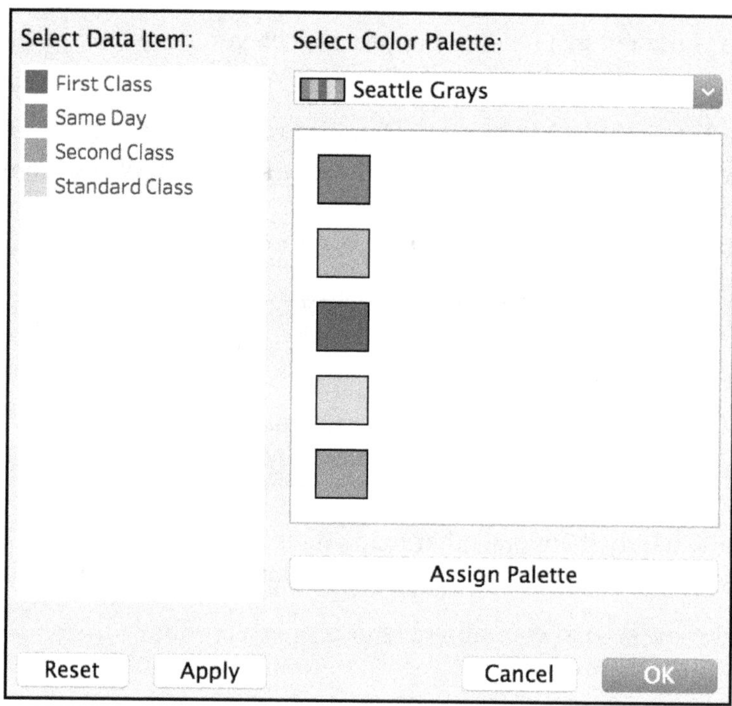

After that, if you build a visualization with **Ship Mode** in **Color**, you'll see that Tableau uses the default color you assigned.

This option is a time saver. When you use a field with a default color, you won't have to assign them again. The next option, **Shape**, is only available for Dimension and is similar to **Color...**.

Shape

The **Shape...** default property works the same as the **Color** one. The only difference is that you are not affecting different colors, but different shapes. Every time you use a field with a Shape default property in **Shape**, Tableau uses the ones you have assigned.

The next option is also available only for Dimension but is quite different.

Sort

The **Sort...** default property opens a new window where you can specify the sort order. You can choose between three options:

- **Data Source** order, ascending or descending
- **Alphabetic** order, ascending or descending
- **Manual** sort the item in the order of your choice

After defining the default sort option, Tableau will always display the values in the order you specified.

If you have a default sort, a new option appears in Default Properties where you can clear sort.

Let's continue with the Measure default properties, starting with the **Number format...**.

Number format

The **Number format...** property allows you to specify the format of numbers. When you click on the option, this is the menu that opens:

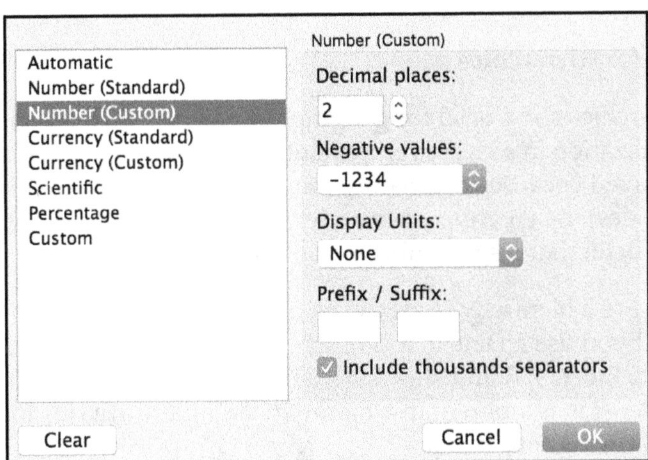

You can use the menu to choose between the four main formats, Number, Currency, Scientific, Percentage, or you can add a Custom format. When you select **Number (Custom)** or **Currency (Custom)**, you have a few options to create the format of your choice.

Once you specify a default format, Tableau will use it every time you use the Measure. The last two default properties are about aggregation.

Aggregation and total using

As you know, Tableau aggregates the Measure when you use it. By default, Tableau usually uses a sum. With the **Aggregation** default property, you can change that. For example, in the `Sample Superstore` Excel file, **Discount** is not a Measure that you can sum. You can change the default **Aggregation** to **Average**.

Total using is quite similar; here, you can specify the aggregation used to display totals.

That's it for the default properties. These options are used to increase your speed in Tableau and are helpful if you want to share your Data Source. Another great way to customize your Data Source is to add hierarchies.

Hierarchies

Hierarchies are quite special. They regroup multiple Dimensions. However, a Hierarchy doesn't just affect the Data Source, but also the visualization and the way the users can interact with it. A hierarchy creates a relationship between different Dimensions, such as a parent-child relationship.

The dedicated icon for **Hierarchies** is .

Hierarchies are crucial for geographical roles. If you try to build a visualization in a city level without a hierarchy, lots of cities won't be displayed because their names are ambiguous (they exist in multiple countries). By creating a hierarchy with a country-level field and a region-level field, there is no ambiguity anymore.

Dates, for example, are a hierarchy. A day is included in a week, which is included in a month and a year. If you use a Date in a Worksheet, such as **Order Date**, Tableau automatically selects the **YEAR** and shows a small **+** in the pill, at the left of the name. It means that the Dimension is a parent in a hierarchy and there are children. This is illustrated in the following screenshot:

Once you click on the **+**, the child is added next to the parent, and the **+** switched to a **-** to remove the child. The child can also be a parent of another Dimension, and so on. You can see, in the following screenshot, where the **YEAR** of **Order Date** is a parent of the **QUARTER**, and the **QUARTER** is a parent of another dimension:

Enough for the theory, let's create a hierarchy and use it. You can reproduce the following example with the `Sample - Superstore` dataset:

1. Select the Dimensions you want to combine in a Hierarchy. For this example, select **Category** and **Sub-Category**.
2. Right-click on one of the selected Dimensions and go to **Hierarchy**, then **Create Hierarchy...**:

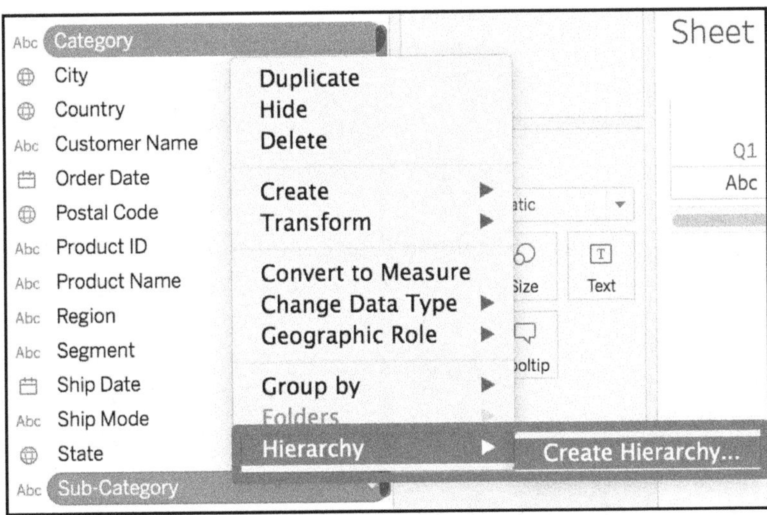

3. A new window opens asking for the name of the Hierarchy. Let's name it `Products`.

4. The Hierarchy is created, and you should see a new icon in your **Data** pane, with the **Category** and **Sub-Category** (in that order) under it. Your Hierarchy should look similar to the following screenshot:

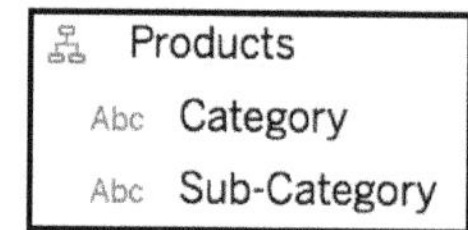

If the order is different, you can easily drag and drop the field to change the order.

5. Let's add the **Product Name** in the Hierarchy, at the last position. To do that, you can drag and drop the field under **Sub-Category**:

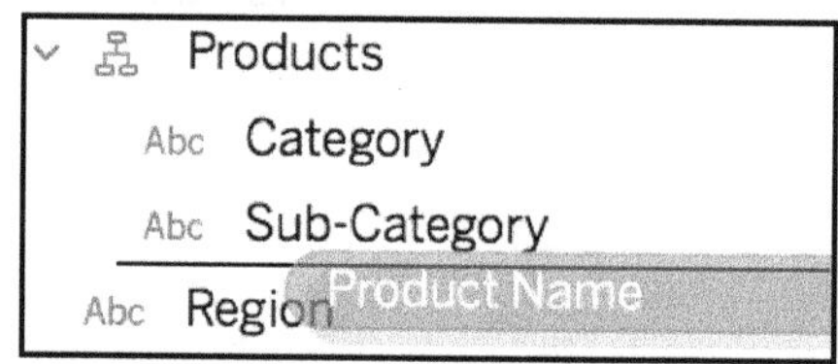

6. Double-click on **Category**, then on **Profit**. It creates a simple table. You can see the + next to the **Category** pill. You can also see the +, when you hover over the values in the visualization:

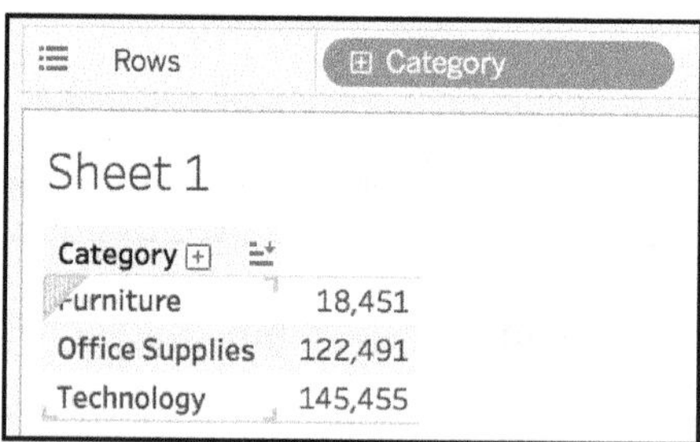

7. Click on +. Tableau automatically adds the child, **Sub-Category**. From here, you can go deeper with + or remove **Sub-Category** with -. Here's the final result:

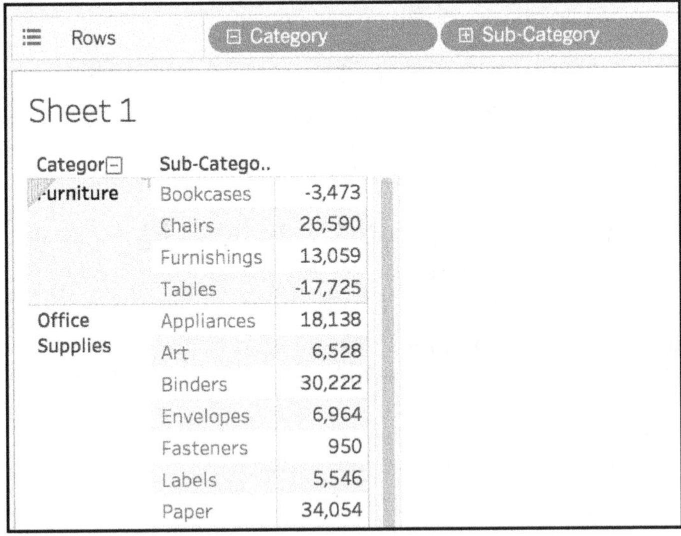

Rows
Category
Sub-Category
Sheet 1
Categor
Sub-Catego..
Furniture
Bookcases -3,473
Chairs 26,590
Furnishings 13,059
Tables -17,725
Office Supplies
Appliances 18,138
Art 6,528
Binders 30,222
Envelopes 6,964
Fasteners 950
Labels 5,546
Paper 34,054

Hierarchies are a useful and powerful tool. Use them when you can! Let's finish this chapter with the last option: creating Groups, Sets, and Bins.

Groups, Sets, and Bins

Groups, Sets, and Bins are synonyms, but they are fundamentally different in Tableau:

- Groups and Sets are created from Dimensions. Bins are created from Measures.
- Groups and Bins are Dimensions, but Sets are a different Tableau element

A bit lost? That's normal! Let's see some examples that you can reproduce with the `Sample-Superstore` dataset, starting with Groups.

Groups

A Group is a way to create a new Dimension that gathers different values of another Dimension. A Group is static; you need to modify it manually.

A Group is characterized by the icon.

There are two ways to create a Group:

- Manually, with a menu, when you know in advance how to gather the values.
- Visually, in the view, when there are too many insignificant values.

Let's start by creating a Group, manually, with Sample Superstore:

1. Right-click on **Sub-Category**, go to **Create**, then click on **Group**.
2. A new window opens where you see the list of the values in that Dimension. In this menu, you can manage the Groups.
3. To create a new group of values, select some values and click on the **Group** button at the bottom. Create a group with **Tables** and **Chairs**:

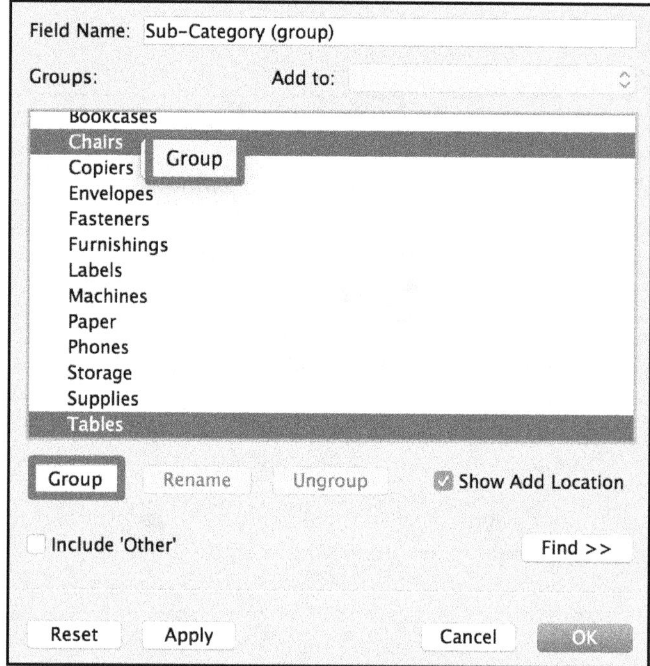

4. By default, Tableau names the new group of values with a concatenation of the values. However, it's possible to rename it by clicking on the **Rename** button. Rename the group `Desk Furniture`.
5. You can add as many groups as you want here. You can also automatically create an `Other` group that contains every ungrouped values. When you finish, click on **OK**.

6. After clicking on **OK**, a new Dimension is created. If you didn't change the name, it is called `Sub-Category (group)`. Your data source should look as follows:

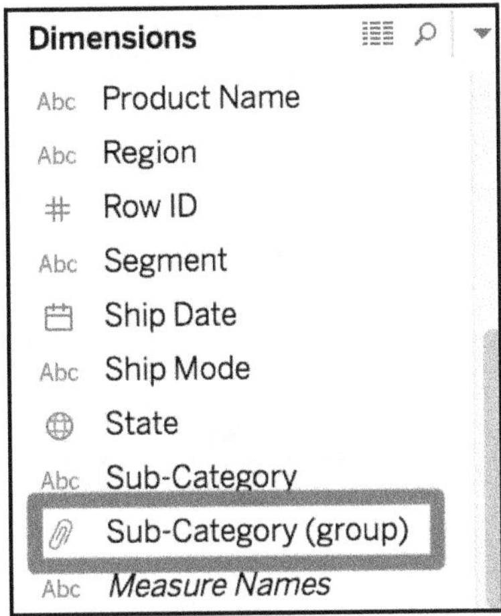

7. To test the Group, create a simple visualization: double-click on **Profit**, then double-click on **Sub-Category (group)**. As you can see in the following screenshot, Tables and Chairs are combined in a group called **Desk Furniture**:

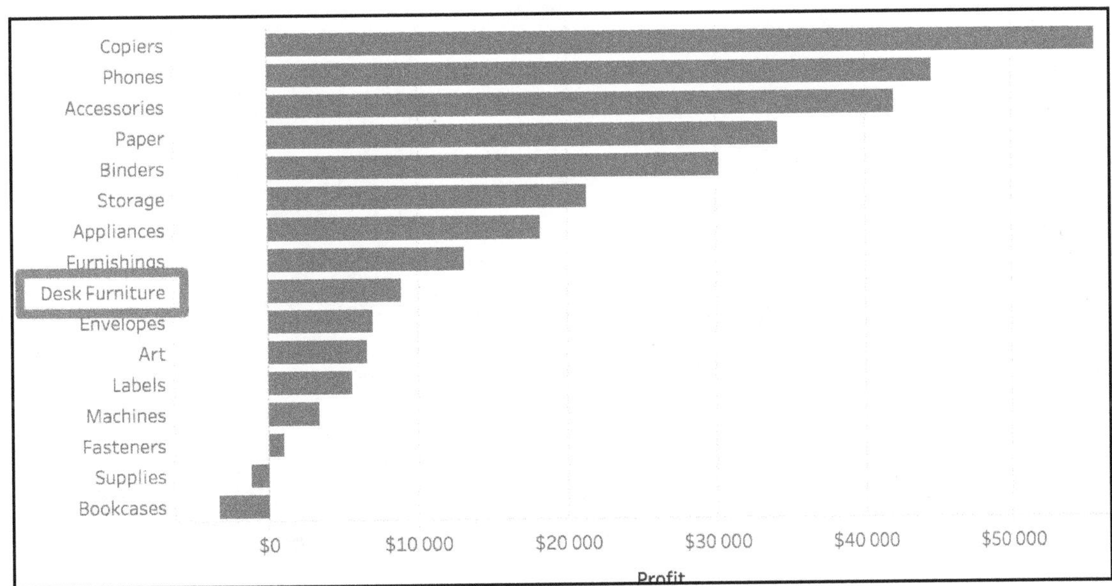

If you have too many values and you want to group them to reduce the number of non-important values, you can use the visual way. Let's see how to do this with Sample Superstore:

1. One a new Worksheet, double-click on **Sales**, then double-click on **Sub-Category** to create a simple visualization.
2. Use the button in the top menu to swap and sort the values as descending. As you can see, there are five sub-categories with small numbers of sales. They are not important so we want to group them.
3. Select the five bottom values by clicking on their names in the header (do not select the bars, it's crucial), and, in the menu that appears, you can click on the **Group** icon to create a group. The icon is highlighted in the following screenshot:

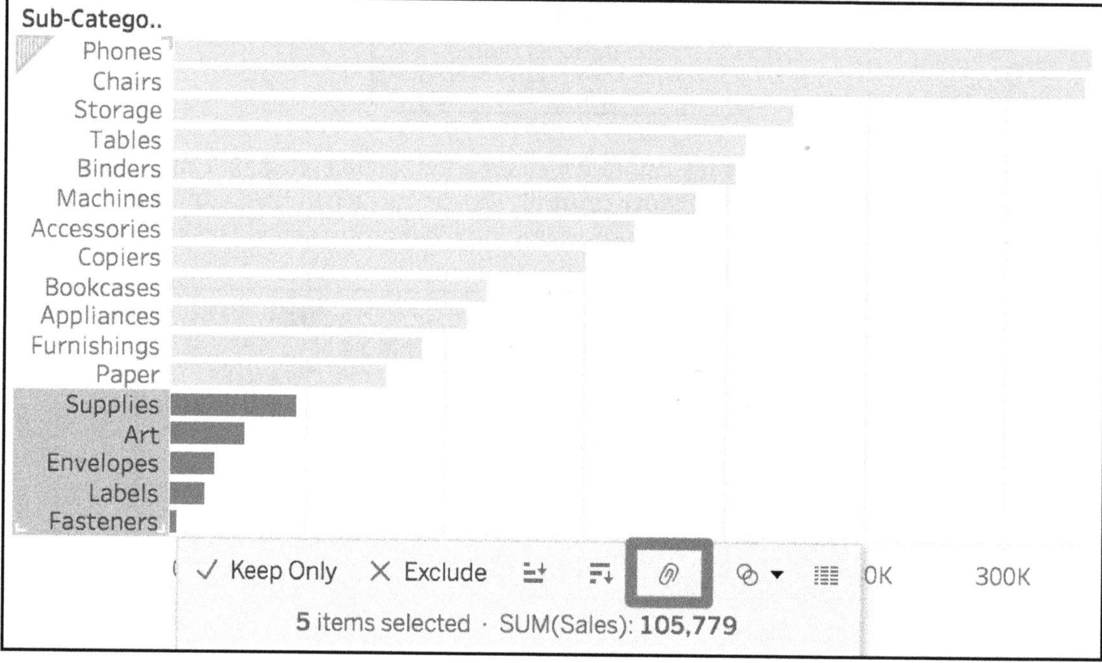

4. Again, you can rename the group by editing it on the **Data** pane, or with a right-click on it in the View to edit the aliases. Choose your favorite way and rename the group **Small Sales**. The final result is displayed as follows:

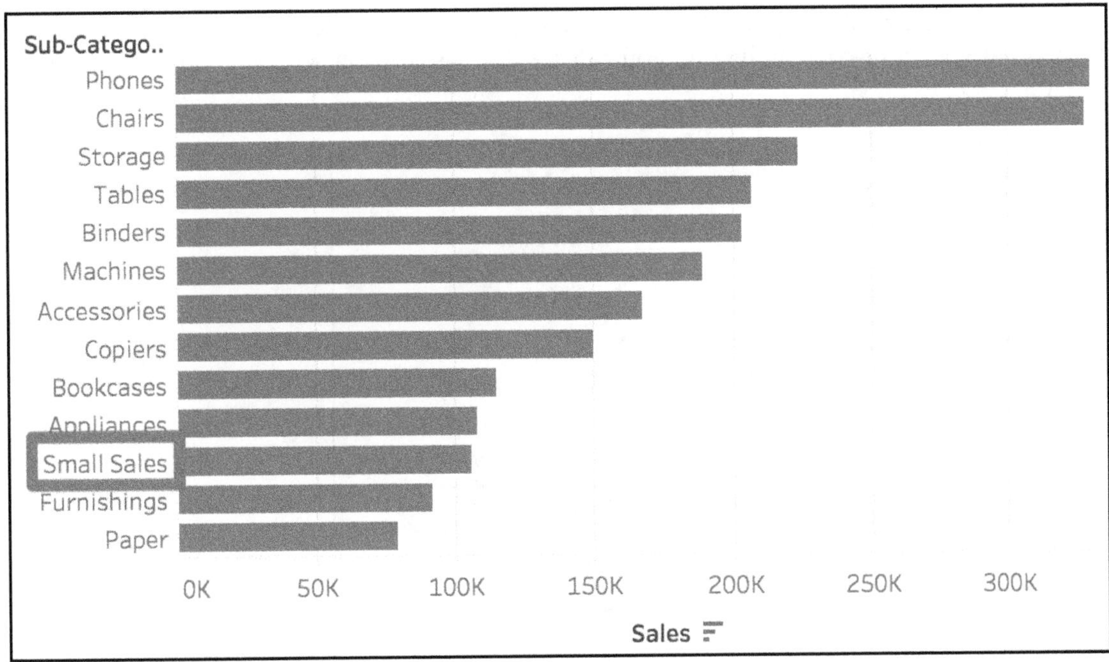

Creating a Group visually is an excellent way to reduce the number of insignificant values and help to focus on what matters. Another perfect use case is when there is a typo, and you want to combine the wrong value with the correct one.

As we said at the beginning, a Group is not dynamic. But Sets are! Let's see how to use them.

Sets

Sets are a different Tableau element. A Set is based on a Dimension. Unlike Groups, Sets are dynamic. With Sets, the values are either **In** the Set or **Out** .

Sets have a special icon: ⦾.

Sets have two ways of being displayed in a Worksheet. By default, a Set will return **In** or **Out**, but if you right-click on its pill, you can see that it's possible to show the members that are in:

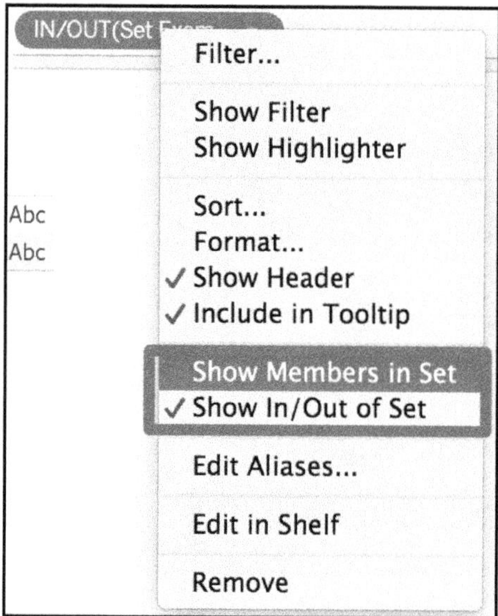

To create a Set, right-click on a Dimension, go to **Create**, and then **Set**. A new window opens with three tabs:

- The first tab, **General**, allows you to select the values that will be in the Set.
- The second tab, **Condition**, automatically puts the values in the Set if the condition is fulfilled. For example, in the following screenshot, the values of the Dimension will be in the Set if the **Profit** is greater than zero:

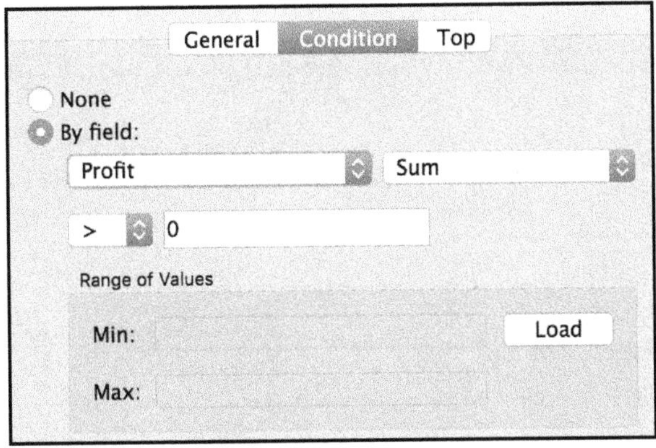

- The last one, **Top**, puts the values in the Set if they are the top (or bottom) ones based on the limit number and a Measure. This last option is used in the next example.

Let's create, together, a concrete Sets example with Sample Superstore:

1. On the **Data** pane, right-click on **State**, navigate to **Create**, then click on **Set**.
2. A new window opens. Change the name of the Set to `Top 5 State by Profit`.
3. Click on **Top** tab and select **By field**. Keep **Top**, and write `5` instead of `10`. Select the **Profit** field, and keep the **Sum** for aggregation. The configuration window of your Set should look like this:

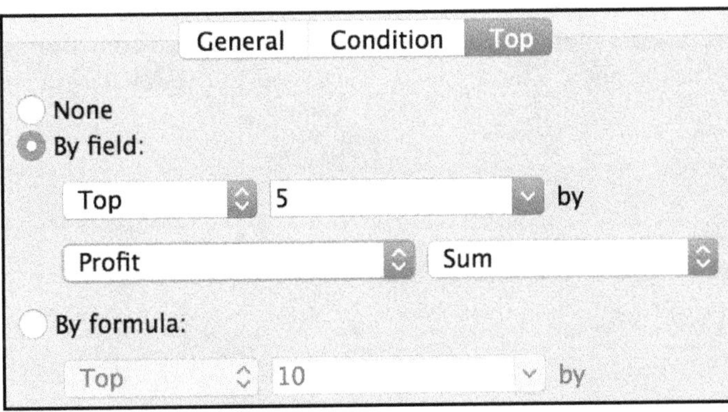

4. Click on **OK**. You should see a new **Sets** element in your data source.

5. In a new Worksheet, double-click on **State** to show a map, then drag and drop **Top 5 State by Profit** (your new Set) onto **Color,** as in the following screenshot:

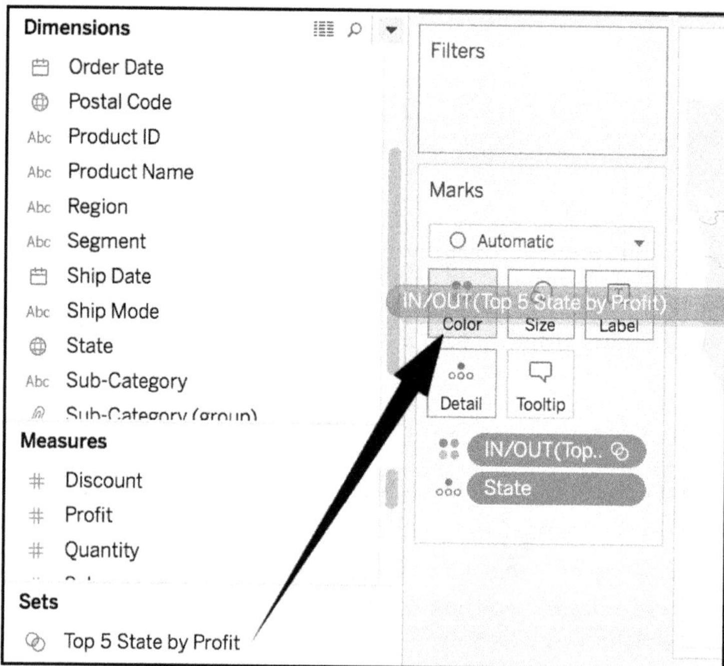

6. You should see a map with five states highlighted. Those five states are the five most profitable ones. The result is displayed in the following screenshot:

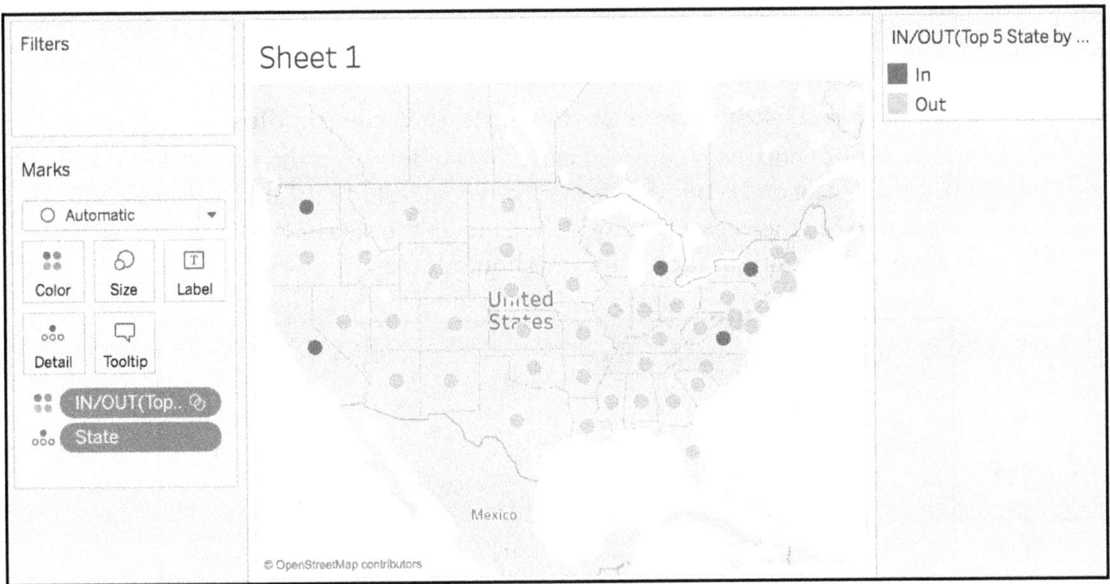

7. The great feature with Sets is that they are dynamic. It means that, if at the next refresh, *Texas* become one of the five most profitable states, its dot will automatically be highlighted.

Sets and Groups are both based on Dimensions, but their use is very different from our last item, Bins.

Bins

A Bin is a Dimension. Unlike Groups and Sets, Bins are based on a Measure. The purpose of Bins is to group the different values of a Measure in bins.

Bins have a special icon: .ılı. .

As always, the best way to understand is with examples. Let's create Bins with Sample Superstore:

1. Right-click on **Discount**, navigate to **Create**, then click on **Bins....**
2. A new window opens where you can edit the Bin. Keep the name `Discount (bin)`. The size of the bin is automatically suggested by Tableau, but in our case, we want to see the reparation by 10%. Change the size of the Bin to `0,1`. Here's how your Bin configuration window should look:

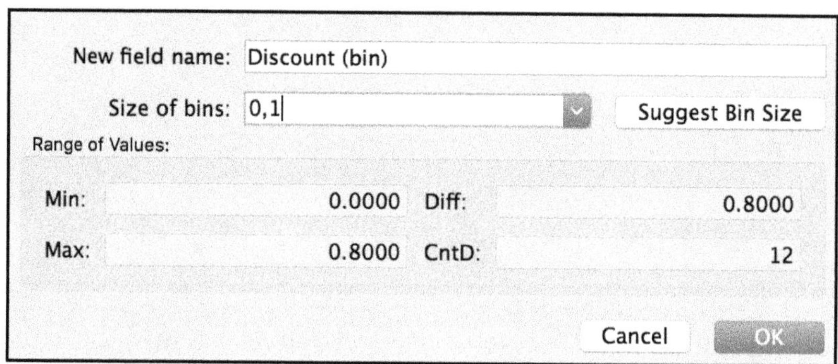

3. Click on **OK**. A new Dimension is created. You should find the Bin in your data source, as shown in the following screenshot:

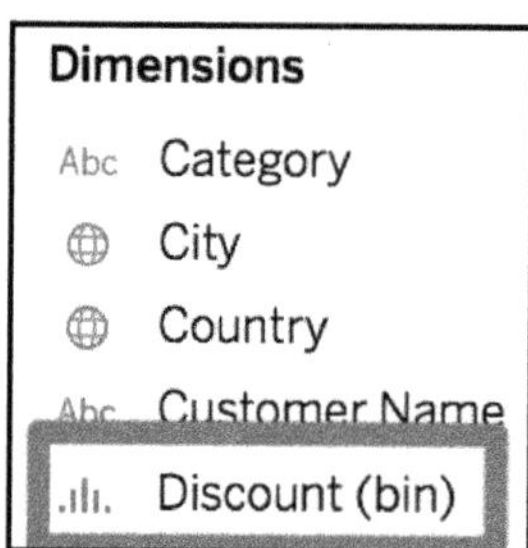

4. Let's use it. Double-click on **Number of Records**, then on **Discount (bin)**. You can now easily see that the majority of the orders have less than a 10% discount, or between 20% and 30%. Here's the final result:

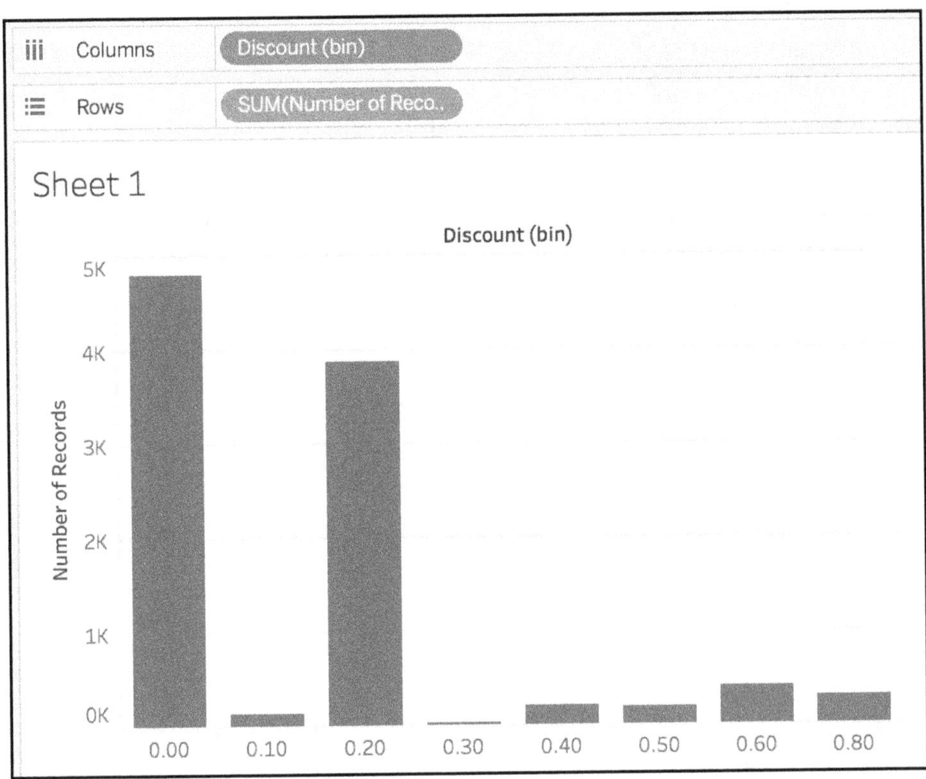

With Groups, Sets, and Bins, we've seen three of the five field-creation capabilities. The last two, Calculated Field and Parameter, are even more interesting than those we just saw. But that's for `Chapter 10`, *An Introduction to Calculations* and `Chapter 11`, *Analytics and Parameters*.

Summary

You've made it! The data source has no surprises for you anymore (or maybe one or two that we'll see later!).

In this chapter, you learned the purpose of a data source, its options, how to refresh it, and how to deal with changes. Then, you saw how to customize a data source with the default properties. Finally, you created Hierarchies, Groups, Sets, and Bins.

Building the data source is not the most exciting thing to do if you, like me, love visualization. However, spending some time creating a good data source and understanding its potential is crucial if you want to create the best analysis.

Speaking of visualization, how about we start using Tableau for its primary purpose? The next chapter is all about data visualization.

6
Design Insightful Visualizations - Part 1

Finally! Visualization! I know it was tempting to skip the last chapters and start here. If you did that, please start at the beginning. It's crucial that you read everything from the start. The reason is not that you won't be able to understand this chapter, but because you'll miss an essential part of what Tableau can do for you.

This chapter is divided into two parts. Creating visualizations is the core of Tableau and there is a lot to say! In this first part, we'll go through three major aspects:

- Creating a visualization the automatic and manual way
- The different Mark types
- Mark properties

In this chapter, for all the examples, we'll use Tableau's **Sample – Superstore** saved Data Source. You can find it on the first page when you open Tableau:

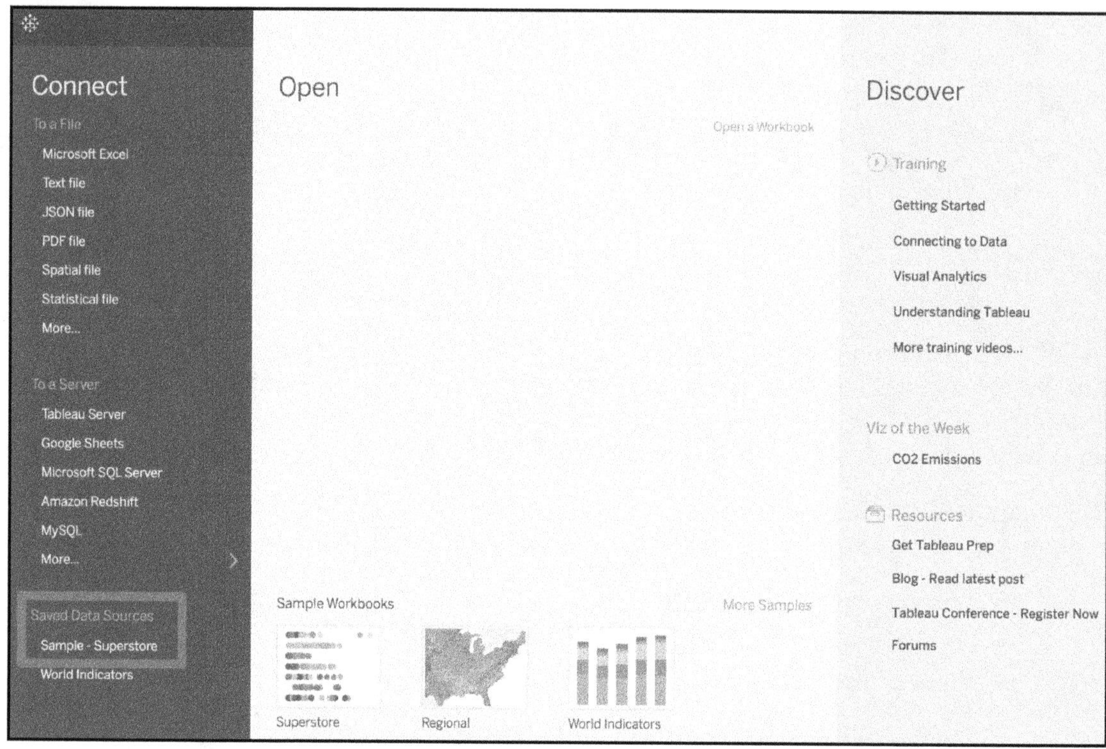

Simply click on it, and you're ready. The Data Source is based on the `Sample Superstore` Excel file and uses many features we saw in the previous chapter (Hierarchies, Folders, Bins, Sets, and so on).

Ready? Let's start with the basics: how to build a visualization in Tableau.

Creating a visualization the automatic and manual way

In Tableau, the only one way to display a visualization is by adding fields in shelves. The different shelves are **Rows**, **Columns**, **Marks**, **Filters**, and **Pages**. When you use a field on a shelf, it becomes a pill.

However, there are two very different ways of adding a field to a shelf: the automatic and the manual way. The automatic way is useful when you want to go fast or if you have no idea how to visualize your data. The manual way is needed when you know exactly what you want to build.

Let's start with the automatic way.

Build a visualization the automatic way

There are two ways of letting Tableau do the job for you.

The first way is the one you've used almost every time in this book since now: double-click. A simple double-click on a field automatically puts it in a shelf.

Double-click

When you double-click on a field in your Data Source, the field is automatically added to a shelf on the Worksheet. Tableau decides where the field should be, based on data visualization best practices.

Of course, there are limitations to what you can do with double-clicks. You won't be able to create a lot of different visualizations. You'll never go outside certain predefined scripts. Very soon, you'll feel limited.

However, a double-click is always the most efficient way to build a map. A simple double-click on any Geographical Dimension and Tableau automatically puts the **Latitude** in **Rows** and the **Longitude** in **Columns**.

The second way of letting Tableau do the work is to use **Show Me**, the menu that appears at the top-right of the toolbar.

Show Me

Show Me is a special menu on the top-right of the toolbar. You can easily spot it with the Show Me icon. If you click on the icon, you can open and close a list of all the predefined **Show Me** visualizations.

In the **Show Me** menu, you can see 24 visualizations. If no fields are selected in your Data Source, all the options are gray. If you choose one or multiple fields (using *Ctrl* or *Command*), you'll see that some options are now available and one of them will have an orange outline (it's the one that Tableau advises you to choose). To use an option, click on it.

Let's do a quick example using Sample - Superstore:

1. Simultaneously select **Order Date**, **Category**, and **Profit** in the **Data** pane
2. Open the **Show Me** menu
3. Click on some of the options to see different results

Show Me is useful when you start in Tableau, and when you have no idea how to visualize your data. You can click on the various options to see different results and use the one you prefer. After some time, you'll use **Show Me** very rarely. That's because, even if you have many possibilities, you are limited by how Tableau arranges the pill.

Show Me is quite powerful to create box-and-whisker and bullet graphs. Without Show Me, those two visualizations require lots of steps if you want to create them manually.

The automatic ways of building visualizations are fast and easy, but quickly limited. Do you remember the very first visualization you did in this book? The next screenshot will refresh your memory:

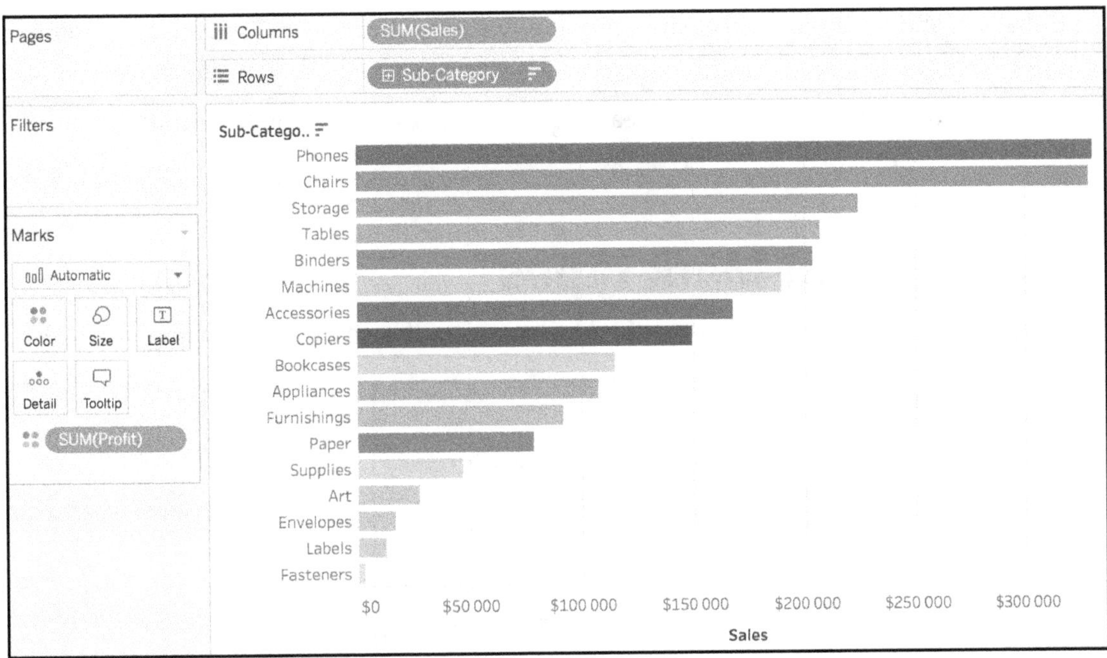

There is no way to create this visualization in an automatic way, either with double-clicks or with the Show Me menu. That's why you need to understand where to put the fields manually to create what you want.

Build a visualization the manual way

It's impossible to describe all the possibilities and combinations to build a visualization in Tableau. You are entirely free to choose where you want to use your fields. However, there are not many places to put them. Here are the different options you have:

- Put fields in **Rows** or **Columns**. If the pill is Discrete (blue), you'll see a header. If the pill is Continuous (green), you'll see an axis.
- Put fields in the **Mark Properties** shelf (Color, Size, Text,...).
- Add fields in **Filters**.
- Add fields in **Page Filter**.

And that's it. With this, you can create every possible visualization in Tableau. No hidden menu, no secret page.

Do you want to learn more? Just keep reading. In the next section, you'll see the different Mark types with an example for each.

The different Mark types

The highlighted menu lets you choose the **Mark** type, as shown in the following screenshot:

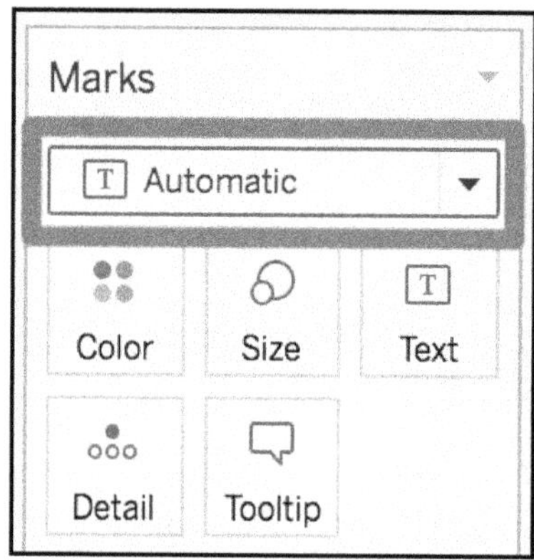

By default, the Mark type is set to **Automatic**. This means that Tableau chooses the best visualization based on the fields (where and which data types you use). For example, if you use a Date and a Measure, Tableau chooses a Line because it's the best way to visualize an evolution.

Of course, you can change the Mark type and use any type you want. For example, if you put **Order Date** in **Columns** and **Profit** in **Rows**, Tableau displays a Line chart. However, by using the Mark type menu, you can select the one you prefer (a **Bar** chart, an **Area** chart, or whatever you think is best).

Here's a list of the different Mark types:

The last one, Density, is available from Tableau 2018.3.

Let's see what you can build with the different Mark types. For each type, there is an example that you can reproduce with **Sample - Superstore**. To reproduce the example, just drag and drop the fields on the same shelves as in the screenshots and select the right Mark type in the menu.

You can also download the `Mark Types` ZIP file from my website `book.ladataviz.com`, on the *Chapter 6: Design Insightful Visualizations* section, or click on this direct link: `https://ladataviz.com/wp-content/uploads/2018/09/Mark-Types.twbx_.zip`. When you unzip the file, you'll find a Tableau Package Workbook with an example of each Mark Type.

Let's start with Bar.

Bar

Bar is represented with the Bar icon.

The Bar is probably the most common and useful Mark type. It's perfect to compare values between multiple categories. When you don't know how to visualize your data, start with a Bar!

Here's an example using a Bar:

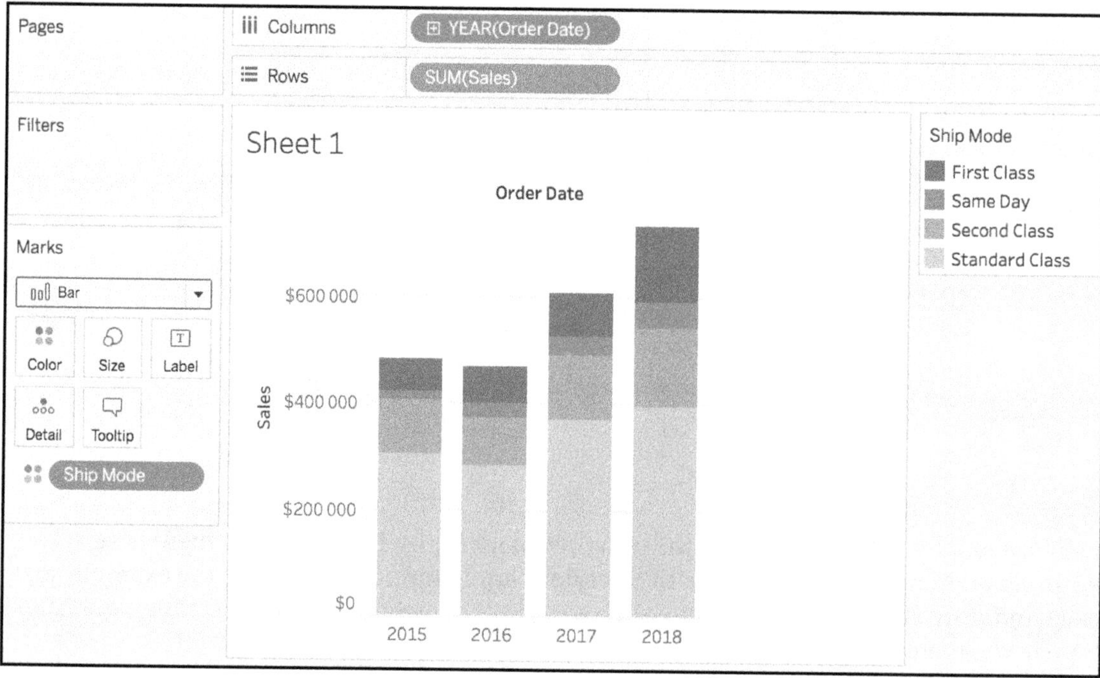

In this screenshot, you can easily see that **2018** is the best year and **2016** the worst in term of sales. You can also see that the **Standard Class** is the one that brings in the most sales and **Same Day** the least.

Let's see how Lines help with your analysis.

Line

A Line is represented with the Line icon.

The Line chart is useful for seeing trends and evolution. When you have multiple Lines, you can easily compare the values. However, it's harder to see the global trend than with Bar.

Here's an example of a visualization using a Line:

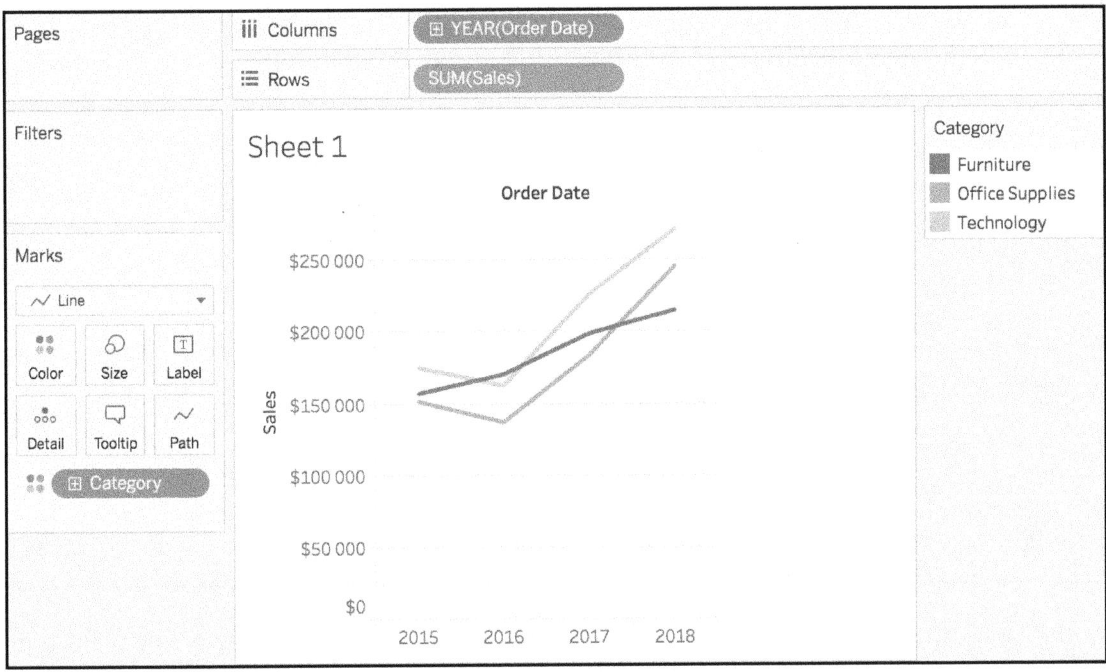

In the preceding screenshot, it's easy to see, in each year, which categories bring in the most sales. Also, Lines allow you to see the trend of each category. You can learn, for example, that in **2016**, **Furniture** was the best category and now, in **2018**, it's the worst.

The next Mark type is Area. It has some advantages over Bars and Lines, but also some of their disadvantages.

Area

Area is represented with the Area icon.

The Area chart is great to see the global trend. However, it's difficult to see the specific evolution of each value. Here's an example visualization using Area:

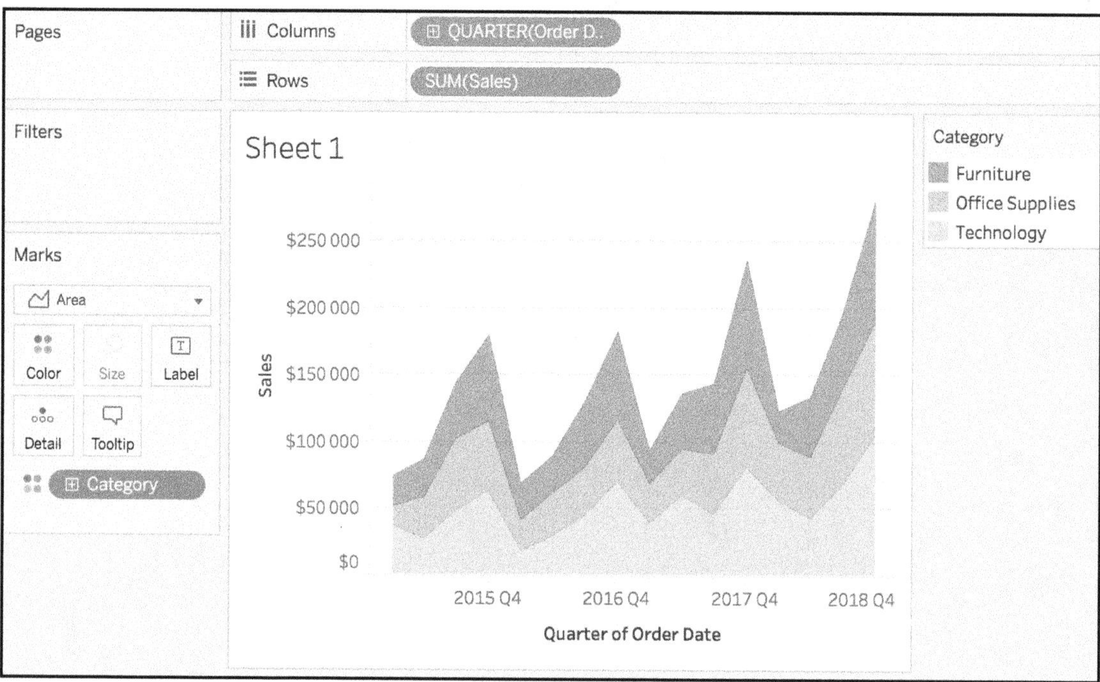

In the preceding screenshot, you can see how, for every year, the best quarter is always the fourth one and the worst quarter is always the first one. For a specific quarter, you can see the contribution of each category. However, as with the Bar chart, it's difficult to see the evolution of one particular category (except for the bottom one).

The next Mark type has nothing in common with the previous one; let's talk about Square.

Square

Square is represented with the ☐ Square icon.

You can create two types of charts with Square: heatmap and treemap.

A heatmap is a table, but better. When you build a table, you have to read every value to compare them. Heatmap gives the same level of granularity (the same amount of information), but with the ability to quickly spot the top and bottom values. Here's an example of a heatmap:

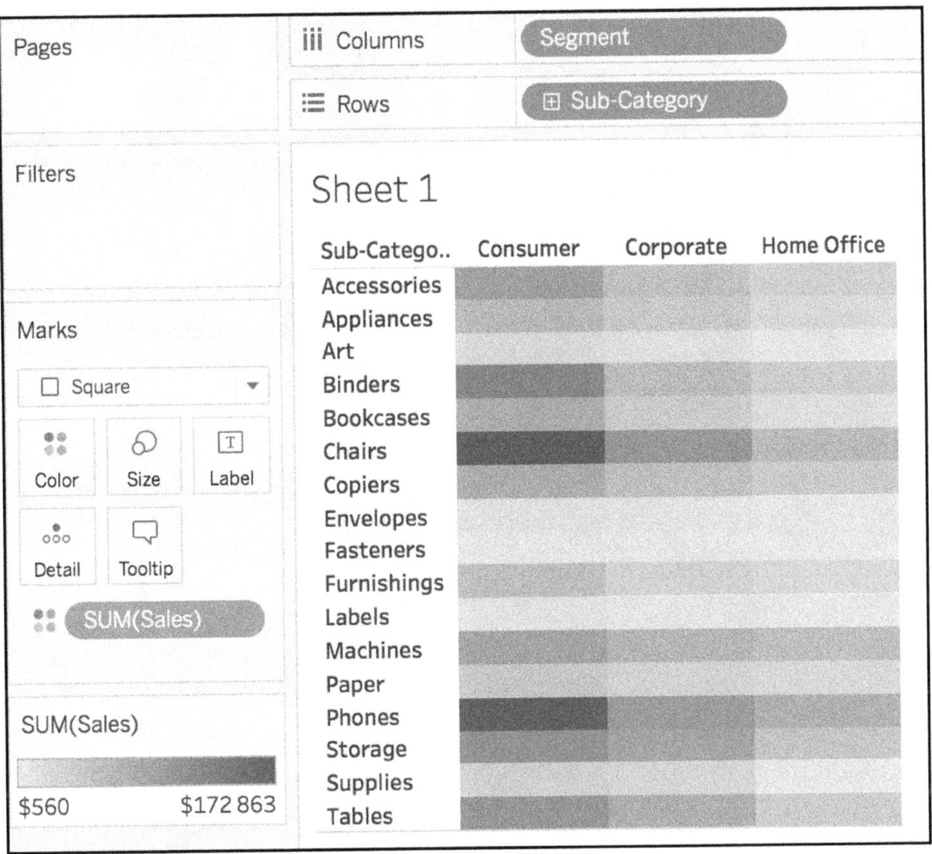

In the preceding screenshot, you can easily see that it's the **Chairs** and **Phones** of the **Consumer** segment that bring in the most money.

A treemap is a hierarchical representation with Squares. The pros of a treemap are that it gives you a quick idea of the number of values and the proportion of each of them. Here's an example of a treemap:

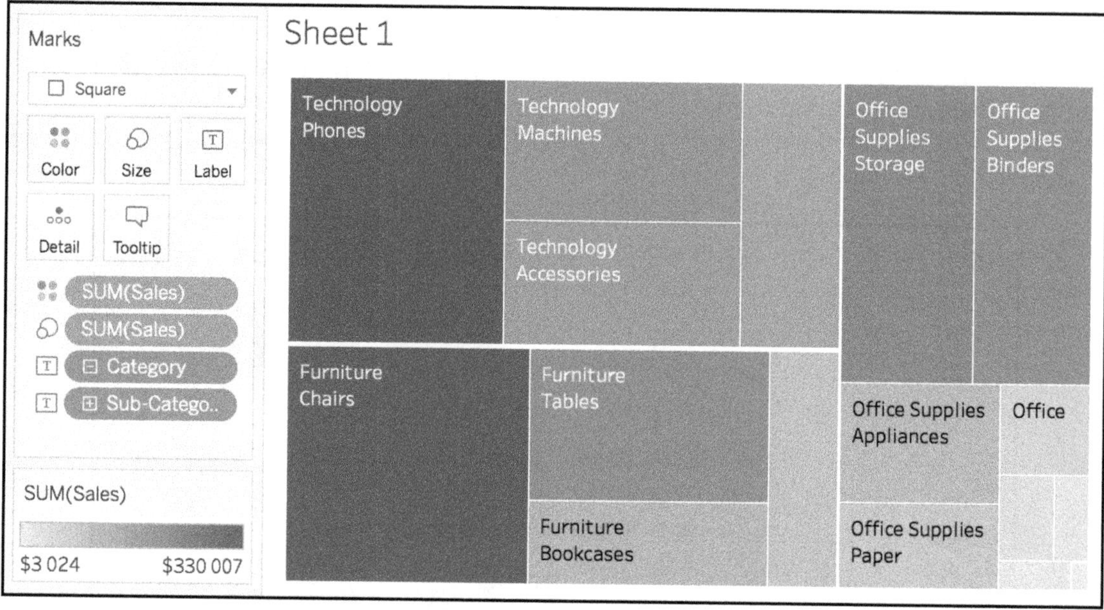

In the previous screenshot, you can easily see the number of sub-categories and the best ones for each category.

The next Mark type, Circle, has a great advantage, which is very useful in data visualization. Continue to discover what it is!

Circle

The Circle Mark type is represented with the ○ Circle icon.

You can use Circles in many different ways. Tableau always represents the values with a filled Circle. The big advantage of this Mark type is that you can easily use two properties: **Color** and **Size**, on top of the position of the circle, as shown in the following screenshot:

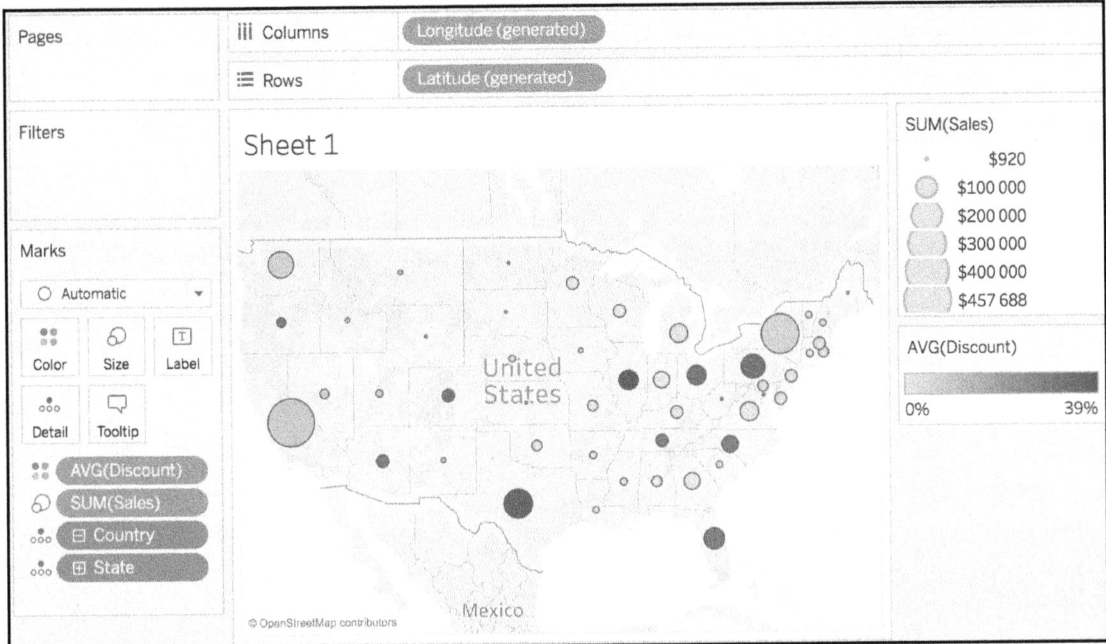

In the example, we represent every State with a Circle. The size of the Circle represents the sales, and the color represents the discount amount. With this visualization, you can see that:

- *California* and *New York* are the best in sales (bigger Circles)
- There are big discounts in *Texas, Ohio,* and *Illinois* (darkest Circles)

The next Mark type is quite fun! Let's talk about Shapes.

Shapes

Shape is represented with the Shape icon.

When you select Shape in the Mark type menu, Tableau uses an empty circle by default and the **Shape** property (the boxes beneath the Mark Type menu) becomes available. To use a Shape, drag and drop a Dimension in the **Shape** property and each value gets a different Shape:

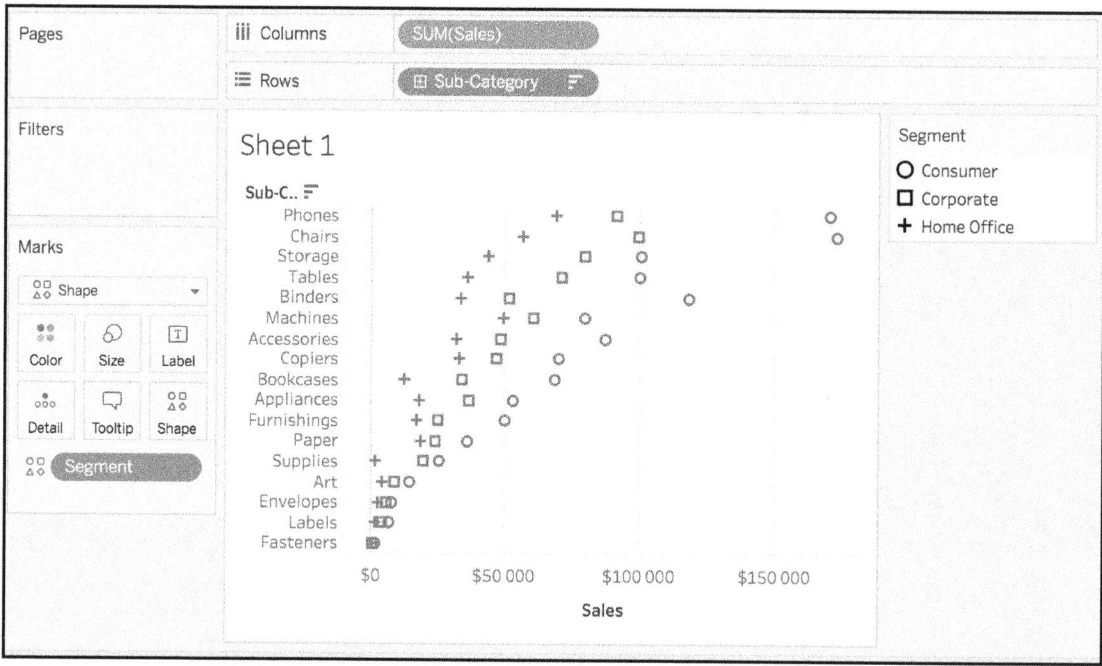

In the preceding example, we sort the sub-categories by sales, and we add the segment in the **Shape** property. So, for each Sub-Category, we can see the contribution of each segment. You can discover that it's always the **Consumer** segment that is the best in term of sales, then **Corporate** in second, and **Home Office** last.

Wait, there's more! Shapes are among the best features to customize your visualization and create something unique. You can add any custom shapes you want in Tableau. You'll learn how to do that in the next section.

Unlike Shapes, a table is not very exciting. However, if you want to create one, you need to use Text.

Text

Text is represented with the [T] Text icon.

Text is, of course, used to build tables but also word clouds.

Tables will always be there. You can build the best visualization ever; there will still be someone asking for a simple table because they need to see the values. You can't do anything about that, so you may as well learn how to create a table.

To create a Table, drag and drop a Dimension to create the headers, and put a Measure in the Text property. You'll learn how to display multiple Measures in `Chapter 7`, *Design Insightful Visualizations - Part 2*.

A word cloud isn't the best visualization to do an analysis. However, it can be used to see the big picture. As with Circle, you can use a Measure in Size and another one in Color. Here's an example of a word cloud:

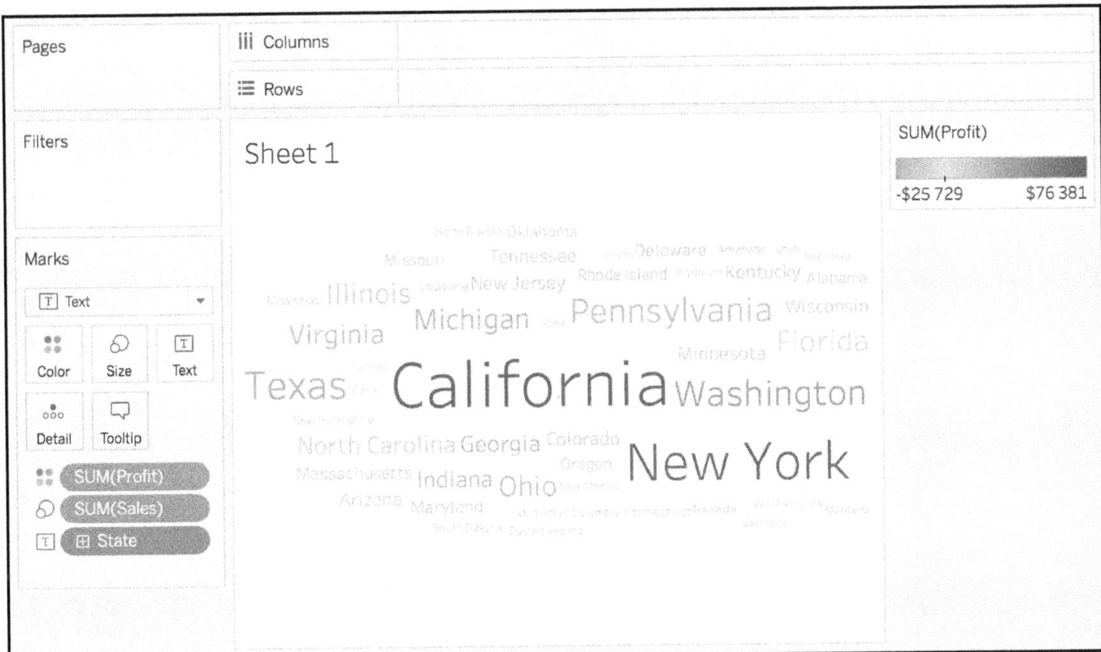

As you can see in the previous screenshot, it's quite difficult to make a precise ranking of the states.

Do you have a geographical role in your Data Source? You need a map!

Map

Map is represented with the Map icon.

To display a Map, you need:

- At least one geographical role in a Mark property (Detail, Color, or Label)
- The **Longitude (generated)** field in columns
- The **Latitude (generated)** field in rows

A Map is great to have a Geographical point of view. However, the biggest disadvantage of a Map is that the small territories are difficult to see. In the United States map, *District of Columbia* is too small to be visible on a Map.

When you display a Map, there are options to search, zoom, and select values in the menu in the top-left of the Map. The following screenshot helps find those options:

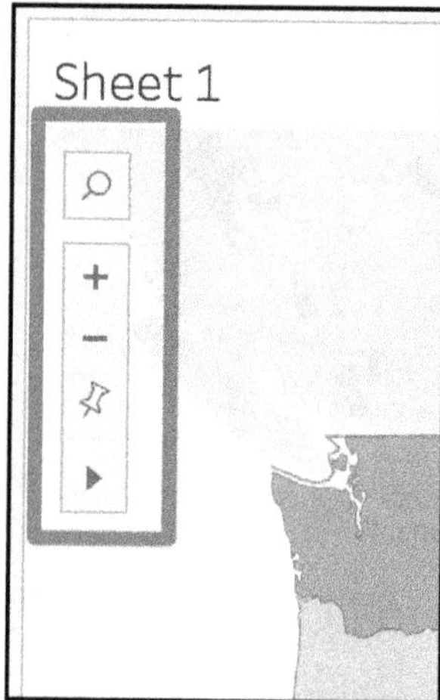

Here's an example of a Map in Tableau:

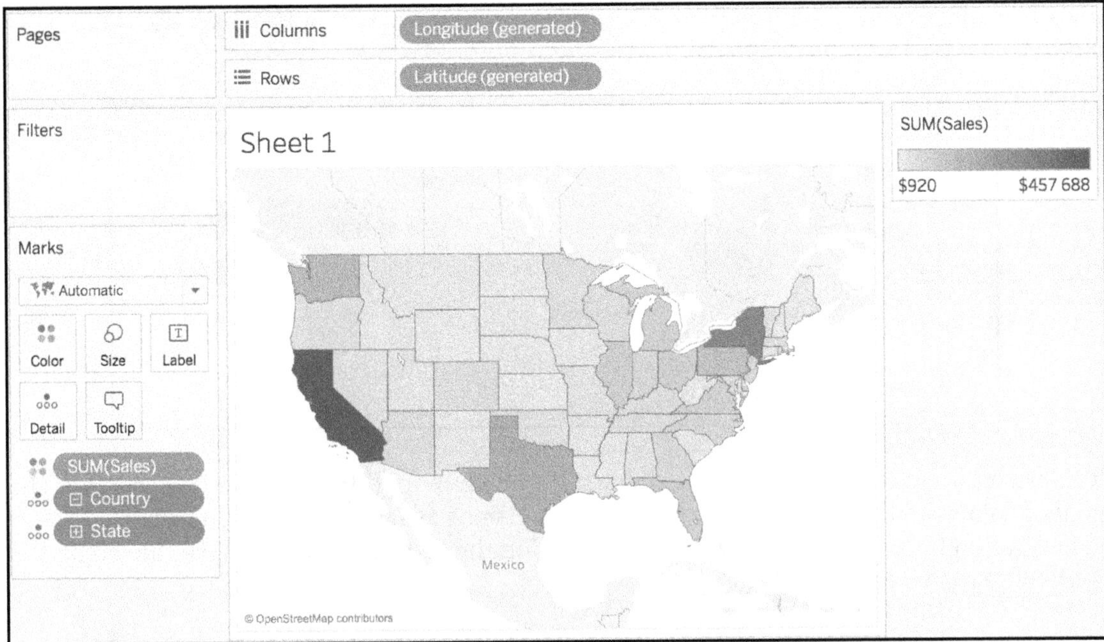

You can use the **Map** menu on top to customize your map: change the layers, the options, and legend.

The next Mark type is not very popular among data visualization people, but it's essential that you know why and when to use it. Let's talk about Pie.

Pie

Pie is represented with the Pie icon.

A Pie works in one specific situation: when you want to compare to the proportion between two values. With more than two values, a Bar is always more efficient. Here's an example of a visualization, representing the unranked sales by category with a Pie chart and a Bar chart:

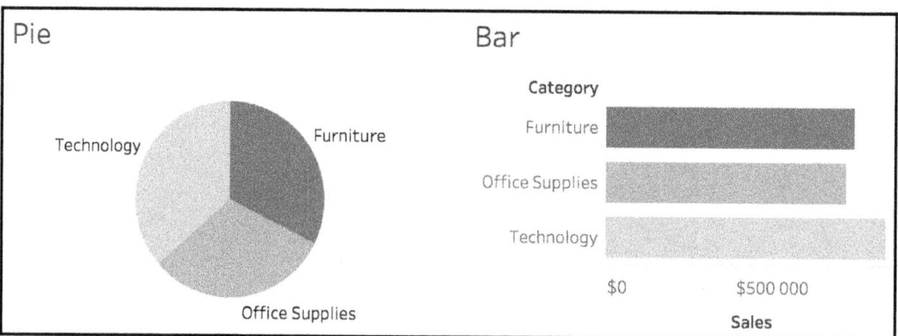

You can easily rank the categories with bars. It's much more difficult to do it with a Pie. The goal of data visualization is to help you make decisions as fast as possible. The best visualization is the one that answers your question the fastest. That's why pies are so bad with more than two values.

When you select Pie in the Mark type selector, a new Property becomes available: **Angle**. To create a Pie, put a Dimension in **Color** and a Measure in the **Angle** property. Here's an example of a Pie chart:

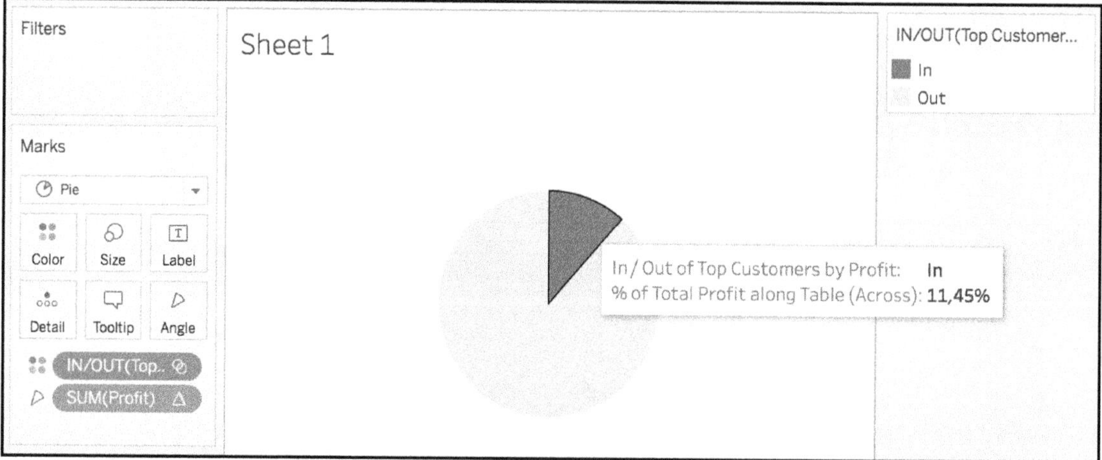

In the preceding screenshot, we represented the percentage of profit generated by the top five customers.

For the next two Mark types, there is no great example to build with Sample Superstore, so I'll show you some use cases. You'll know how and when to use them. The first one is the Gantt Bar.

Gantt Bar

Gantt Bar is represented with the Gantt Bar icon.

A Gantt Bar uses a Continuous field (generally a Date) in **Rows** or **Columns** to set the initial position and another Continuous field in Size. The Gantt Bar is generally used to create a Gantt chart. This visualization is helpful when you manage projects over time or if you want to create a timeline, as in the following screenshot:

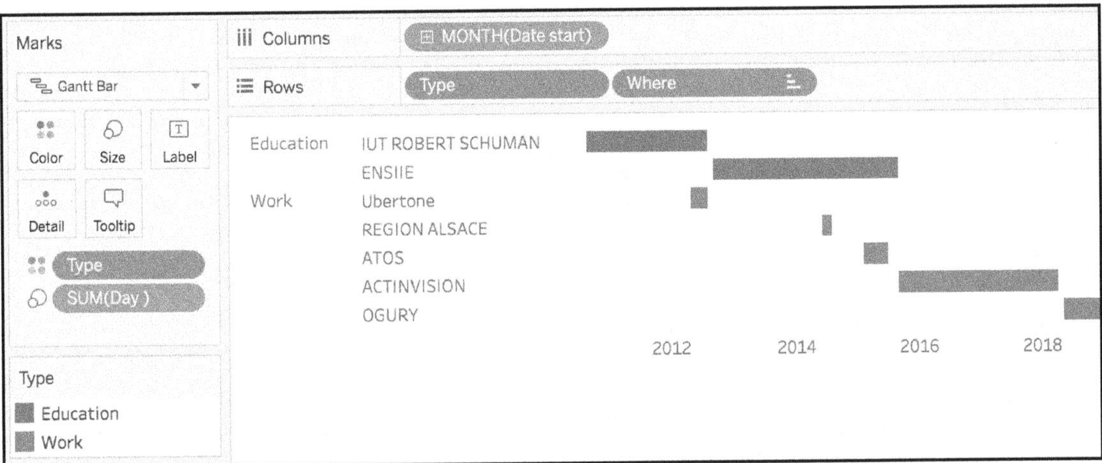

I built this Gantt chart for my resume. As you can see, there is a Continuous Date in columns and the number of days in Size. With this visualization, you can see when the different events started and their length.

The next Mark type is very uncommon, and you'll need a particular dataset to use it: Polygon.

Polygon

Polygon is represented with the Polygon icon.

Polygon exists for when you want to represent something impossible to do in Tableau. When you select Polygon, a new property is available: **Path**. To create a Polygon, you'll need the following:

- A Dimension representing the unique identifier of each Polygon
- A Number in Path to connect the points and draw the shape of the Polygon
- One Continuous field in rows and another one in columns to generate the coordinates

Once you have that, you can create, for example, this:

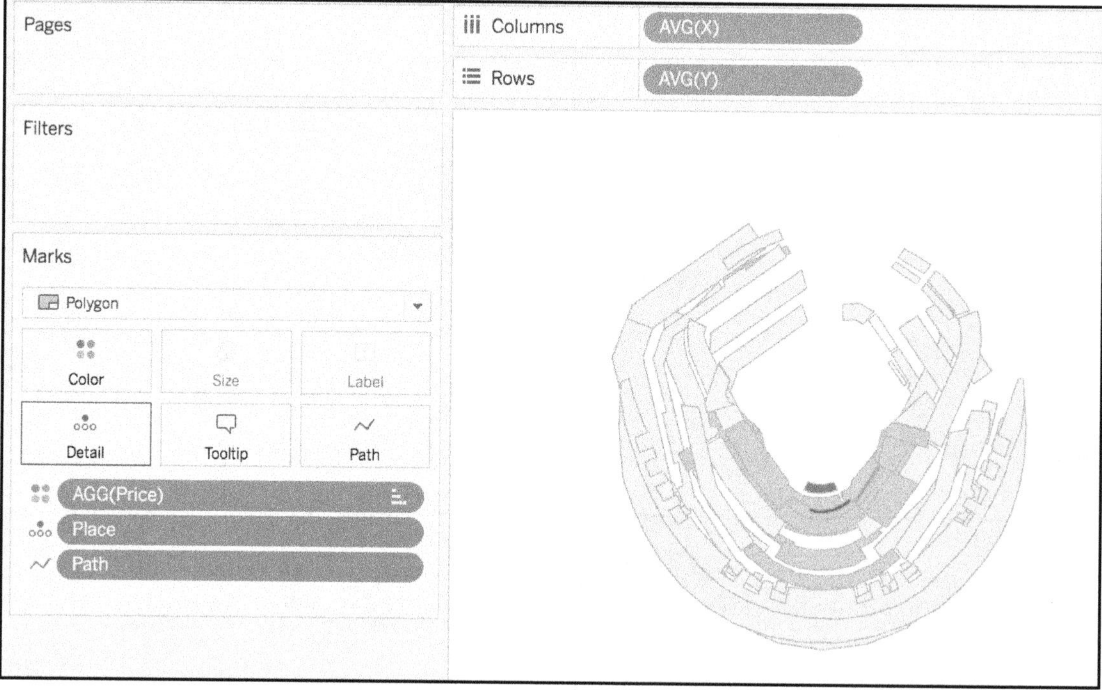

In this screenshot, you can look at the average seat price in a stadium thanks to Polygons. This visualization comes from a tutorial by Ryan Sleeper available in his website: `https://www.ryansleeper.com/how-to-make-a-custom-polygon-map-in-tableau`.

For a long time, Polygons were the only solution to create this kind of visualization. Recently, Tableau introduced the shapefile connector to render spatial objects. However, a shapefile is fixed, and the coordinates of the Polygons aren't. That's why, to create flow diagrams such as a Sankey, the Polygon remains useful.

Let's finish with the most recent addition in the Mark type: Density.

Density

Density is represented with the Density icon.

Density is the newest Mark type, introduced in Tableau 2018.3. It fills a gap: to show the density of Marks. The superposition of multiple Marks determines the color intensity. It's a very simple Mark type; you can use it in various cases as long as you have many Marks overlapping.

In the following example, you can see where the concentration of customers is by sales and quantity:

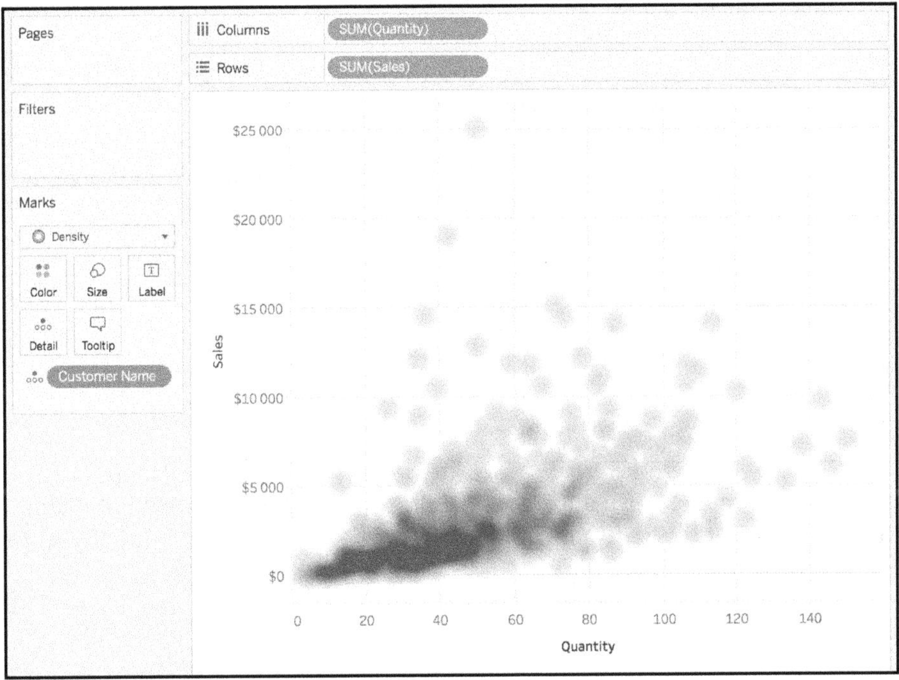

Now that you know how and when to use the 12 different Mark types, it's time to learn how to use another critical part of the Marks shelf: Mark properties.

Mark properties

There are five Mark properties always available: Color, Size, Text/Label, Detail, and Tooltip. There are also three properties available only when using a specific Mark type: Shape, Path, and Angle.

Any field used in a Mark property splits the number of Marks if it returns more than one value (except for the Tooltip). For example, if you put a Dimension that contains three different values on **Color**, the number of Marks is split by three. If you have more than one Dimension in Mark Properties, the number of Marks are defined by the number of existing combinations of the different Dimensions.

Let's see in detail each Property with the different options you have to make better visualizations. Again, for each Property you'll find an example that you can reproduce with **Sample - Superstore** by adding the fields on the same shelves as in the image.

You can also download the `Mark Properties` ZIP file from my website `book.ladataviz.com`, on the *Chapter 6: Design Insightful Visualizations* section, or click on this direct link: `https://ladataviz.com/wp-content/uploads/2018/09/Mark-Properties.twbx_.zip`. When you unzip the file, you'll find a Tableau Package Workbook with an example of each Mark Type.

Let's start with the most used property, Color.

Color

Color is represented with the Color icon.

Color is probably the most useful and most used Property. It can be used to change the color of the Mark, slice it if you use a Dimension, or display another value if you use a Measure.

If you don't place any fields on the **Color** property, clicking on the **Color** button opens a menu where you can select a color and more. Here's a screenshot of the menu:

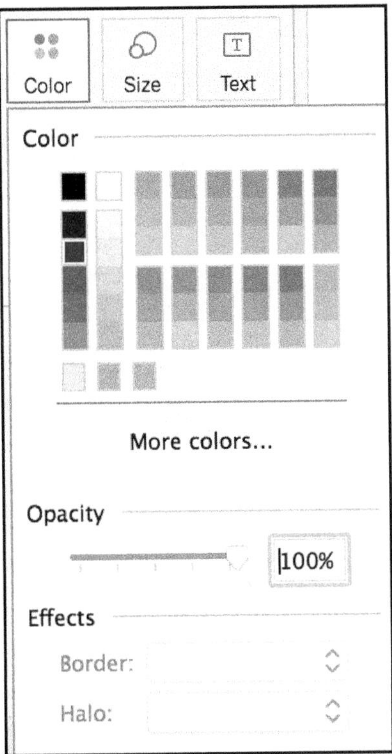

The first part of the menu displays Tableau's default colors, and you can click on one of them to use it. You can also click on **More colors...** to open a menu where you can opt for the color of your choice. On the bottom side of the menu, there are options to change the opacity, add a border, or add a halo.

If you drag and drop a field on Color, Tableau uses color to add a new layer of information. This behavior is different between a Continuous field and a Discrete field.

If you use a Discrete field (in blue, usually a Dimension), each value of the field has a specific color. Tableau uses a default set of colors, but you can edit them by clicking on the **Color** menu. If you click on **Edit Colors**, a new window opens where you can choose between different color palettes and assign a color to the values. Here's the **Edit Colors** menu for the Discrete field:

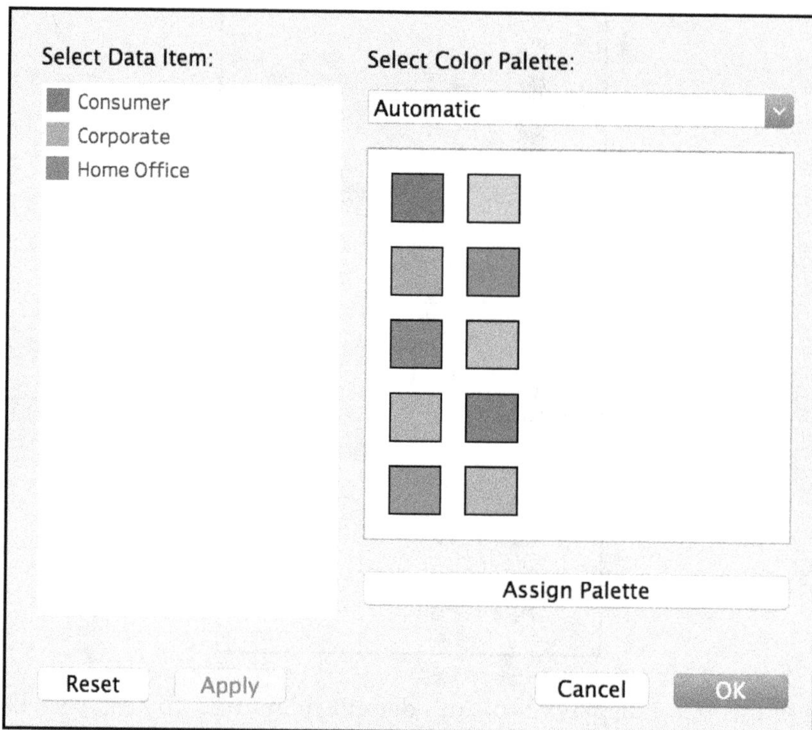

Still on the menu, to personalize your visualization even more, you can double-click on a **Data Item** to open another menu where you pick any color, select one on your screen with a color picker, or enter a color code.

The following screenshot illustrates a Discrete field in **Color**:

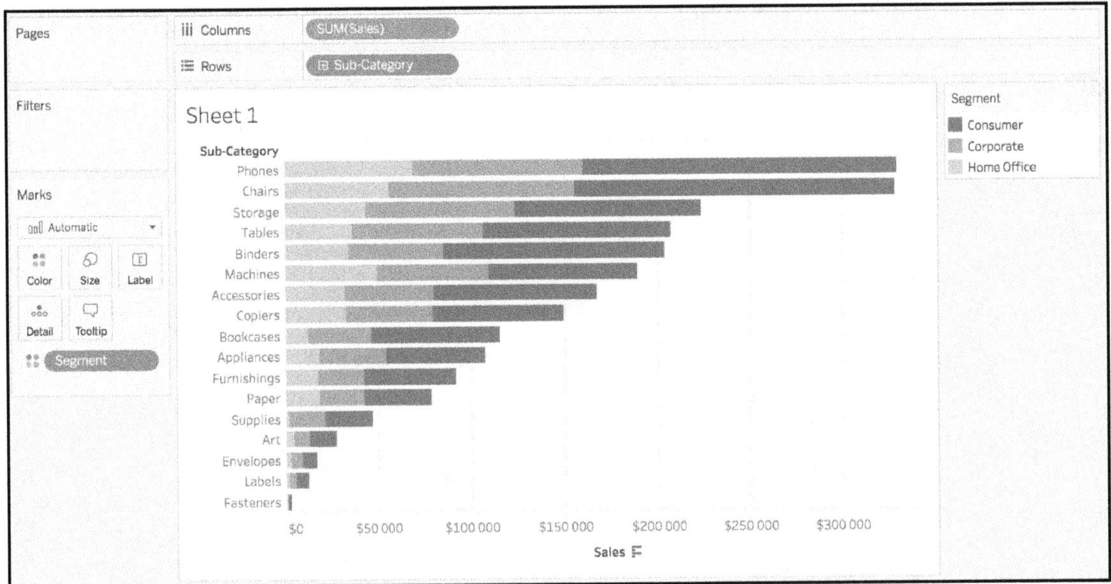

It's possible to add a custom color palette by editing `Preference.tps` in your Tableau repository as explained in the Tableau documentation: `https://onlinehelp.tableau.com/current/pro/desktop/en-us/formatting_create_custom_colors.html`

If you use a Continuous field (in green, usually a Measure), Tableau uses a color gradient from the minimum value to the maximum. If there are positive and negative values, Tableau chooses a diverging palette. Again, Tableau selects a default color palette that you can edit by clicking on the **Color** menu. If you edit the color of a Continuous field, a different window opens. Here's the **Edit Colors** menu for the Continuous field:

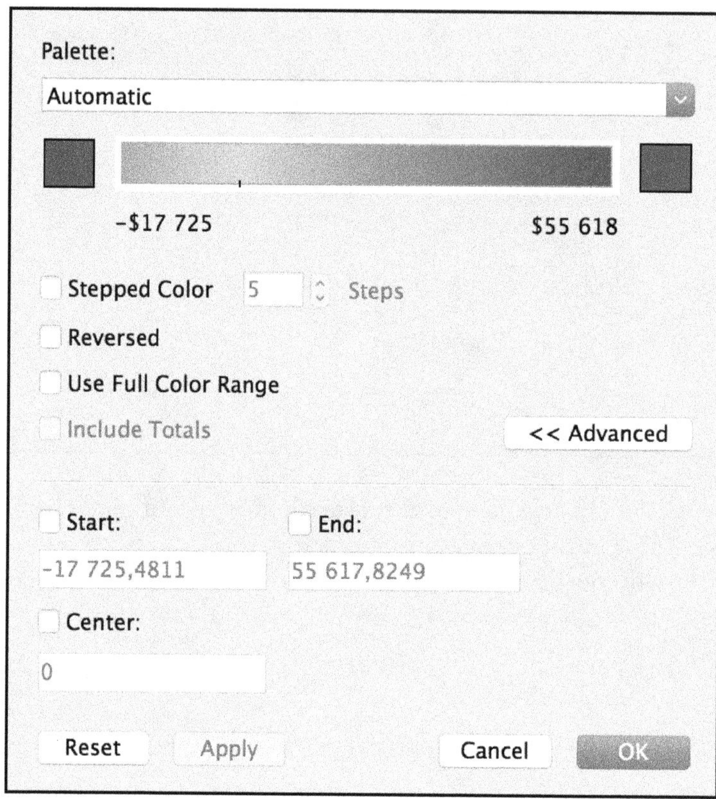

In this menu, you have many options to configure your palette. Again, if you click on a color box, it opens a menu to choose the exact color of your choice.

The following screenshot illustrates a **Continuous** field in Color:

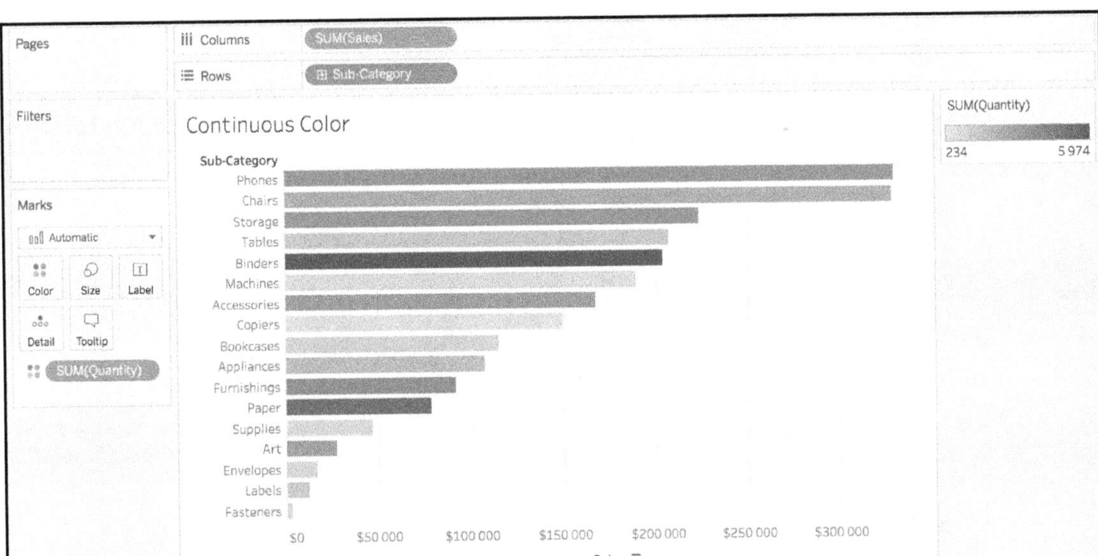

After Color, the second property is Size.

Size

Size is represented with the Size icon.

Size is used almost all the time when designing a visualization. It can be used to change the size of the Marks or, as with Color, to add more information.

If you don't put any fields on the Size property, clicking on the **Size** button opens a small menu where you can change the size of the Marks.

If you put a field on Size, new information is added to the visualization. If you use a Discrete field, each value has a specific size. If you use a Continuous field, Tableau uses a range of size from the minimum to the maximum.

The following screenshot is an example of a Continuous field in Size:

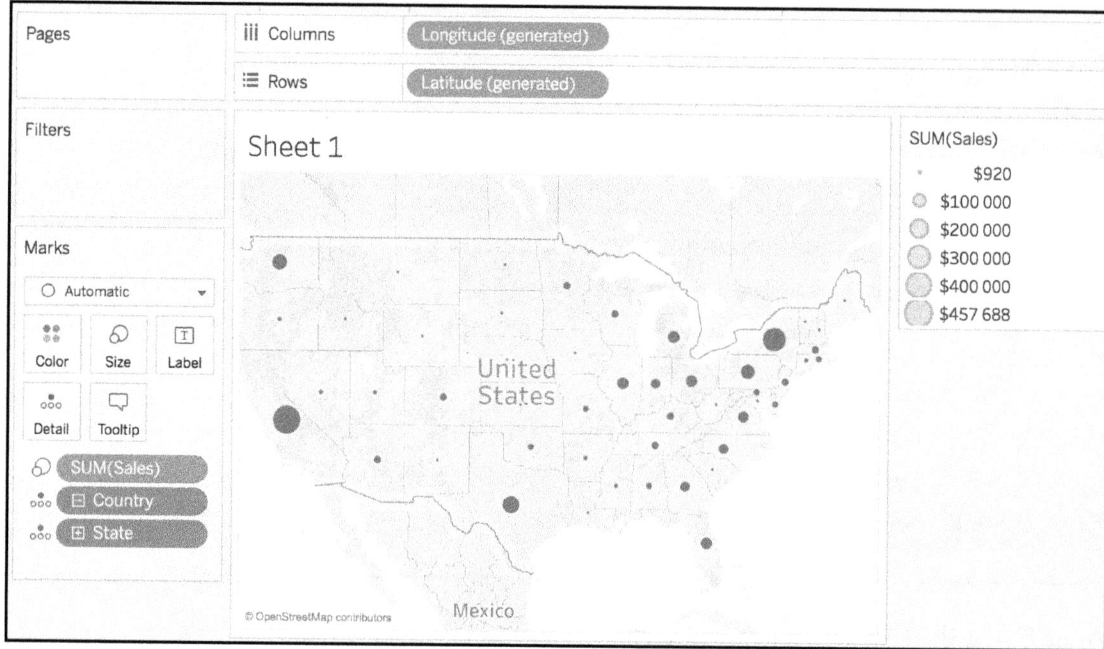

When using a field on Size, a Size legend appears (usually on the right). If you double-click on the Legend, a new menu opens. In this menu, you can choose how the size varies but also the start, end, and size range. Here's the menu:

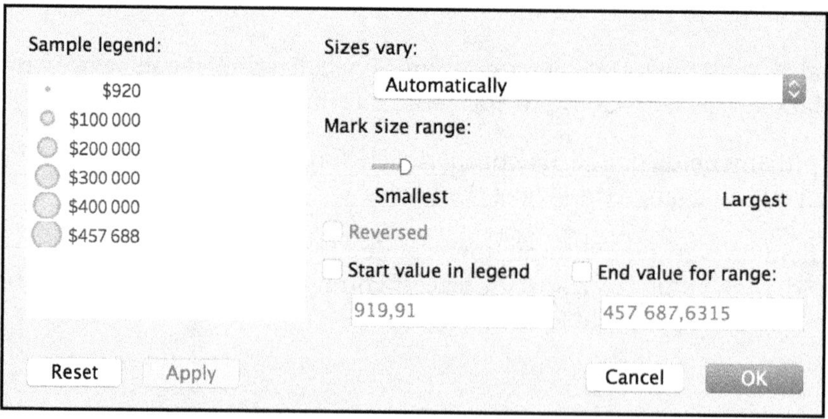

The next property reacts differently depending on the Mark type.

Label (Text)

Label (or Text) is represented with the Label icon.

There are two different cases: when you use the **Text** Mark type and if you use any other type.

If you use the Text Mark type, this property is also named **Text**. You can drag and drop multiple fields on **Text**. If you put a Measure, the aggregated value is displayed, but if you put a Dimension, all the different values are displayed (multiplying the number of Marks).

If you click on the **Text** button, you'll find an option to change the alignment and, if you click on the box with the three dots (...), Tableau opens a new window. This window is a text editor where you can modify the font, the size, the color but, more than that, you can write any text you want. Here's an example of **Sales** and **Quantity** in **Text** with the **Edit Label** window and the result in the View:

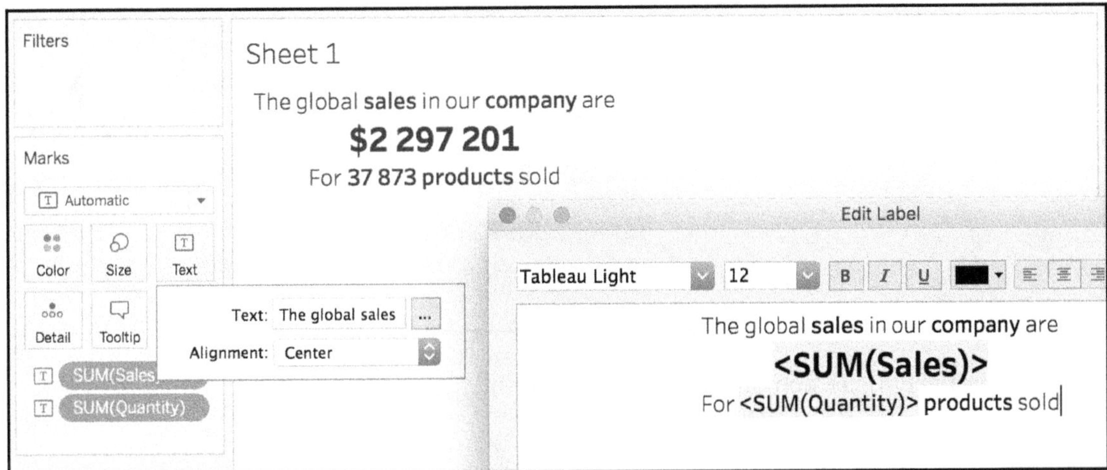

If you use any Mark type other than Text, this property is named **Label**. You can also drag and drop multiple fields on **Label**. A Measure is simply displayed in the visualization; a Dimension also splits the number of Marks. When you click on the **Label** button, you'll find many options:

- **Show Mark labels** is the same as clicking on the icon in the toolbar.
- **Label Appearance** allows you to change the text, the font, and the alignment.

- **Marks to Label** allows you to choose which Marks will have a Label. You can add a Label to all the Marks, only to the maximum or minimum, only if selected, or to the highlighted ones.
- The last option allows the Labels to overlap. By default, Tableau chooses to show the Labels only if they don't overlap.

The following screenshot is an example of Label use:

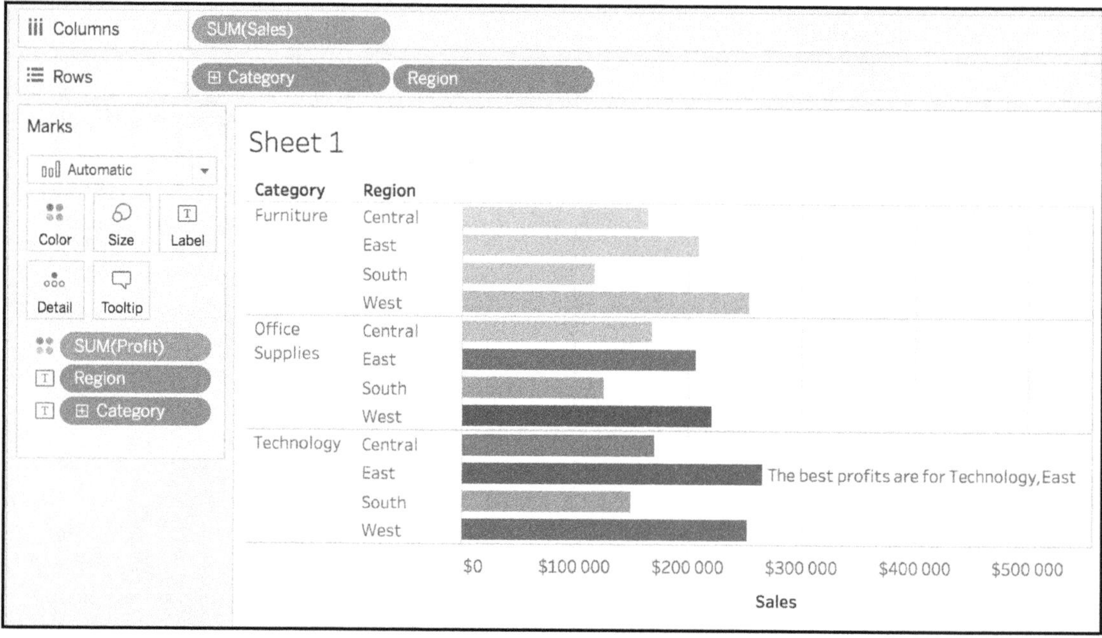

The next property is elementary but also very useful!

Detail

Detail is represented with the icon.

Like the previous Mark properties, dropping a Dimension on **Detail** splits the Marks. And that's it. The **Detail** property does nothing more than split the Marks. There are no different colors, sizes, or labels.

You can use Detail to show your data at a less aggregated level. Here's an example:

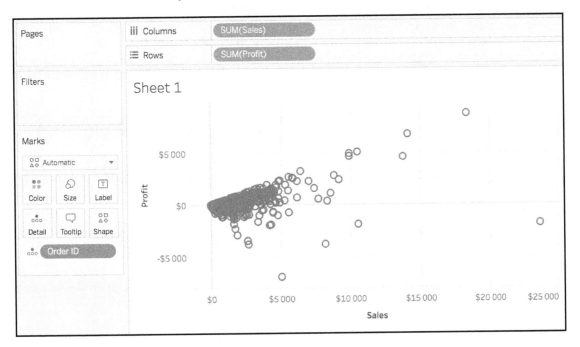

Tooltip is the next property, and it's the only one that doesn't split the Marks.

Tooltip

Tooltip is represented with the Tooltip icon.

A tooltip is displayed when you hover over a Mark.

Any field that you drop on **Tooltip** is added to the tooltip box. The fields in the tooltip are always aggregated. However, you can still add a Dimension to the tooltip. Tableau uses a special aggregation, **ATTR**, to display it. This aggregation returns the value if it's unique, or shows * if not. That symbol means that there is more than one value.

Clicking on the **Tooltip** button opens a window where you can edit the text and change a few options. Those options allow you to:

- Choose whether you want to show the Tooltip
- Include the command buttons (Keep Only, Exclude, Group, Set, and so on) or not
- Allow selection by category or not

Here's an example of **Tooltip** use:

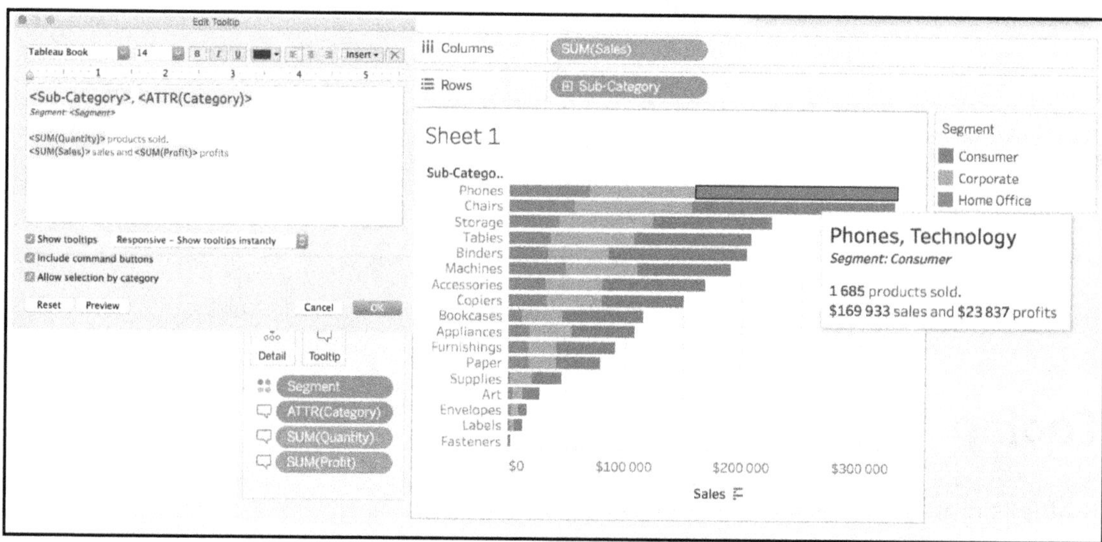

You can also add other Worksheets in the Tooltip. This functionality is called **Viz in Tooltip**. In the Tooltip editing window, you have the option to insert objects on the top-left. Here, it's possible to select a Worksheet. You can modify the width, height, and filters of the Viz in Tooltip. Here's an example of a Viz in Tooltip:

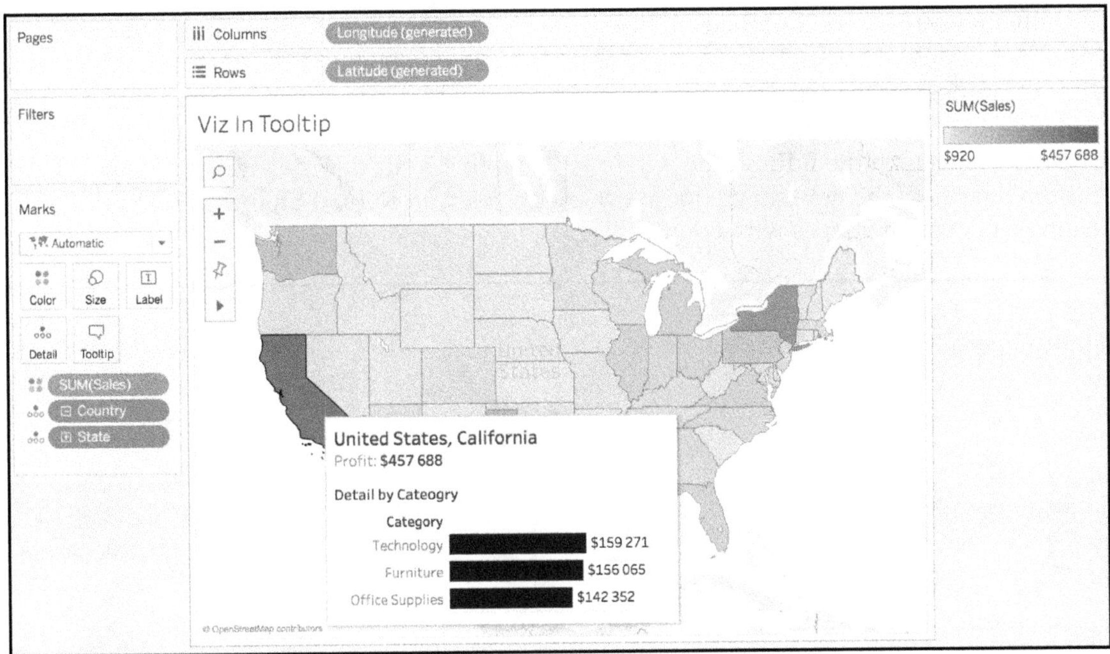

The next property, Shape, is only available with the Mark type of the same name.

Shape

Shape is represented with the Shape icon.

You can only use a Discrete field in Shape, and it works the same as if you a Discrete field in Color.

When you put a field in **Shape**, the different values of the field have different shapes. When you click on the **Shape** button, Tableau opens a new window where you can, as with Color, select predefined Shapes palettes and add them to the values.

A really interesting aspect of Shapes is that you can add custom shapes. To do that, find the `Shapes` folder in your Tableau repository (usually inside the `My Documents` folder on your computer). In the `Shape` folder, there is one subfolder by palette. You can create a new folder (of the name of your choice) and put different images in it (PNG, JPG, BMP, or GIF). Then, in Tableau, in the **Edit Shape** window, you'll find your new palette with your custom Shapes (if the new shape doesn't show up, click on **Reload Shapes**). Here's an example of custom Shapes with country flags:

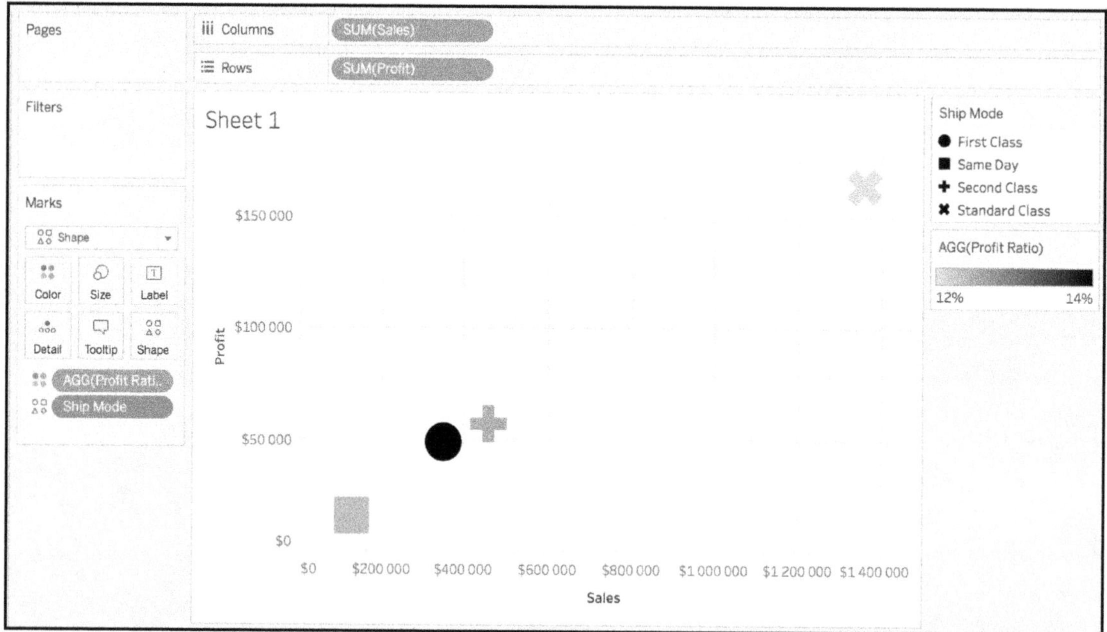

The next property exists for both Line and Polygon.

Path

Path is represented with the icon.

Path is a property available for both Line and Polygon.

Since 2018.1, when using the Line Mark type, clicking on the **Path** button opens a menu where you can select the Line type: Linear, Step, or Jump. Here's an example of a Step Line:

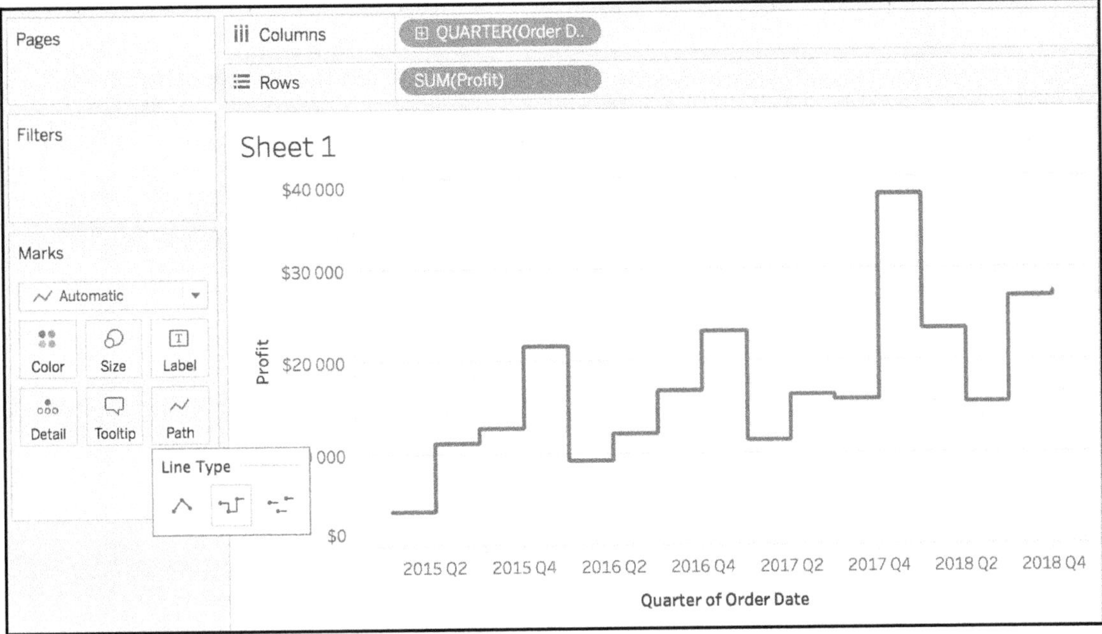

This property allows you to choose the order to connect the Marks. You can use either a Dimension or a Measure.

It's quite rare to use this property. Usually, you only use it if, in your data, there is a special order to connect the Marks to create a specific visualization.

The next and last property only exists for Pie.

Angle

Angle is represented with the Angle icon.

Angle is a simple property that exists only for Pie. More than that, you have to use Angle to display a Pie chart. You can only put a Continuous field on **Angle**. When you use a field on **Angle**, the values are used to calculate the angle of the different portions of the Pie.

You now have all the knowledge to build almost every visualization in Tableau. I say *almost* because some other essential features are waiting for you in `Chapter 7`, *Design Insightful Visualizations - Part 2*.

Summary

That's it for the first part of this chapter on building visualization in Tableau.

You have all the keys to build your first visualizations, automatically or manually. The different Mark types and Mark properties hold no mystery for you anymore.

In the second part of this chapter, we'll focus on how to build visualizations with multiple Measures, how to use filters and Pages filters, and, finally, all the Worksheet options and formatting.

7
Design Insightful Visualizations - Part 2

Ready to continue the chapter about visualizations? In this second part, we'll take a closer look at the following points:

- Using multiple measures
- Filters
- Pages
- Worksheet options and format

Again, you can reproduce all the examples with the **Sample - Superstore** Data Source, which that you can open on the first page. To begin, let's see how to build a visualization with multiple Measures.

Using multiple Measures

In the previous chapter, you only used one Measure at a time on the row or column shelf. Let's see what happens when you use more than one.

To be precise, we'll see what happens when you use more than one Continuous field at a time in the row or column shelf. However, in the majority of cases, the Measures are Continuous and the Dimensions are Discrete.

If you use more than one Continuous field at a time in row or column, Tableau creates different axes, and the Marks shelf splits by the number of Continuous fields (plus one for **All**). Each Marks shelf can have a different type and properties. If you change the Marks type or properties for All, all the Marks are affected.

Let's build an example together:

1. Put the Continuous Quarter of **Order Date** in **Columns**, then **Profit** and **Profit Ratio** in **Rows**. The Marks are split into three, one for **All** and two others for the different Measures, as you can see in the framed area:

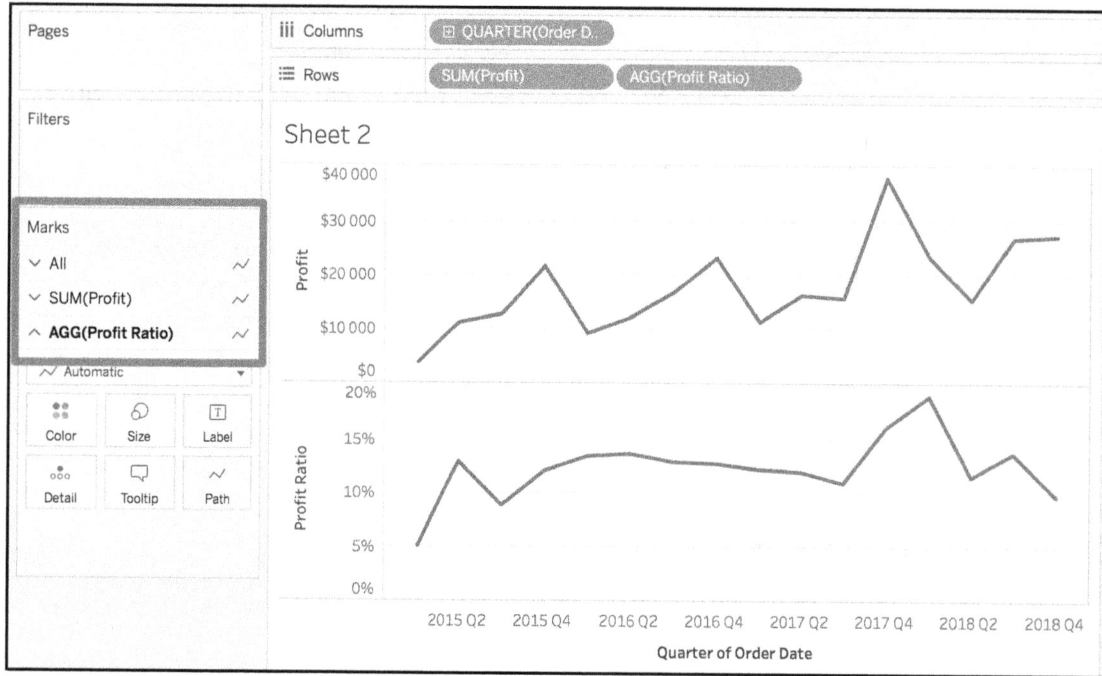

2. Click on the **SUM(Profit)** Marks shelf and change the Marks type to a **Bar** and the **Color** to black as illustrated here:

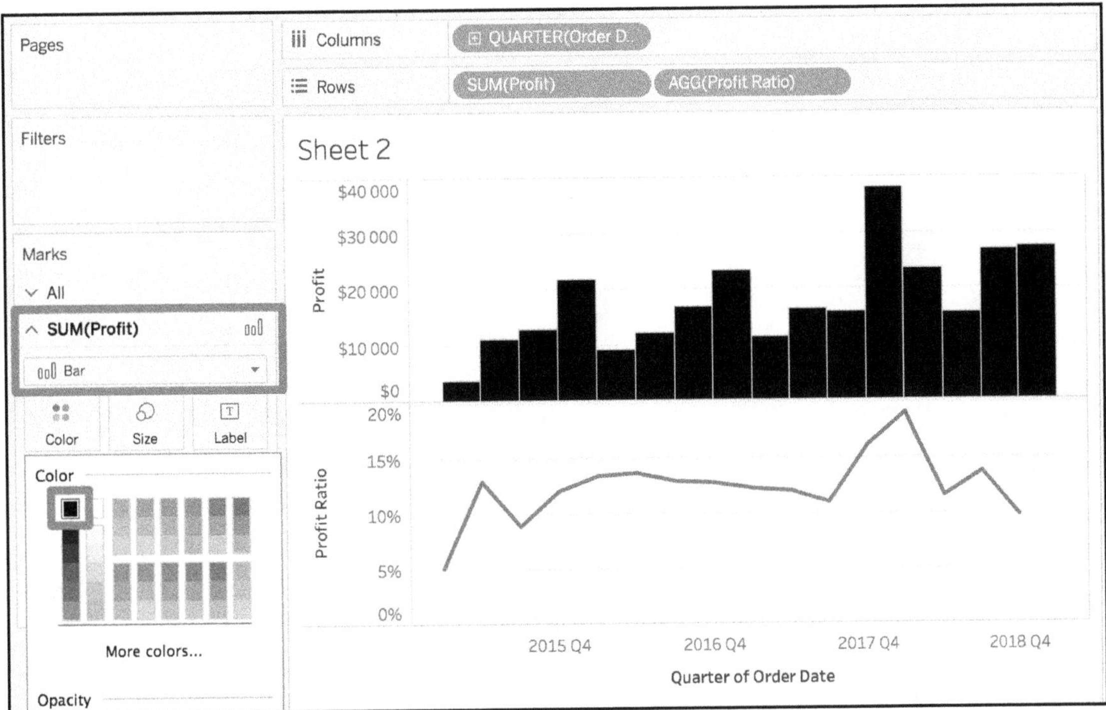

Keep the visualization for the next section!

As you can see, you can edit the different Marks shelves of the different Continuous fields independently.

Can we do more than that? Yes! Let's talk about Dual Axis and Measure Values/Names.

Dual Axis

When you want to combine two Continuous fields, it is possible to create a Dual Axis. With a Dual Axis, there is one axis on the left, one on the right, and the Marks are superimposed. To create a Dual Axis, right-click on the second Continuous field and select **Dual Axis**, as shown in the following screenshot:

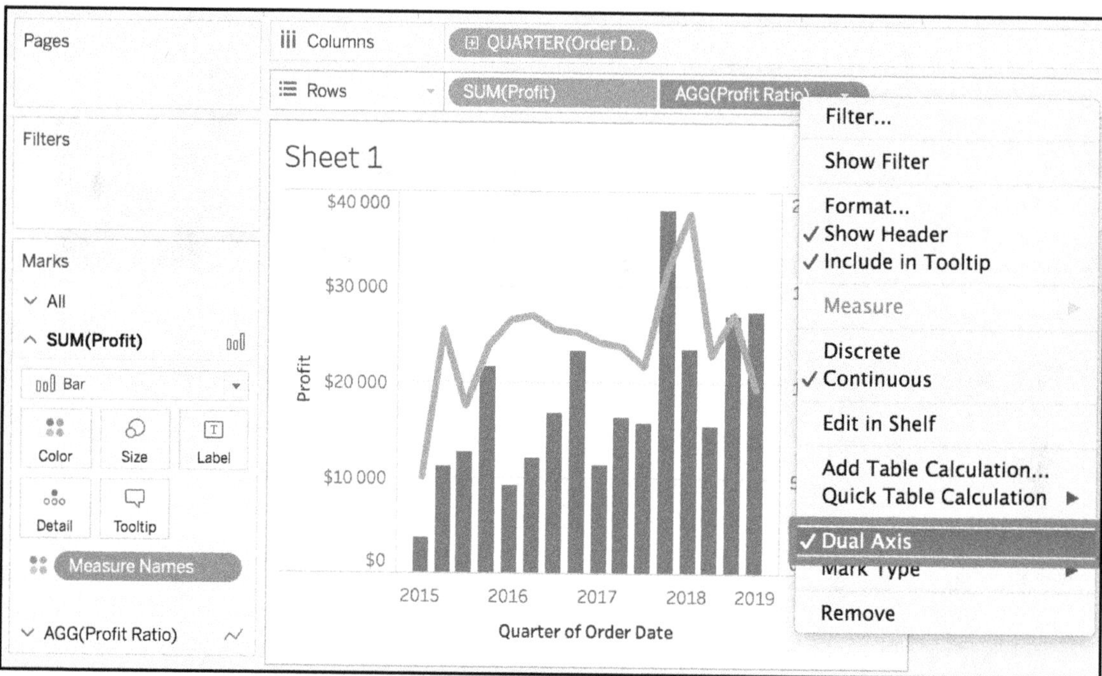

When using Dual Axis, the pills are merged in the Rows or Columns shelves. If the Mark types are set to **Automatic**, they might change while using Dual Axis. However, it's still possible to edit them individually by using the different Marks shelves. By default, Tableau also puts **Measure Names** in Color to distinguish the two fields. You can modify Color or remove it.

The Dual Axis allows you to build new types of visualization like Donut Chart (`https://kb.tableau.com/articles/issue/creating-donut-charts`), Dual Axis Map (`https://onlinehelp.tableau.com/current/pro/desktop/en-us/maps_dualaxis.html`) or Lollipop Chart (`https://www.tableau.com/fr-fr/about/blog/2017/1/viz-whiz-when-use-lollipop-chart-and-how-build-one-64267`)

With Dual Axis, the range of the two different axes can be different. For example, it's possible to compare the sales in dollars and discount in percentages. The two axes don't necessarily have the same range. However, if you're comparing values with a similar scale (such as the sales of the current year and the sales of the last year), the axes need to be in the same range. To do that, right-click on an axis and select **Synchronize Axis.**

You can create a Dual Axis between any sorts of Continuous fields (even between a Continuous Date and a Longitude if you want!).

What if you need to compare more than two Measures? To do that, you'll use Measure Names and Measure Values.

Measure Names and Measure Values

If you remember, in the Data Source there is one special Dimension named **Measure Names**, and one special Measure named **Measure Values**. Measure Values returns the values of the different Measures and Measure Names returns their names. You can use them to display as many Measures as you want.

When you use Measure Values, Tableau displays the Measure Values shelf where you can add as many Measures as you want. You can only put Measures on that shelf.

The easiest way to display multiple Measures with Measure Values and Measure Names is the following:

1. Put the **Continuous Quarter** of **Order Date** in **Columns** and **Sales** in **Rows**.
2. Drag and drop a second Field, **Profit**, on the existing axis (you can visually see the different icon when you're hovering the axis) as shown in the following screenshot:

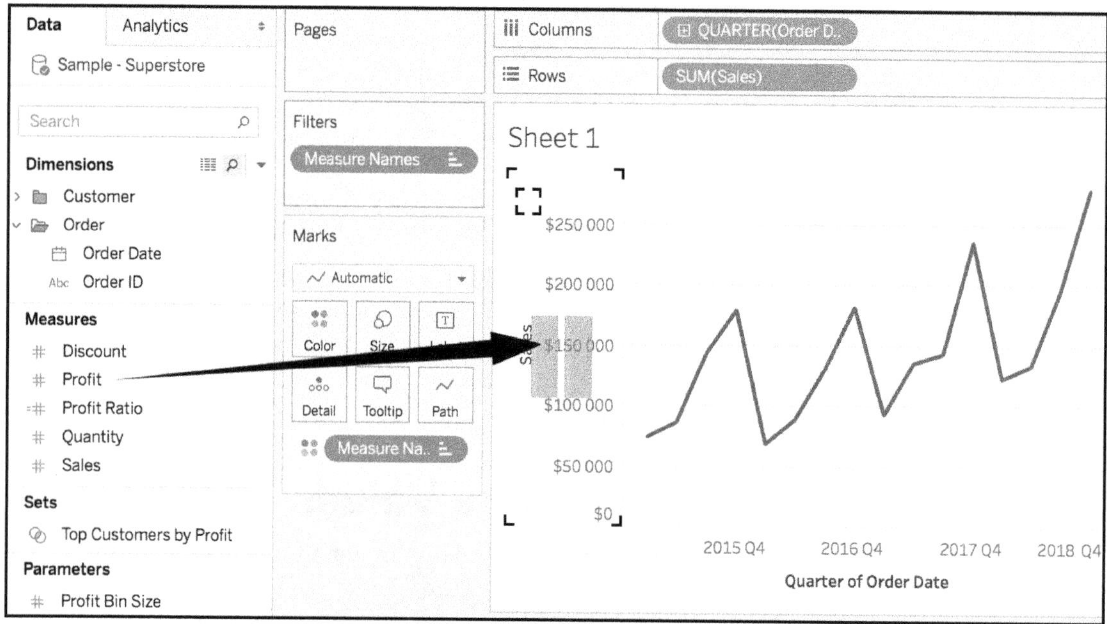

3. Tableau automatically replaces the **Sales** pill by **Measure Values**, puts **Measure Names** in **Color**, and places it on the **Filters** shelf.

4. Add **Quantity** to the **Measure Values** shelf, as shown in the following screenshot:

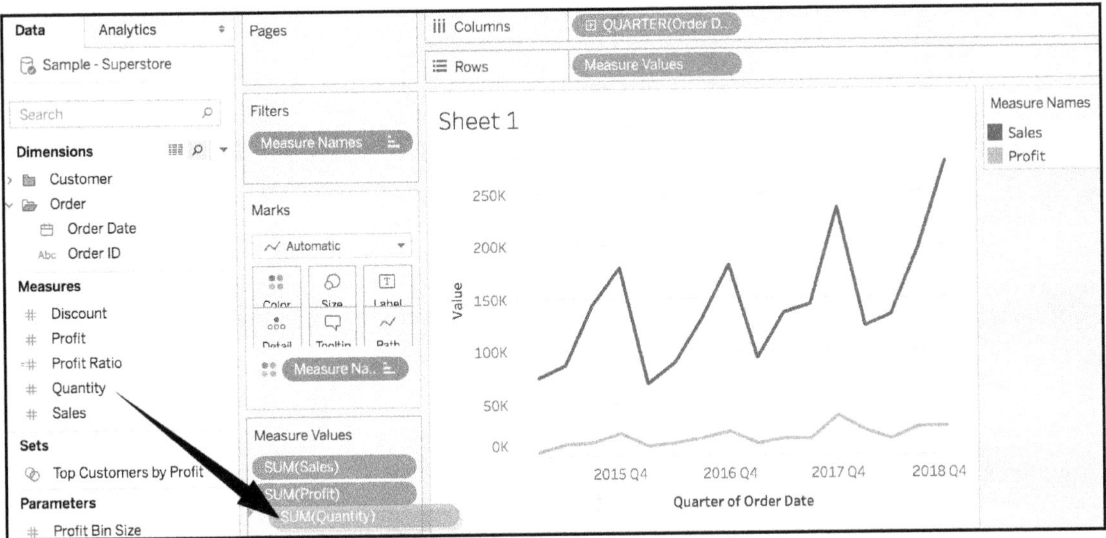

Another way to add another measure is by editing the Measure Names filter and selecting the measure you want.

5. In contrary to Dual Axis, there is only one axis here, meaning that you can have only one scale. If the different Measures you use have a significant scale difference, it may be hard to see the variation. In the following screenshot, you can see that the **Quantity** values are too small, when compared to **Sales** and **Profit**, to be readable:

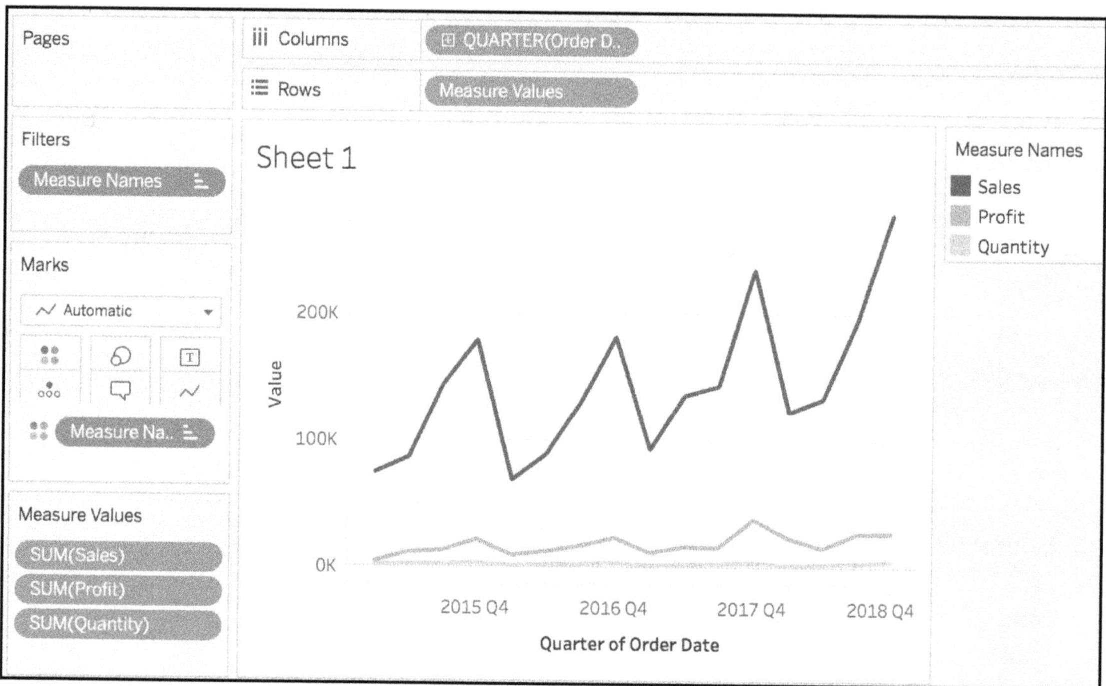

A significant difference with Dual Axis is that there is only one Marks shelf because there is only one Continuous field, Measure Values, in Rows or Columns. It means that you cannot control the Mark types or properties for each different Measure.

With Dual Axis, you can only combine two Continuous fields, but they can have different Mark types and properties and different axis ranges. With Measure Values and Measure Names, you can use as many Measures as you want but only one Axis and one Marks shelf. The choice is yours, so use the best option!

The next section is an unavoidable piece of Tableau, Filters.

Filters

Filters are among the most used features in Tableau. To create a Filter, drag and drop any field onto the **Filters** shelf. You can filter as many fields as you want. Here's an example of adding a Filter on **Sub-Category**:

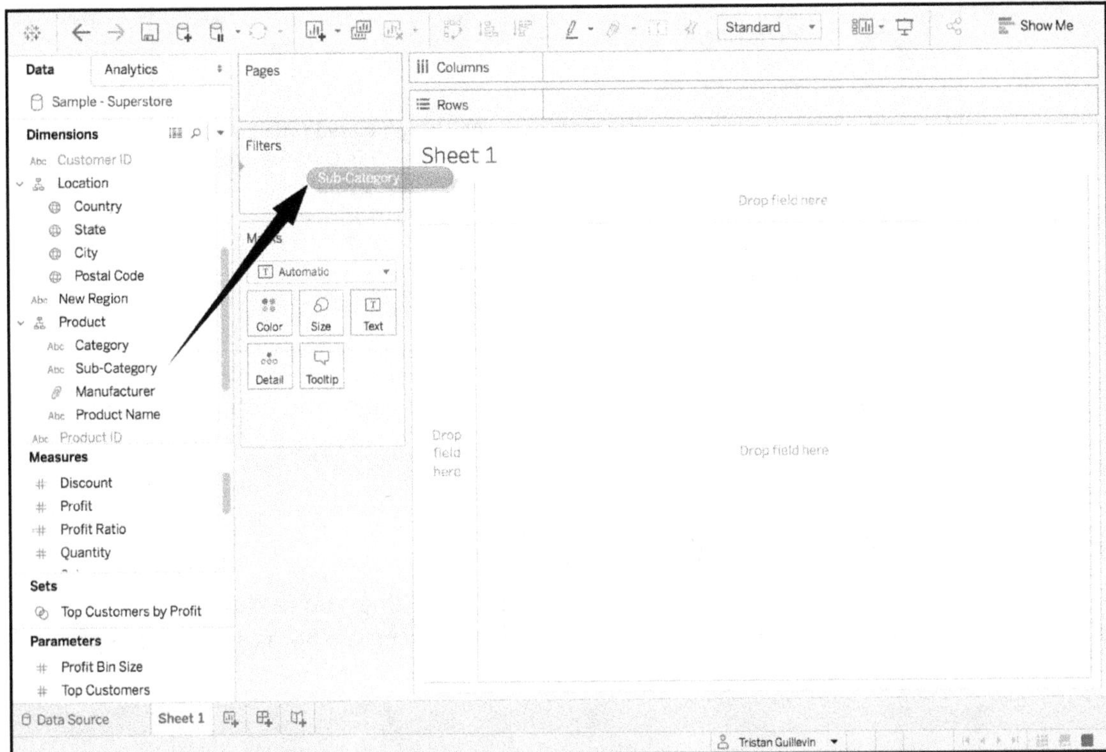

A Filter can be applied on:

- The current Worksheet you're working on (by default)
- A list of selected Worksheets (you can select them with a menu)
- All the Worksheets that use the same Data Source
- All the Worksheets that use the same or a different Data Source that contains the same filtered field

To decide where a Filter should be applied, right-click on its pill in the **Filters** shelf, and use the following options:

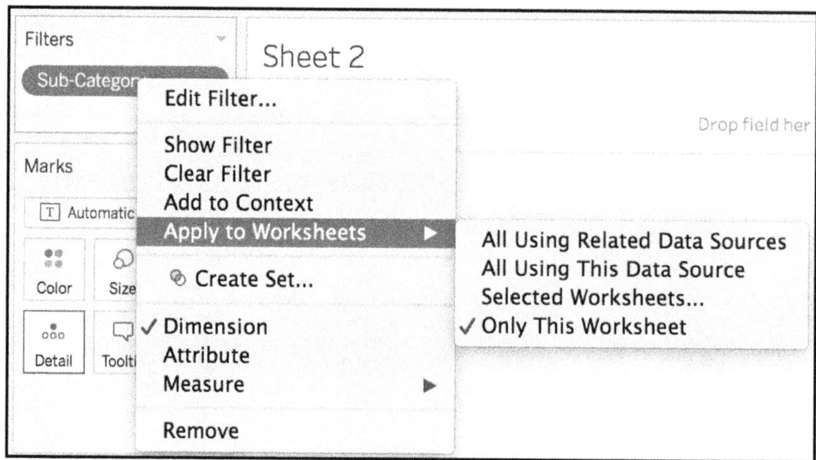

There are differences between a Discrete and a Continuous field, and with Dates compared to other data types.

Filtering a continuous field

If a continuous field is a Measure, a new window opens asking you to choose an aggregation or **All values** (no aggregation). The following screenshot is an example of adding **Profit** to a **Filter**:

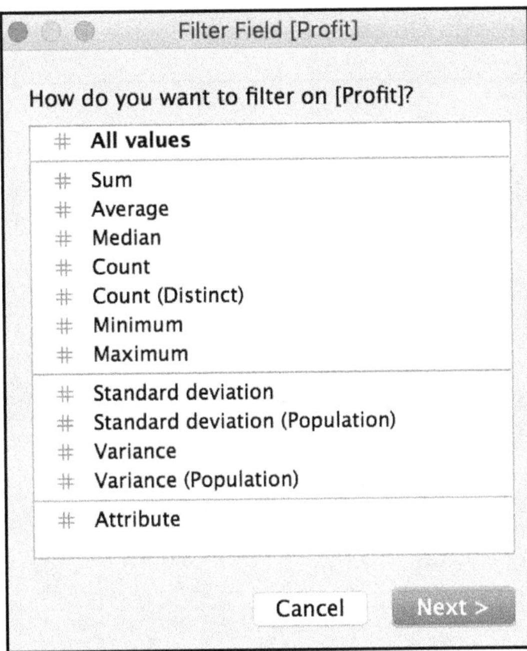

After clicking on **Next**, Tableau opens the continuous filters window. In this window, you have four options:

- **Range of values**: Select the minimum and maximum value, everything outside is excluded
- **At least**: Select the minimum value, everything lower is excluded
- **At most**: Select the maximum value, everything higher is excluded
- **Special**: You can filter only the null or only the non-null values

Here's an example of a Filter on **Quantity** to keep only orders with at least ten items:

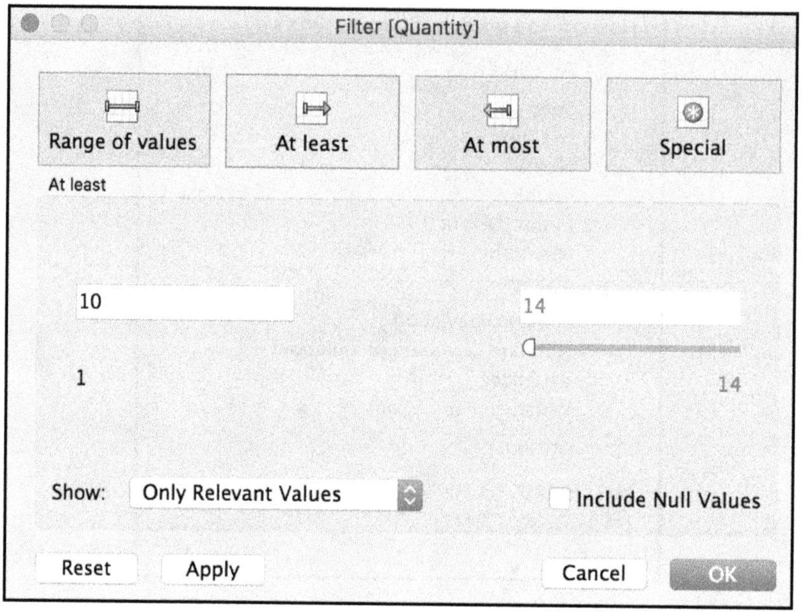

Let's see what happens when using a discrete field on filters.

Filter a discrete field

When you use a discrete field on filters, a new window automatically opens. In this window, you have four tabs with different options, which are as follows:

- General
- Wildcard
- Condition
- Top

The conditions you set on each tab are combined. Let's see how to use the different tabs.

General

On the **General** tab, you can select the values you want to keep (or to exclude if you check the **Exclude** box). At the bottom, there are buttons to select all the values or none. At the top, you can choose between:

- **Select from list**, the default option, where you can select each item
- **Custom value list**, where you can enter a list of custom values to keep or exclude
- **Use all**, to keep all the values

The following screenshot is an example of a **General** filter on **Sub-Category** where **Accessories** and **Envelopes** are excluded:

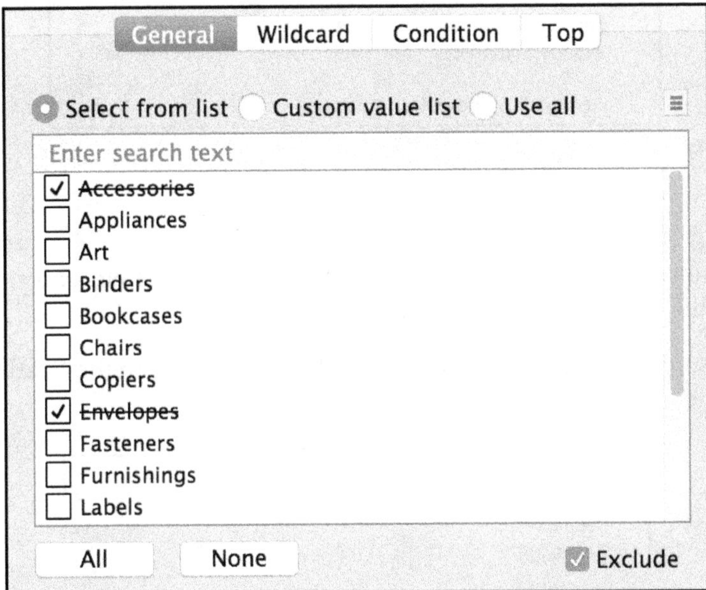

Wildcard

On the **Wildcard** tab, enter some text so that the filter keeps (or excludes) the values that:

- **Contains** the text
- **Starts with** the text

- **Ends with** the text
- **Exactly matches** the text

The following screenshot illustrates a Wildcard filter on a product item that keeps values that start with `Acco`:

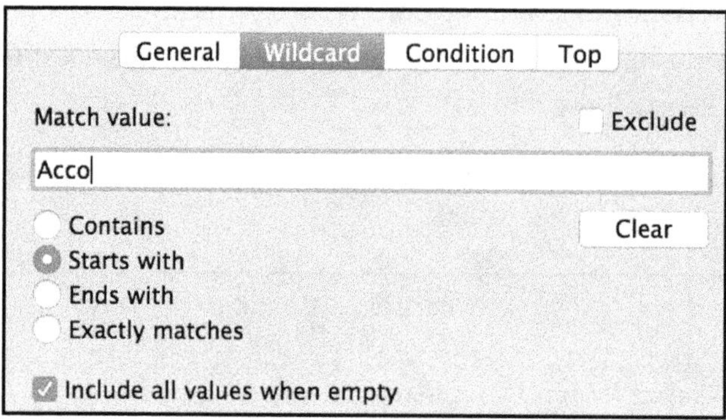

Condition

With the **Condition** tab, you can specify a condition based on a field or formula. The filter keeps only the values that fulfill the condition.

In the following screenshot, the filter keeps only the values where the **Profit** is lower than `1,000`:

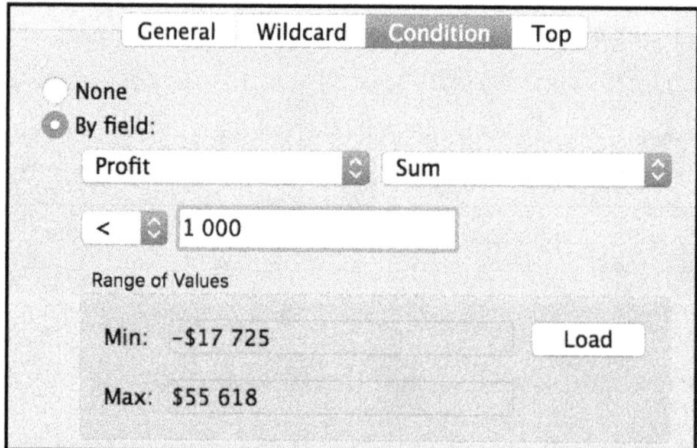

Top

On the **Top** tab, there are four drop-down menus to configure the filter. With them, you can:

- Choose between the **Top** and **Bottom** values
- Specify the number of values to keep (with a Number, a Parameter, or a Set)
- Select the field and aggregation to calculate the Top or Bottom

Here's an example of keeping the five sub-categories with the highest number of **Sales**:

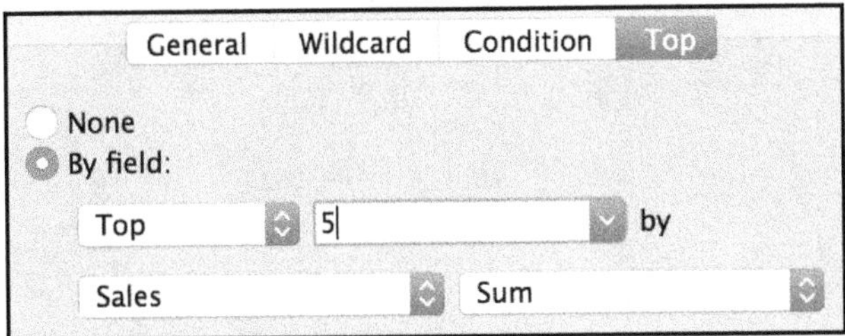

As always, using a Discrete or a Continuous field on a filter produces different results. It's the same with quick filters.

Quick filters

With a right-click on a pill in the filters shelf, you can find the **Show Filter** option. It's, in fact, an option available when you click on any pill, but it deserve a focusing on in this section. It's the first option we have seen in this book that adds interactivity in Tableau. A click on **Show Filter** opens a quick filter card on the Worksheet.

You can automatically add a quick filter by right-clicking on a field in the **Data** pane or a pill in the **View** and selecting **Show Filter**. This shortcut only works when there is at least one pill in the View.

The quick filter allows you, and the people who interact with the visualization, to filter the values without having to open a menu. Here's an example of a quick filter on **Category**, where **Furniture** has been deselected:

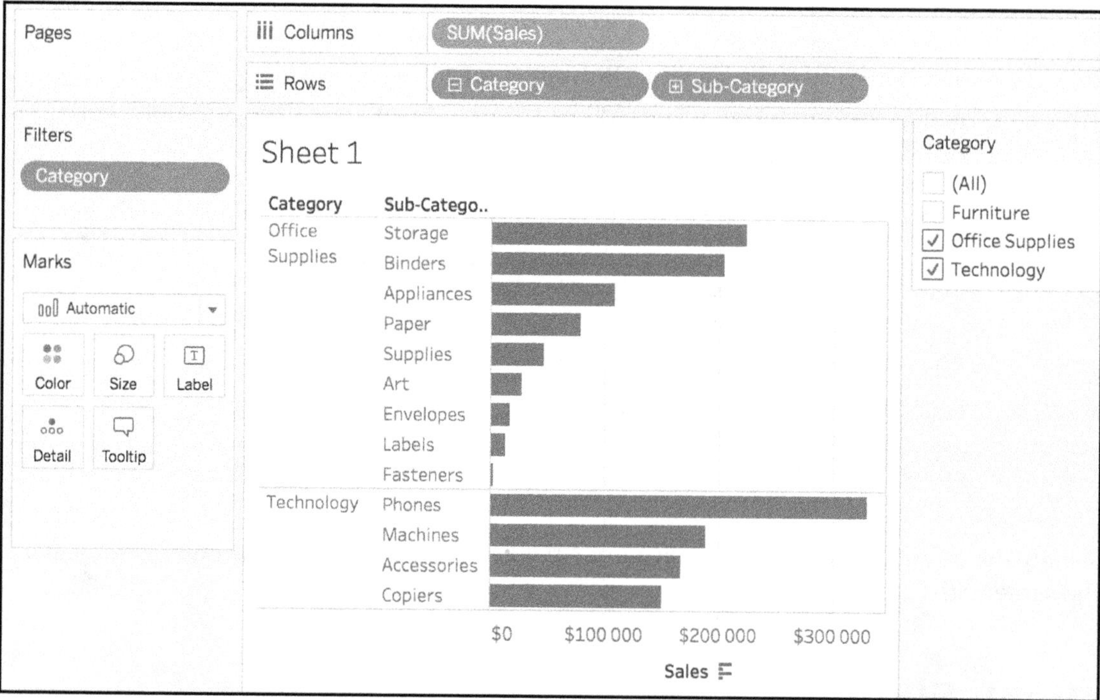

There are many interesting options when you click on the arrow on the top right of the quick filter card, as highlighted in the following screenshot:

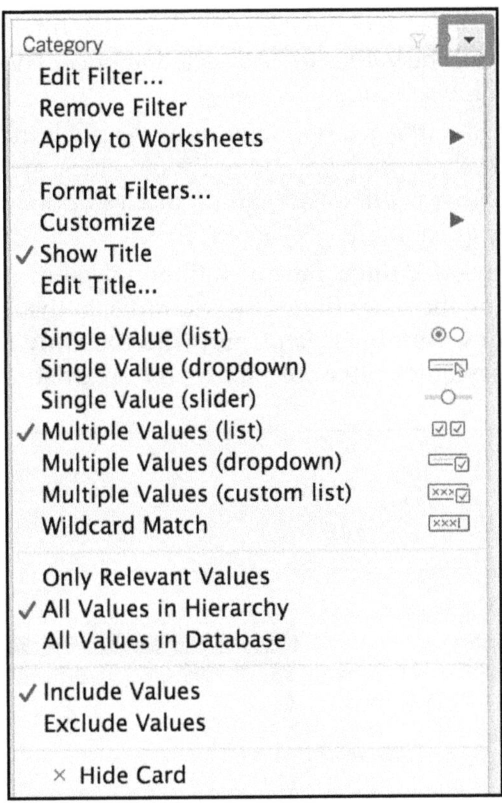

Here's a selection of the most important options:

- You can allow single selections or multiple selections. For both options, you can choose between a list, a dropdown list, or a slider. The **Wildcard Match** is a bit different, as it allows any values to be entered. The following screenshot displays the different quick filters display for a Discrete field:

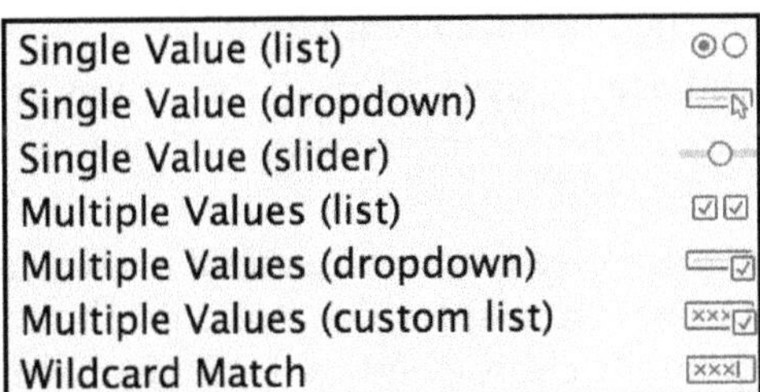

- In **Customize**, you can remove **All** from the quick filter list. It may be crucial that you don't allow all the values to be selected at once. This option is often used with a Single Value selection.
- In **Customize** again, the last option adds an **Apply** button to the quick filter. It's useful when you have a long list of values, and you don't want the visualization to refresh after each selection. This option is often used with a Multiple Values quick filter.
- With **Only Relevant Values**, the quick filter only shows the possible values when considering the other filters. For example, in the following screenshot, only **State: District of Columbia** is kept, and with the **Only Relevant Values** option, the **Sub-Category** quick filter only shows the six existing values:

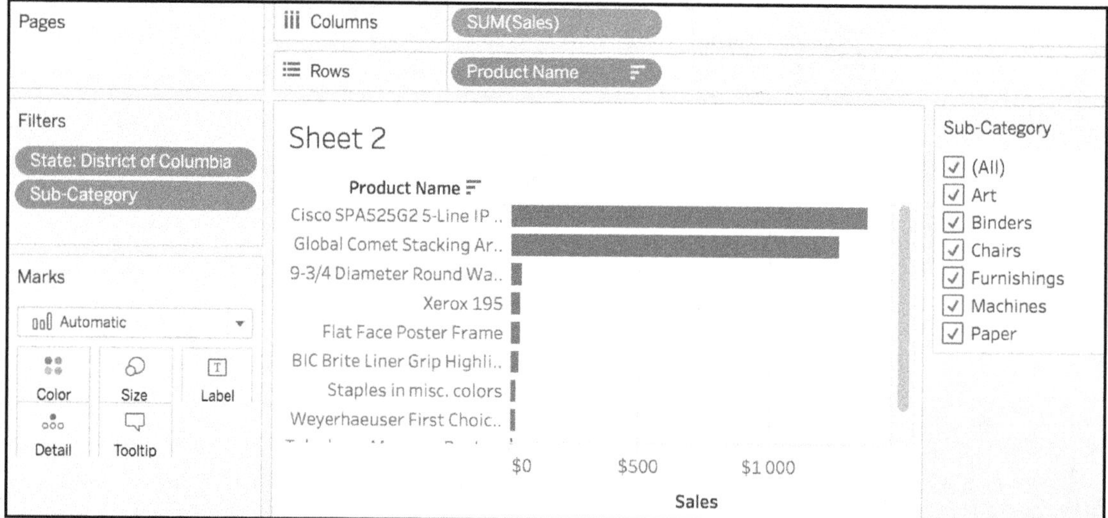

- **All Values in Hierarchy** is automatically applied when you are using fields from a common hierarchy. With this option, the quick filter shows only the possible values considering the filtered parent value.
- **All Values in Database** always shows all the values of the field, even if the combination of the different filters returns no lines.

A quick filter based on a Continuous field is always represented by a *slider*. You can customize it to display the readouts, the slider, and the null controls. You can also visually choose between Range of Values, At Least, or At Most.

Now that you know how to add filters and play with quick filters, let's talk about the hierarchies between the filters.

Filter hierarchy

All Dimension filters are applied at the same time. There is, by default, no hierarchy between them, but you can add one with Context.

Context

Using Context is a way to add a hierarchy between the different Dimension filters. Consider the following example:

1. Create a visualization with **City** in **Rows** and **Sales** in **Columns**. Add **City** in **Filters** and select the top five by **Sales**, as shown in the following screenshot:

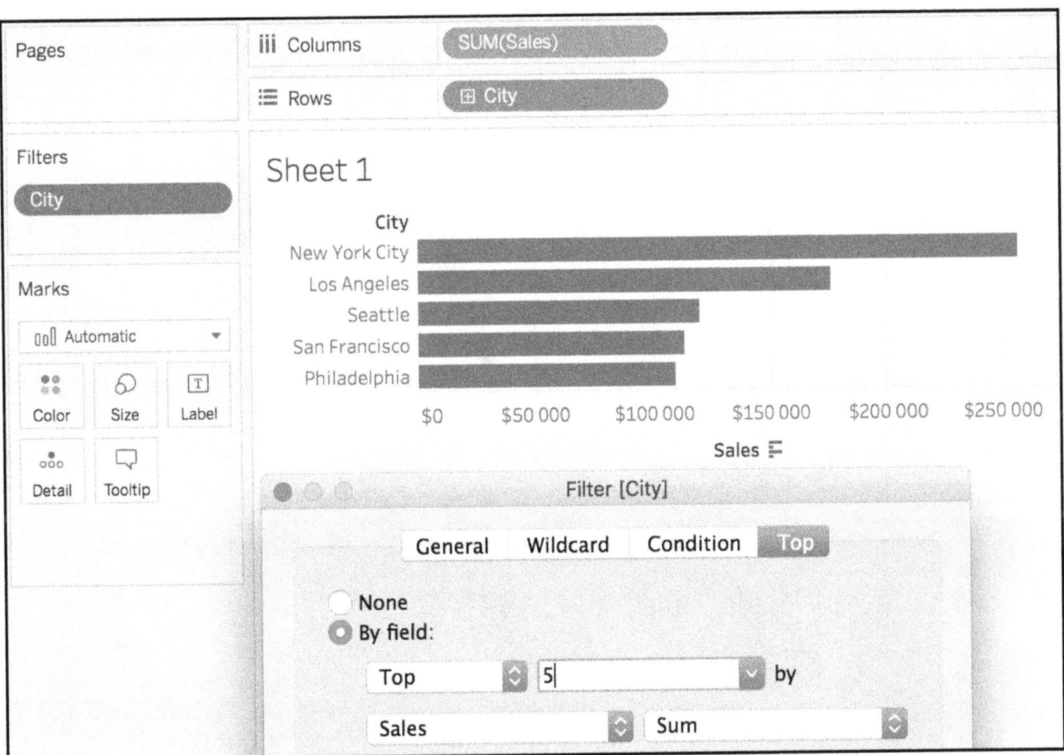

2. Add a quick filter for **State** (you can do this very easily by right-clicking on the field in the Data Source and selecting **Show Filter**).
3. In the quick filter, select only the State of **California**. Tableau combines the two filters and looks for cities that are both in the top five and in *California*. As you can see in the following screenshot, there are only two remaining cities, *Los Angeles* and *San Francisco*:

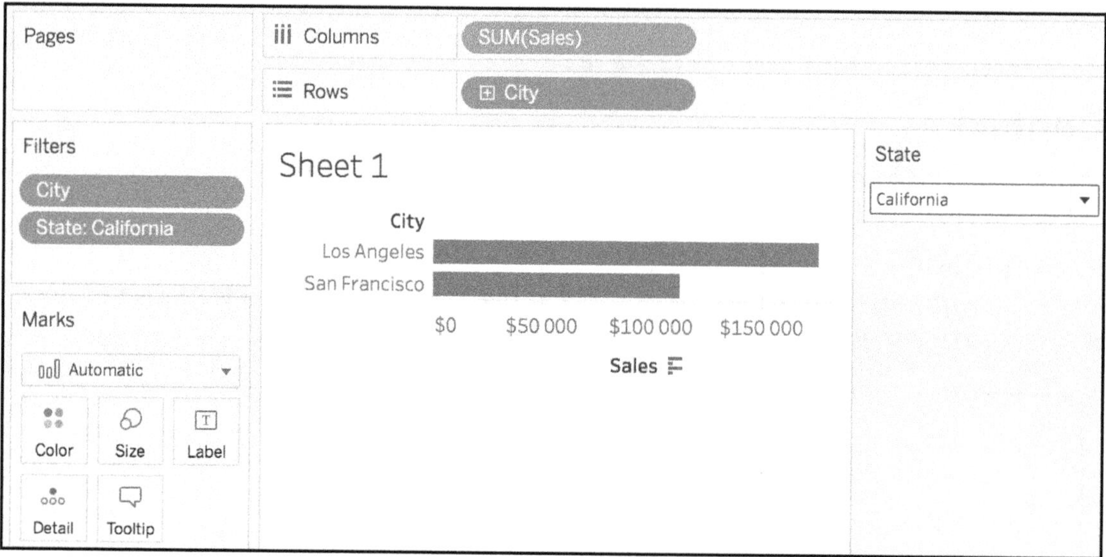

4. Right-click on **State** on the **Filters** shelf and select **Add to Context**. The pill automatically turns gray and goes above the **City** pill.
5. You can now select any State from the quick filter and see the top five cities in that State. Thanks to **Context**, Tableau first filters the states, then keeps the top five cities. Here's the final result:

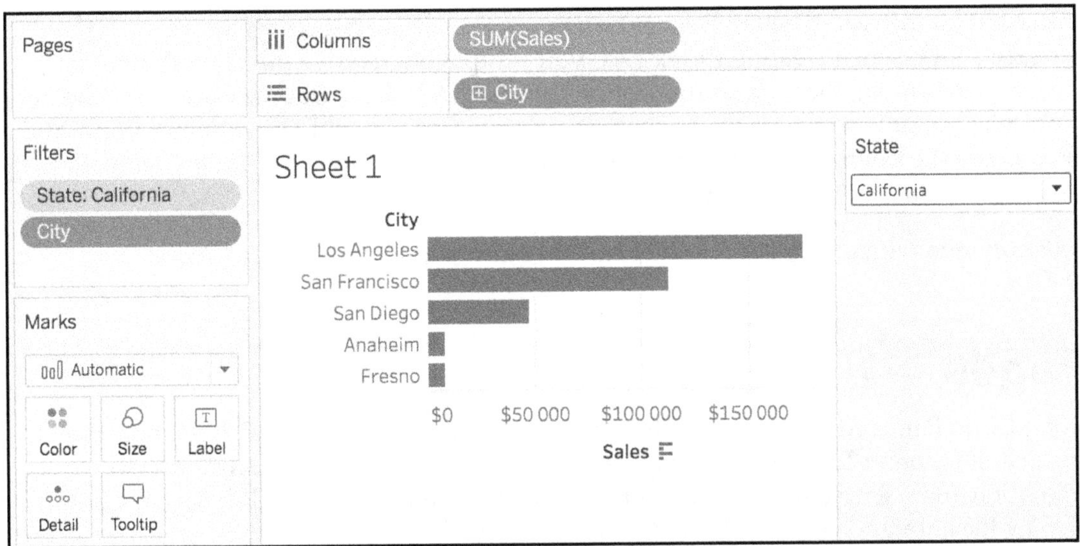

Context is a great way to put hierarchies between your different filters. To end this section about Filters, let's see the general hierarchies between different Filters.

Global filter hierarchy

Always keep this book close to you when using Tableau, and look at the following screenshot if you need to ask yourself a question about the hierarchy between filters:

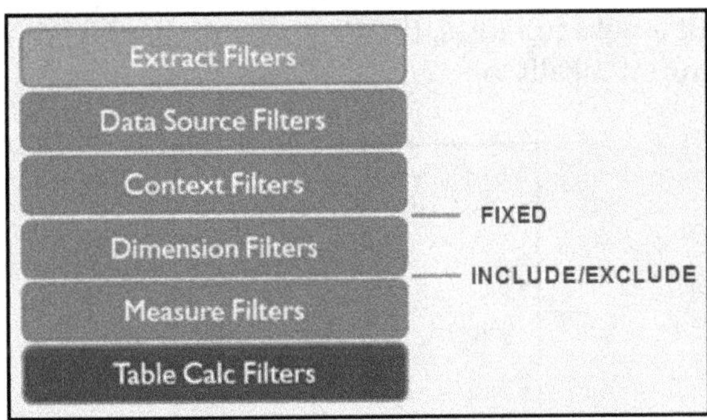

Of course, on top, you find the **Extract Filters**. As the extract is a local copy of your data, if you add a filter when creating the extract, you completely remove the filtered data. In second place among the data source options, you can add **Data Source Filters**. All the data is present, but only some are used. Then, as we saw, **Context** and **Dimension Filters**, and at the bottom, the filters based on Measure. Fixed, Include/Exclude, and Table Calculation are advanced techniques we'll address later.

Let's continue with a very special shelf called **Pages**.

Pages

Not only do Pages add interactivity to your visualization, but they're also the only way to create animation in Tableau. You may have never seen a Tableau visualization with animation, for a simple reason: currently, Tableau Server/Online and Tableau Public can't display the animations. That's why Pages are not much used. But what exactly are Pages?

Page basics

Pages act like filters but only show one value at a time. Each value is a Page, and you can click on the **Play** button to go through all the Pages and create an animation.

A few things to have in mind before we look at any concrete examples:

- You can only use Discrete fields in Pages
- When you put a field in Pages, the Pages card, displayed in the following screenshot, automatically opens:

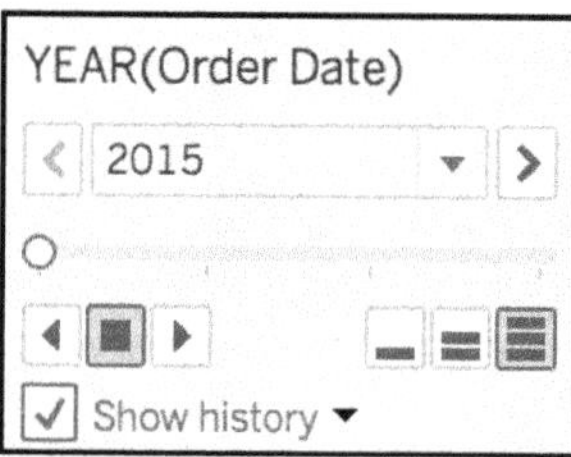

Here are some things about the Page card:

- The first line displays the selected value, and the arrows allow you to go to the next or previous value.
- The slider shows how many Pages (values) there are, and you move the cursor to go through them.
- On the third line, on the left, you can see the animation buttons. You can use them to automatically go through all the Pages from the first to the last, the other way, or stop the animation. On the same line, on the right, you see the speed buttons. They define how fast Tableau changes the Page.
- At the bottom, you can show the history, or not.

If you decide to **Show history**, a new menu opens:

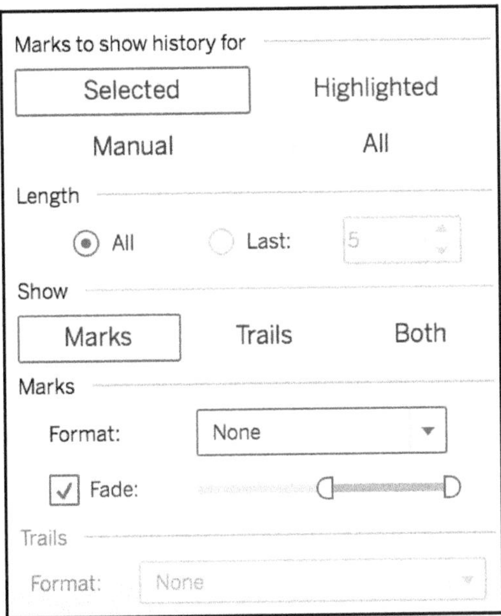

In this menu, you can configure how to display the previous Marks (the ones from the preceding Pages). Let's quickly see the different options if you decide to show the history:

- In the first part, you specify which Marks should display the history
- In the second part, you define how many historical Marks to show (all or the last number of your choice)

- The third part allows you to choose between showing the historical Marks as they were, only the trails (the path of the prior point to the next), or both
- Finally, in the two other parts, you can customize the format of the historical Marks or the trails

That's it for the theory, let's build an example together.

Guided tutorial with Pages

Ready to play with Pages and animate your visualization? Follow these steps:

1. Put **Discount** in **Columns**, **Profit** in **Rows**, and **Segment** in **Color**.
2. To see the points more easily, change the Marks type to **Circle** rather than **Shapes**. The visualization should look like this:

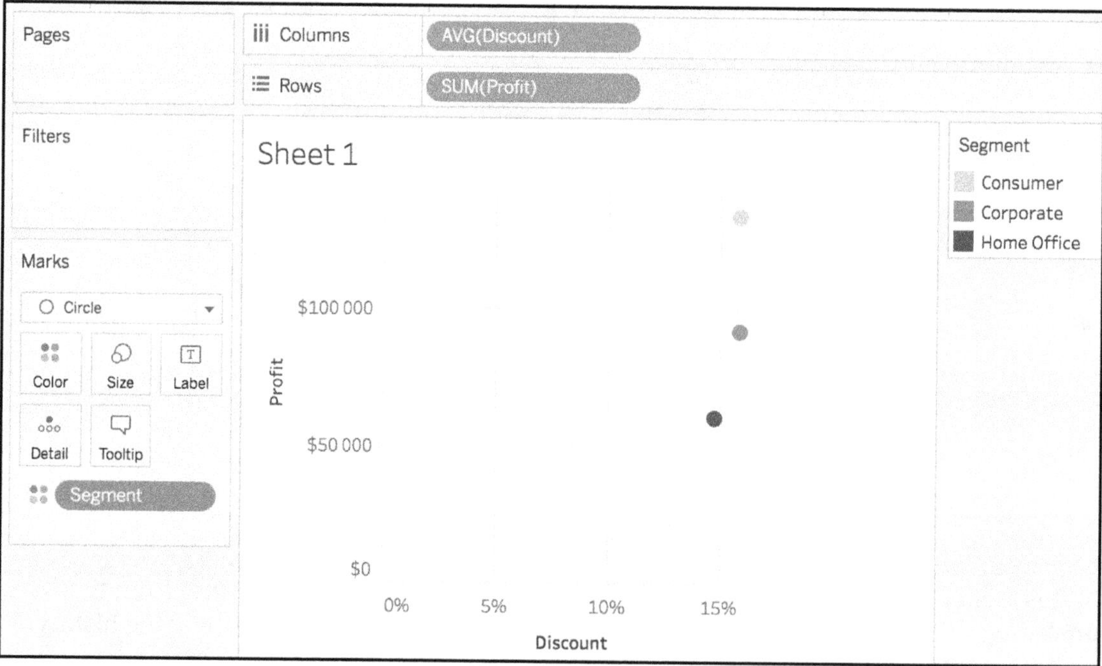

3. Put **Order Date** in **Pages**. By default, the visualization is now filtered into *2015*. You can use the arrows to look at the other years or use the animation buttons.
4. Verify that the **Show history** box is selected and open the menu.
5. Configure **Show history** to display only the **Trails** of the last 5 Marks for **All** the Marks, as shown in the following screenshot:

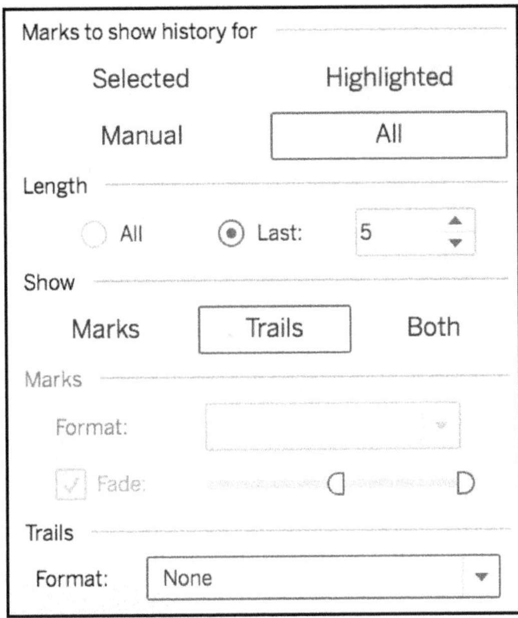

6. Use the slider to go to **2018**. You should now see the trails of each segment and do some analysis. You can see that the **Home Office** and **Consumer** segments have constantly increased in profit, but not **Corporate**. You can also clearly see how the average discounts have increased from **2015** to **2017** in the **Home Office** segment. Here's the final result:

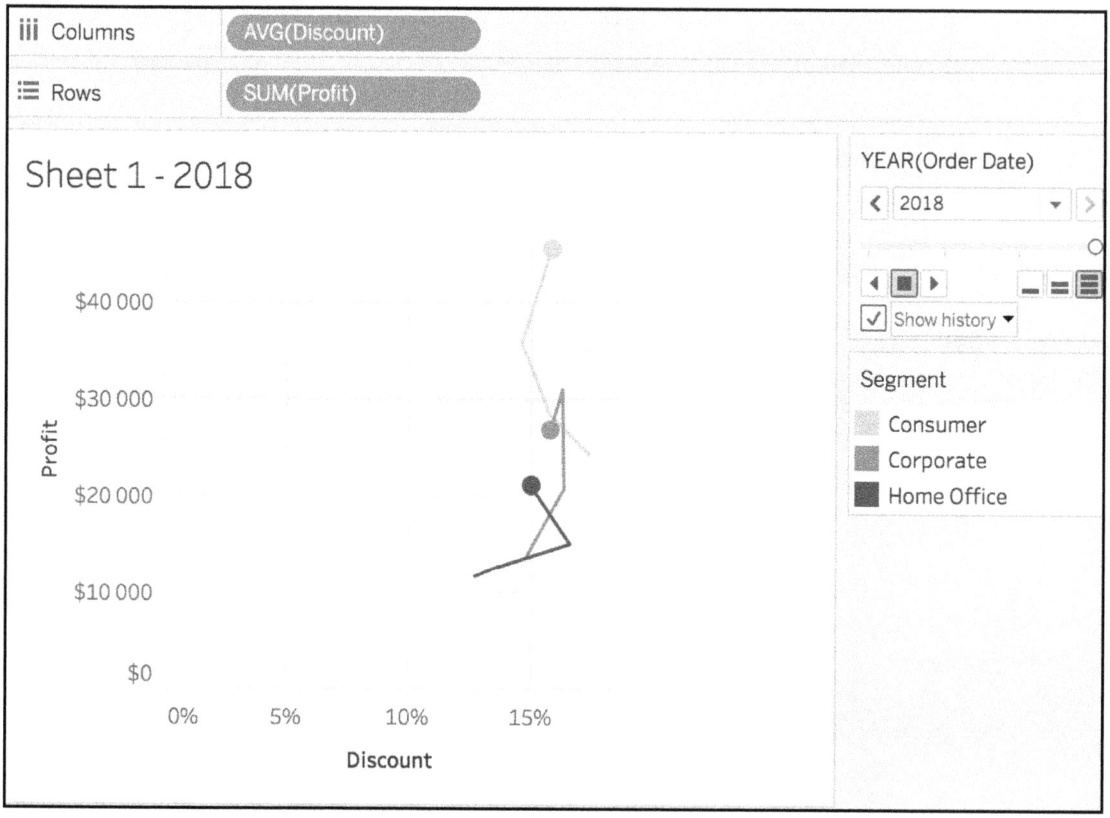

Columns AVG(Discount)
Rows SUM(Profit)
Sheet 1 - 2018
YEAR(Order Date)
2018
Show history
Segment
Consumer
Corporate
Home Office
$40 000
$30 000
$20 000
$10 000
$0
Profit
0%
5%
10%
15%
Discount

Pages are great for presentation. You can give life to your visualization. If you want to see concrete, real-life use of Pages, I advise you to look at the Iron Viz 2017 competition on YouTube: `https://www.youtube.com/watch?v=1P7r_G1k0FU` ;-)

We have seen all the different shelves available in Tableau. To conclude this chapter, let's take a look at the various options in a Worksheet.

Worksheet options and format

There are lots of options available in a Worksheet, and you can find them in many different places. You can right-click almost anywhere, and you'll get a list of options. The three significant places to find options are:

- With a right-click on a pill
- In the **Worksheet** menu at the top
- With a right-click on the **View** (or on a **Mark**)

Let's go through a selection of the most useful options for each place, starting with the pill options.

Pill options

All the pill options are available by right-clicking on a pill. There are some differences between Continuous and Discrete pill options. The following screenshot shows the options available for a Continuous pill:

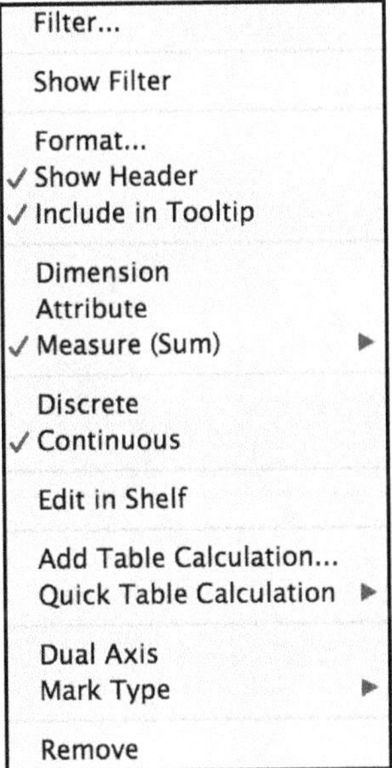

Among the most important options, you'll find the following:

- **Filter...**: A shortcut to the pill in the Filters shelf that opens the **Edit Filter** window
- **Show Filter**: Automatically puts the pill in the Filters shelf and displays the quick filter
- **Show Highlighter (only for Discrete pills)**: Opens the Highlighter card, which allows you to highlight a specific value, as shown in the following screenshot:

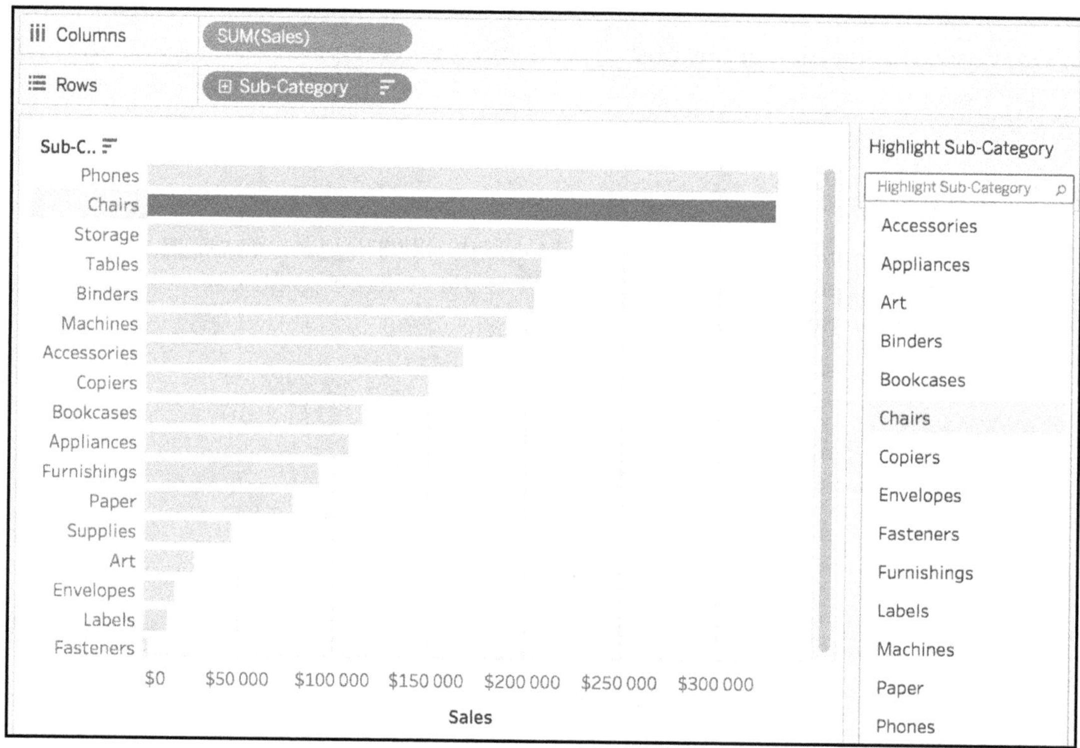

- **Sort (only for Discrete pills)**: Opens the **Sort** window where you can change the sort order of the values. Here's an example of an ascending Sort based on sales:

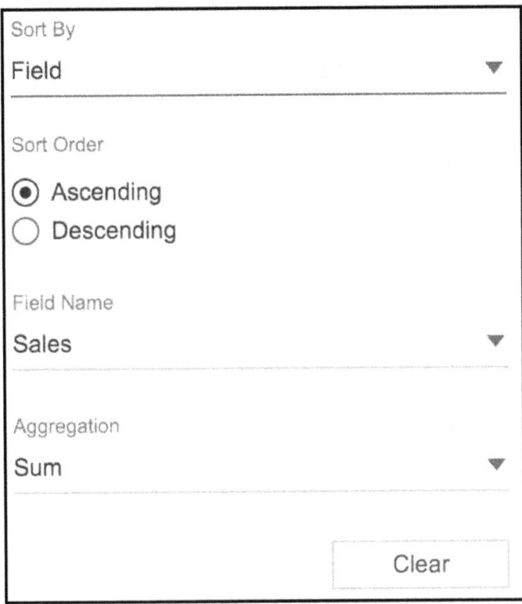

You can also transform the pill into a Dimension, an Attribute, or a Measure and, if the pill returns a number, you can choose between Discrete and Continuous. If the pill is a Measure, you can also create Table Calculations, but that's for another chapter.

Next, we'll see the options available in the Worksheet menu.

Worksheet menu options

At the top, among the different menus of Tableau, you can find the Worksheet menu, which contains a few interesting options:

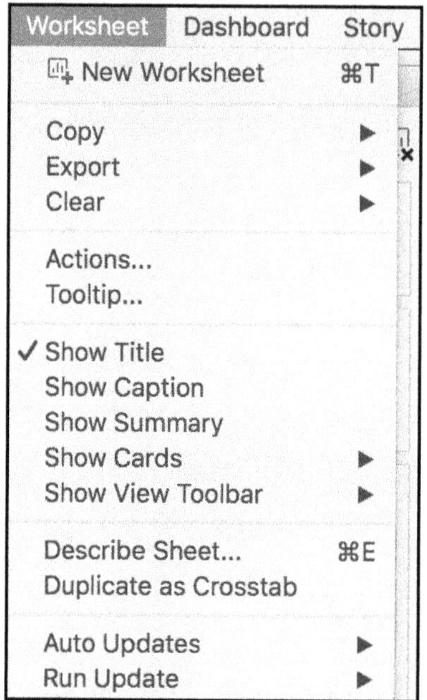

Again, let's focus on the more important ones:

- **Export** allows you to export the Worksheet as an image, a CSV file, or an Excel cross-tab. If you choose the image, a new window opens where you can customize the result. The Data and Excel exports both convert the visualization into a table.
- **Tooltip...** is a shortcut to edit the tooltip.
- With the different **Show** ... options, you can display or hide many different shelves or cards. The **Caption** is a quick description of the Worksheet, and the **Summary** adds statistical information. Both are displayed in the following screenshot:

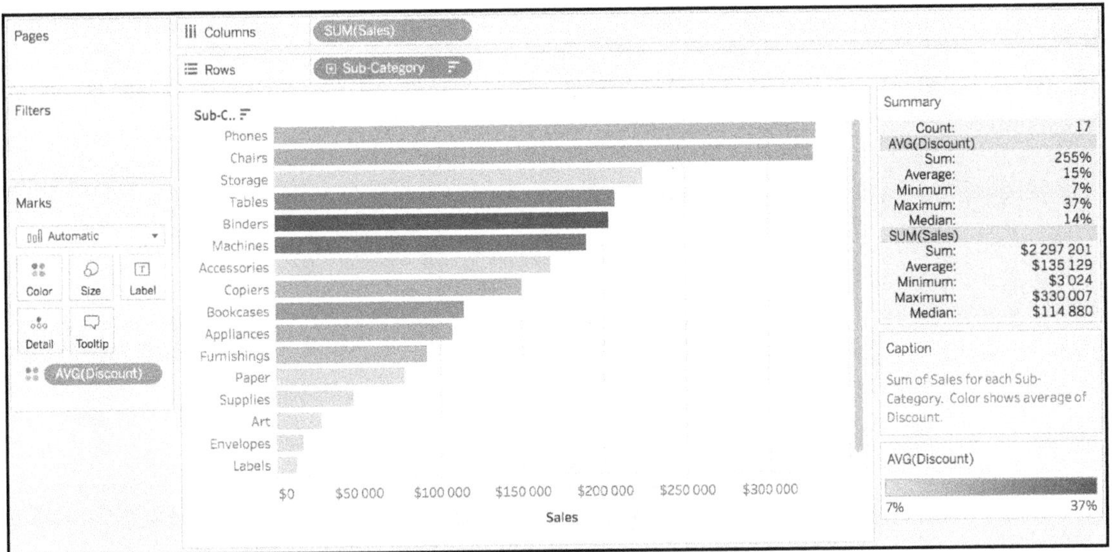

- **Describe Sheet...** opens a window with a complete description of the Worksheet.
- **Duplicate as Crosstab** duplicates your current Worksheet in a new one, and transforms the visualization into a table.

With a right-click on the Worksheet tab, at the bottom, you can also duplicate the Worksheet as a cross table.

The last sets of options are available with a right-click on the **View**.

View options

In a Worksheet, the part that displays the visualization and contains the **Headers**, **Axes**, and **Marks** is called the **View**. When you right-click on the different elements of the View, you may find appealing options. The following screenshot is an example of the options available when you click on a **Mark**:

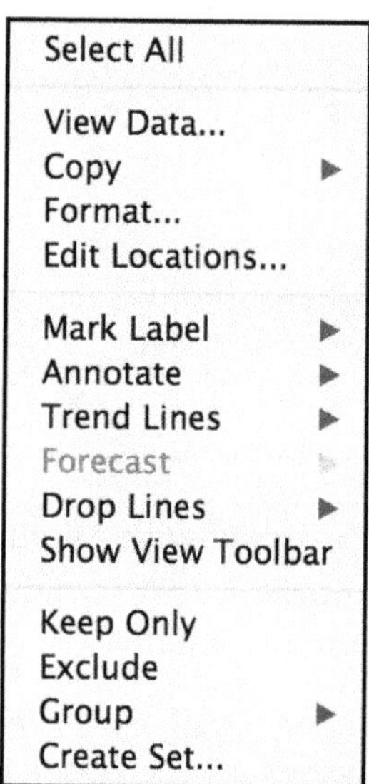

As before, you'll find here a list and description of the most useful options:

- **View Data** opens a new window with, by default, a **Summary** of the displayed data, or the **Full Data**, which shows all the lines that are used to build the visualization. From the **View Data** window, you can also copy or export the current selection in a CSV.

- **Edit Locations...** is available when the Mark has a geographical role and lets you configure the locations in a new window.
- With **Mark Label**, you can force the Mark to always, or never, show the Label.
- **Annotate** lets you add an annotation to a specific Mark, point, or area in the View. When you select one of the three options, Tableau opens the **Edit annotation** window, where you can customize the text. Adding an annotation is an excellent way to add context to your visualization. Here's an example of annotation:

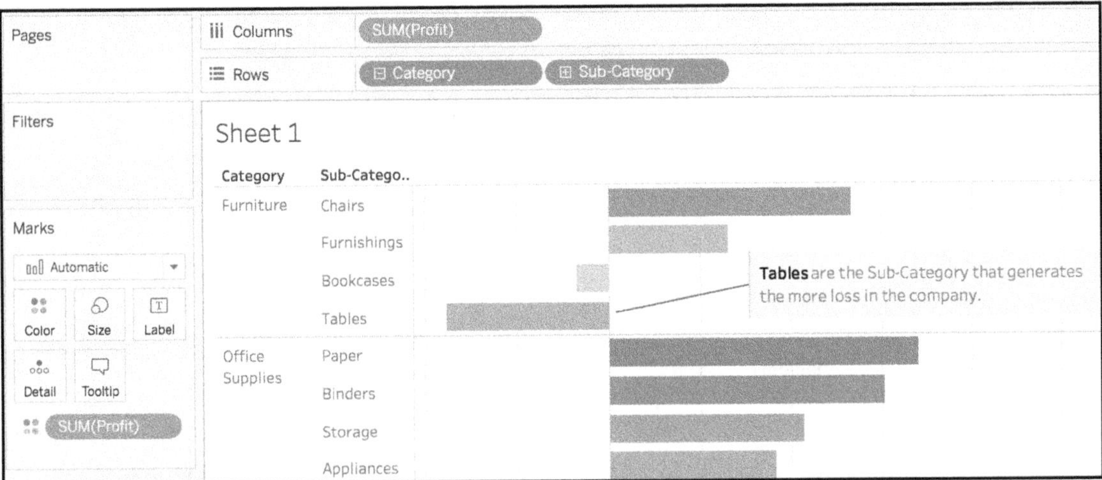

- **Keep Only** and **Exclude** are options that are available with a simple left-click on a Mark. **Keep Only** automatically adds a filter that includes only the value of the selected Mark. **Exclude** also adds a filter, but this time the filter excludes the selected value. Both options can be handy for focusing on the interesting values and eliminating mistakes in your data.

If you right-click on an axis, you can edit it. Tableau opens the **Edit Axis** window, where you can configure many aspects of the axis such as the range, the scale, the titles, and the tick marks. Here's the **Edit Axis** configuration window:

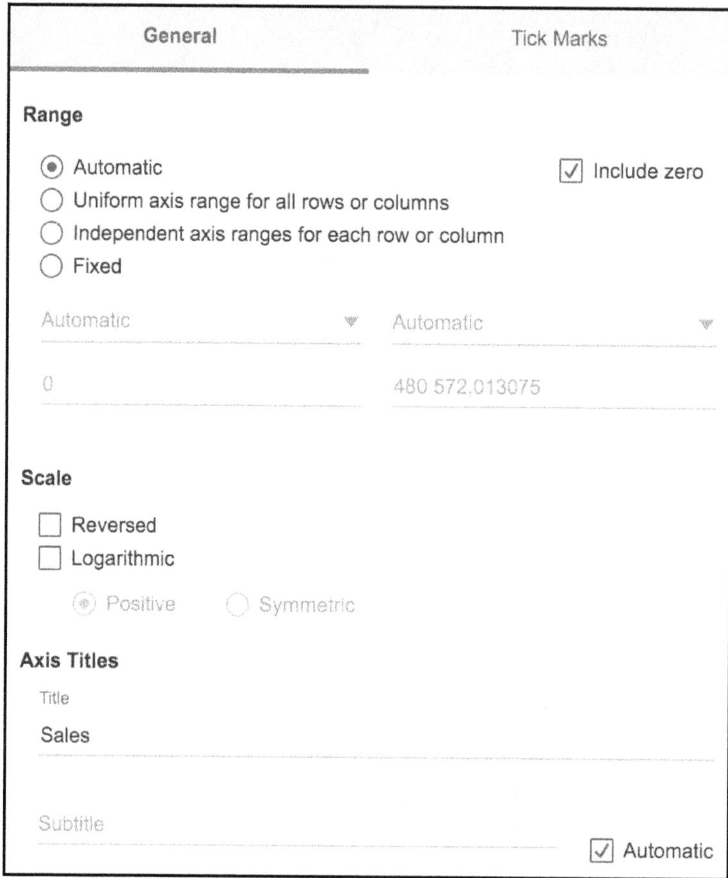

Always remember that if you are searching for how to configure or edit something in Tableau, a simple right-click is almost always enough.

A recurring option, available almost everywhere, is Format.

Format

When you click on **Format**, Tableau opens a whole new pane on the left, instead of the Data Source one. The formatting pane is highlighted in this screenshot:

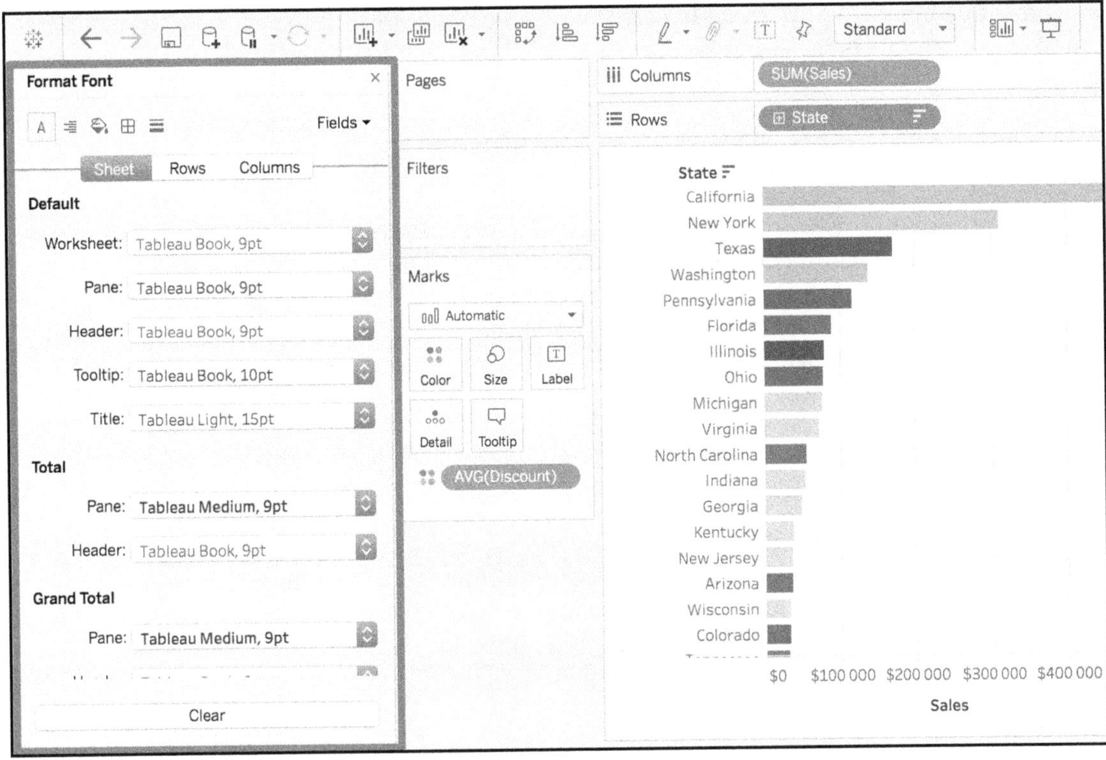

There are five different icons for the various formatting options available. For each option, the formatting can be applied on the Worksheet, the Rows, or the Columns, and on different parts of the View (Worksheet, Pane, Header, Title, and so on). The five formatting options allow you to:

- **Format Font**: Select the font type, size, and color
- **Format Alignment**: Change the text alignment, direction, and wrapping
- **Format Shading**: Add a background color, and column or row banding
- **Format Borders**: Add a border and column or row dividers
- **Format Lines**: Change the format (plain, dotted) of the different lines in Tableau (grid lines, zero lines, trends lines, and so on)

There is an entire **Format** menu on top, where you can change the format of almost everything in Tableau. In this menu, you can open the **Format Workbook** pane, which is very useful for configuring the format of the entire Workbook in a few clicks.

With those options, you can quickly make everything beautiful or ugly. The only advice I can give you on this is to keep it simple, readable, and easy to understand!

Summary

In this chapter, you first learned how to build a visualization with more than two Measures using Dual Axis, Measure Names, and Measure Values. The second section was about Filters and how to use them to your advantage to focus on the right data. Then, we looked at Pages and how to add interactivity to Tableau! To finish, we saw an overview of the most useful options, where to find them, and how to use them.

If we combine its two parts, this chapter is the longest and most important one in the book. It's the core of Tableau and where you'll spend a major part of your time. I'm sure you'll enjoy building many different visualizations to find the ones that make your data shine.

Once you find the best visualizations to understand your data and answer your questions, it's time to assemble them in a Dashboard. You probably guessed where this is going. The next chapter is about building Dashboards, how to create them and make them interactive, and, of course, this will be a chapter containing all the best advice and lots of examples.

8
Create Powerful Dashboards and Stories

A **Dashboard** is a composition of multiple Worksheets but also other **objects**, such as **Container**, **Text**, and **Image**. The goal of a Dashboard is to provide insights on a regular basis, with each update. A **Story** is a composition of **Worksheets** and **Dashboards.** You can use a Story to do a presentation, or if you've found an interesting story in your data and you want to tell it with **Story points** and **captions**.

In this chapter, we'll cover the following topics:

- Dashboard basics
- Tiled, Floating, and Container Layouts
- Dashboard Actions
- Create a Story

Before starting with the Dashboard basics, let's configure our work environment.

Before we start

For this chapter, we'll use the saved Data Source, **Sample-Superstore**, again. As the focus is on the Dashboard, the examples will start as if three Worksheets were already built. The Worksheets are the following:

- **Sales and Profit by Sub-Category**: **Sub-Category** in **Rows**, **Sales** in **Columns**, and **Profit** in **Color**, as illustrated here:

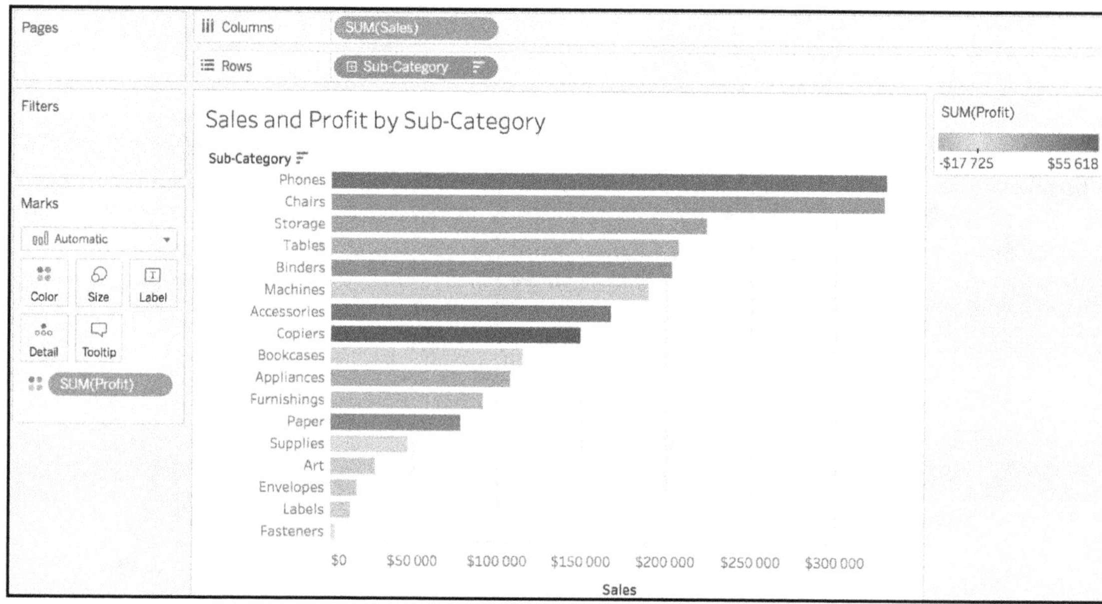

- **Profit Evolution**: **Continuous Quarter** of **Order Date** in **Columns** and **Profit** in **Rows**, as illustrated here:

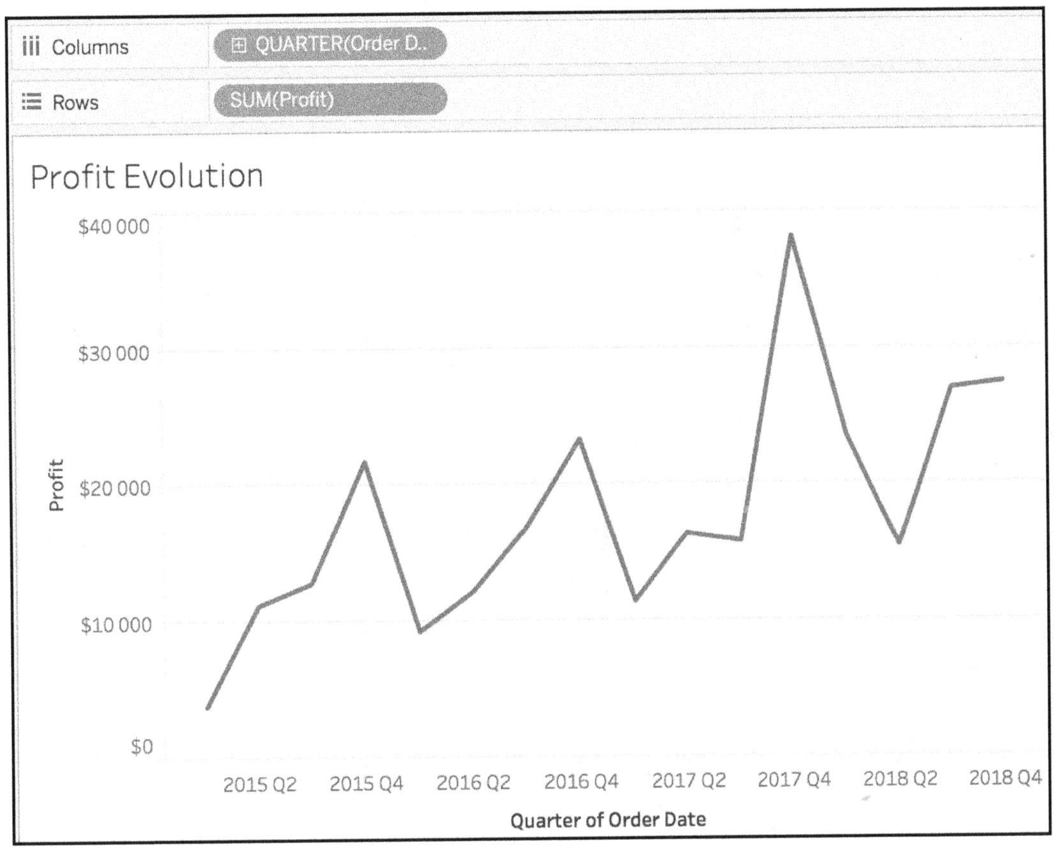

- **Profit by State**: A **Map** of each **State** with **Profit** in **Color**, as illustrated here:

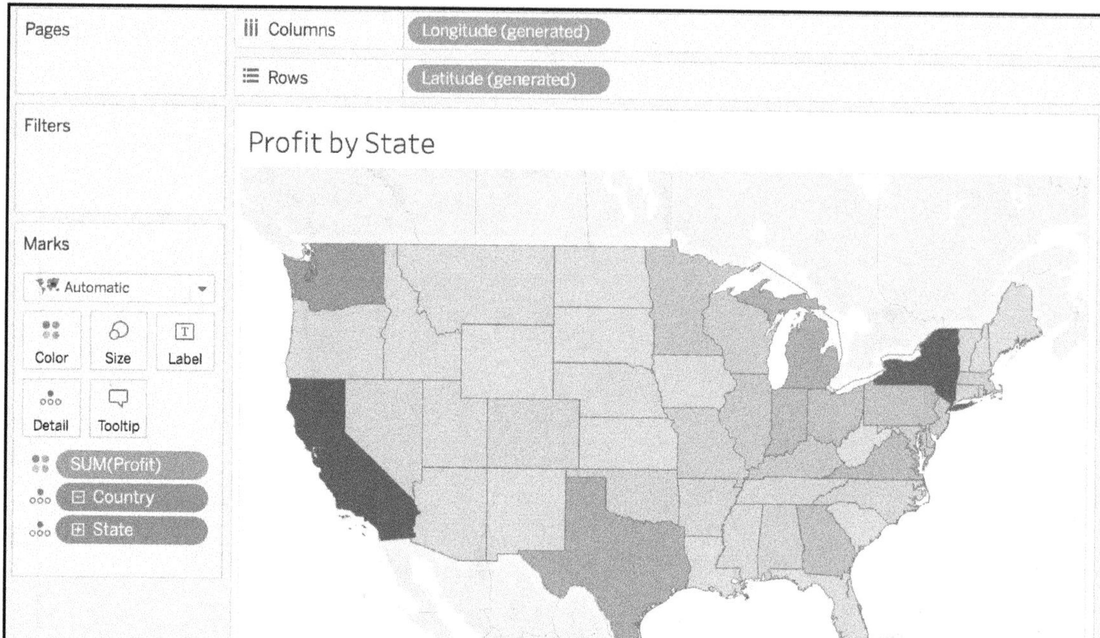

You can download the ZIP file `Dashboard Start` from the *Chapter 8: Create Powerful Dashboards and Stories* section of my website, `book.ladataviz.com` (or, browse to `https://ladataviz.com/wp-content/uploads/2018/09/Dashboard-Start.twbx_.zip`). When you unzip the file, you'll find a Tableau Package Workbook that contains the three Worksheets. However, don't hesitate to recreate them yourself to practice!

Dashboard basics

If a Worksheet is one idea, a Dashboard is a way to combine all those ideas. With a Dashboard, you can create interaction between the Worksheets, and add pictures, web pages, and other objects to create a unique page that will answer all your questions.

To add a new Dashboard, you can either click on the icon at the bottom-right, click on **New Dashboard** from the **Dashboard** top menu, or use the **New Dashboard** button in the toolbar, as highlighted in the following screenshot:

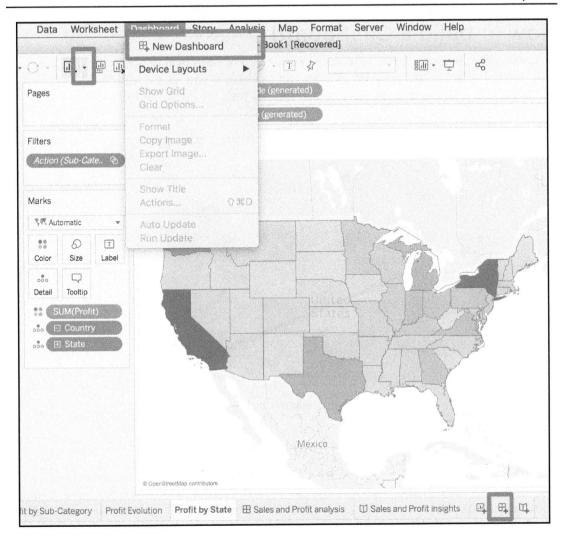

The Dashboard workplace is composed of a central blank part where you can drop Worksheets and objects. On the left pane, you can find two tabs: **Dashboard** and **Layout**.

You can't see the data pane on the Dashboard anymore. If you need to modify it, you have to go on a Worksheet or create a temporary new Worksheet that you can delete afterwards.

Let's start by seeing how to build a Dashboard; then, we'll focus on the two different tabs.

How to build a Dashboard

To create a Dashboard, you have to drag Worksheets or objects to the central blank area (you can also double-click on a Worksheet, but as always, you let Tableau build it for you). By default, the Worksheets are **Tiled**, meaning that they are added in *boxes*, as shown in the following screenshot:

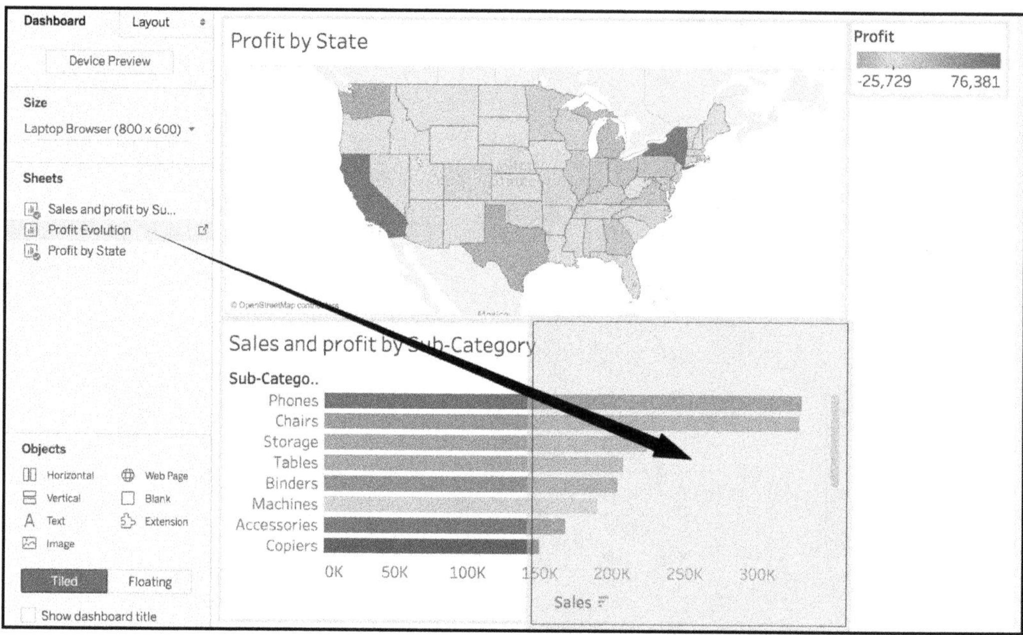

A Worksheet that you add in a Dashboard is the Worksheet itself; It means that it's not a copy and if you modify the Worksheet (either from the Dashboard by changing the format or from the Worksheet by adding a new field, for example), you'll see the change in both the Dashboard and the Worksheet.

Usually, the purpose of a Worksheet is to end up in a Dashboard. If you create a Workbook with many Dashboards that contain many Worksheets, the bottom part with all the tabs will rapidly become crowded. You can hide all the Worksheets that are in a Dashboard by using the **Hide All Sheets** option when you right-click on a **Dashboard** tab. You can, of course, unhide them as easily.

You cannot modify any of the Worksheet shelves from the Dashboard. However, you can still use all the toolbar buttons (to sort, add labels, swap, create groups, and so on) and use a right-click and all the options available with it.

When you click on a Worksheet, its outline will turn gray, and you'll see four or five icons:

- The first removes the Worksheet from the Dashboard
- The second takes you to the Worksheet to modify it
- The third is a shortcut to put a Filter action on the Worksheet (detailed in a later section)
- The fourth icon can be used to fix the width or height of the Worksheet if it's inside a Horizontal or Vertical Container
- The last one, the small arrow, opens a list of options, as you can see in the following screenshot:

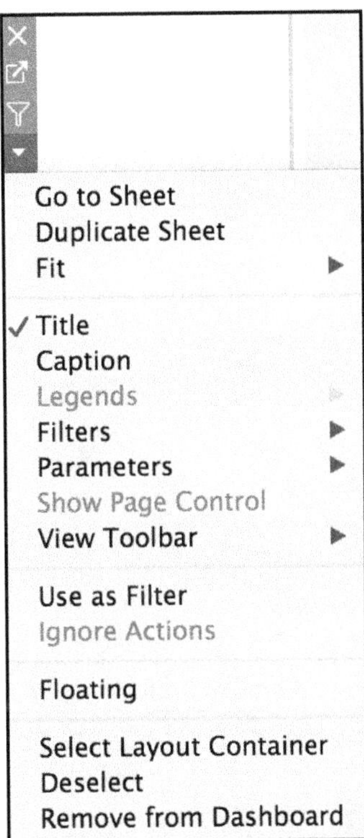

Many of those options can be found elsewhere among the Worksheets or Dashboard options. The most useful options are probably **Legends**, **Filters**, and **Parameters**, which allow you to quickly add the Legends, Filters, or Parameters that exist on the Worksheet to the Dashboard. You can also click on **Ignore Actions** to remove a Worksheet from the impacted Action Filters from other Worksheets.

Speaking of options, let's discover what you can do with the **Dashboard** pane on the left.

Dashboard pane

Here's a screenshot of the Dashboard pane:

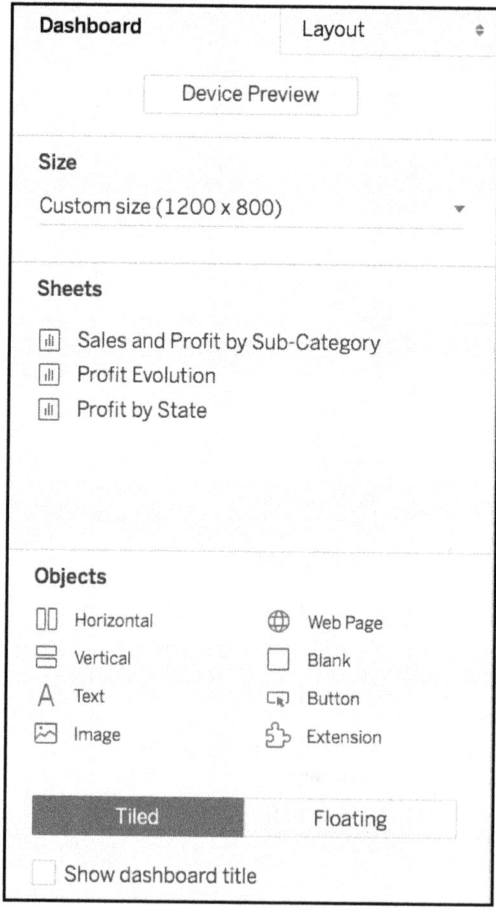

On this pane, the part you'll use the most is **Sheets**. Here, you'll find all the different Worksheets in your Workbook, as long as they are not hidden (*you understand, now, why giving a meaningful name to each of them is crucial*).

A second—more important than you think—useful option is **Size**. Here you can set the size of your Dashboard to *fixed* (with a list of standard sizes and also the option to set the height and width manually), *automatic* (the Dashboard will resize to fit the screen), or *range* with a minimum and maximum range.

Automatic may seem to be the best option, but it is probably the worst. The ratio between height and width is critical in data visualization, and in automatic you have no control. A bad ratio can lead your Dashboard to look very bad, even unusable. My advice is to go with fixed size when you want absolute power over the looks of your visualization, or choose *range* to allow resizing when the Dashboard will be displayed on many different screen sizes.

You'll also find a button to create a **Device Preview** and, beneath the list of Worksheets, the different **Objects** you can add to your Dashboard, and the option to choose between **Tiled** and **Floating**. All these essential functionalities will be seen in detail in this chapter.

To finish, at the very bottom, you can use the checkbox to choose whether to show the Dashboard title. Let's continue with the Layout pane.

Layout pane

Here's a screenshot of the **Layout** pane:

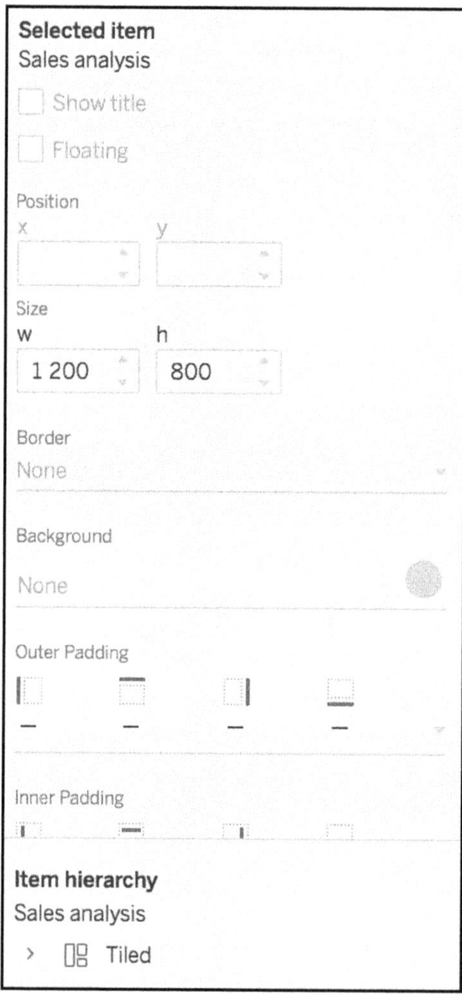

This second pane is handy when you select a Worksheet or Container in the Dashboard. You can show or hide its title, make it floating or not, change its position and size (only for Floating items), add a border, modify the background, and add outer and inner padding. All of that just by using the different options here. Don't be afraid to try those different options, especially the padding, to add some space to your Dashboard.

At the bottom, you'll find the **Item hierarchy**, where you can unfold all your Dashboard items to find them and edit or remove them. Among the different elements, you'll of course see the added Worksheets, but also the different Dashboard objects. Time to discuss them!

Dashboard objects

Most of the objects are very simple. Drag and drop them on the Dashboard to use them. They can be either Floating or Tiled. Here's a list of existing objects:

- **Horizontal/Vertical Container**: Adding these is a great way to control the way the items are added. We'll focus on Containers in the *Tiled, Floating, and Containers Layouts* section.
- **Text**: Adds free text. Great for titles, explanations, credits, and so on.
- **Image**: You can add almost any image files. Great for logos or to add some context to your Dashboard. Once you've added an image, you have a few options when you right-click on it, such as fit or center the image, or add a target URL when someone clicks on the picture.
- **Web Page**: More useful than you think! Of course, you can use it to display a web page in your Dashboard, but you can also link this Web Page to a Dashboard Action to load different URLs based on your data. We will look at this in more detail in the *Go to URL* action section.
- **Blank**: Inserts a blank (such as a void Text); you can use it to add some space.
- **Extensions (2018.2)**: A new feature that enables you to integrate and interact with data from other applications. A list of Extensions is available here: `https://extensiongallery.tableau.com/`.
- **Button (2018.3)**: A very recent feature to navigate between your Dashboards or Worksheets: It adds a button that you can, with a right-click, configure (to specify where to navigate) and personalize (change the image or add a Tooltip).

As you can see, most of the objects are easy to understand and use.

To finish, let's discover the other Dashboard options.

Dashboard options

In the top menu, between **Worksheet** and **Story**, you can find the following options for Dashboards:

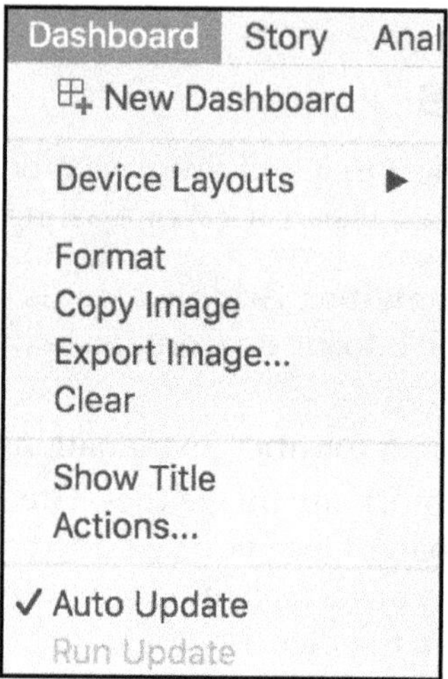

Among those options, the most important one surely is **Actions....** There is a focus on Actions in a later section. **Format** is also handy as you can configure the Dashboard color background, titles, and text objects. The **Grid** is a great new feature if, like me, you like when everything is properly aligned. You can decide whether to show the Grid, and how to configure its size.

To show or hide the Grid, you can also press the *G* key on your keyboard!

All the other options are either straightforward to understand and use (such as **Export Image...**) or just duplicates of option in different places (such as **Device Layouts, Show Title**, and **Auto Update**).

That's it for the basics, but you still have many things to learn about Dashboards! The next section is about building a Dashboard with one of the most significant divisions between Tableau users: Tiled or Floating.

Tiled, Floating, and Container Layouts

When you drag and drop a Worksheet or an object on your Dashboard, you can either use Tiled or Floating Layouts. Some users don't like Tiled; others consider Floating dangerous. Let's see the pros, cons, and how the Containers (once understood) can make you enjoy building Dashboard.

Tiled

Tiled is the default way to add elements on a Dashboard. At the beginning it seems perfect: the grey part where you're dragging an element helps you to see where it'll go, the different items are distributed evenly, and it stays like that when you resize the Dashboard. But rapidly, you'll notice the limits of that technique.

Many cons make it hard to create a great Dashboard with Tiled Layouts:

- You have low control over the size and position of the elements
- Achieving a pixel-perfect Dashboard is a big fight (maybe a little less now that the Grid exists)
- You cannot add a border or a background that outlines multiple items
- You cannot move multiple items at the same time

What about the Floating Layout, then?

Floating

The Floating Layout often became the default layout for people who had terrible experiences with Tiled. With this layout, you can drag and drop any element wherever you want. With the **Layout** pane, you can define the exact position and size of every item. Even better, since 2018.2, you have the Grid, and you can move any Floating elements with your keyword arrows, making it very easy to create a pixel-perfect Dashboard. Among the Worksheet or object options (with the small descending arrow), you can also specify the Floating order to move the element to the back or the front.

The Floating Layout seems to be far better than Tiled, but it's more time-consuming to define the position and size of everything on the Dashboard. Also, the main problem is the time you have to spend if you need to make changes in your Dashboard. Let's say that you want to add a new Worksheet before all the existing ones—you'll need to reset the position and size of all the existing elements on your Dashboard, one by one. And you'll have to do so for every change. That's also the case when you resize the Dashboard (even if Tableau gets better and better at dealing with Floating elements when resizing the Dashboard).

What is the solution if both Tiled and Floating Layouts are not perfect? You guessed right: Containers.

Containers

The purpose of a Container is to group elements inside a shared space and allow you to have better control over those elements inside. Containers can be added both as Tiled or Floating (in the end it's your decision, and both solutions work fine). They can be Horizontal or Vertical. The following screenshots will help you see the difference. First, here's an example of a Horizontal Container:

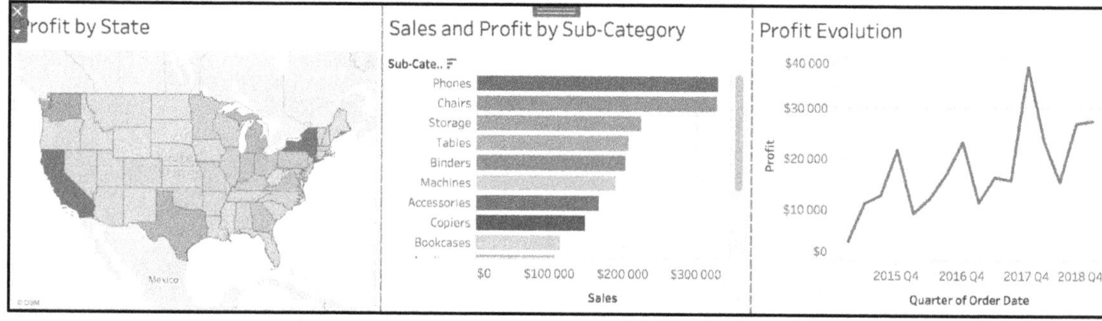

And here's an example of a Vertical Container:

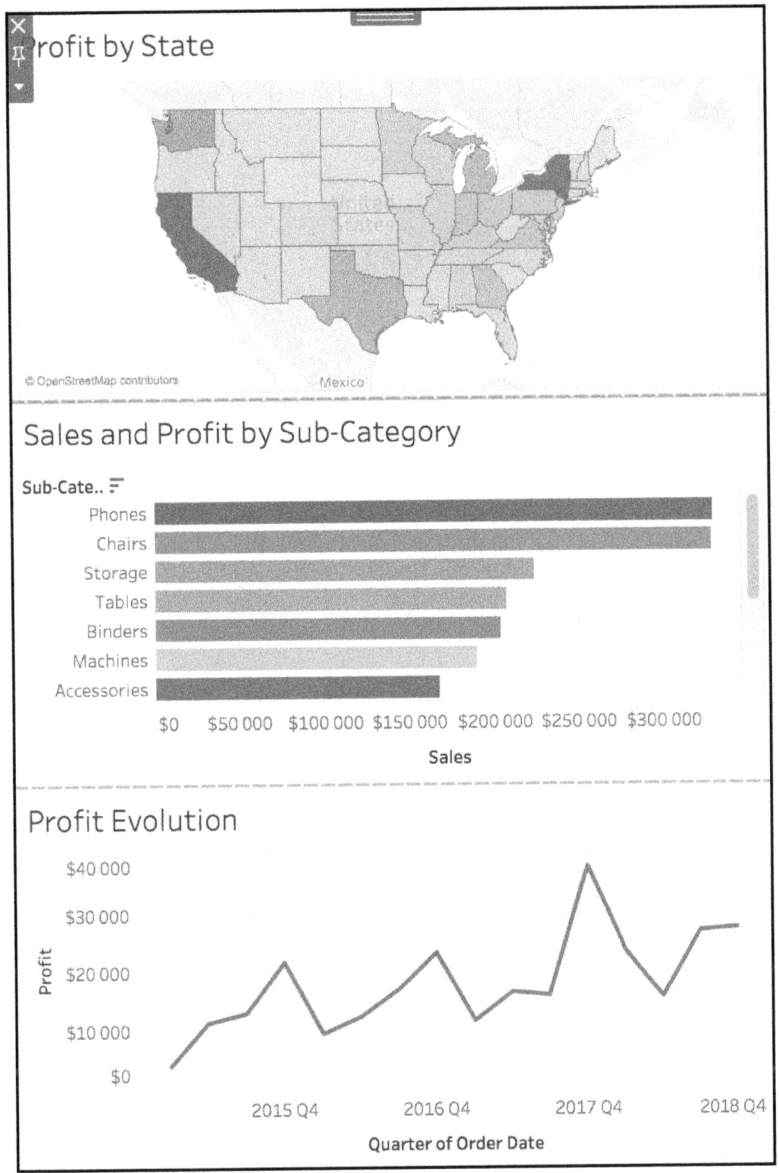

When you add a Container, it'll be empty. Then, you can drag and drop Worksheets or objects inside the Container. You can also add another Container inside a Container, and so on; it's a good practice that I advise you to adopt.

To select the parent layout Container, you can click on **Select Layout Container** among the options (available with a click on the small arrow from a select element), or you can also simply double-click on the *grip* part of every element, as highlighted in the following screenshot:

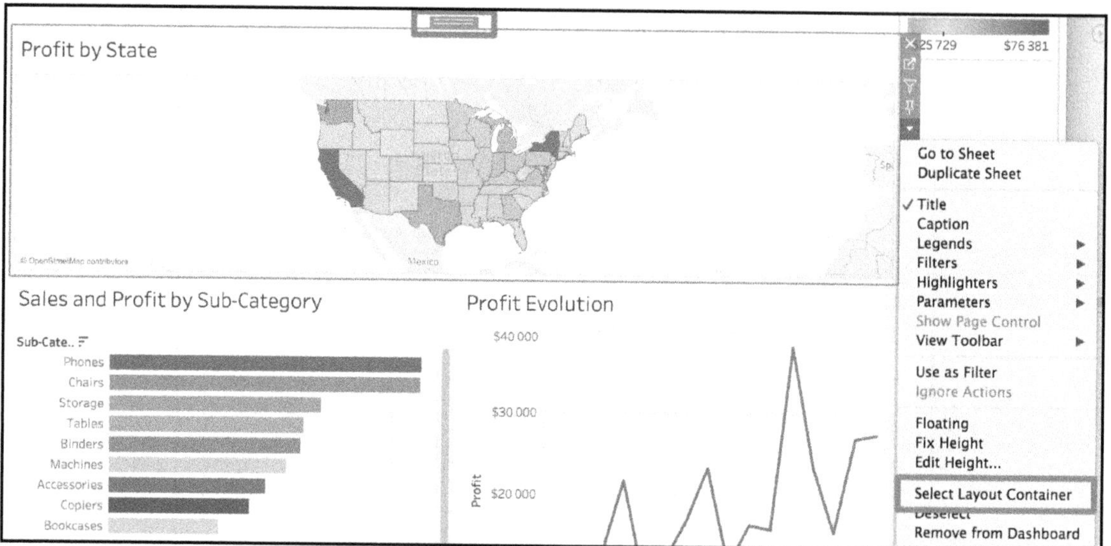

Another way to select a specific Container is to use the **Item hierarchy** in the **Layout** pane.

Containers act like the other elements in a Dashboard. The only difference is that their outline is blue when selected (while the other items are grey).

So why exactly are Containers a good solution? First, every element inside a Container has two great new options:

- **Fix Width** for Horizontal Container or **Fix Height** for Vertical Container. If this option is ticked, the width/height of the element will not change. So if you change the size of your Dashboard or add new elements, the size of the fixed item won't move.

In a Container, you should always have, at least, one element whose width/height is not fixed so it can fill the space or shrink.

- **Edit Width...** for Horizontal Container or **Edit Height...** for Vertical Container. This option allows you to set a specific width/height, in pixels, for every element inside the Container. Did you want pixel-perfect options as you had with the Floating Layout? You have it!

The second reason is that among the Container options, you'll find **Distribute Evenly**, which you can see in the following screenshot:

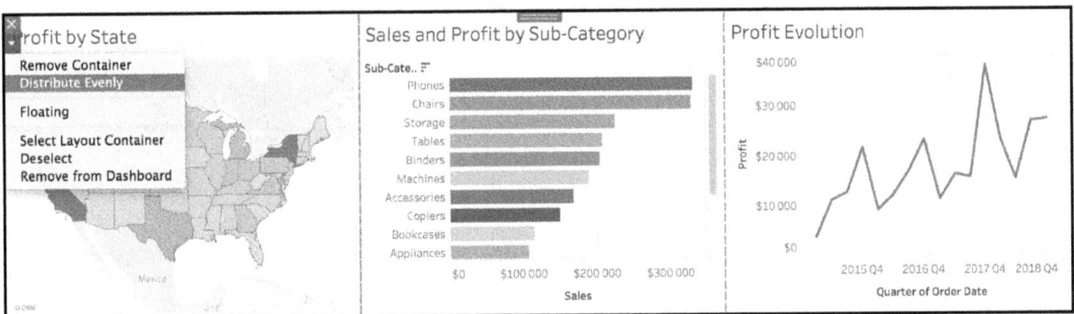

If you select this option, every element inside the Container will have the same width (or height, depending on the Container type) and will resize if you add another item and change the size of the Dashboard.

With Containers, you can set the size of any element to the last pixels, or distribute them evenly. By adding Containers into Containers, you can use all those features at the same time.

Now, let's look at creating your very first Dashboard, the proper way.

A step-by-step guide to building a Dashboard with Containers

We'll start this step-by-step guide with the `Dashboard Start` file mentioned in the introduction. The default Layout is *Tiled* and, to test the functionalities, even if it's generally not a good thing to do, you can set the size of the Dashboard to automatic. Then, follow these steps:

1. Create a new Dashboard and add a **Vertical** Container. As a general rule, you should always start with a Container.
2. Add **Profit by State** in the Container.
3. Add a **Horizontal** Container beneath the map. As you may notice, the grayed area that helps you see where the elements will go is much smaller than with Tiled. Here's what it looks like:

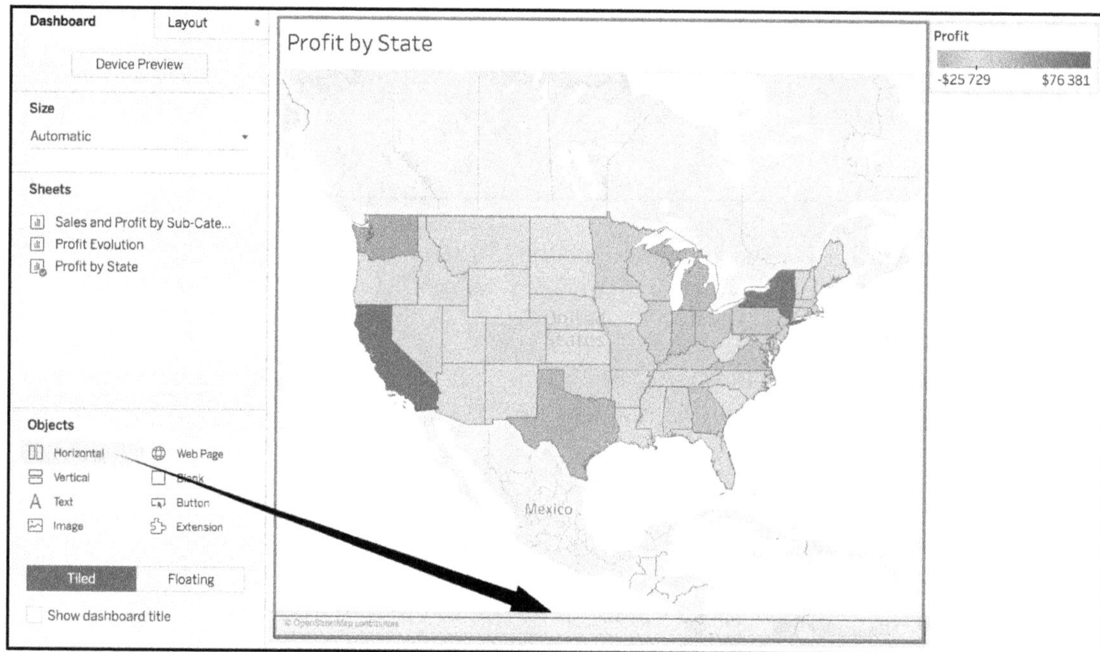

4. Add **Sales and Profit by Sub-Category** in your new Horizontal Container and then add **Profit Evolution** to its right, as displayed in the next screenshot:

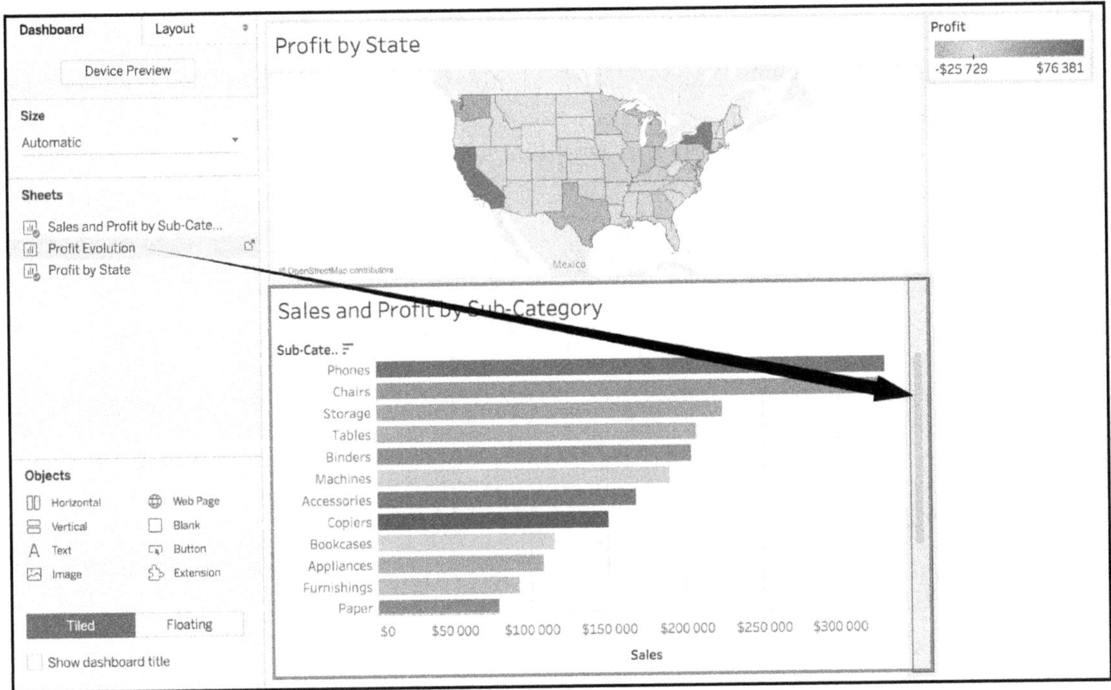

You should now have a Dashboard very similar to the first one presented in this book. Let's see how Containers change everything:

1. We will consider that our most crucial visualization here is the map. We don't want the map to become too small or to resize. Select the Profit by State Worksheet, and click on **Edit Height...** from the options.
2. In the new window that appears, set your desired height (depending on your screen resolution, the right size could be `300` or `600` pixels; try different numbers until the map is close to half the height of the Dashboard). Now, if you play with the size of the Tableau window, you'll see that the map doesn't resize.
3. For the bottom part, we want all elements to have the same size. To do that, first select the Horizontal Container (among the Worksheet options or with a double-click on one of the *grip*, as seen previously) and choose **Distribute Evenly** from the Container options. To test, you can, for example, add a **Blank** next to **Profit Evolution**. All the elements will resize to have the same width.

Mastering the Containers requires a bit of patience and time, but in the end, you'll be able to create great new dashboard very fast and efficiently. Let's continue to explore the uses of Dashboard and add a bit of Action!

Dashboard Actions

Actions are the more common way to add interactivity in Tableau, as well as being the easiest way. Actions have at least one Worksheet as a Source, and a Target (except for URL actions). Depending on the Action type, the target can be another Worksheet, a Dashboard, a Field, or a Set.

You can also add Actions on Worksheets directly. Most of the time, Actions are used to create interactions between the Worksheets in a Dashboard. Anyway, the features are the same.

There are three ways to trigger an Action:

- **Hover**: Just put your mouse over a Mark, and the Action is triggered.
- **Select**: The Action is triggered when you click on a Mark.
- **Menu**: A link is added at the bottom of the tooltip when clicking on a Mark, but the Action is only triggered if you click on that link. The text of the link can be customized.

You'll find the option to add an Action in the top menu, among the other Dashboard options. When you click on **Actions**, a new window opens where you can add different types of Actions, as you can see in the following screenshot:

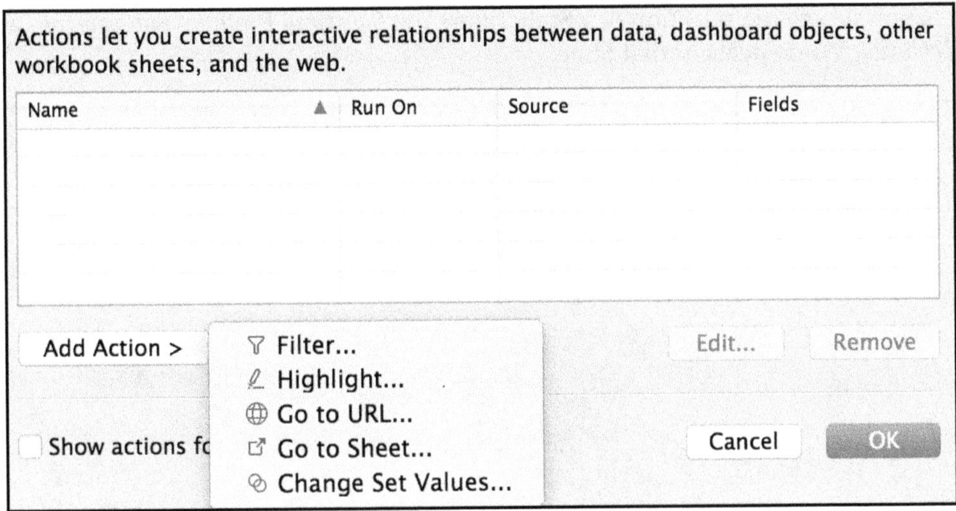

From version 2018.3, there are five different Actions: **Filter...**, **Highlight...**, **Go to URL...**, **Go to Sheet...**, and **Change Set Values...**.

You can download a ZIP file `Actions` from the *Chapter 8: Create Powerful Dashboards and Stories* section of my website, `book.ladataviz.com` (or, browse to `https://ladataviz.com/wp-content/uploads/2018/09/Actions.twbx_.zip`). When you unzip the file, you'll find a Tableau Package Workbook that contains an example for each Actions.

Let's now look at the different types of Actions, starting with the most common one: Filter.

Filter

The Filter action is the most common. From one or multiple Source Worksheets, you can filter one or numerous target Worksheets. The next screenshot is an example of a Filter action where the selection of a State filters the *Sales and Profit by Sub-category* and *Profit Evolution* Worksheets in that State:

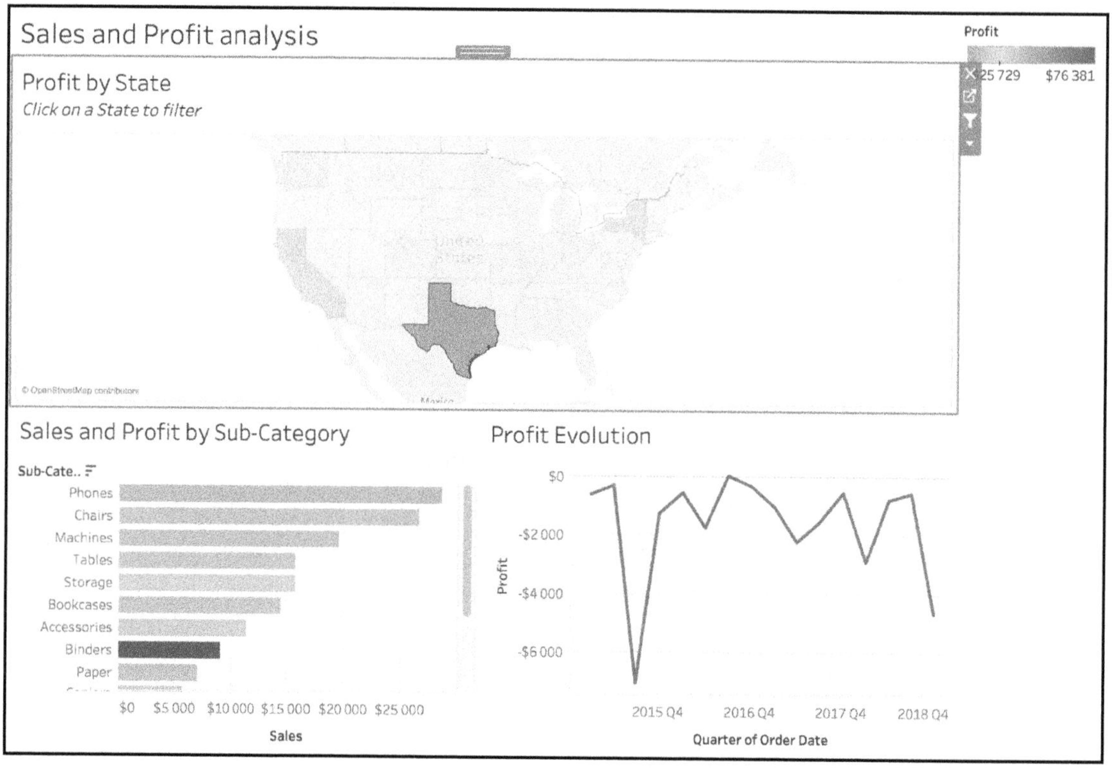

Make sure to specify, in the subtitle of the Worksheet, for example, that there is an Action. Not everyone is aware of Tableau's capabilities and at ease with interactivity in Dashboards.

The **Filter** is the only Action with a quick shortcut: when you select a Worksheet, click on the funnel icon, **Use as Filter**, and a Filter Action is automatically generated with the selected Worksheet as Source and all the others as targets.

If you want to remove a Worksheet from the targeted ones, you can select **Ignore Actions**.

You can, of course, also add a **Filter...** Action from the **Action** menu. You can only edit and configure the Action Filter from the Action menu. Here's the configuration window of the example at the beginning of this section:

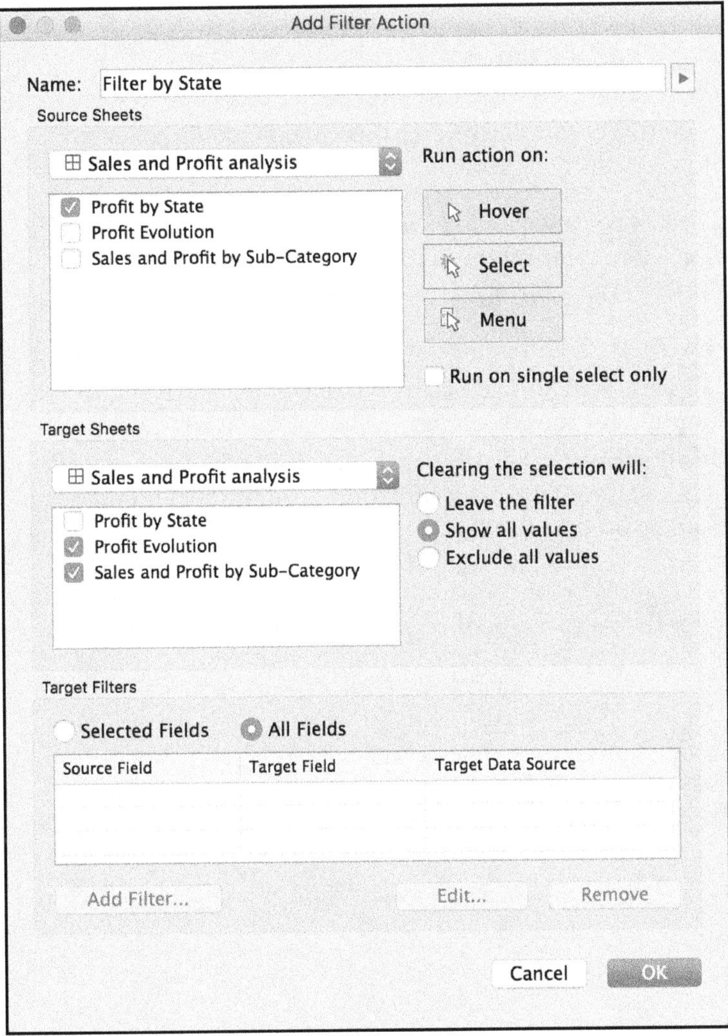

In the configuration window, you can specify:

- The **Name** of the Action—here `Filter by State`
- The **Source Sheets**—in the example, only the **Profit by State** Worksheet triggers an Action
- The trigger—**Select** (a click on Mark) in the example
- The **Target Sheets**—**Sales and Profit by Sub-category** and **Profit Evolution** Worksheets are the Target
- The comportment when clearing the selection—in the preceding example, we decided to **Show all values**
- The **Target Filter**—fields, by default **All Fields** from the Source are filtered on the Targeted Worksheets, but it's possible, by using **Selected Fields**, to choose which fields should be used

With the Action Filter, you can specify exactly which fields need to be filtered. You can also dictate the behavior when clearing the Action (removing the mouse from a Mark for *Hover*, or unselecting it for *Select* and *Menu*). There are three different behaviors:

- **Leave the filter**: When you clear the selection, the Filter stays as it is.
- **Show all values**: When you clear the selection, you'll see all the values. It's the default option for the *Select* trigger.
- **Exclude all values**: When you clear the selection, the target Worksheets turn blank as all values have been excluded. It's only when you trigger the Action again that they'll display some data.

The Target Worksheets can be in another Dashboard. Then, when you trigger the Action, you'll be automatically redirected to that Dashboard.

The next Action is **Highlight**. It's a great way to help the users understand the related Fields in your Dashboard.

Highlight

The Highlight action is also used quite often. From one or multiple Source Worksheets, you can highlight fields on one or multiple Target Worksheets. The next screenshot is an example of a Highlight Action where hovering over a category from one of the two bottom Worksheets automatically highlights it on both visualizations:

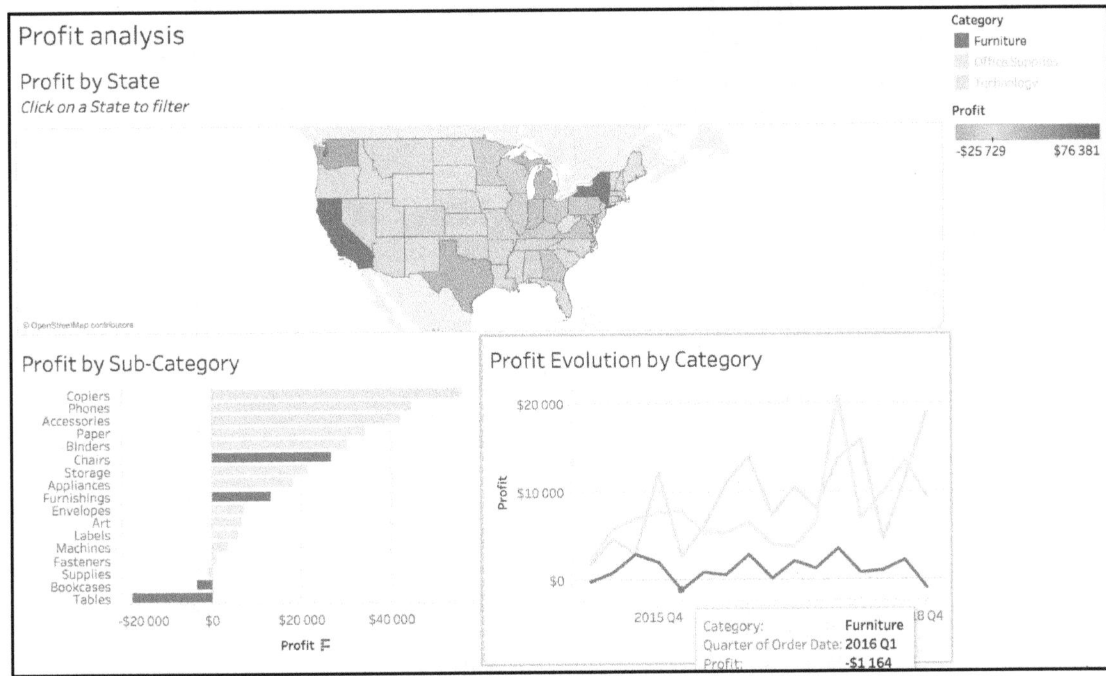

In the preceding screenshot, we hover over the **Furniture** category in the **Profit Evolution by Category** Worksheet, and thanks to the Highlight Action, we can easily spot this category on the *Profit by Sub-Category* Worksheet.

As for the Action filter, you can specify what fields will be highlighted.

Contrary to the Action filter, the fields that you want to highlight needs to exist in both the Source and the Target Worksheets (no matter where, it can be in the **Detail** Mark property, for example).

When you add a Highlight action, a new window opens where you can configure it. Here's the configuration window of the preceding Highlight example:

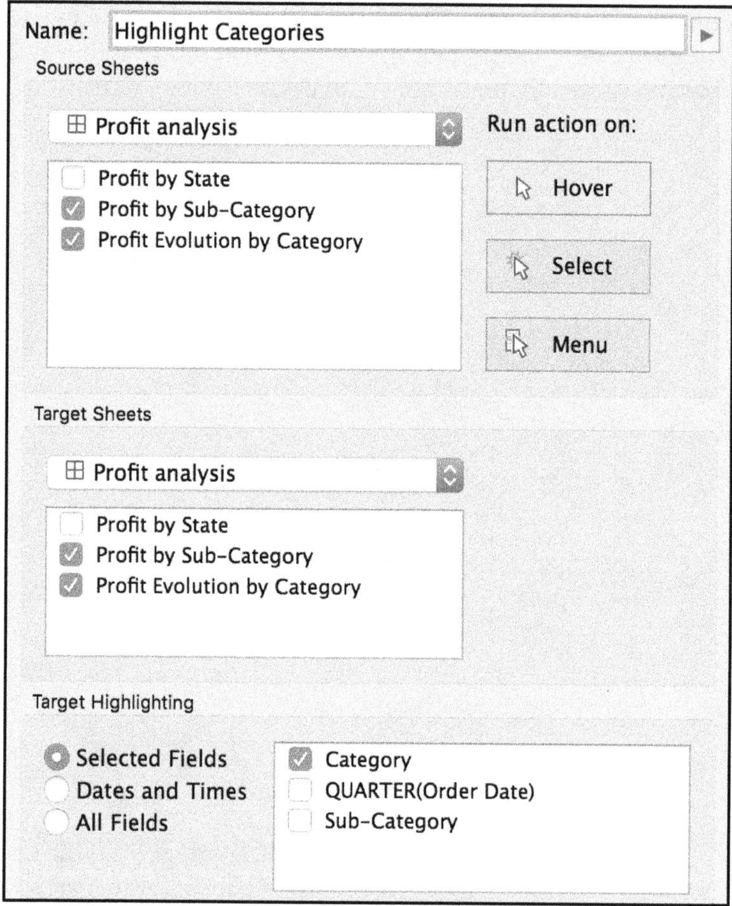

In the configuration window, you can specify the following:

- The **Name** of the Action — here `Highlight Categories`.
- The **Source Sheets**—in the example, the Action sources are both **Profit Evolution by Category** and **Profit by Sub-Category**.
- The trigger, a **Hover** on a Mark in the example.
- The **Target Sheets**—the same as the Source here, as we want to highlight both Worksheets at the same time.

- The **Target Highlighting** fields (by default, **All Fields** from the source are highlighted on the Targeted Worksheets, but it's possible, by using **Selected Fields**, to choose which ones to use) — in the example, we want to highlight only the **Category**.

The next Action, **Go to URL...**, is a great way to add interaction with the outside world to Tableau.

Go to URL

The **Go to URL...** action allows you to open a website directly inside the Dashboard or in a new window. If there is a **Web Page** object in your Dashboard, the website will open inside it; if not, the site will load in a new browser window. But there is more: you can create dynamic URLs based on the fields in the Worksheets to open different web pages based on your data.

The following screenshot is an example of a Go to URL Action that you can easily reproduce (just put the **Profit by State** Worksheet on the left, a **Web Page** object on the right, and follow the configuration window):

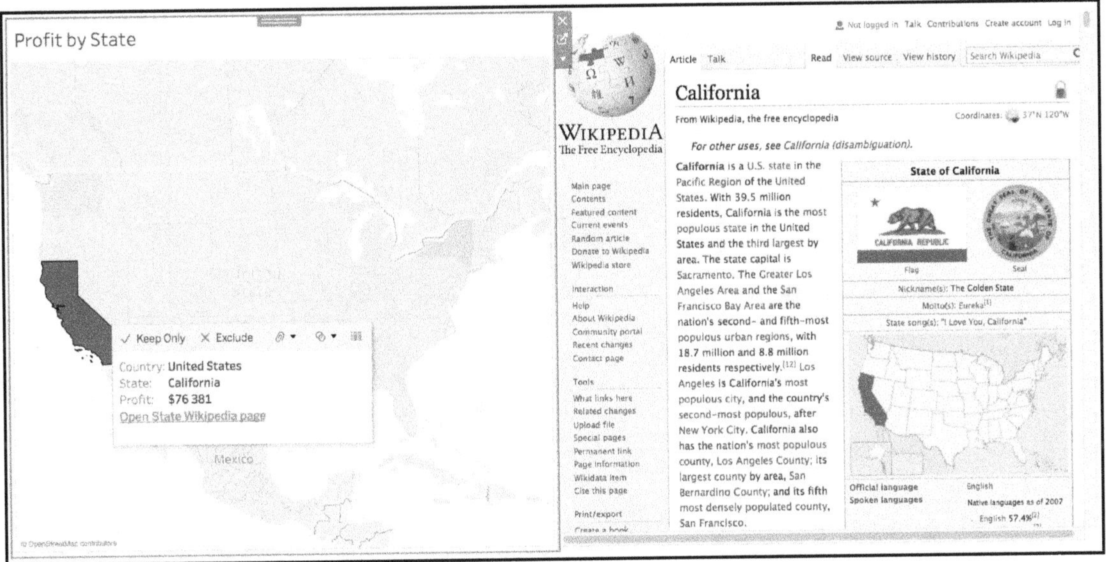

In this example, when you click on a *State* in the map, you have a menu saying **Open State Wikipedia page**. If you click on the link, the Wikipedia page of the State opens on the right, in a Web Page object.

When you add a **Go to URL...** Action, a new window opens where you can configure it. Here's the configuration window of the preceding example:

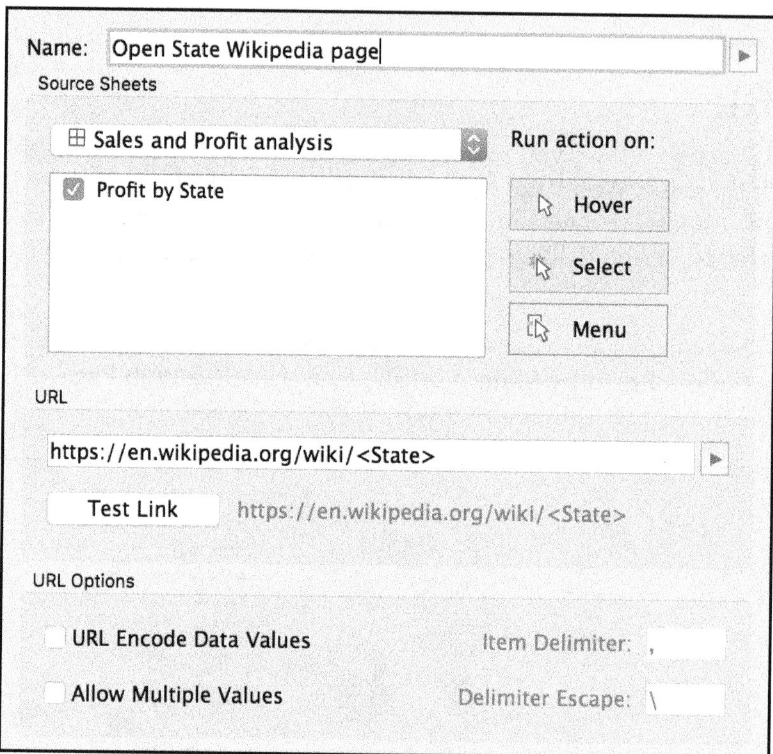

In the configuration window, you can specify the following:

- The **Name** of the Action — `Open State Wikipedia page` here.
- The **Source Sheets**—in the example, we have only one Worksheet, **Profit by State**.
- The trigger—in the example, a **Menu** that opens when you click on a Mark.
- The **URL**—you can write any URL you want, and add, thanks to the small arrow at the end, fields from the Worksheet. In the example, we wrote `https://en.wikipedia.org/wiki/` and we added the **State** field at the end. You can use the **Test Link** button to verify that your URL is working.

There are also two options. The first, **URL Encode Data Values**, needs to be set if the field's value contains special characters (such as `&`). The second needs to be set if the URL accepts a list of values as a parameter. If you check the second option, you'll also need to specify the **Item Delimiter** and **Delimiter Escape** escape.

Before Tableau 2018.3, those were the only three actions available. In the new version of Tableau, two further Actions are available. Let's get started with *Go to Sheet.*

Go to Sheet

The **Go to Sheet...** Action is very simple. From one or multiple Source Worksheets, you can navigate to a Target Worksheet or Dashboard.

Here's the configuration window when you add a **Go to Sheet...** Action:

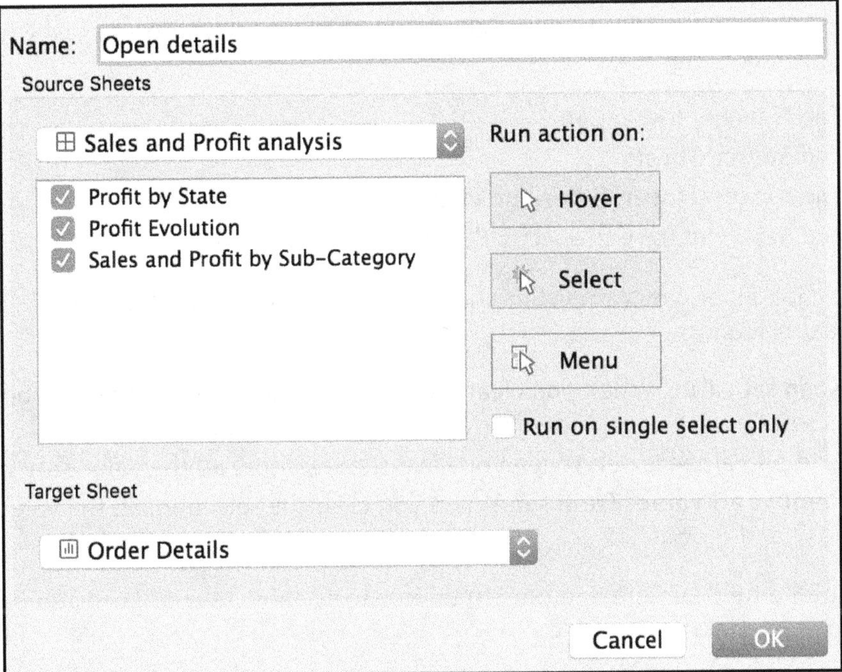

In this configuration window, you can specify the following:

- The name of the Action
- The Source Sheets
- The trigger
- The Target Sheet—it can be a Worksheet or a Dashboard

The next Action allows you to play with Sets!

Change Set Values

The **Change Set Values** Action allows you to select, visually, the values to put in a Set. From one or multiple Source Worksheets, you can update the values of a Set in your data source to impact other visualizations in your Workbook.

When you create a Change Set Values Action, a configuration window opens where you can specify the following:

- The **Name** of the Action
- The **Source Sheets**
- The trigger (**Hover**, **Select**, or **Menu**)
- The **Set**—you have to specify the Data Source and the Set

As for the Action Filter, you can dictate the behavior when clearing the Action. There are three different behaviors:

- **Keep set value**: When you clear the selection, the current values of the Set stays as selected
- **Add all values to set**: When you clear the selection, all the values are In the Set
- **Remove all values from set**: When you clear the selection, all the values will be Out of the Set.

Let's do a guided tutorial with Sample-Superstore to see how to configure and use this new Action:

1. Create a first Worksheet, `Sales by State`, which is a map of each **State** with **Sales** in **Color**:

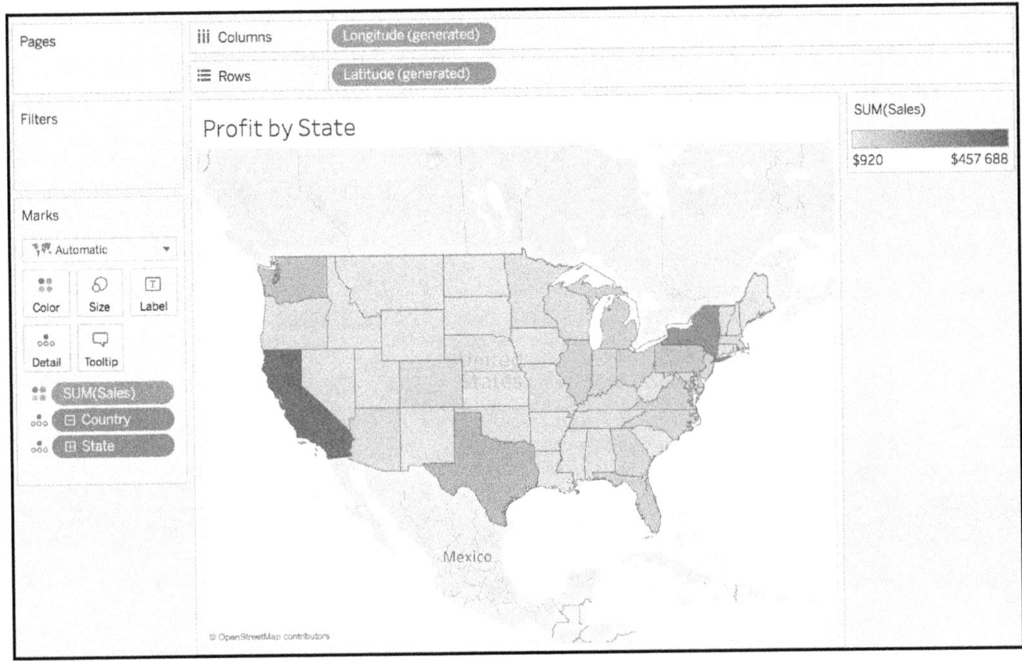

2. Create a Set, `State Set`, based on **State** (right-click on the **State** field and go to **Create**, then **Set**). In the **Edit Set** window, select **Use all**:

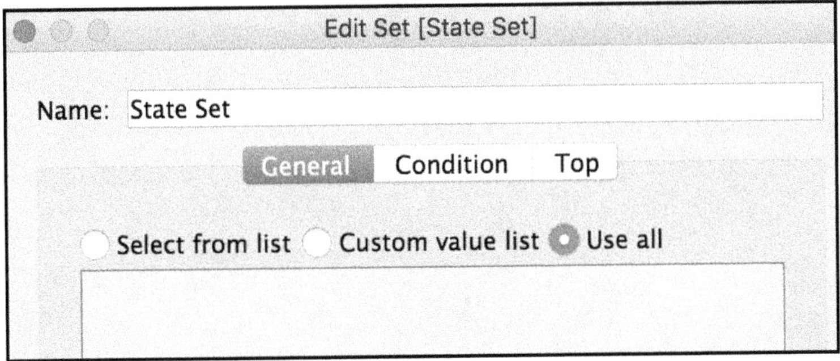

3. Create a second Worksheet, `Sales by Sub-Category`, with **Sales** in **Rows**, **Sub-Category** in **Columns**, and the new set, **State Set** in **Color**. Here's how your Worksheet should look:

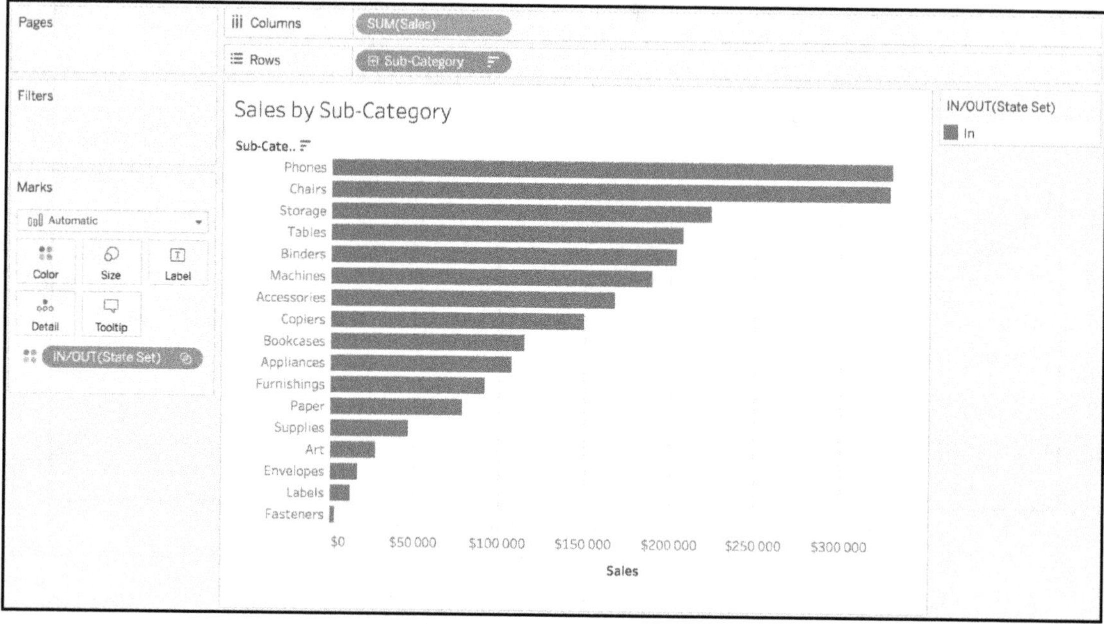

4. Create a Dashboard: first add **Sales by State**, then **Sales by Sub-Category** on its right. Add an Action and choose **Change Set Values....** We want to update the **State Set** when we click on a State on the Map. When we clear the selection, all the values will be **In** the Set. The next screenshot illustrates the configuration of the Action to do that:

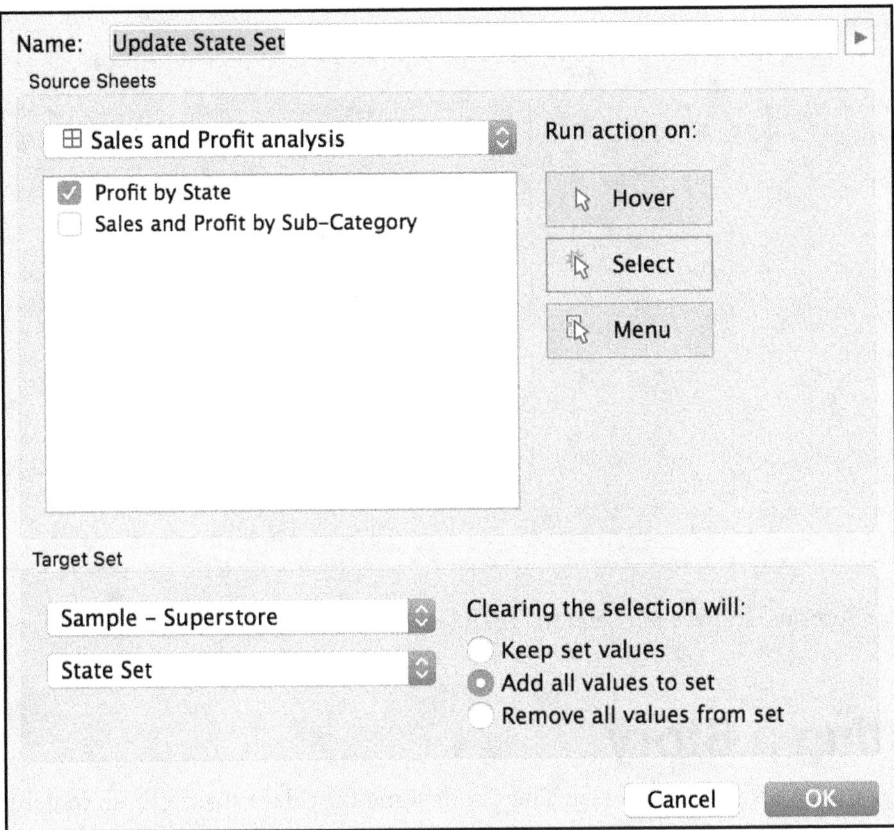

5. Let's test our Action! When you select one or multiple States on the map, you should see, on the right, the portion of sales coming from the selected State. In the following screenshot, you can see the portion of sales coming from the State of *California*:

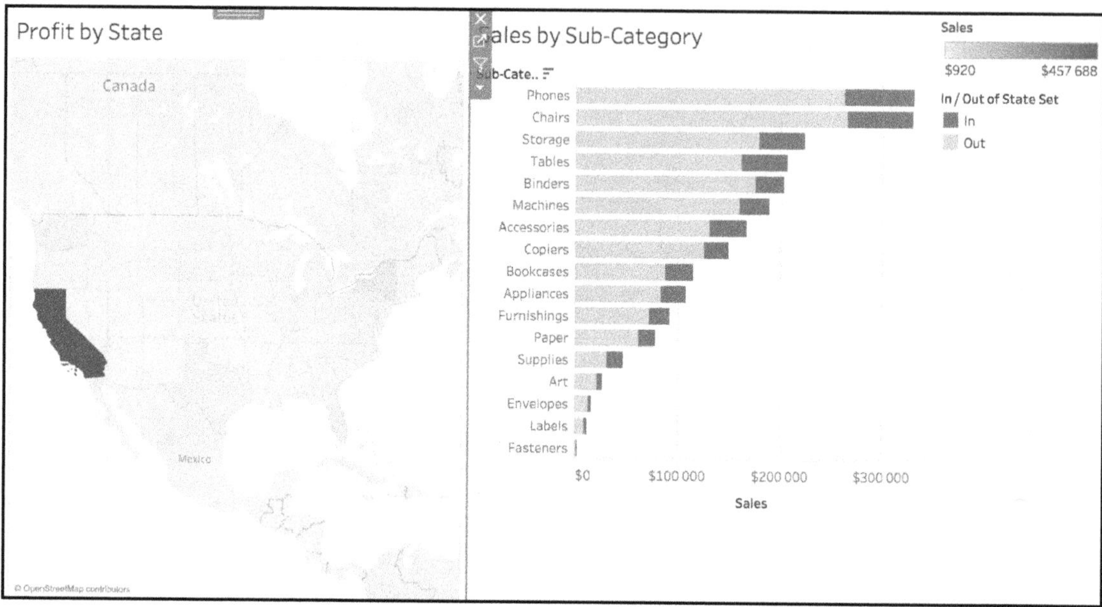

That's it for Actions. In the next section, we'll see how to create a **Story**.

Creating a Story

Stories in Tableau are often misused. They're designed for data storytelling, to control what the users will discover, in which order, and to add annotations and explanations while the Story goes on. Do not add a Story to use it as a menu to navigate between the Dashboard. For that, you have the Buttons object and the Go to Sheet Action.

To add a Story, you can either click on the icon at the bottom right, click on **New Story** from the **Story** top menu, or use the **New Story** button in the toolbar, highlighted in the following screenshot:

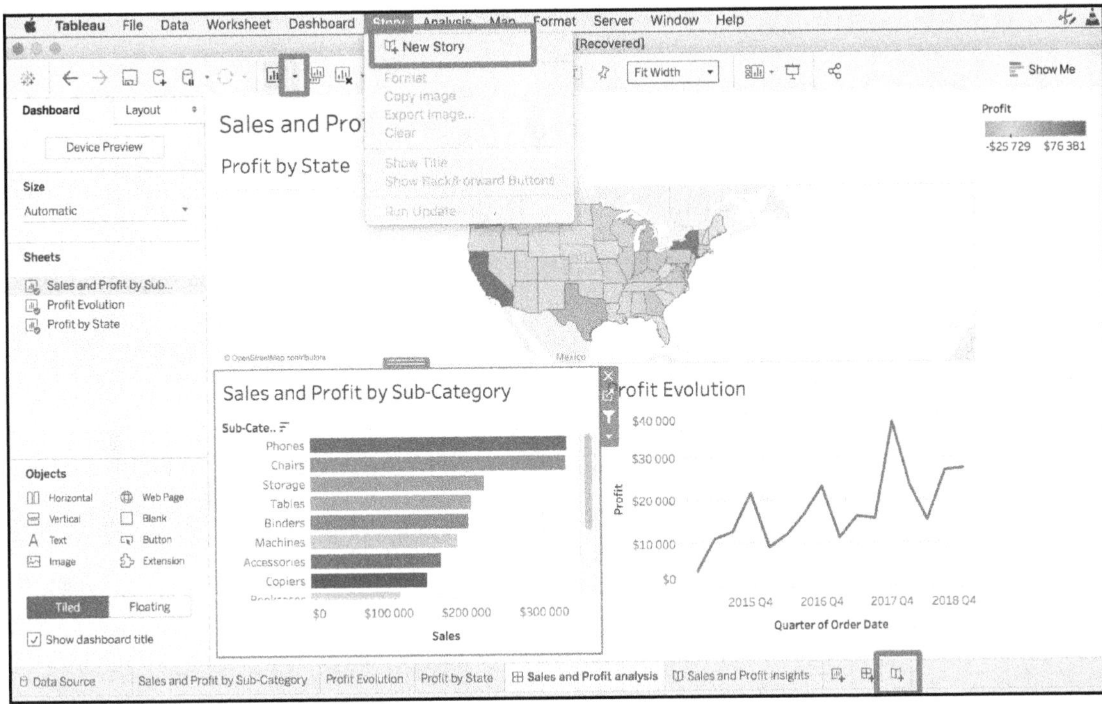

The Story workplace is quite similar to the Dashboard one. You'll find a central blank part where you can drop Worksheets and Dashboards. Again, modifying the Dashboards or Worksheets will impact the Story. On the left pane, you can also find two tabs: **Story** and **Layout**.

The main difference with Dashboards is the **Story points**. A Story is usually composed of multiple Story points. Each of them can contain only one Worksheet or one Dashboard. Here's an example of three Story points:

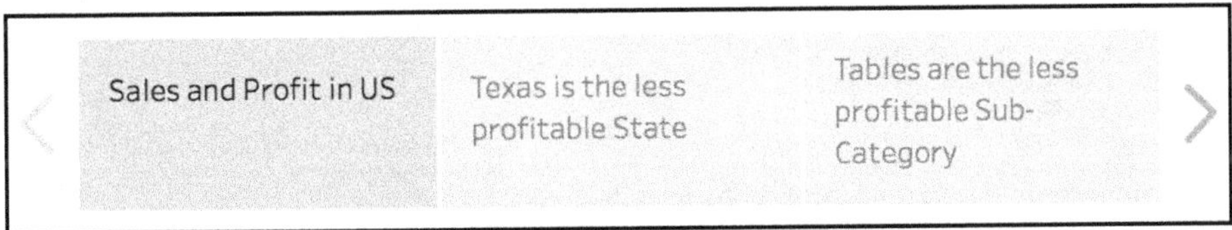

When you hover over a Story point, you'll see these four icons:

Each icon has a unique function:

- The first one lets you remove the Story point
- The second icon reverts the changes to the latest updated state
- The third one refreshes the Story point and memorizes the changes
- The last icon saves the current changes in a new Story point

Now that we've seen the basics, let's start to create a Story.

How to build a Story

You begin to build a Story in a Story point. Each Story point contains one Worksheet or one Dashboard. You can add them with a simple drag and drop to the central blank area (or use double-click). Then, you can create a new blank Story point and add another Sheet, or duplicate the existing one to Highlight or Filter a specific element. The Story keeps the selection, Highlights, and Filter added on each Story point.

We will now create a Story together. To reproduce the example, you can use the Dashboard that we built earlier (with a Filter Action when you click on the map):

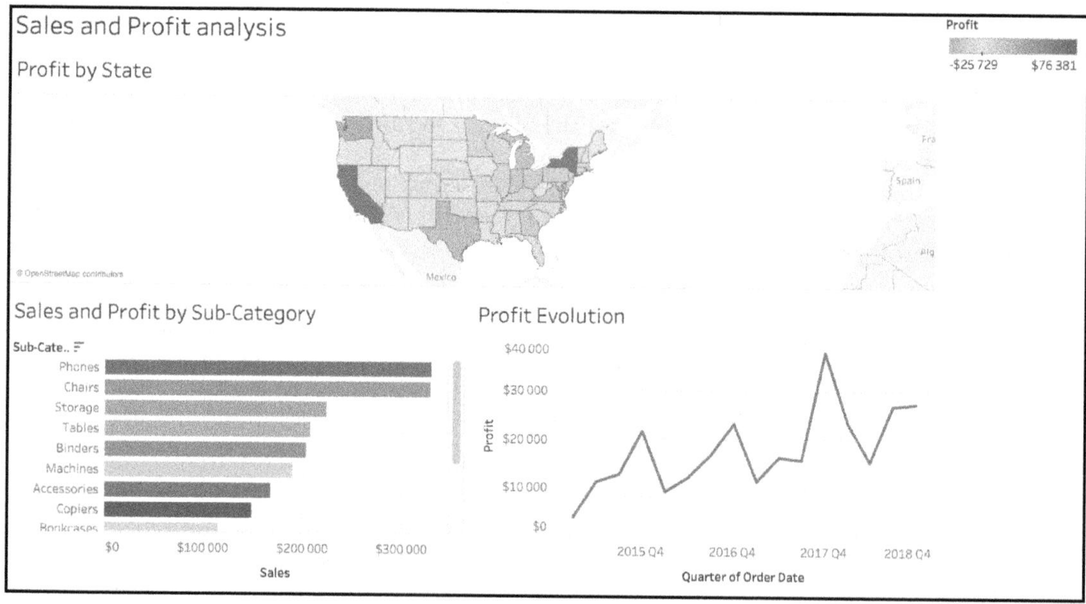

Let's start:

1. Create a new Story and call it `Sales and Profit Insights`.
2. Drag and drop the **Sales and Profit Analysis** Dashboard in the Story, and change the caption of the Story point to `Sales and Profit Analysis`:

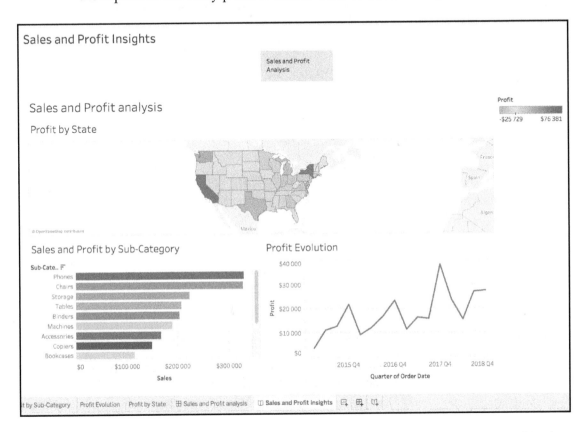

3. Duplicate the current Story point with the button on the right, highlighted in the following screenshot:

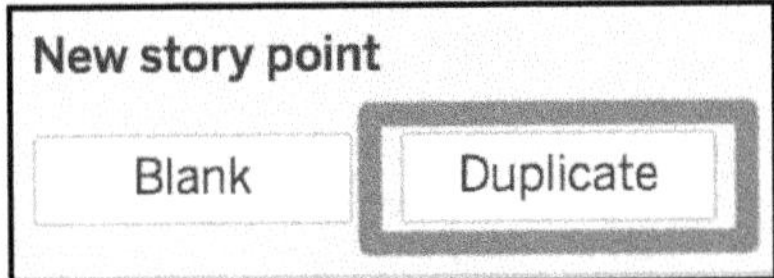

4. On this new Story point, click on the State of *Texas*, change the caption to `Texas is the less profitable State`, and click on the **Update** button in the Story point to save the changes. Here is how your **Story** should look, and where to find the button to update:

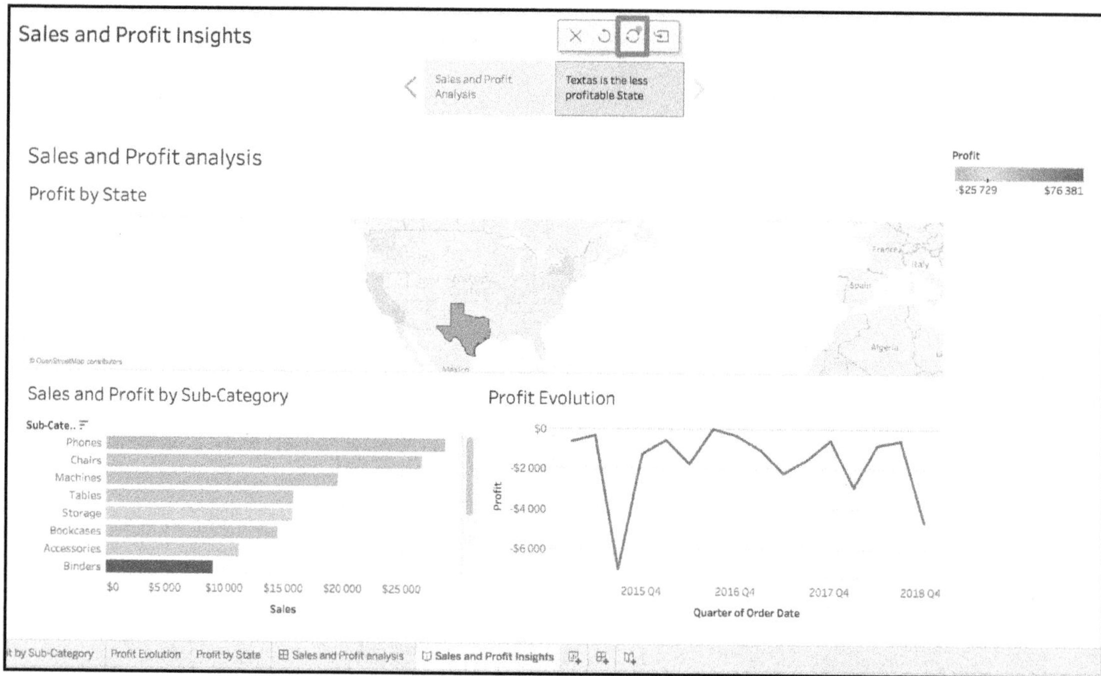

5. On the **Texas is the less profitable State** Story point, click on the State of *California* and then click on the **Save as New** button:

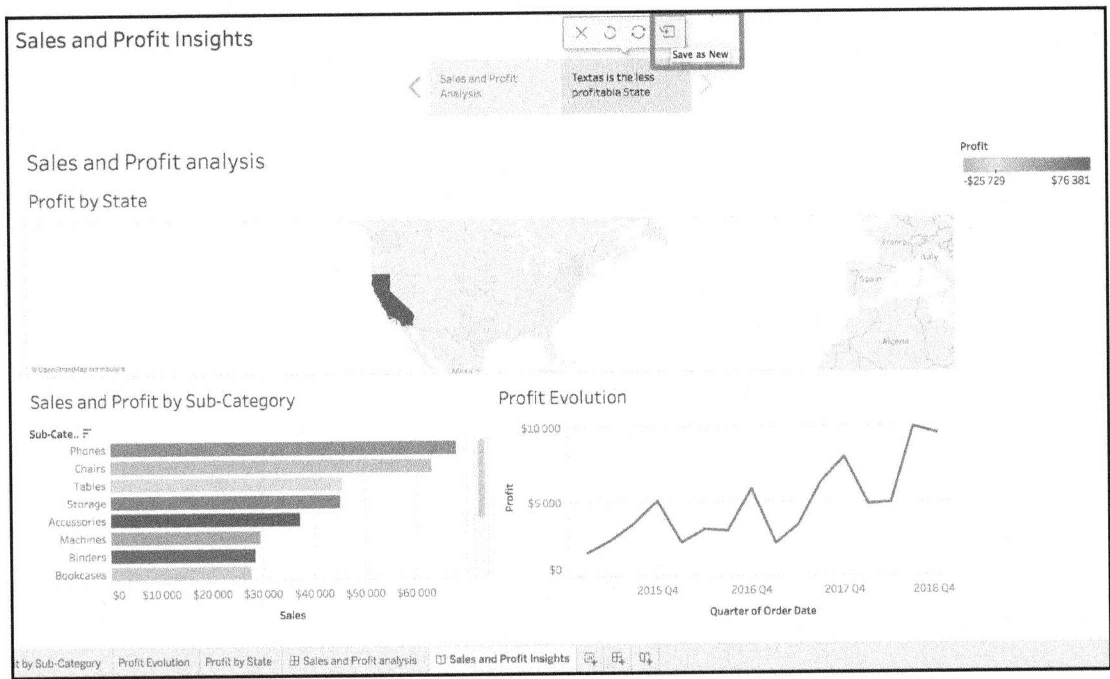

6. The **Save as New** button will take the current state of the Story point and copy it into a new Story point while reverting the changes of the existing one to the last updated state. You can change the caption of the new Story point to `California is the most profitable State`. Here's the final look of your Story, with three Story points:

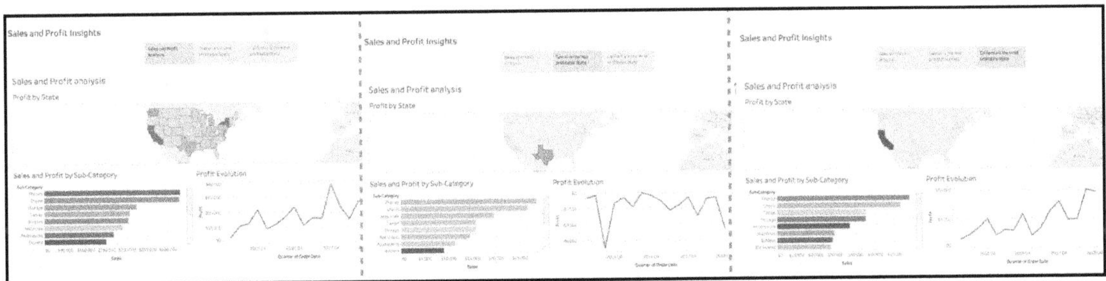

Now that you know how to build a Story, let's see how to customize it.

Story options

There are not many options to customize a Story.

On the left, at the bottom of the **Story** pane, you'll find three options:

- Add floating Text to add some context
- Show or hide the title of the Story
- Change the size of the Story

On the **Layout** pane, you can change the style of the Story navigator. There are four different styles:

- **Caption boxes** (the default style):

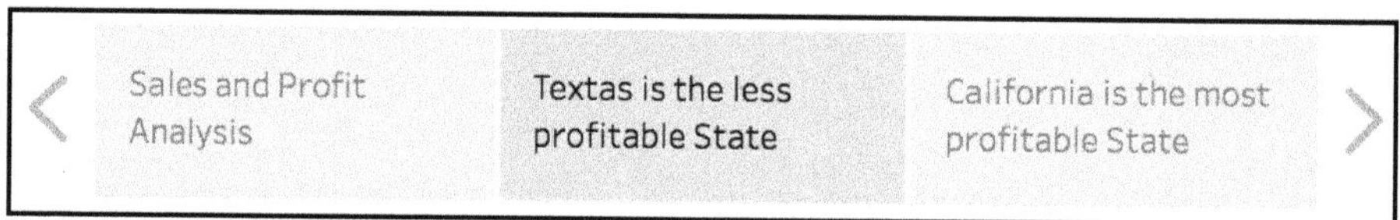

- **Numbers**:

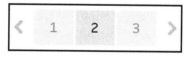

- **Dots**:

- **Arrows only**:

On the same pane, you can also show or hide the arrows.

Finally, on the **Story** top menu, you'll find similar options as for Dashboards: **Format**, **Copy Image**, **Export Image**, and **Clear**.

Stories should not be a mystery to you anymore. Use them to amaze your audience with great insights from your data!

Summary

Congratulations! This chapter was one of the longest while being one of the most important. Building Dashboards is an essential feature of Tableau.

We started with the basics of how to build a Dashboard and the different panes in the workplace, we also saw the objects that you can add to personalize it. Then, we explored the different types of Layout with all the pros and cons of Tiled, Floating, and Containers. To finish with the Dashboard part, we focused on Actions, how to use them, and how they can add interactivity. After that, we learned about Stories. You learned how, and when, to build and customize them.

In the next chapter, we'll discover a new Tableau product: Tableau Server. All the things you learned from the beginning of the book were about creation—how to create Data Sources, how to create Worksheets, and how to create Dashboards and Stories. The next chapter is about sharing; we'll look at how to publish your work to make it globally accessible. Ready to go online?

9
Publish and Interact in Tableau Server

Time to share your work! This chapter is the culmination of everything you've learned since the beginning of the book. It's also the first chapter where you'll use a tool other than Tableau Desktop: Tableau Server/Online.

As Tableau Server and Tableau Online are almost the same product (learn more in `Chapter 2`, *The Tableau Core*), we will use the name Tableau Server for both products throughout this book.

Thanks to Tableau Server, users can connect to new or published Data Sources to create new analyses, and open published Workbooks to interact with them. In this chapter, our main focuses are:

- Introduction to Tableau Server
- Tableau Server Contents
- Publishing and modifying Contents
- Interacting with published Contents
- Device layout

This book doesn't cover Tableau Server installation and configuration. It's a technical aspect that requires you to work with your IT team. You can find all the useful information and guidance for installation on the Tableau website: `https://onlinehelp.tableau.com/current/guides/everybody-install/en-us/everybody_admin_intro.htm`.

To reproduce the example in this chapter, you need access to Tableau Server. Also, we are going to use a Tableau Workbook example: **World Indicators**. You can find it on the Start page when you open Tableau, highlighted in the following screenshot:

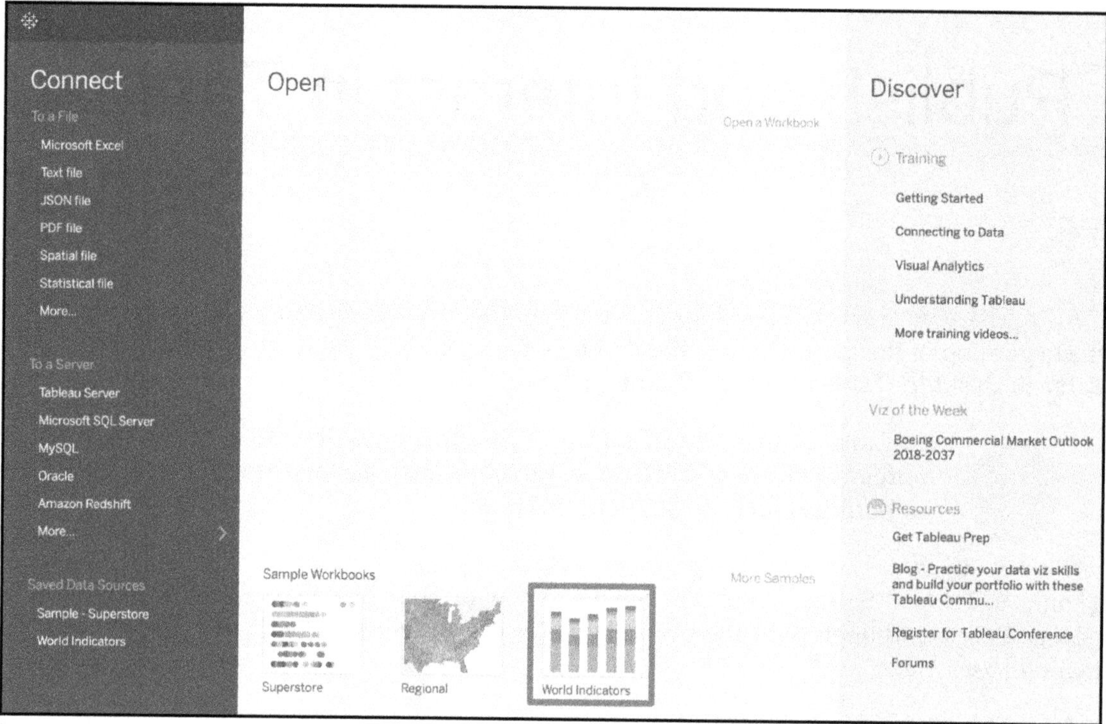

Introduction to Tableau Server

Tableau Server is an online tool made for sharing Workbooks and Data Sources. Usually, only a few people use Tableau Desktop to build Data Sources and Workbooks. They can publish their work on Tableau Server, making it available to many users who can access them using Tableau Server on the web. There are two ways of using Tableau Server:

- In a browser, to access the Tableau Server web page and interact with published content (Data Sources, Workbooks, and Views)
- In Tableau Desktop, to publish Data Sources and Workbooks, or connect to published Data Sources and open published Workbooks

To connect to Tableau Server on a browser, you have to write the URL of your server and enter your login and password. If you're using Tableau Online, the URL is `https://sso.online.tableau.com`.

Tableau Server can have multiple sites. Each site is a different environment with different Users, Groups, and Content.

Once you're logged in, you can access the Tableau Server **Content** page:

Tableau Server Content page

Depending on your accreditations, on the top menu you'll see either:

- Different tabs to create new Users, Groups, Schedules, and configure the server
- A search bar to look for published Contents

On the web, you also have different ways to interact with Workbooks (create custom views, comment, subscribe) and you can use Web Authoring to create new Workbooks based on new or published Data Sources. All the interactions are detailed in the *Interacting with published Contents* section of this chapter.

To connect to Tableau Server on Tableau Desktop, go to the **Server** menu and select **Sign in**. A new window opens where you can enter your credentials. Once logged in, you can open published Data Sources from the **Connect** pane and open published Workbooks from the **Server** menu. You can also publish Content on Tableau Server from Tableau Desktop.

Let's explore the different Content you can find on Tableau Server.

Tableau Server contents

There are four different types of content on Tableau Server:

- **Projects**: The highest level; it is like a folder. You can only create new projects from the web. A project can contain other Sub-Projects, Workbooks, and Data Sources.
- **Workbooks**: Either created on Tableau Desktop and published here, or directly created in Tableau Server. Each Workbook is composed of one or multiple Views.
- **Views**: All the different Worksheets, Dashboards, and Stories in the Workbooks.
- **Data Sources**: Created on Tableau Desktop and published here. You can use them to build new analyses directly on the web.

Tableau Server has two ways of displaying Content. Since the 2018.3 version, the default way is called **Mixed Content** and shows different types of Content in the same place.

As you can see in the following screenshot, in the **Sales** project, there is one other Sub-Project, one Workbook, and one Data Source, all displayed in the same place:

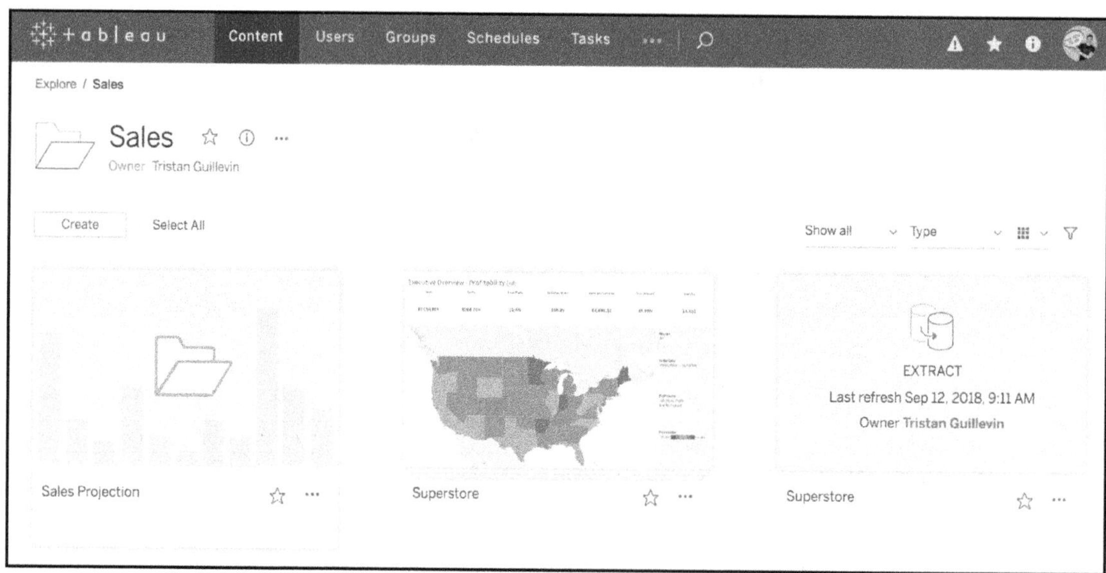

The Sales project dashboard

Before Tableau Server 2018.3, the different types of Content were separated into different tabs, and you needed to select a specific tab to see its Content. You can see, in the following screenshot, the same **Sales** project, traditionally displayed:

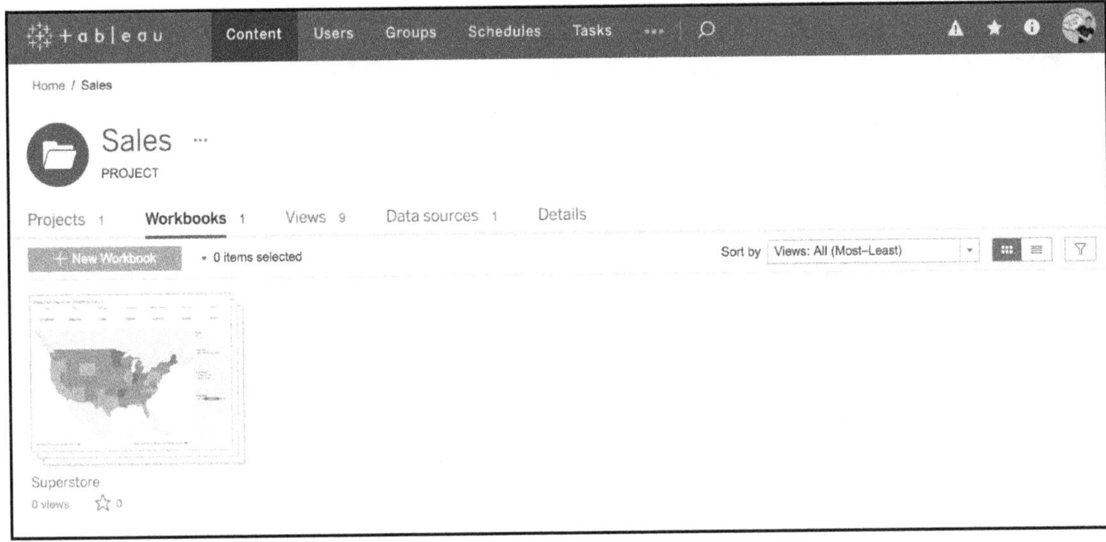

Workbooks in Sales project

Let's look at how to publish Data Sources and Workbooks from Tableau Desktop.

Publishing and modifying contents

On Tableau Desktop, you can connect to Tableau Server from the **Sign In...** option on the **Server** menu, highlighted in the following screenshot:

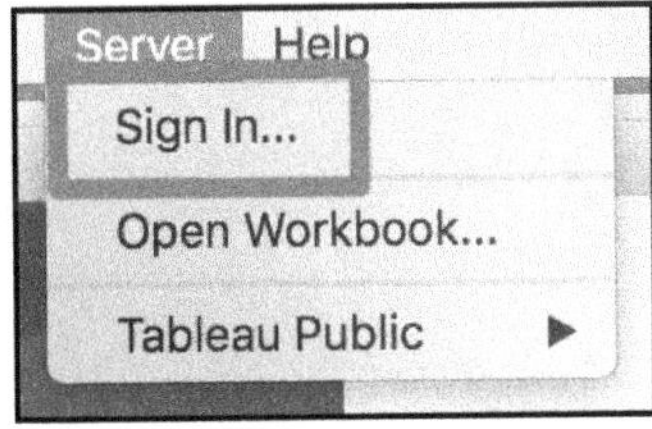

Then, you can publish the Data Source and the Workbook individually. The most common way to work with Tableau Server is first to publish the Data Source (usually an Extract), then the Workbook.

Why and how to publish a data source

Tableau Desktop is the only tool that allows you to connect to a Dataset, create an Extract, publish it to Tableau Server, and schedule an automatic refresh. Publishing a Data Source offers multiple advantages:

- All the customization (aliases, default properties, hidden or renamed fields, and so on) is saved. If you, or another Tableau Server User, uses the published Data Sources, all the customization work is already done.
- All the newly created fields (Calculated Field, Sets, Groups, Parameters, Bins, and so on) are also saved. All Workbooks based on the same published Data Source use the same calculation. If, for any reason, a calculation needs to change, all the Workbooks are impacted at the same time.
- On Tableau Server, you can plan to refresh published Data Sources automatically. All the Workbooks connected to the same published Data Source are updated at the same time. You are alerted if a refresh fails.
- Tableau Server users who don't have Tableau Desktop can create new analyses on the web, based on published Data Sources.

As you can see, if you plan to work in a professional environment with Tableau, publishing Data Source is crucial.

Publishing a Data Source is easy: on a Worksheet, right-click on the Data Sources name and click on **Publish to Server** (you can also find this option from the **Data** menu on top). When you click on this option, a new window opens to configure the published Data Source:

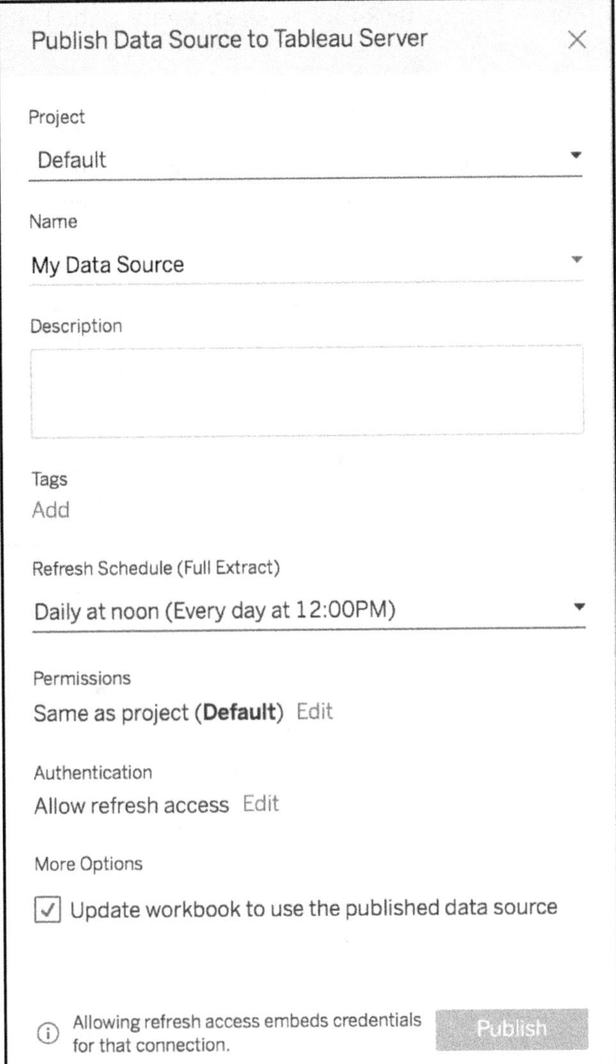

In this window, you can do the following:

- Select the Project associated with the Data Source
- Change the name of the published Data Source
- Add a description to help the users understand it (optional)
- Add tags to find it more easily (optional)

- Schedule a refresh Extract task (optional, and only if the Data Source is an Extract connected to a server)
- Modify the Permissions, by default similar to the Project (you will learn more about permissions and security in `Chapter 13`, *Deal with Security*)
- Allow the refresh or not by including the credentials in the Data Source
- Update the Workbook to use the published Data Source or not (I advise you to validate this option)

You can't publish a Live Data Source connected to a file; Tableau automatically generates an Extract before publishing.

When the Data Source is published, a new web page opens, letting you know that it is ready, as you can see here:

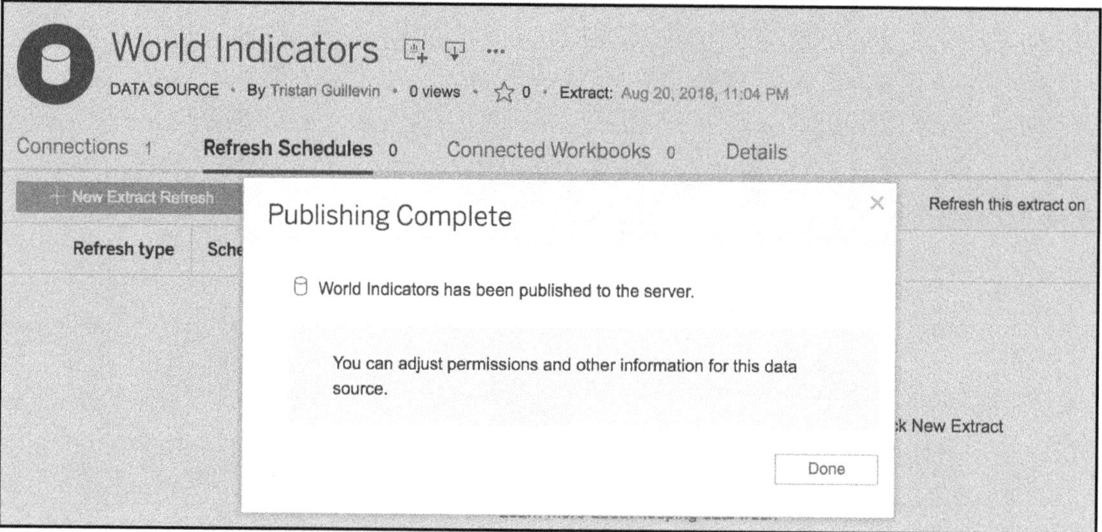

We will see, in the *Interacting with published Contents* section, how you can interact with published Data Sources on the web.

Using a published Data Source, instead of an Extract, in a Workbook makes it lighter (the Extract is no longer inside the Workbook), more secure (you can control who has access), and sustainable (the changes and updates in the Data Source are automatically impacted in the Workbook).

Fortunately, only you and the Users of your choice can modify a published Data Source, making it secure and preventing anyone from making unwanted changes. Unfortunately, this security makes it a bit more complicated to modify a Data Source. Let's discover how to do it.

Modifying a published Data Source

A published data source cannot be modified. You cannot change the aliases or the Groups, for example, and if you try to edit a Calculated Field, Tableau creates a copy; the original calculation cannot be edited.

To modify a published Data Source, you need to download it, edit the local file on your computer with Tableau Desktop, and republish it. Don't worry; it's easier than it sounds!

Instead of **Publish to Server**, a published data source has another option, **Create Local Copy**:

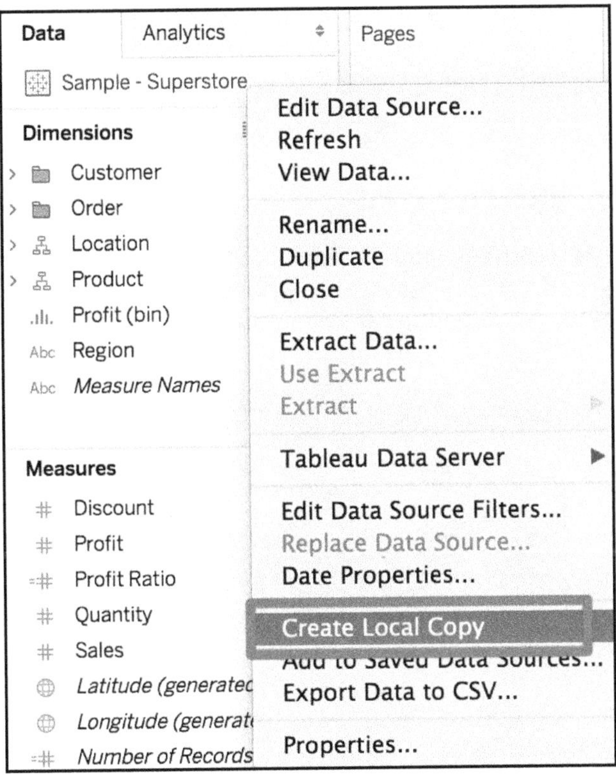

This option automatically downloads the Data Source and adds it to the Workbook as a second source. When you create a local copy, it appears directly in the **Data** pane:

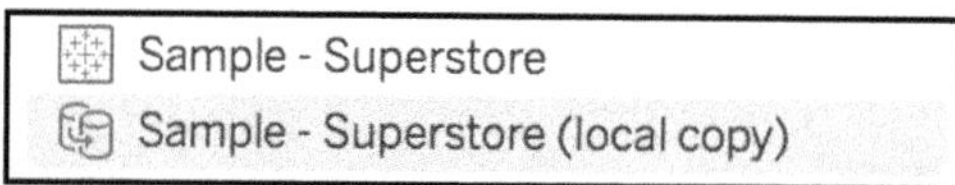

You can make all the modifications you want on the local copy. Then, when you are done, publish it again with the same name to replace it. When publishing a Data Source with the aim of replacing an existing one, be sure you see this message:

If you still feel a bit uncomfortable with this process, there is a step-by-step guide at the end of this section where we will go through all the processes.

Publishing a Workbook

Publishing a Workbook is the best way to share your work. You can control who has access to your visualizations, and Tableau Server users have many ways of interacting with it. It's easy to publish a Workbook; in the **Server** menu, you have the **Publish Workbook...** option:

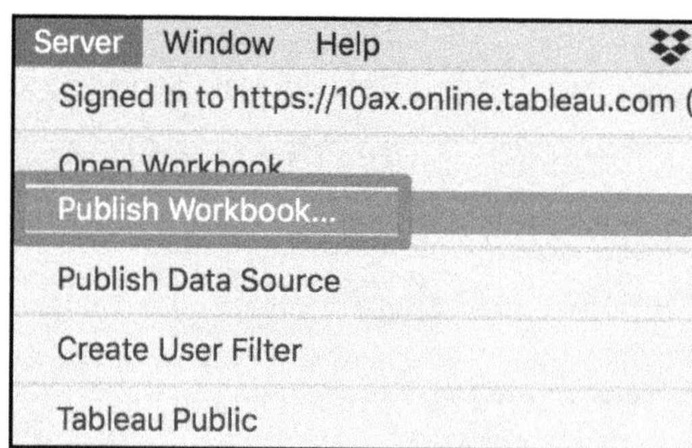

You can publish a Workbook without publishing the Data Source. In that case, the Data Source is embedded inside the Workbook. You can also plan a refresh for Workbooks with embedded Data Sources (with the condition that you integrate the credentials).

When publishing a Workbook, a new window opens, as illustrated here:

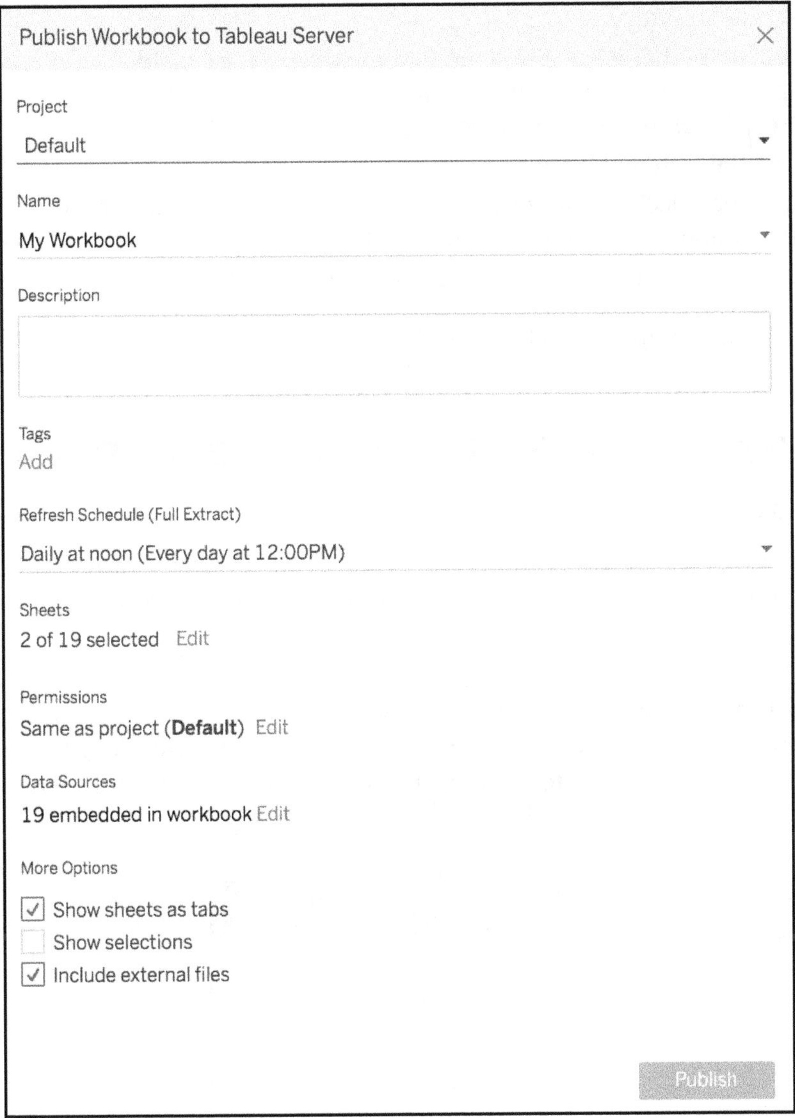

In this window, you'll find similar options as when you publish a Data Source (choose the project, change the name, add a description and tags, set the Permissions, and schedule a refresh Extract). However, there are a few new options:

- Select the visible Sheets (Worksheets, Dashboard, and Stories). The Sheets you decide not to publish are hidden, but still available if you open the Workbook in Tableau Desktop.
- Decide whether you want to embed the data source inside the Workbook or publish it separately and automatically. You can also decide here to allow a refresh by embedding the credentials or not.
- Show the different Sheets as tabs or not
- Show the selections or not (usually not, unless you want to highlight specific information every time a user opens the Workbook)
- Include external files or not (usually yes to include shapes and pictures)

To finish, let's go through a concrete example.

Step-by-step guide – publishing and modifying your work

In the tutorial, we'll go through all the steps: create a new Project on Tableau Server, publish the Data Source, the Workbook, and modify the Data Source.

Ready? Let's go:

1. On Tableau Server, create a new project and name it `World Indicators Tutorial`. You can create a new project from the **Content** page. In the following screenshot is the **Create** | **Project** button on the new Mixed Content browsing experience is highlighted:

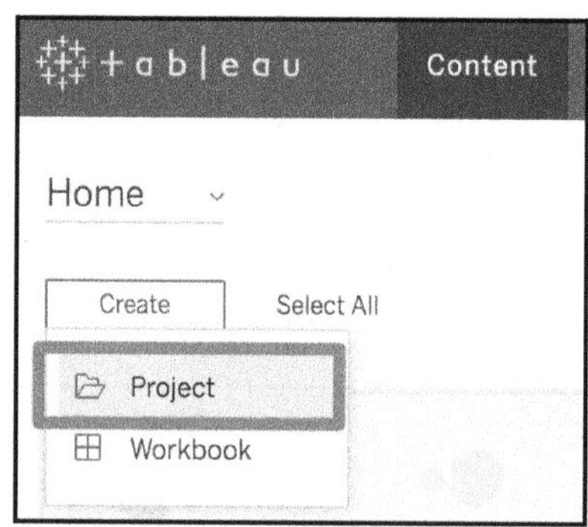

Alternatively, in the traditional browsing experience, highlighted here:

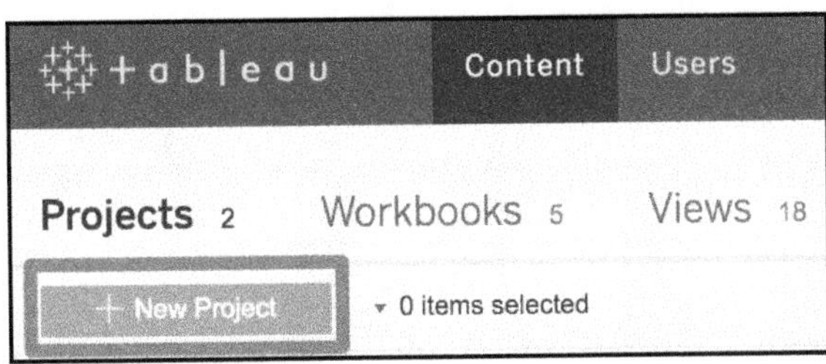

2. Open Tableau Desktop and sign in on Tableau Server (from the **Server** menu)
3. Open the **World Indicators** sample Workbook from the start page
4. On the first Worksheet, *Population*, right-click on the Data Source and select **Publish to Server**.
5. On the **Publish Data Source** configuration window, select the **World Indicators Tutorial** project, be sure that **Update workbook to use the published data source** is checked, and click on **Publish** (an Extract is automatically generated because the Data Source is connected to a file).
6. When the Data Source is published, a new web page opens where you can check in that it's in the right project, as highlighted in the screenshot:

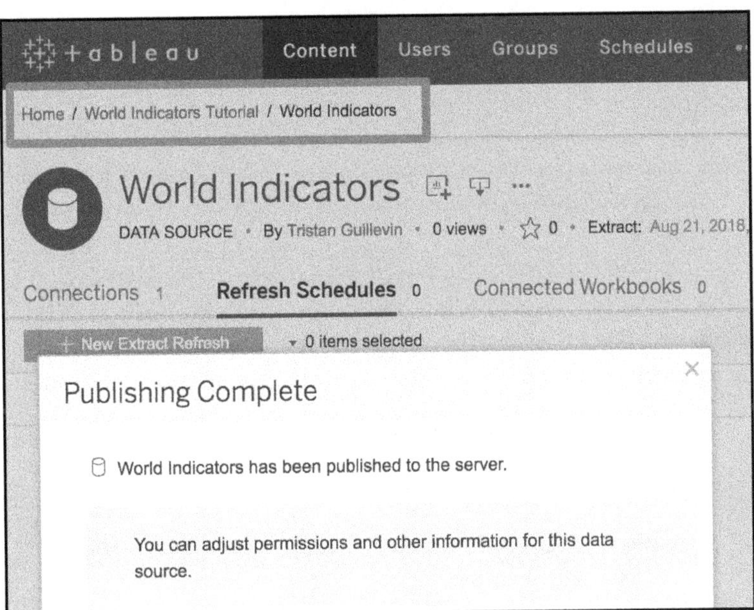

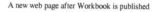

7. In Tableau Desktop, click on the **Server** top menu, and click on **Publish Workbook**.
8. Publish the Workbook in the **World Indicators Tutorial** project (be sure that the **Show sheets as tabs** option is checked).
9. A new web page opens that displays the different Views:

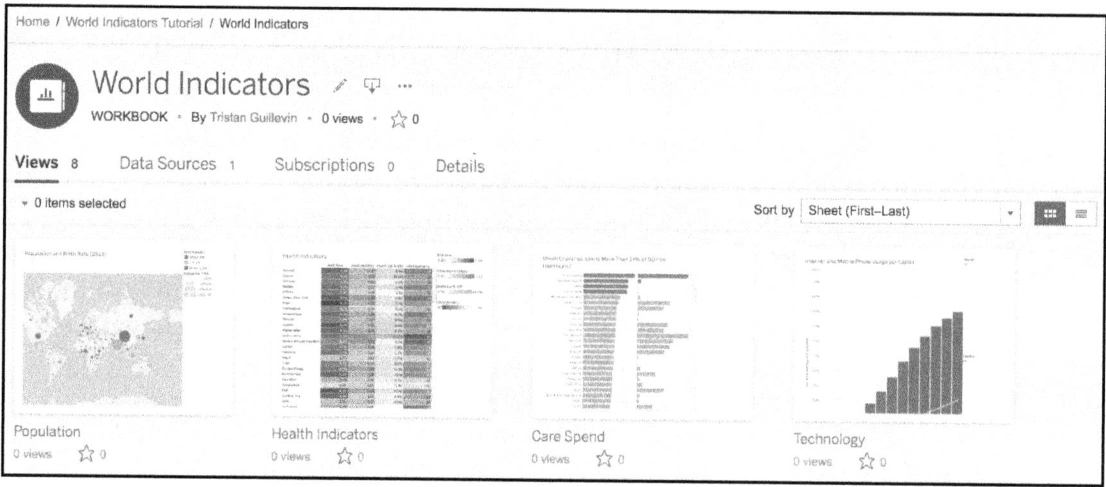

A new web page after Workbook is published

Wait! You forget to add the **GDP per Capita** field in a folder! You need to modify the published Data Source:

1. On Tableau Desktop, right-click on the published Data Source, select **Create Local Copy**, and chose a location in your computer (you can delete the file afterwards).
2. To make sure that the changes have no impact on the visualization, you can replace the published Data Source with the local copy. To do that, right-click on the published Data Source, then choose **Replace Data Source**. A new window appears where you have to select the local copy as the replacement:

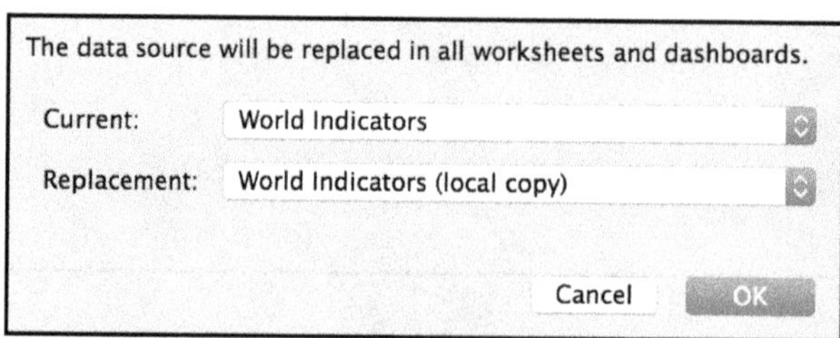

3. Verify that Tableau uses the local copy instead of the published Data Source—the check mark (✓) next to the icon indicates which Data Source is used.
4. Right-click on the published Data Source and select **Close** to remove it. It should be removed instantly (if there is an error message, it means that some Worksheets are still using this Data Source).
5. On the **World Indicators (local copy) Data Source**, right-click on the **GDP per Capita field**, and go to **Folders**, then **Add to Folder**, and select **Development**:

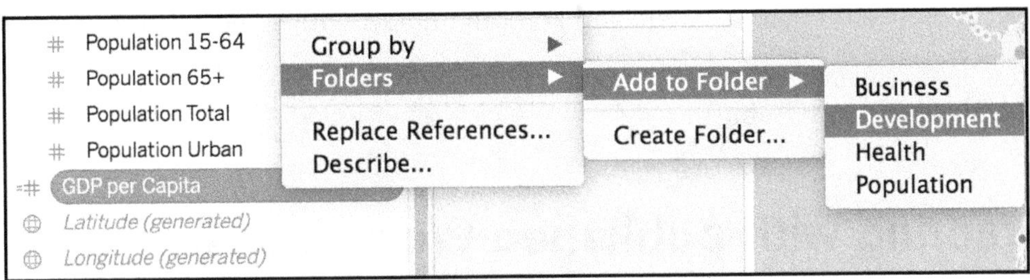

6. Right-click on the **World Indicators (local copy)** Data Source and click on **Publish to Server**.
7. In the configuration window, be sure to select the **World Indicators Tutorial** project and change the name to `World Indicators`. A message should warn you that you will replace an existing Data Source:

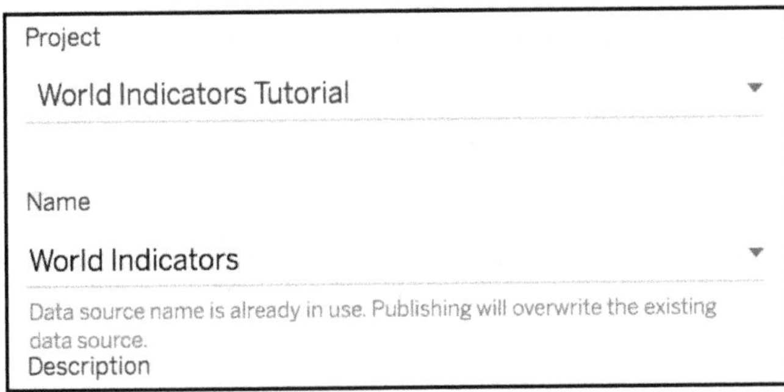

8. The Data Source is now updated! You don't need to republish the Workbook because it uses the published Data Source that you updated.

Keep this Project and the two published contents, as we'll use them in later sections.

You can verify in Tableau Server that, in your **World Indicators Tutorial** project, you can see the Workbook and Data Source. Now that you have some published Content, let's see how to interact with it!

Interacting with published Contents

Publishing your Workbooks and Data Sources presents many advantages. Tableau Server users can interact with your Content, and you can interact with someone else's Content.

Let's start by discovering all the options you have when you open a published Workbook on Tableau.

Interacting with published Workbooks

When you click on a Workbook on Tableau Server, you can see all its Views (Worksheets, Dashboards, and Stories). Then, when you click on a View, Tableau Server opens it in reader mode. You cannot modify it, but you can use the Filters, Highlighters, Parameters, and Actions, and see the Tooltips.

Above the visualization, there is a special toolbar with some new features, only available on Tableau Server. The left part, not very interesting even if useful, allows you to undo, redo, or revert all your actions, and refresh or pause the Data Source. You won't use that part much. However, the right part of the toolbar, displayed in the following screenshot, is very interesting:

There are height features available on Tableau Server only. **Edit** is explained in the next part about Web Authoring, **Share** provides a link to the View and the code for embedding it in a web page, and **Full Screen** speaks for itself. We'll focus more on the five remaining features. For each feature, you can test and reproduce the examples with the **Tourism** View of the **World Indicators** Workbook published earlier, highlighted here:

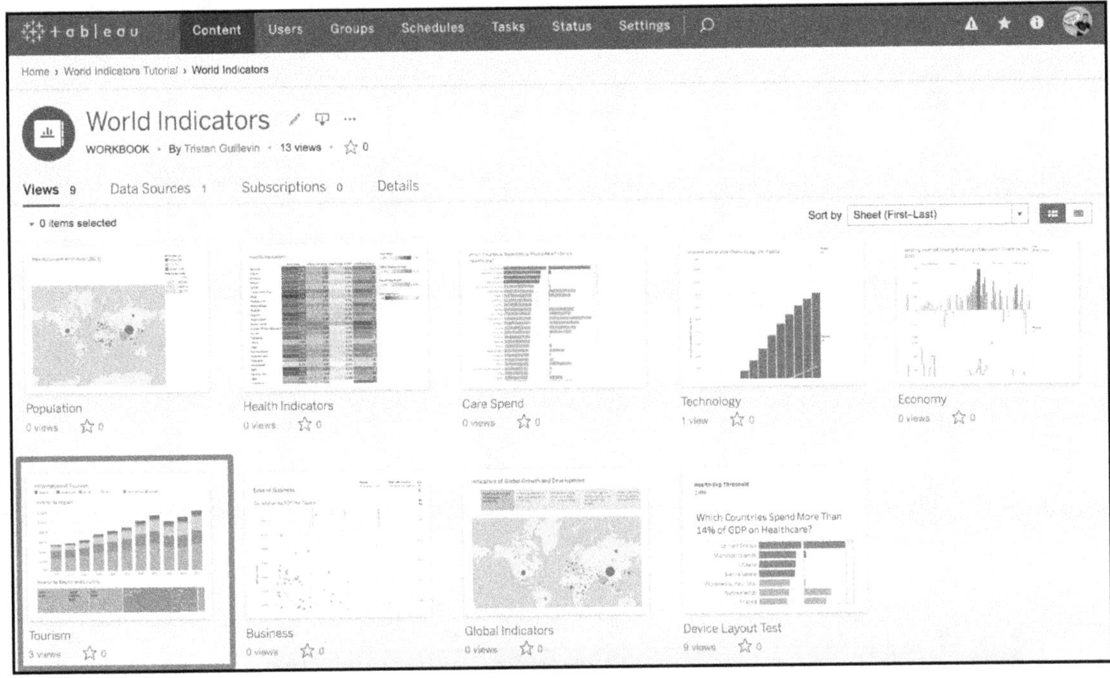

Tourism View of the World Indicators Workbook

Let's start with Custom Views.

Custom Views

A Custom View is a way two save the current state of a visualization to reopen it later. Imagine that, in a Dashboard, you need to select different values in ten different filters to focus the visualization on what interests you. Without Custom Views, you'll have to apply the different filters each time you open the Workbook. With Custom Views, you can save a state where all the filters are applied and reopen it when you want. All the filters will be applied at once.

The default View is **Original**. It's the View as the author of the Workbook published it.

To add a Custom View, click on the **View: Original** button to open the configuration window. Here's a screenshot of the configuration window:

This window offers the following options:

- Give a name to your Custom View.
- **Make it my default**—replace the Original default View with your Custom one. Each time you open the Workbook, the default Custom View opens.
- **Make it public**—the other Tableau Server users will be able to see and use your Custom View.
- **My Views**—a list of all the Custom Views you created.
- **Other Views**—a list of all the other public Custom Views created by other users, and the Original one.
- With the **Manage** button, you can rename, delete, or hide your Custom Views.

Let's see a quick example on the Tourism View together:

1. Use the Quick Filters to start the **Year Range** in `2005` and select only **Europe** in **Region.**
2. Click on **View: Original**.
3. In the configuration window, name your Custom View `Europe, starting in 2005`, make it public and your default, and click on **Save**. The configuration window should look like the preceding screenshot used to illustrated the Custom View configuration window.
4. Get back to the list of all the Views in the Workbook.
5. Reopen the **Tourism** View; you should be automatically filtered in *Europe*, between 2005 and 2012.

This option is a time saver when you have to apply many different filters or if a team only focuses on a subset of the data. The second feature is probably as important and useful!

Alert

With Alerts, Tableau sends you an email when a condition is fulfilled in your data after a refresh. For example, if you have a visualization with daily sales, you can configure an Alert to receive an email when the sales are above or below a certain amount. An Alert is a great way to allow you to do something other than check your data every day on Tableau Server. You can set an Alert on any visualization as long as it has an axis.

Be sure that the SMTP server is configured and that you have specified a correct email address to receive Tableau Server emails.

To create an Alert, click on the axis, then on the **Alert** button on the toolbar. A new window opens to configure the Alert, illustrated here:

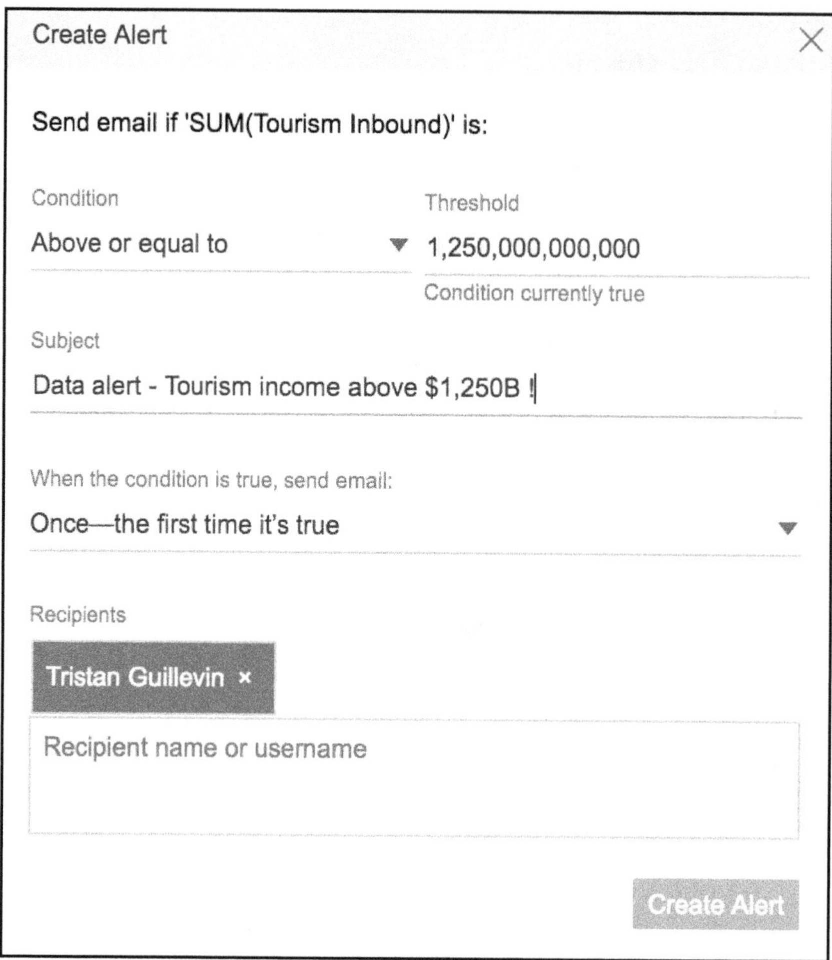

Alert configuration window

In this window, you can set the following:

- The **Condition** (*Above, Above or equal to, Below, Below or equal to,* or *Equal to*) and the **Threshold** to trigger the Alert. Tableau indicates to you whether the condition is currently true or not.
- The **Subject** of the email.
- The frequency of the emails (only the first time that the condition is true or *Daily at most,* for example).
- The **Recipients** of the email (you can specify multiple users who will receive the email).

Let's create an Alert on the Tourism View:

1. Click on the axis of the *Income by Region* visualization (it turns blue when selected).
2. Click on the **Alert** button.
3. Configure the Alert to send you an email with a subject of `Tourism Income above 1,250B!` when the value is equal to or above `1,250,000,000,000`. If you didn't filter a specific Region, the condition is true for the year 2012. The configuration window should look like the preceding screenshot used to illustrated the *Alert configuration window.*
4. Click on the **Create Alert** button.
5. Click on the **Refresh** button in the toolbar.

6. You should have received an email like this one, with a screenshot of the Alert:

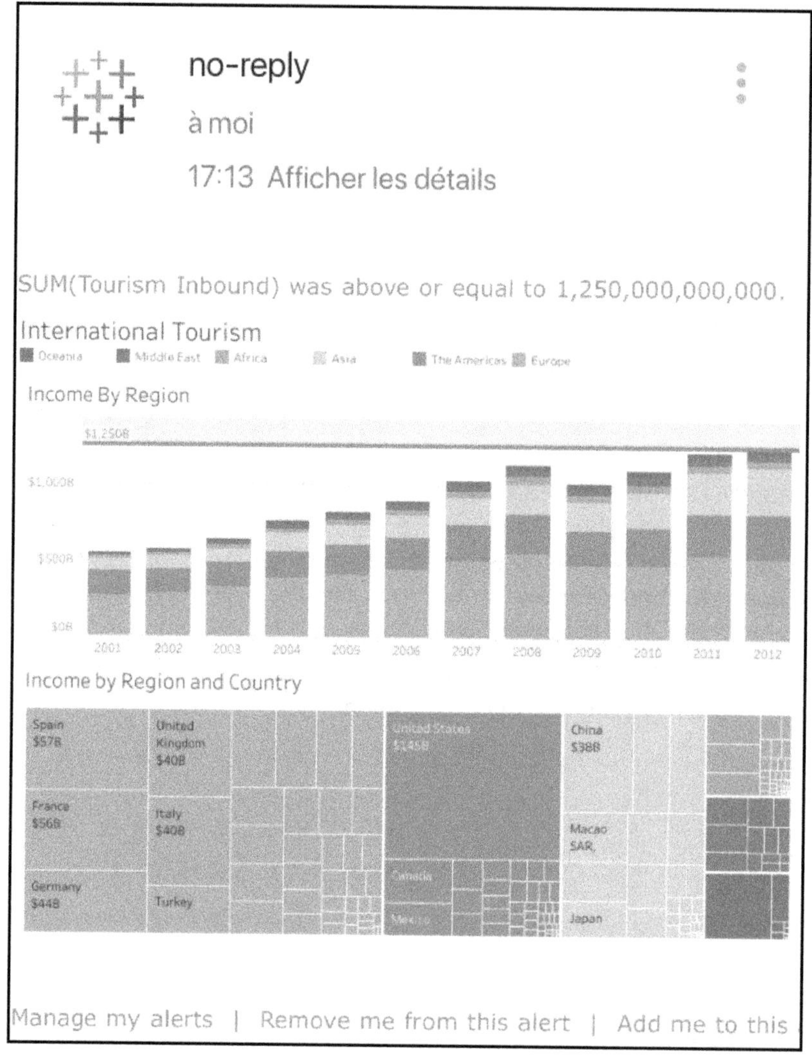

Alert screenshot

As you can see, the Alert feature is very useful, probably as much as the next one: Subscribe!

Subscribe

If you Subscribe to a View or Workbook, you'll receive, at a chosen frequency, an email with snapshots of your visualizations. Like Alerts, it's a useful feature that allows you to receive insights directly into your inbox, without having to connect to Tableau Server. Each snapshot contains a link to the published visualizations, so if you spot something intriguing, click on the picture to automatically open the View in Tableau Server and start your analysis.

To subscribe, click on the **Subscribe** button in the toolbar and configure it on the window that opens. Here's an illustration of the **Subscribe** configuration window:

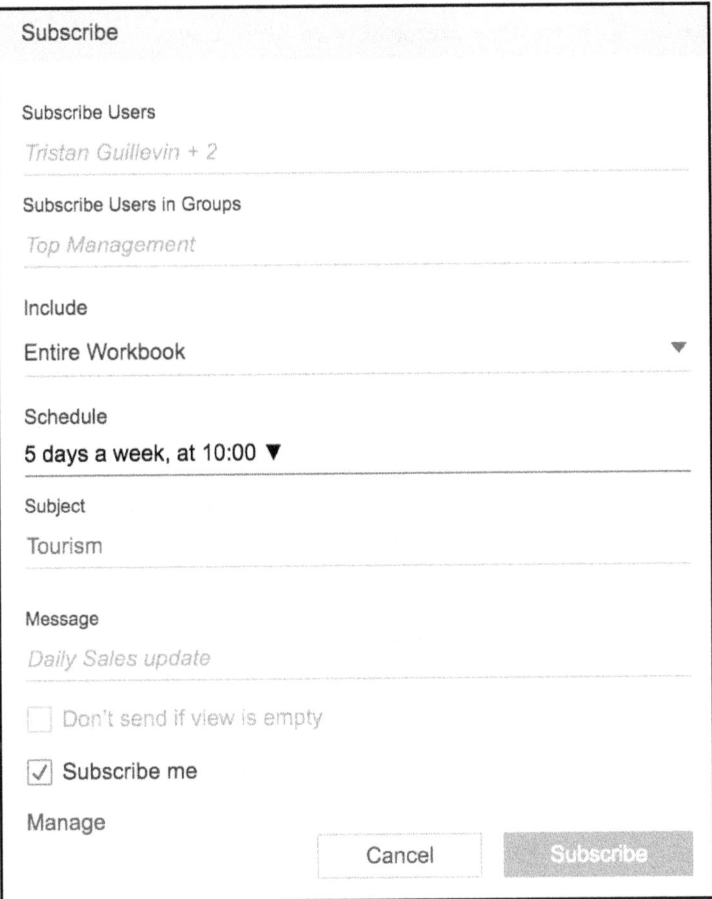

There are many interesting options in this window:

- Define the **Users** and **Groups** who will receive the emails
- Specify whether the Subscription is only for the current View or the entire Workbook (there will be a snapshot of every View in the Workbook in the email)
- Specify the **Schedule** and repetition of the emails
- Modify the **Subject** of the email and add a **Message**
- Configure the Subscription not to send an email if the View is empty (in case of a problem during the refresh)
- Add yourself to the Subscribed Users
- **Manage** the subscriptions and add or remove Users

The next useful feature to discover is Download.

Download

When you click on the **Download** button, a new window opens with five options. Three options are available by default:

- **Image**: Generates a picture of the View.
- **PDF**: Generates a PDF of the current View or the entire Workbook. You can specify the scaling and format of the PDF.
- **Workbooks**: Downloads the file.

To activate the two other options, you need to click on a visualization. If you click on a Mark, you will download the data of that Mark. Unfortunately, there is no way to see which Worksheet is selected. The two options are:

- **Data**: Opens the summary data but you can also get the full data on the second tab
- **Crosstab**: Generates a CSV that you can download

The last feature, unlike the previous ones, isn't about interacting with the View, but with other Users.

Comment

When you click on the **Comments** button, a left-hand pane opens where you can chat with other Users. Each Workbook's Views have their proper comments. Any User (who is allowed to do so) can add a comment, mention other users, and add a snapshot of the current View.

Comments are a great way for you to add more information about your Views. Other users can also use this feature if they spot mistakes or if they have questions.

As you saw, publishing a Workbook isn't just about making it safe and visible for other users. Some features, such as Alerts or Subscribe, open completely new ways of working with your data. Let's see another way of interacting with Tableau Server Contents with Web Authoring.

Web Authoring

Web Authoring is the ability to add a new Data Sources and build new Workbooks directly from Tableau Server on the web. There are three main ways of opening the Web Authoring mode.

This first way is with the feature we skipped on the Tableau Server toolbar: **Edit**. If you click on this button, Tableau opens the Web Authoring mode where you can modify your Workbook without leaving Tableau Server. It's a great way to fix small issues.

The second way is starting a new Workbook from a published Data Source. A Tableau Server User can use a published Data Source to create a new analysis without Tableau Desktop. You can find the options to create a new Workbook among the Data Source options (the three little dots next to its name), or from the Data Source page, as highlighted here:

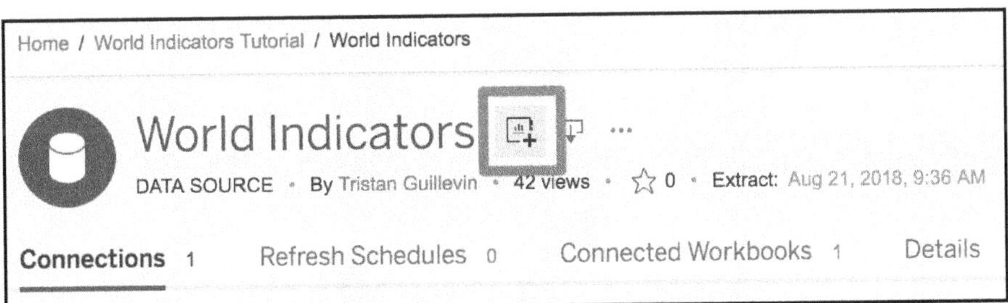

When you start the Web Authoring mode from a Data Source, you won't be lost! The interface is almost identical to Tableau Desktop, with the **Data** pane on the left. You can create new Worksheets, new Dashboards, and Stories. Here's the start page for Web Authoring when doing a new analysis from a published Data Source:

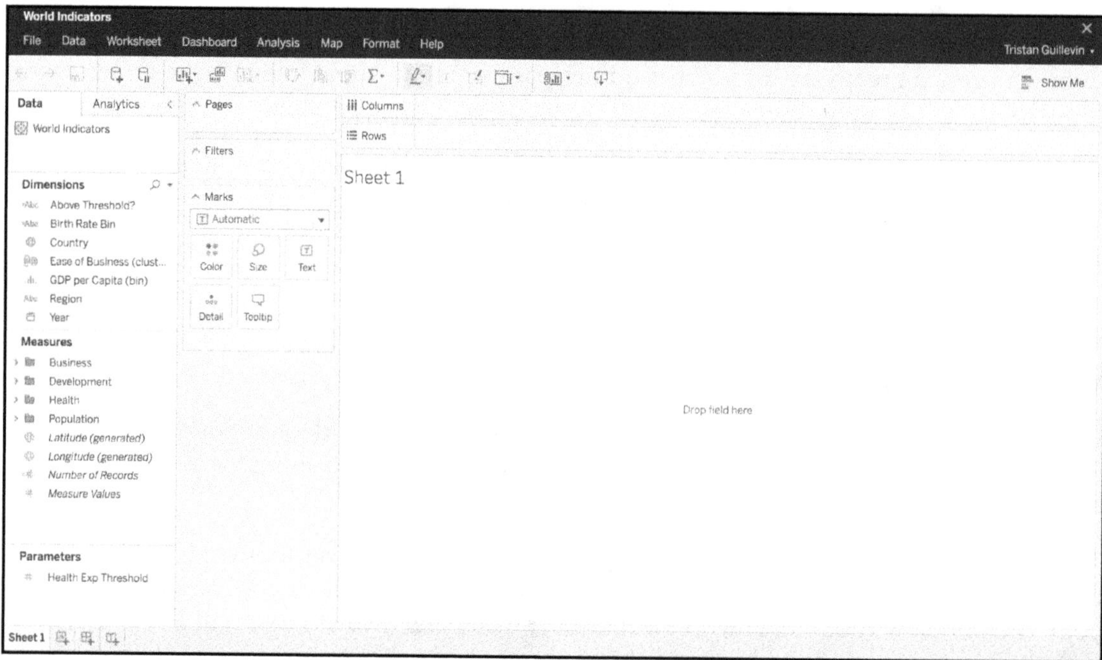

The last way is to use the option to create a new Workbook on Tableau Server. You can find this button among the **Create** options in the new browsing experience:

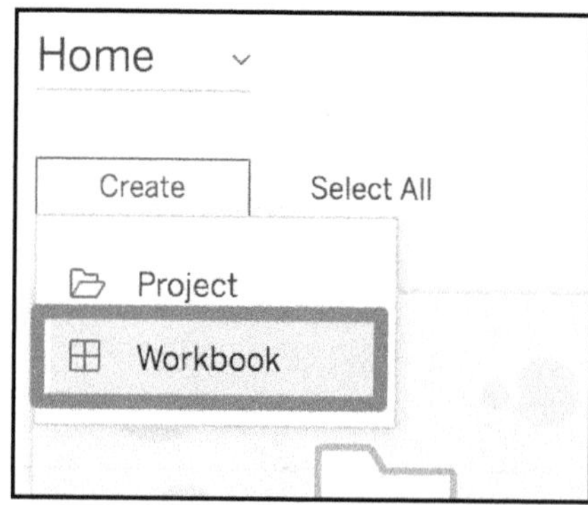

If you are using the traditional display mode, you can find this option on the **Workbooks** tab, as highlighted in this screenshot:

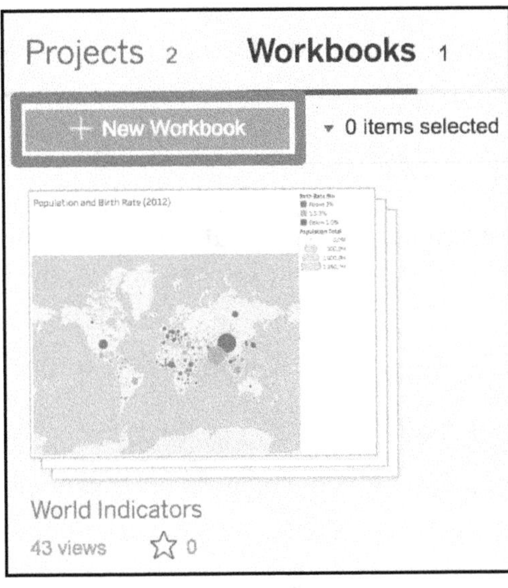

New Workbook tab

If you use this way, Tableau opens the Web Authoring mode and starts by asking you to connect to data. Since Tableau 2018.1, with a Creator license you can connect to files and servers directly from the web! There are four types of data connections available:

- **File**: Drag and drop an Excel file or CSV on the web page; you can choose the Sheets and build a new Data Source
- **Connectors**: A list of server-hosted databases available directly from Tableau Server
- **On this site**: Use an existing published Data Source
- **Dashboard Starters**: Start with prebuilt templates of cloud-based systems

Again, you won't be lost; all the different Workspaces are similar to Tableau Desktop.

Users who don't have a Creator License can always use published Data Sources to create new analyses, but they can't connect to new data from files or servers.

Not all the functionalities of Tableau Desktop are available yet on the web, but it's getting closer and closer after each new version of Tableau Server. It is, however, an excellent way of allowing web users to create their analyses and train future Tableau Desktop users.

To finish this chapter, let's see how to build a Dashboard with specific Layouts for mobile.

Device layout

On Tableau Desktop, you can create device layouts for your Dashboard. Then, depending on the device used to open the Workbook on Tableau Server, the right layout is automatically chosen.

Device Layouts also works when publishing a Dashboard on Tableau Public.

For example, here's a Dashboard displayed on a computer:

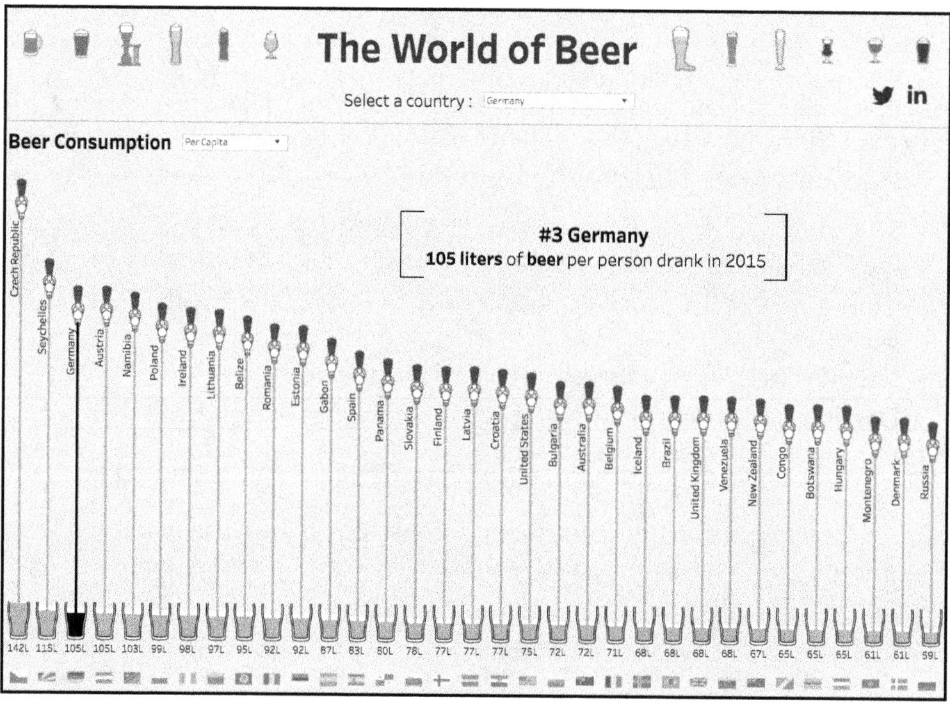

Here is the same Dashboard if you open it on a mobile:

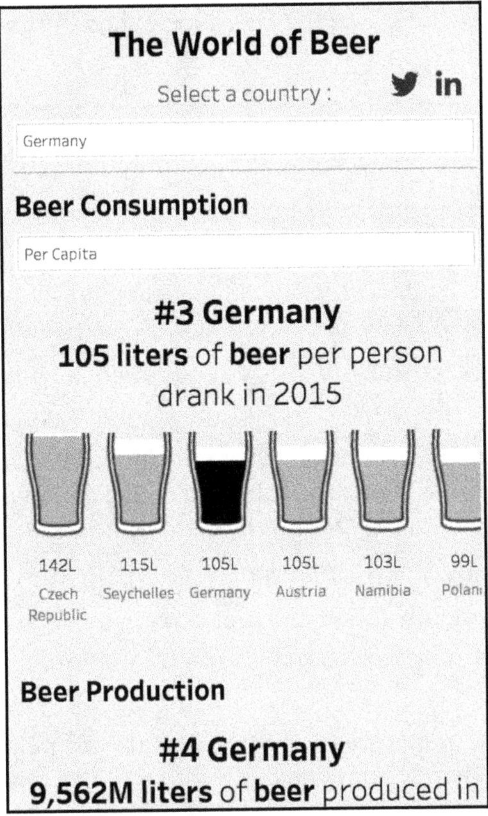

As you can see, the ideas and insights are visible in both layouts, but are adapted for each device.

Are you interested in beer consumption or do you want to learn how to build this visualization? All my Tableau Public Workbooks are downloadable: `https://public.tableau.com/profile/guillevin#!/`.

The section is divided into two parts. First, we'll see how to create a Device layout, then how to preview the results on Tableau Desktop.

Creating a Device layout

To create a Device layout, first click on the **Device Preview** button on a Dashboard to open the Device layout toolbar:

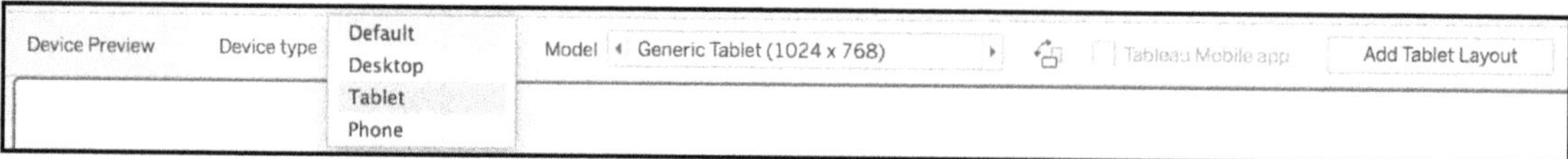

On this toolbar, you need to do the following:

- Select the type of Device
- Select a specific or generic model
- Select the orientation of the Device

When you're done, click on the last button to add the layout and start personalizing it. You can add three different layouts: **Desktop**, **Tablet**, and **Phone**. If you only specify a layout for Phone, Tableau uses the **Default** layout for the other types of devices.

Usually, creating a layout for Phone is enough because the Default one works fine for both Tablet and Desktop.

When you add a new layout, you can see it in the **Dashboard** pane on the left. You can click on the different layouts to switch from one to the other. On a Device layout, you have a few more options. You can specify the fit (usually **Fit width** for Phone because it's easy to scroll down) and the height of the Dashboard. You can also see the different items and choose to keep or remove them (they are only removed from the selected layout and not from the other layouts). Here's an example of a Phone Layout configuration:

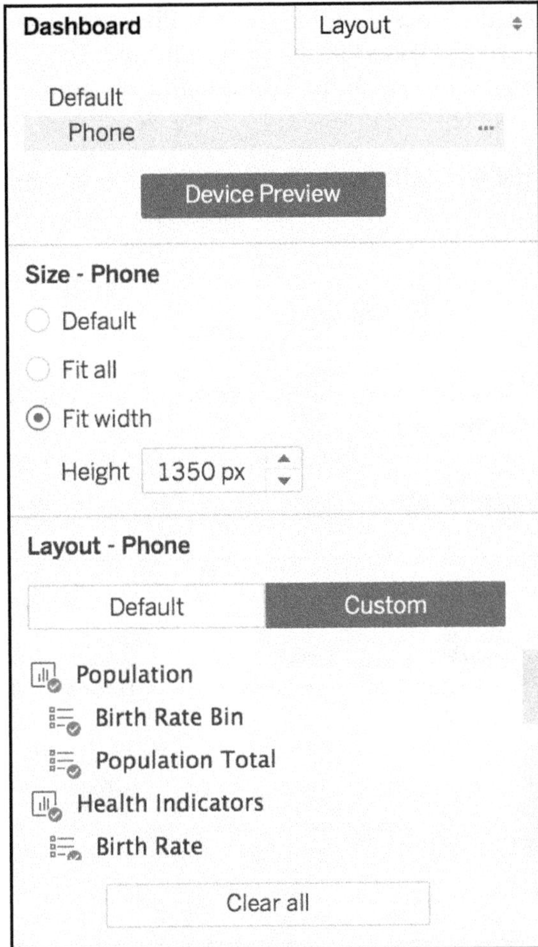

Since Tableau 2018.2, Tableau automatically rearranges the layout for Phone and Tablet, so they are ready to use. In the previous versions, you had to reorder them yourself to make them pleasant.

Let's build a new Dashboard with a device layout for Phones in the *World Indicators* Workbook that we published in the *Publishing and modifying Contents* section. If you didn't keep it, no worries, just open the *World Indicators* sample Workbooks and skip the two first points.

This example was built with Tableau 2018.2. If you are using Tableau 2018.1 or older, you'll have to rearrange the Layout yourself between *step 4* and *step 6*.

Follow these steps:

1. Open Tableau Desktop, go to the **Server** menu, and click on **Open Workbook** (you may have to sign in).
2. In the window that opens, open the **World Indicators** Workbooks, as shown in the following screenshot:

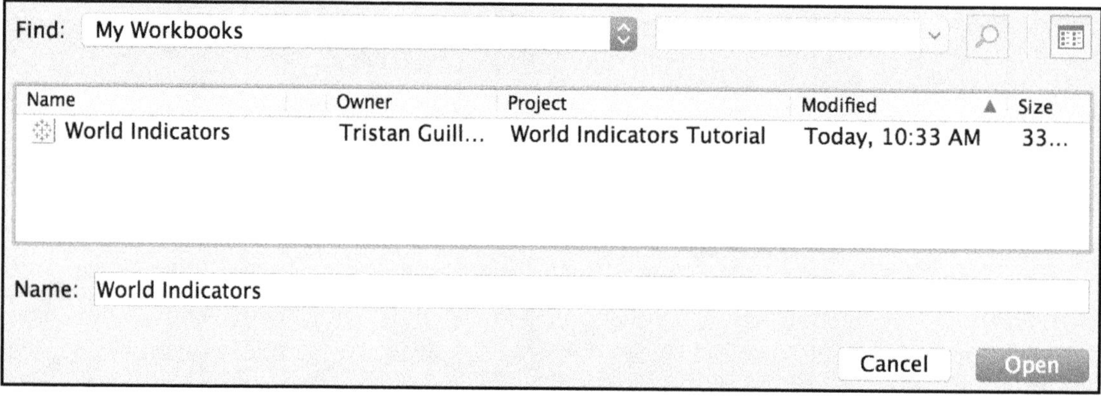

3. In the Workbook, create a new Dashboard, and name it `Device Layout Test.` Start by adding the **Population** Worksheet, then **Care Spend** below, and ,finally, **Health Indicators** on the right of **Care Spend** (don't bother with Containers here, it's just a quick example). Your Dashboard should look like this:

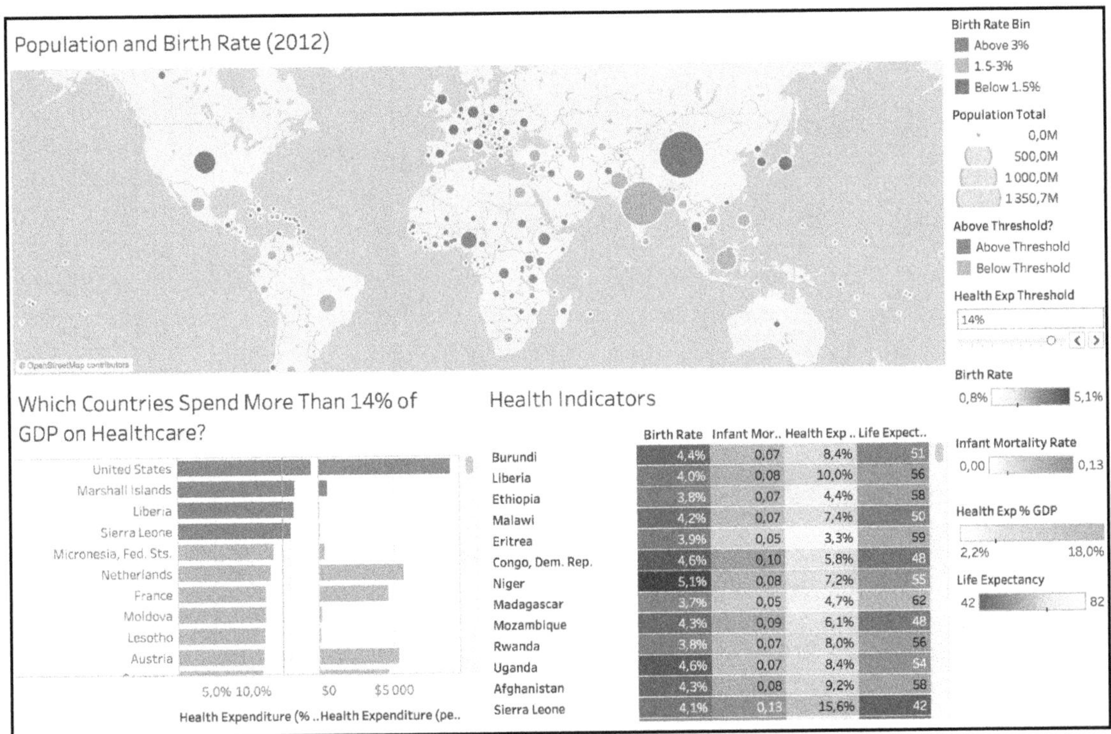

4. Click on **Device Preview**, select **Phone** as the Device type, and click on the **Add Phone Layout** button.

5. Tableau automatically chooses **Fit width** and rearranges the items. However, as you can see, the map is not very readable, so we can remove it:

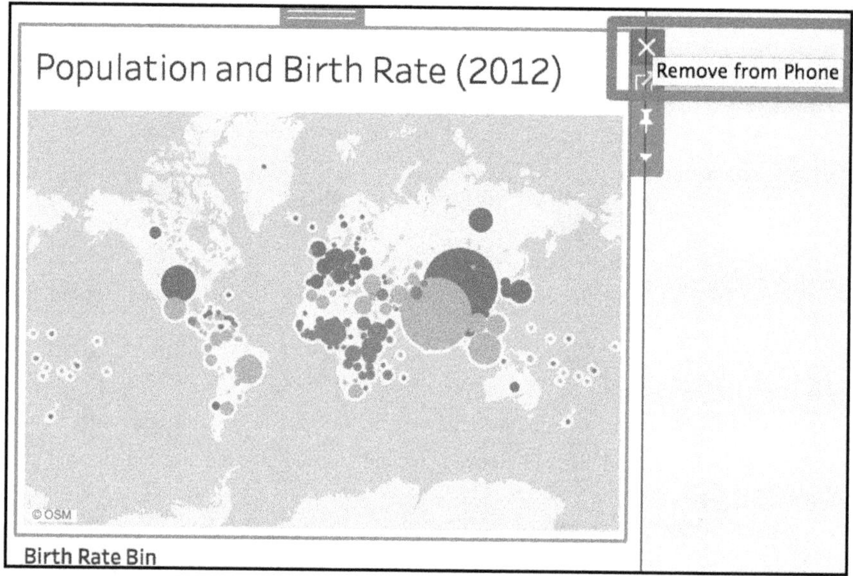

6. You can click on **Rearrange layout** among the Phone Layout options to automatically change the height (only from Tableau 2018.2) . The option is highlighted in the following screenshot:

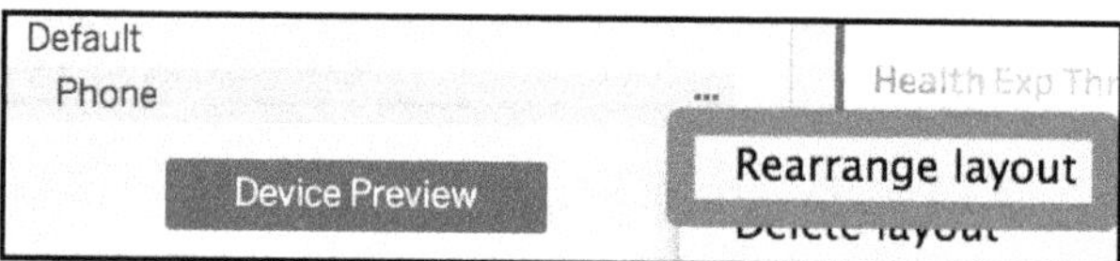

7. You now have two different layouts, one for **Phone** and the **Default** one for other devices.

8. To finish, go to the **Server** menu and click on **Publish your Workbook**. Be sure to replace the old Workbook by checking the following warning:

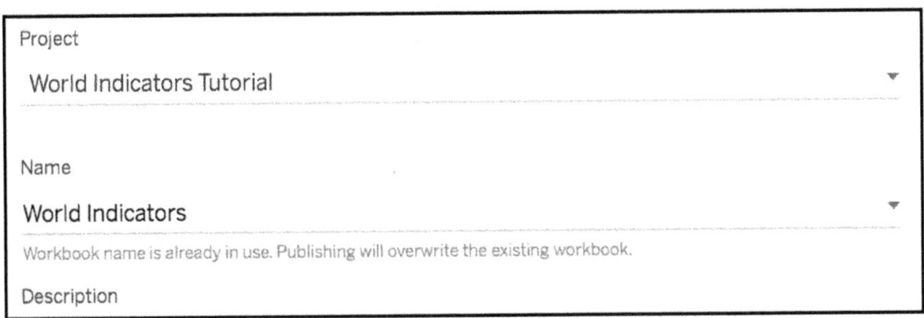

Now that your Workbook is published, you can test the rendering of your Device layout on Tableau Server.

Mobile layout preview

Since Tableau 2018.3, you can preview the different layouts on Tableau Server. Above the toolbar, a new button, **Preview Device Layouts**, is now available:

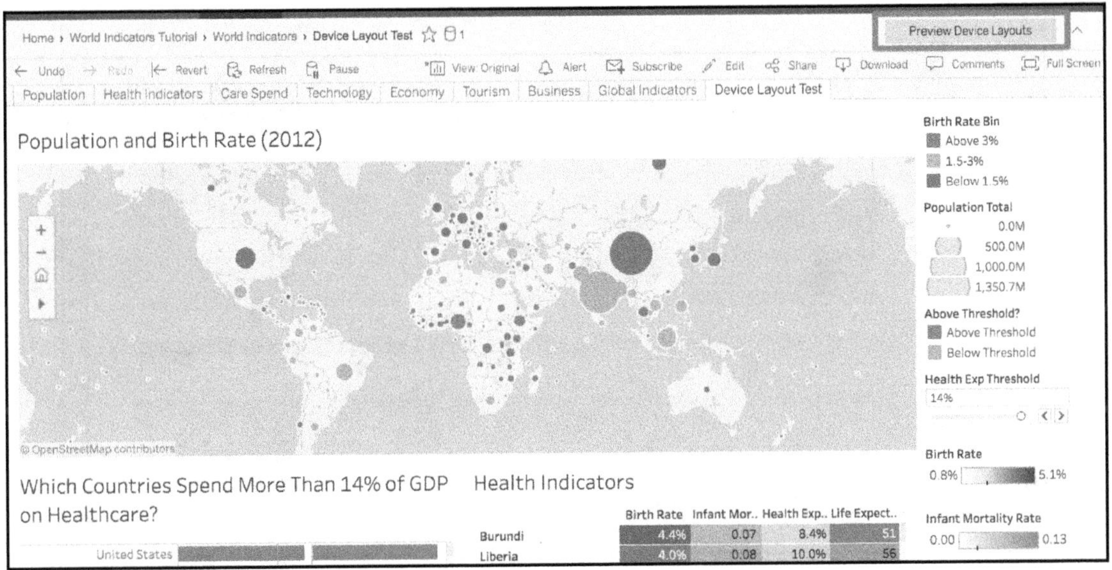

When you click on the button, Tableau opens the preview mode where you can select **Laptop**, **Tablet**, or **Phone** to see how your Dashboard renders. For example, if you preview the Dashboard you created before, you can see your special Phone Layout:

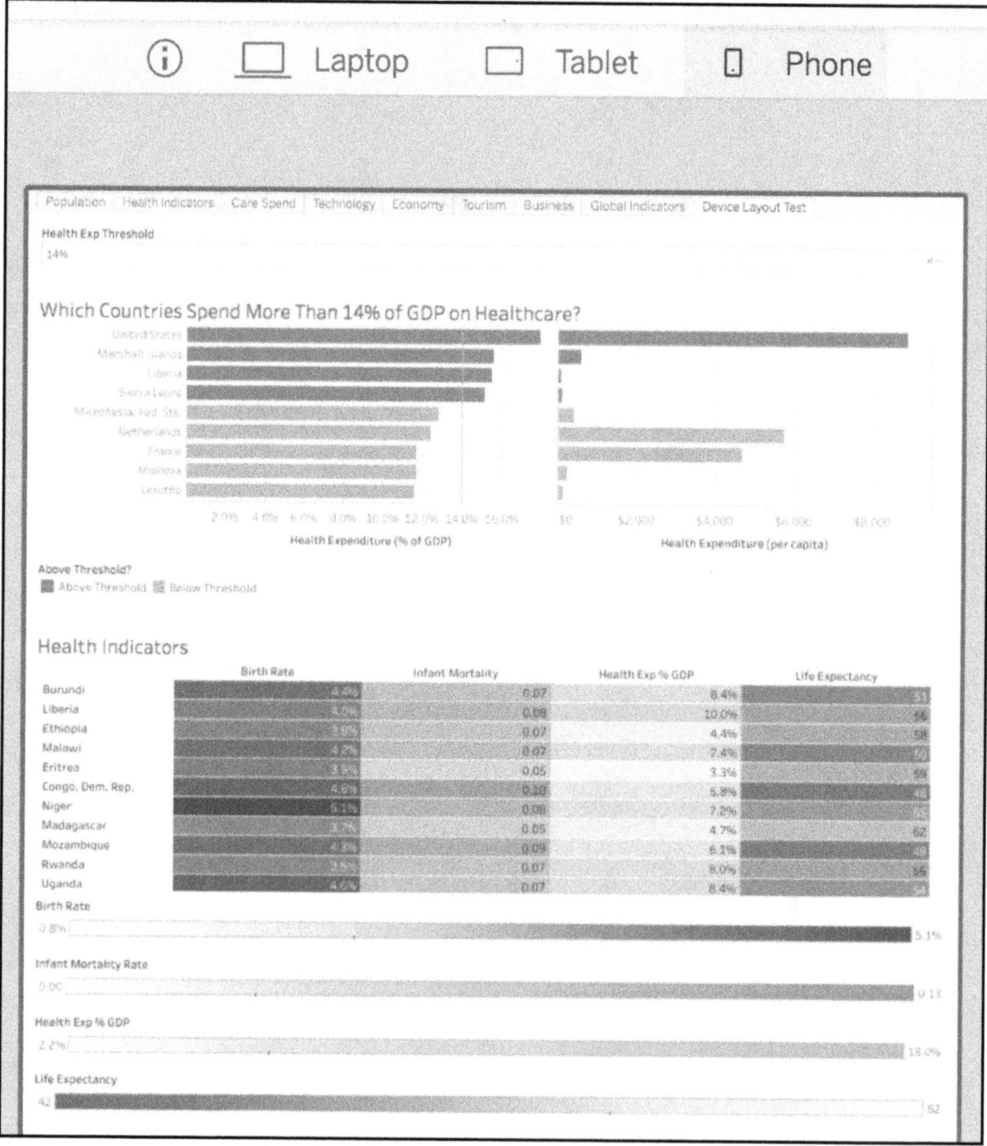

Phone Layout

This new feature is a great addition to test your different layouts without having to use those devices or special tools.

Summary

Now that you've learned how to use Tableau Server, you have a complete view of what Tableau can do as a data visualization and analysis tool. We looked at connecting data to Tableau Desktop, building your Data Source, Worksheets and Dashboards, and finally publishing all your work online for you and other users to interact with. What a journey!

This chapter was the last piece of the puzzle in understanding how to use Tableau. You started by understanding what Tableau Server is and what kind of content you can find in it. Then, you saw how to publish your Content, modify it, and interact with it on the web. Finally, you learned how to build specific Device layouts so any user, with any device, can see your visualization correctly.

This summary may sound like the end. What else could be left to see now? A lot! In the next chapters, we'll get our hands back on Tableau Desktop to discover many other crucial and advanced features. Creating Parameters, using the Analytics built-in tools, using data blending, securing your data, and many more features are waiting for you to discover. Without more teasing, let's start with Calculated Fields, or how to unlock unlimited power on Tableau Desktop.

10
An Introduction to Calculations

Congratulations! You have reached the first advanced chapter of this book! It's a challenging chapter, yet essential if you want to use Tableau without limitations. Indeed, to build the best analysis, you'll need to create Calculations. But let me reassure you: if you are traumatized by words such as *universe*, *cube*, or *MDX*, you can breathe. Creating a calculation in Tableau is straightforward and the language is very close to what you know in Excel. This chapter is split into two main sections:

- Calculated field basics
- Advanced functions

In this chapter, some examples use the Sample-Superstore saved Data Source, but others require special files. You can find the files that are used for the tutorials on my website, `http://book.ladataviz.com`, in the *Chapter 10: An introduction to calculations* section.

Calculated Field basics

A Calculated Field is a new field in your data source. It can have any data type. You can build a calculated Measure or Dimension. To differentiate a field from the Calculated Field, each data type icon has a small equals symbol in front of it, as you can see in the following screenshot:

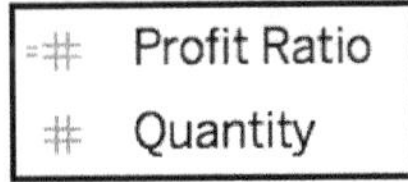

Let's start by learning how to create a Calculated Field.

Creating a Calculated Field

To create a new Calculated Field, go through the following steps:

1. Click on the small arrow next to **Dimensions** in the **Data** pane, highlighted in the following screenshot:

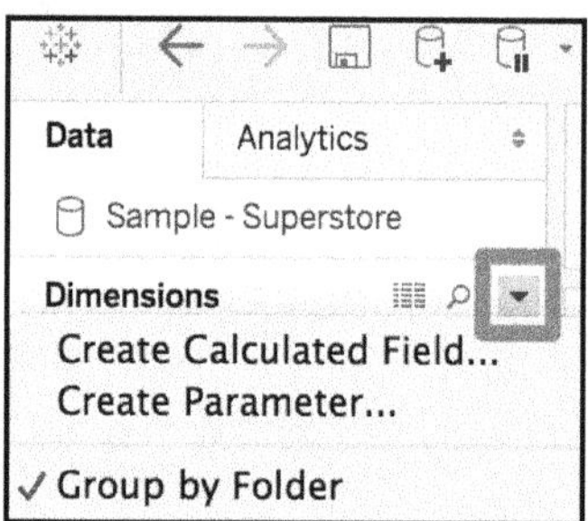

It's also possible to right-click on a field and go to **Create** to start a new **Calculated Field** based on this field. You can edit a Calculated Field when you right-click on it.

2. When you create a new Calculated Field, a new window opens where you have to write a formula. The formula can be based on other fields, calculated or not, and use functions.
3. On the right, when you click on the arrow, you can open the list of functions.
4. When you write a formula, at the bottom of the window, Tableau indicates to you whether the calculation is valid or not. You can also see the dependencies (other Calculated Fields and Sheets that use this Calculated Field).
5. Click on **OK** when you are done and the calculation is valid.

Here's an example of the calculation window with a list of functions open:

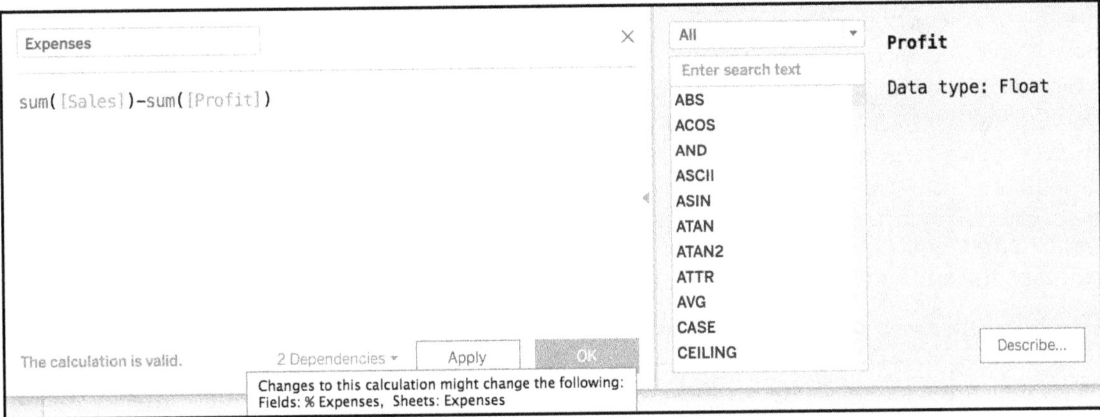

When you write a formula, the fields are in orange and between brackets, and the functions are in blue.

There is auto-completion, meaning that when you start writing at least one character, Tableau opens a list of suggestions based on all the fields and functions available. You just have to press *Enter* or click on the desired element. Here's an example of auto-completion:

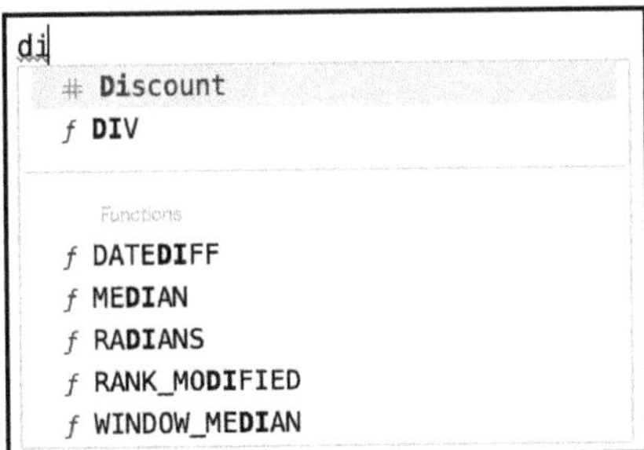

You can also drag and drop any field in the calculation window to add it to the formula.

When using fields in a formula, you can decide whether to aggregate them or not; let's discover what the difference is.

To aggregate or not to aggregate fields?

The main rule with Calculated Field is to think about aggregation when you create a new Measure. As you know, a Measure is, by default, aggregated and so are Calculated Measures. You can specify the aggregation inside the formula or not. If you aggregate the data inside the formula, the pill of the Calculated Measure will start with AGG. If you don't specify the aggregation in the formula, a default one is added when you use the Calculated Measure, as for any normal Measure.

For example, the Calculated Measure **Profit Ratio**, in the **Sample - Superstore** Data Source, contains the aggregations inside the formula, so its pill starts with **AGG** displayed as follows:

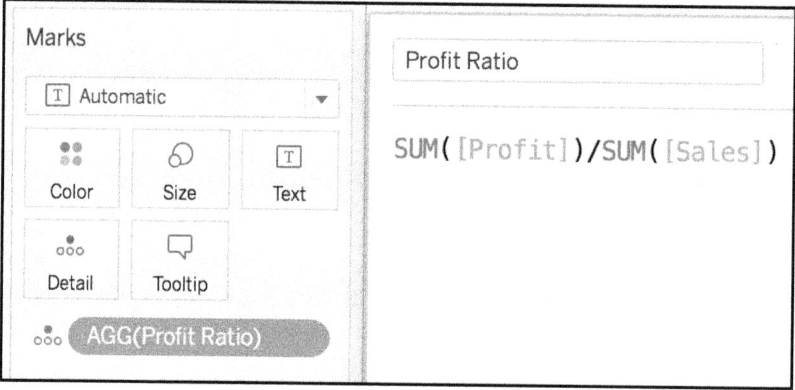

A Calculated Field cannot contain aggregated and non-aggregated fields in the same formula. Remember that you can aggregate a Dimension with the `ATTR()` function.

Often, there is a significant difference between adding the aggregation inside the formula and not. For the calculation of Profit Ratio, Tableau first aggregates the Profit and the Sales separately, then divides the two results.

An incorrect way of calculating the Profit Ratio would be `[Profit]/[Sales]`. With this calculation, Tableau divided the value of the Profit by the Sales at each line of the Data Source, then aggregates the result of all the divisions. To illustrate, I created a Calculated Field, `Wrong Profit Ratio`, with the incorrect formula. Here's the difference between the two calculations:

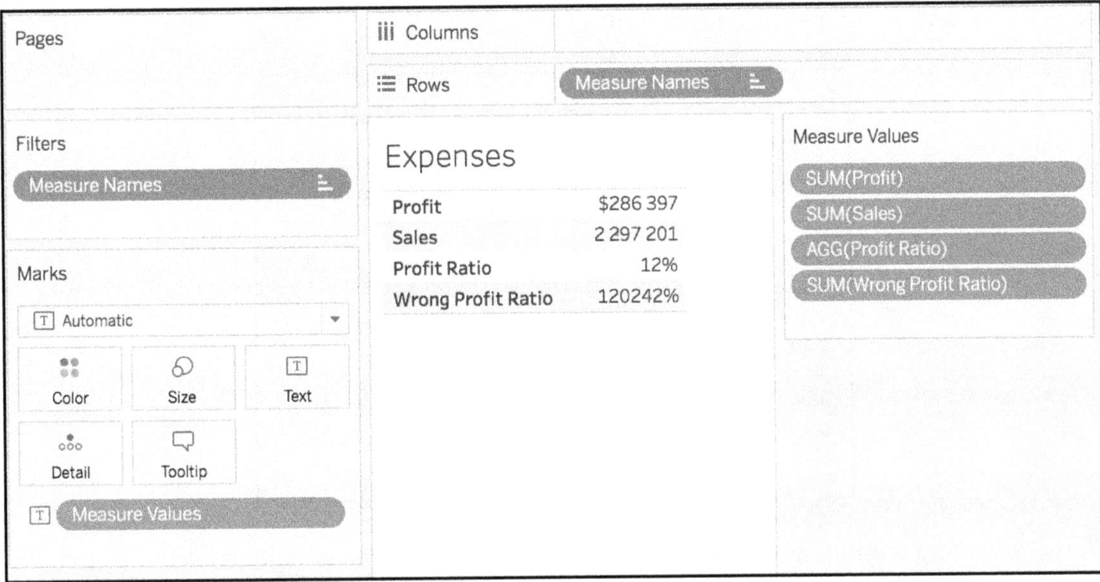

As you can see, if Tableau sums the result of all the divisions rather than dividing two aggregated values, the result is incorrect. Always keep this principle in mind.

Using calculation functions

Of course, you can create Calculated Fields based on a calculation between different fields (such as the Profit Ratio). However, the really interesting aspect of Calculated Fields is the functions. There are many different functions, some basic, some hard to understand. Each function returns a specific data type, and some require arguments.

Tableau has made it easy: each function has a clear description and examples for learning how to use them.

Going through all the functions and repeating the description and example already available in Tableau doesn't add any value. My strong advice for you is to take fifteen minutes to look at all the functions to have a clear overview of what you can and can't do.

Here's an example for the round function:

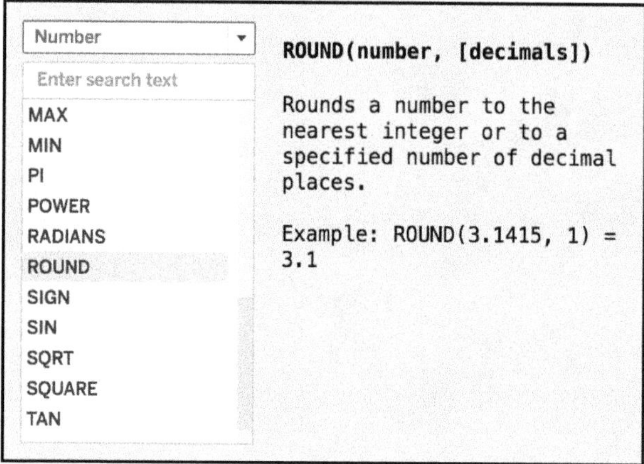

In the following sections and chapters, we'll often use calculations, so don't be afraid, you'll practice them. Speaking of practice, it's time for a guided tutorial!

Example – highlight values

Probably the most common use of calculation is to highlight values. Let's create a calculation that returns different text values depending on sales:

1. Open Tableau Desktop and click on the **Sample - Superstore** saved Data Source.
2. Create a new Calculated Field and name it `Sales Highlight`.
3. Write the following formula and check that the calculation is valid: `if SUM([Sales]) > 300000 then "Great" ELSEIF SUM([Sales]) < 50000 then "Bad" else "Average" END`.

This formula is a conditional test. If the sum of sales is higher than 300 000, the formula returns the text *Great*, if the sum of sales is lower than 50 000, the formula returns *Bad*, and in the other cases (when the sales are between 50 000 and 300 000, the formula returns *Average*.

4. Create a visualization with **Sales** in **Columns**, **Sub-Category** in **Rows**, and **Sales Highlight** in **Color**.

5. You can change the color of the three values to make it easier to see the difference between great and bad values. Here's the final result:

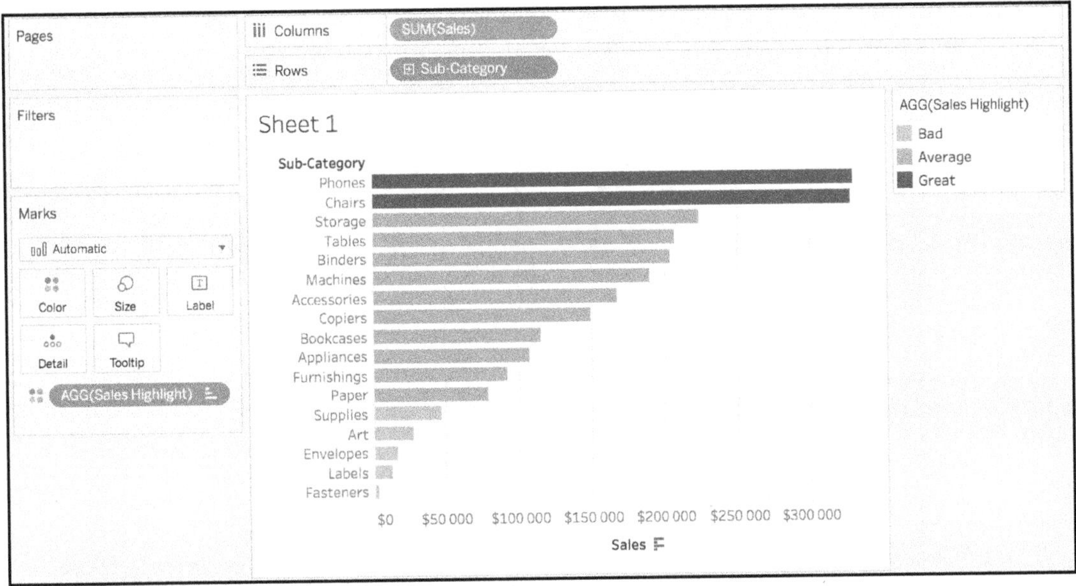

Keep this example, as we'll see how to make it better in the following section.

As you can see, simple calculations can already be useful. In the next section, we'll see how to use two sorts of advanced functions: Table Calculation and Level of Detail.

Advanced functions

There are two type of functions that are different from each other: Table Calculation and Level of Detail.

Table Calculation functions

The Table Calculation functions are special in many ways. Mastering them requires practice, but many useful functions are Table Calculation. It's important to understand how they work, and how to use them. Let's start with the basics.

Table function basics

Table Calculation functions allow you to calculate the rank, the percentage of total, the difference, and much more. Here is an example of the same Measure, Quantity, with different table functions:

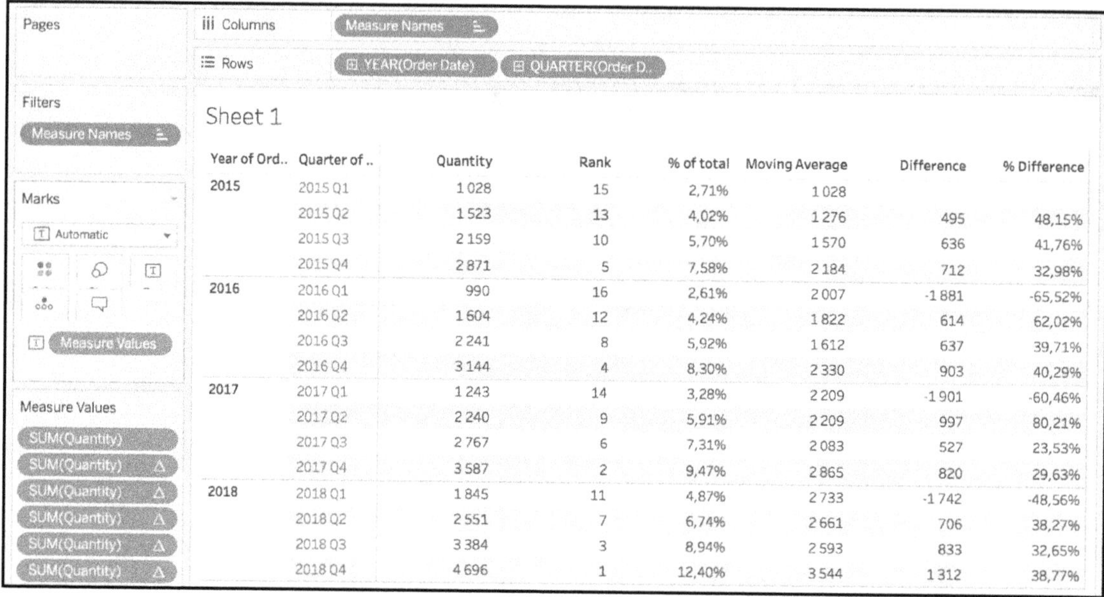

Year of Ord..	Quarter of ..	Quantity	Rank	% of total	Moving Average	Difference	% Difference
2015	2015 Q1	1 028	15	2,71%	1 028		
	2015 Q2	1 523	13	4,02%	1 276	495	48,15%
	2015 Q3	2 159	10	5,70%	1 570	636	41,76%
	2015 Q4	2 871	5	7,58%	2 184	712	32,98%
2016	2016 Q1	990	16	2,61%	2 007	-1 881	-65,52%
	2016 Q2	1 604	12	4,24%	1 822	614	62,02%
	2016 Q3	2 241	8	5,92%	1 612	637	39,71%
	2016 Q4	3 144	4	8,30%	2 330	903	40,29%
2017	2017 Q1	1 243	14	3,28%	2 209	-1 901	-60,46%
	2017 Q2	2 240	9	5,91%	2 209	997	80,21%
	2017 Q3	2 767	6	7,31%	2 083	527	23,53%
	2017 Q4	3 587	2	9,47%	2 865	820	29,63%
2018	2018 Q1	1 845	11	4,87%	2 733	-1 742	-48,56%
	2018 Q2	2 551	7	6,74%	2 661	706	38,27%
	2018 Q3	3 384	3	8,94%	2 593	833	32,65%
	2018 Q4	4 696	1	12,40%	3 544	1 312	38,77%

In the preceding screenshot you can see, by Year and Quarter, in the following:

- The sum of the quantity, the initial Measure.
- The rank—which quarter is the best across all Years and Quarters.
- The percentage of total—*Q4 2018*, for example, represents 12% of the total quantity of products purchased.
- Moving average—the value of each quarter is the average of the current value and the two previous. This table function is useful to smooth an evolution. For example, in *Q3 2015*, the moving average of the quantity is `(2159+1523+1028)/3 = 1570`.
- Difference—calculates the difference from one quarter to another, in value. For example, in *Q1 2016*, the difference in `1243-3144`, so there were `1901` fewer quantity purchased.
- Percentage of difference—the same as the difference but expressed in percentage.

A normal Calculated Field is computed for every row in the Data Source, then aggregated (if it's a Measure) when used in the view. You can see the Calculated Field in the View Data window, with **Profit Ratio**:

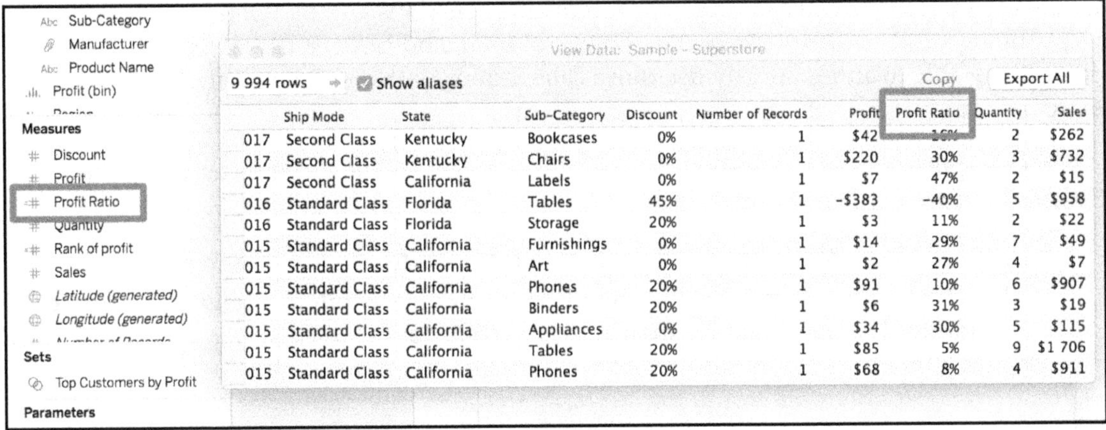

If you use a Table function in a Calculated Field, it's different:

1. First, it doesn't appear in the detailed table.
2. Second, the calculation is computed after the aggregation, and it's based on the displayed result in the View. Modifying the View (the position of the pills for example) directly affects the table calculation.
3. Third, when you use the Calculated Field in the View, you can choose how to compute the calculation with a right-click, as displayed here:

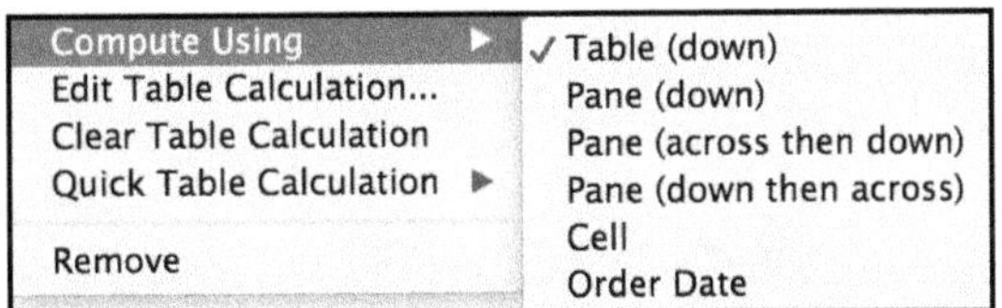

You can also click on **Edit Table Calculation...** to open a new window where you can use the calculation assistance to help you see how the calculation will be computed. Table calculations have another particularity: **Quick Table Calculation**.

Quick Table Calculation

Quick Table Calculation is an option available with a right-click on every Measure. It automatically changes the Measure to a Calculated Measure using a Table Calculation function. You can find very interesting functions among the table calculations list; running sum, rank, difference, percentage of total, and more, all available with a right-click. Being able to automatically use those calculations with a simple right-click is extremely useful.

As an example, let's compare, for each year, the cumulative sales by quarter using the Sample - Superstore Data Source:

1. On a blank Worksheet, add **Order Date** in **Columns** and **Sales** in **Rows**.
2. Click on the + button next to the **YEAR(Order Date)** pill to open the quarter to add to. The visualization should look as follows:

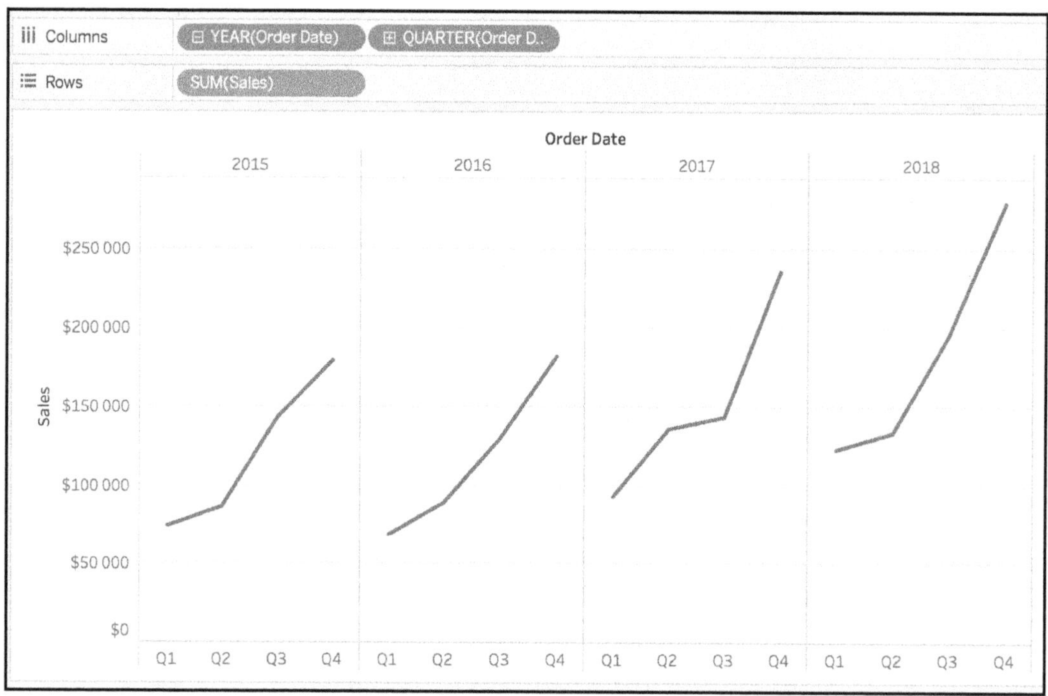

3. Right-click on **Sales**, go to **Quick-Table Calculation**, and select **Running Total**. What you see is the running total of the sales among all years and quarters.

4. Put the **YEAR(Order Date)** pill in **Color**. It's now very easy to see which year ends with the most sales generated at the end of the year; you can observe this in the following screenshot:

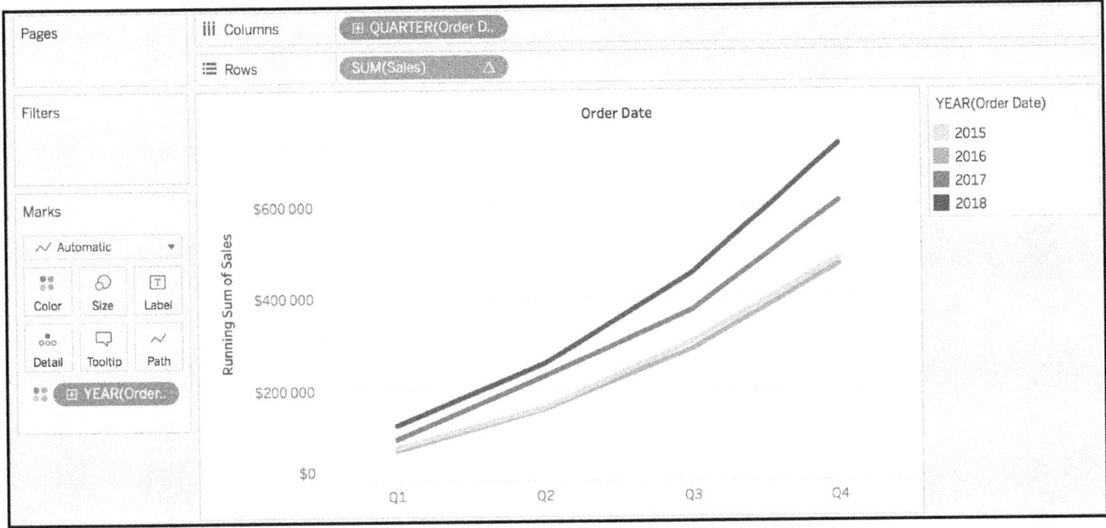

To finish with table calculation functions, let's see another example.

Hands-on Table Calculation functions

Let's create a visualization with two table functions computed at different levels using Sample - Superstore. Let's start with the following:

1. On a blank Worksheet, put **Sub-Category** in **Rows**, and **Segment** and **Sales** in **Columns**.
2. Put **Sales** also in **Label**.

We'd like to see the weight of each segment in a sub-category:

1. Right-click on the **Sales** pill used in the **Label** and select **Quick-Table Calculation**, then **Percent of Total**. Currently, you can see the weight of each sub-category by segment, which is not precisely what we want.
2. Right-click on the same pill again, go to **Compute Using**, and select **Table (across)**. That's it; you can see that the **Consumer** segment is always the biggest part.

Your visualization should look like this (check the figures):

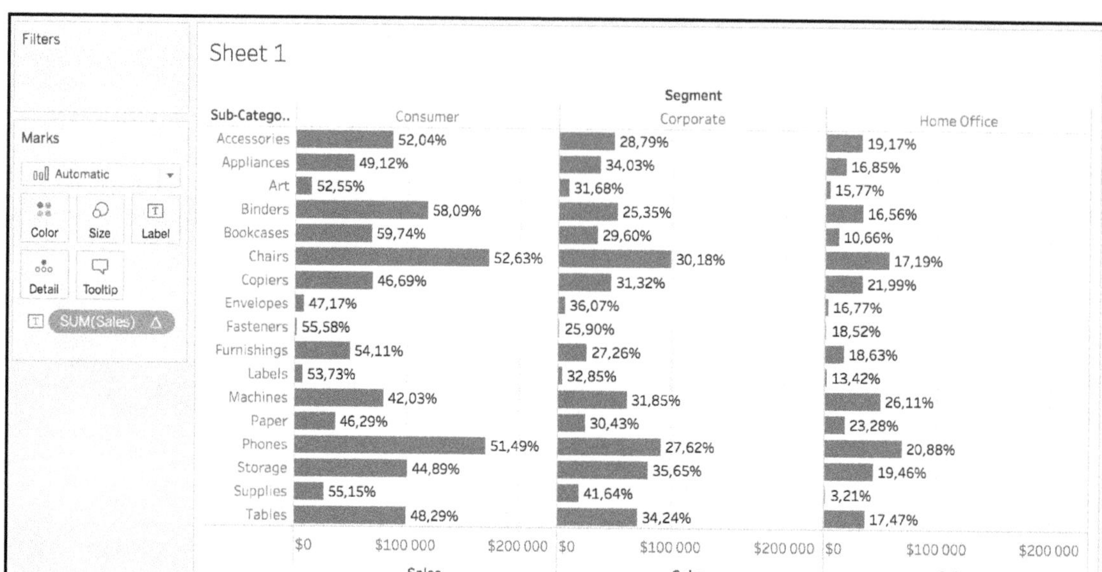

Now, we want to see the sub-categories beneath the average sales visually. To do that, we are using the `WINDOW_AVG` table function, which returns the global average value of a Measure. Let's continue:

1. Create a new Calculated Field and name it `Sales Highlight Average`.
2. Write the following calculation and check that it is valid: `if SUM([Sales]) > WINDOW_AVG(SUM([Sales])) then "Great" else "Bad" END`.
3. Put the calculation in **Color**.
4. Check that the calculation is computed using **Table (down)**.

You can now easily see which sub-categories are higher or lower than the average. It's interesting, for example, to see that **Bookcases** are only above the average in the **Consumer** segment. Here's the final result:

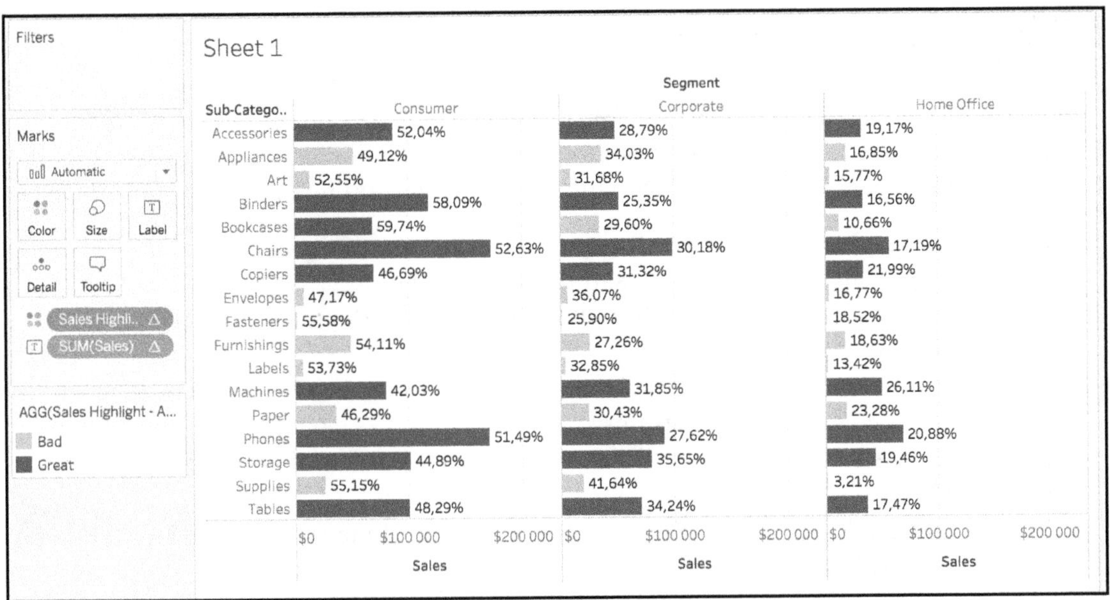

As you can see, it's possible to have multiple table calculations computed in different ways on the same Worksheet. Table calculation functions aren't easy to understand, and they will require practice to be mastered. It's important that you know they exist, what you can do with them, and how to use them.

The next set of functions is called **Level of Detail** (**LOD**) and are not easier to understand, but even more powerful.

Level of Detail

LOD functions were introduced in version 9 of Tableau and, today, it's hard to believe that there was a time without them! These functions are probably the most powerful ones. The Fixed function, in particular, allows you to ignore Filters, ignore duplication in your data, and return a Measure in any desired LOD. Let's start with the basics of these functions.

LOD function basics

As you know, each Dimension in the View splits the number of Marks and defines the level of detail for the Measure. However, at some point, you will probably need to aggregate a Measure at a different level than the View. To do that, you can use one of the three LOD functions. The three LODs are Include, Exclude, and Fixed:

- **Include** adds the specified Dimensions to the level of detail of an aggregated Measure. For example, the calculation `{ INCLUDE [Region]: SUM([Sales])}` computes the sum of the sales by Region and all the other Dimensions in the View.
- **Exclude** removes the specified Dimensions from the level of detail of an aggregated Measure. For example, the calculation `{ EXCLUDE [Region]: SUM([Sales])}` computes the sum of the sales without the Region if it exists in the View.
- **Fixed** can do both, as you have to specify all the Dimensions of the level of detail precisely. For example, the calculation `{ FIXED [Region]: SUM([Sales])}` computes the sum of the sales with Region only, no matter the other Dimension in the View.

Include and Exclude calculations are always Measures and consequently are aggregated. The default aggregation for Measures using the Exclude function is `ATTR()`, because the aggregation is at a higher level than the View. Fixed can be both Dimension and Measure.

Let's start with the Include and Exclude functions.

Include and Exclude

The best way to understand these is with an example. In the following diagram, you can see three measures, according to Category and Sub-Category:

- A normal aggregation, the maximum of sales: `MAX([Sales])`
- An attribute aggregation of a Calculated Measure using an Exclude function: `ATTR( { EXCLUDE [Sub-Category]: MAX([Sales]) } )`
- An average aggregation of a Calculated Measure using an Include function: `AVG( { INCLUDE [Segment]: MAX([Sales]) } )`

Here's the result:

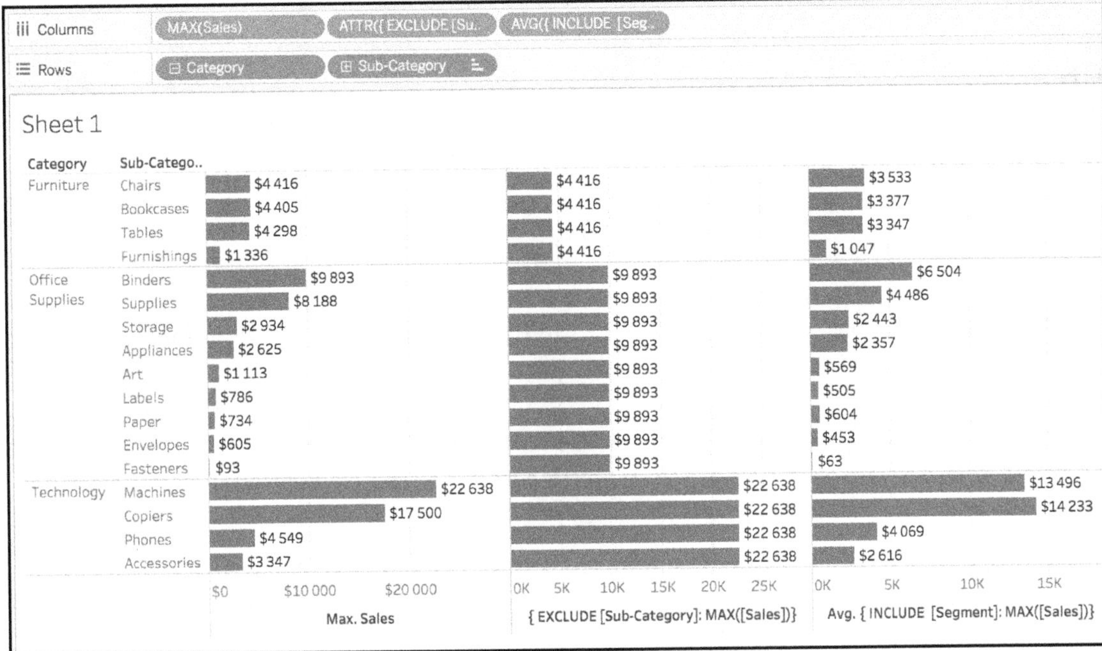

Let's spend some time understanding what you see:

- The first value is a simple aggregation. It returns the highest sales value by Category and Sub-Category, which are the levels of detail in the View.
- The second calculation, `ATTR( { EXCLUDE [Sub-Category]: MAX([Sales]) } )`, excludes the Sub-Category from the calculation. The result shows the maximum sales value of the Category, even if the Sub-Category is in the View. The level of detail of the calculation is higher than the level of detail in the View, so Tableau uses the `ATTR()` aggregation. There are more Marks than returned values, so the same value is repeated multiple times.
- The third calculation, `AVG( { INCLUDE [Segment]: MAX([Sales]) } )`, includes the Segment in the calculation. The result shows the averages of the maximum sales by Category, Sub-Category, and Segment. The level of detail of the calculation is lower than the level of detail in the View. An aggregation is needed because the calculation returns more different values than Marks.

You can write all the Include and Exclude functions with Fixed. Let's focus on the third LOD function, which is even more powerful.

Fixed

With Fixed, all the Dimensions that you want to include in the level of detail must be specified. So, if you want to exclude an existing Dimension, don't specify it, and if you want to include one, specify it. Here's how to rewrite the two previous LOD calculations with Fixed:

- `{ EXCLUDE [Sub-Category]: MAX([Sales]) }` is equivalent to `{ FIXED [Category] : MAX([Sales]) }` in the previous example. If you want to remove the Sub-Category, you don't specify it.
- `AVG( { INCLUDE [Segment]: MAX([Sales]) } )` is equivalent to `AVG( { FIXED [Category],[Sub-Category],[Segment]: MAX([Sales]) } )` in the previous example. If you want to add the Segment, you have to add all the existing Dimensions, plus the Segment.

Calculated Fields that use a Fixed function have three advantages. First, they are easier to understand. You write all the Dimensions that you want to use, and that's it, Tableau only uses them to aggregate the calculation, no matter what's in the View.

The second advantage is even more interesting: Fixed calculations are not impacted by Dimension Filters. If you remember, the Filter hierarchy looks like this:

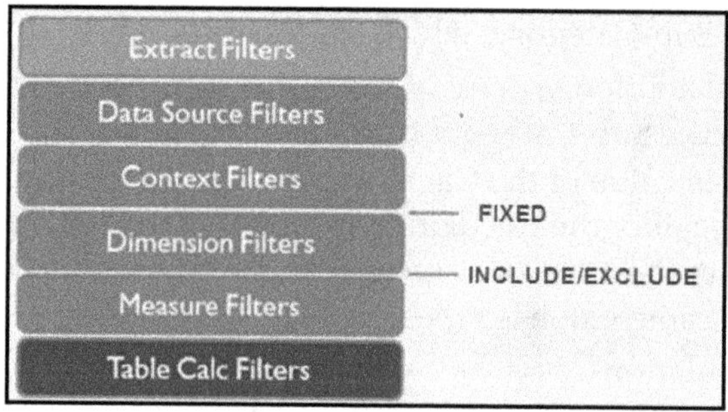

As you can see, the Include and Exclude functions are impacted by the Dimension Filters, but not Fixed, unless they are in Context.

Let's see how to use this to your advantage with an example. Let's display, by Sub-Category, and with a Filter on State keeping only California, the following three Measures:

- A normal aggregation, the sum of sales: `SUM([Sales])`
- A Fixed calculation: `SUM( { FIXED [Sub-Category]: SUM([Sales]) } )`
- The ratio of the two previous Measures: `SUM([Sales]) / SUM( { FIXED [Sub-Category]: SUM([Sales]) } )`

Here's the result:

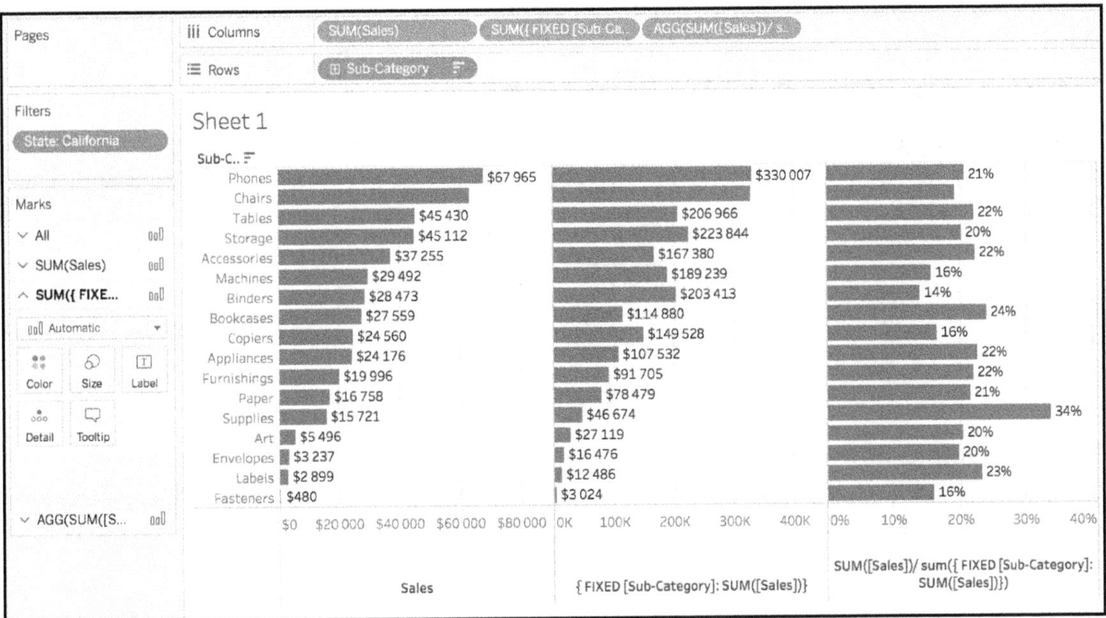

As before, let's spend some time understanding it:

- The first value is a simple aggregation. It returns the sum of sales by Sub-Category, filtered on *California*.
- The second calculation, `SUM( { FIXED [Sub-Category]: SUM([Sales]) } )`, returns the sum of sales by Sub-Category for all States. As State is not specified in the list of Dimensions in the Fixed function, the filter has no power over this calculation.

- The third calculation, `SUM([Sales]) / SUM( { FIXED [Sub-Category]: SUM([Sales]) } )`, calculates the ratio between the two previous calculations. It calculates the percentage of sales in California (the first part of the ratio) against total sales (the second part). It's a typical usecase of the useful Fixed calculation.

The third and last advantage is also very useful: Fixed allows you to remove duplicates in your data. As you can specify the level of detail of a Measure, you can return the unique value of a Measure (with `MAX` or `MIN`) by its unique row identifier. Hard to picture? The following hands-on tutorial shows you how to deduplicate your data.

Hands-on - use a LOD function

In the following example, you'll add a target for the quantity in each Category of Sample - Superstore. The `Target` table contains two columns, `Category` and `Target`, as you can see in this screenshot:

Category	Target
Technology	7000
Office Supplies	20000
Furniture	10000

For this example, download the `Superstore with Target` Excel file from my blog, `book.ladataviz.com`, in the *Chapter 10: An introduction to calculations* section. Here's the direct link: `https://ladataviz.com/wp-content/uploads/2018/09/Superstore-with-Target.xls`. This Excel file contains two sheets, `Orders` and `Target`.

Let's add a target to our orders and deduplicate thanks to Fixed:

1. Open Tableau and connect to the `Superstore with Target` Excel file.
2. Create a Join between the two tables. As you can see, the `Target` value is duplicated:

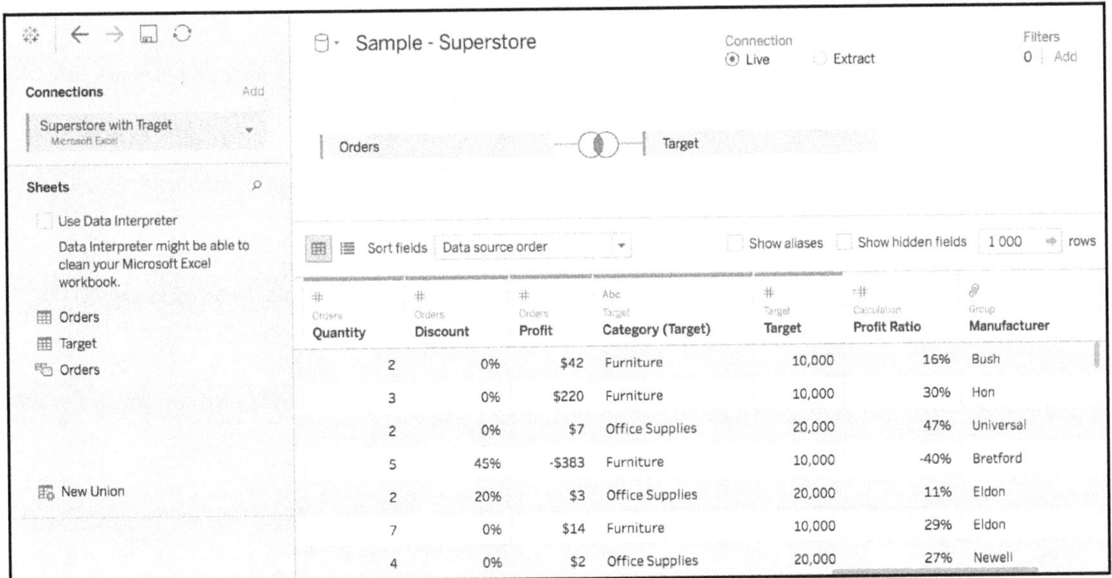

3. In a Worksheet, add **Target** in text. As you can see, the value is way above the expected sum of targets.
4. Create a Calculated Field, name it `Target - fixed`, and write the following calculation: `{FIXED [Category]:MIN([Target])}`.
5. Add the new calculation, **Target - fixed**, in text. You should see *37,000*, the real value of the sum of the targets.

That's it! You can now use the Fixed calculation in all the Worksheets or other calculations; it'll always be calculated correctly.

As you can see, Fixed is a very useful function for removing duplicates, ignoring Filters, and specifying precisely the level of detail of a Measure. Always be careful to put the Filters in Context if you want them to have an impact on the Fixed calculation.

Summary

This chapter is a door that has been opened to so much more. With the right dataset and calculations, you can build absolutely anything you want. Yes, it requires a bit, and sometimes a lot, of practice, but mastering Tableau goes through this. As the title of this book says, we're only getting started here!

In this chapter, you learned the basics of Calculated Fields. With simple examples, you understood why aggregation is so important, created your first calculations, and used your first Tableau functions. In the second part of this chapter, things started to get a bit more complicated with two types of special functions: Table Calculation and LOD. Table functions are applied after the aggregations and can be computed in various ways. You can use them to calculate ranks, difference, percentage of total, and more. LOD can ignore Dimension Filters. Both are powerful; both require practice.

In the next chapter, you'll first learn how to use all the analytics tools provided by Tableau to add Trend Lines, Clusters, Forecasts, and more. Then, you'll create Parameters to bring more interactivity to your visualizations. Finally, with the help of calculations (I told you, this chapter is crucial), you'll create one of the most efficient and useful visualizations, combining Parameters, Analytics tools, and Calculated Fields!

11
Analytics and Parameters

Analysis and Parameters are two significant and easy ways to enhance your work. Analysis tools add new insights, such as **Trend Line**, **Forecast**, or **Cluster**, that are just one drag and drop away. With **Parameters**, you'll discover a new way of bringing interactivity to your visualization with user inputs.

In this chapter, we'll go through the following different sections:

- Using built-in Analytics tools
- How to work with Parameters
- Creating a year-on-year comparison

If you went through all the chapters prior to this one, you know what **Data Source** we'll use! If this is the first chapter you are reading, all the examples and guided tutorial can be reproduced with the **Sample-Superstore** Data Source, which you can find on the first page when opening Tableau.

Using built-in Analytics tools

When creating a visualization on a worksheet, you always use the **Data** pane on the left, where you can find **Dimensions** and **Measures**. Under the aforementioned Data Source, you can see that there are two tabs: **Data** and **Analytics**. If you click on **Analytics**, Tableau opens a new pane, divided into three parts:

- **Summarize**
- **Model**
- **Custom**

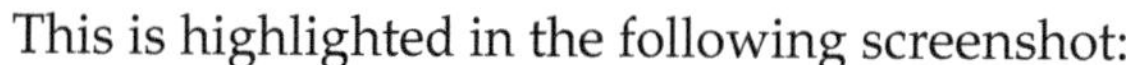

This is highlighted in the following screenshot:

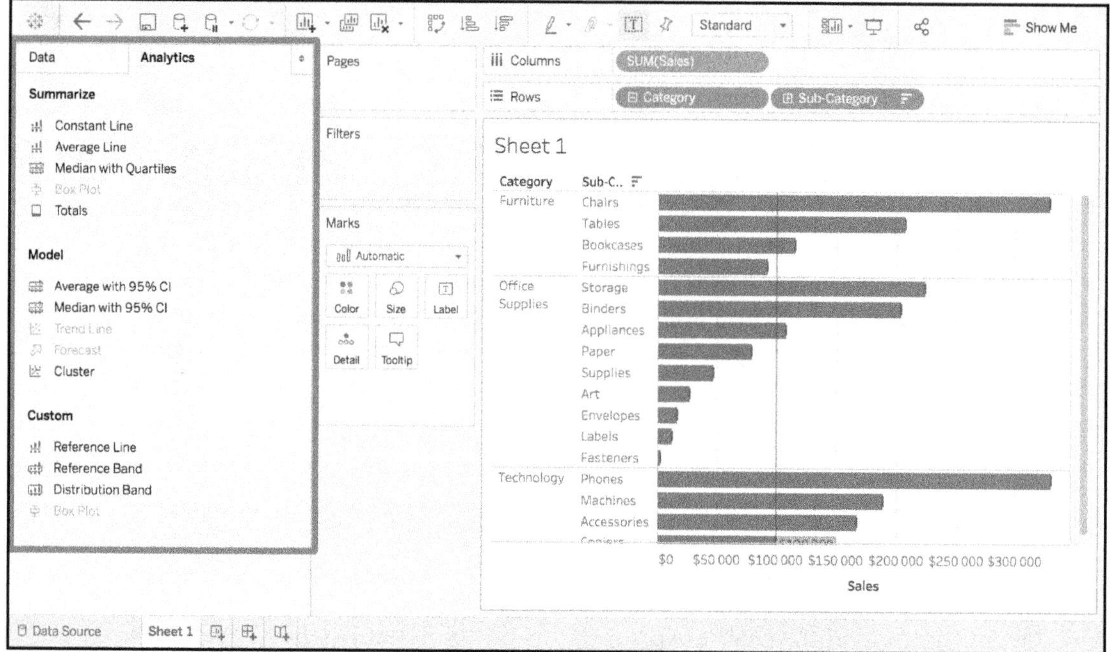

All the options on the **Analytics** pane can be found in other places in Tableau (with a right-click on an axis or the **Analysis** menu on top). The options in the **Analytics** pane are mostly just shortcuts or pre-configured options.

Let's explore all the options of each section. All of them can be used with a simple drag and drop in the View.

The Summarize tab

In Summarize, you can find options to add a Reference Line, Band, Box Plot, or Totals. Let's do a quick overview of each option, starting with the Constant Line.

Constant Line

With a double-click on **Constant Line** or with a drag and drop on the View, you can automatically add a Constant Line to your visualization. When you add it, Tableau opens a small textbox where you can enter the value of the constant. A Constant Line is an excellent way of representing a goal.

For example, the goal could be to have sales above $100,000 for each Sub-Category. As you can see in the following screenshot, it's straightforward to spot the sub-categories that are above or below the goal with a Constant Line:

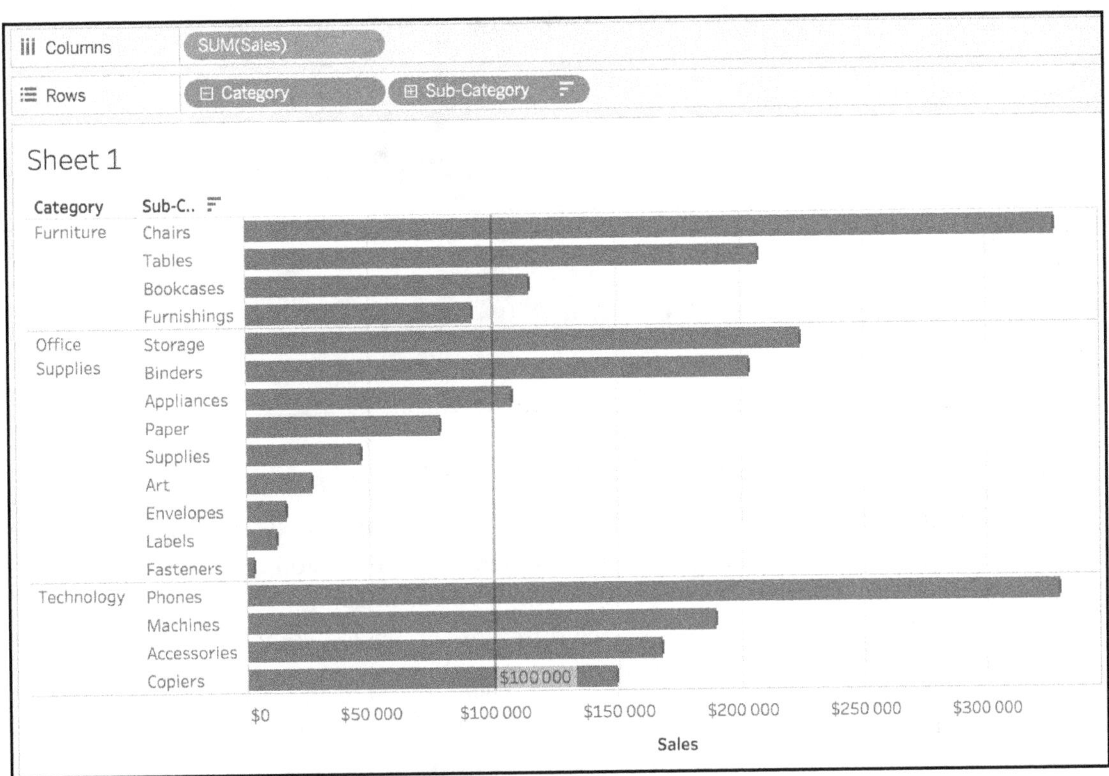

With a simple click on the line, you can change the value of the constant, change its format, or remove it. Let's continue with the second, very similar option; Average Line.

Average Line

An Average Line works in the same way as a *Constant Line*. But unlike it, you don't enter any value. Instead, Tableau automatically calculates the average of the Measure. When you start to drag **Average Line** on the View, Tableau displays a menu where you can drop the option on **Table**, **Pane**, or **Cell** as shown in the following screenshot:

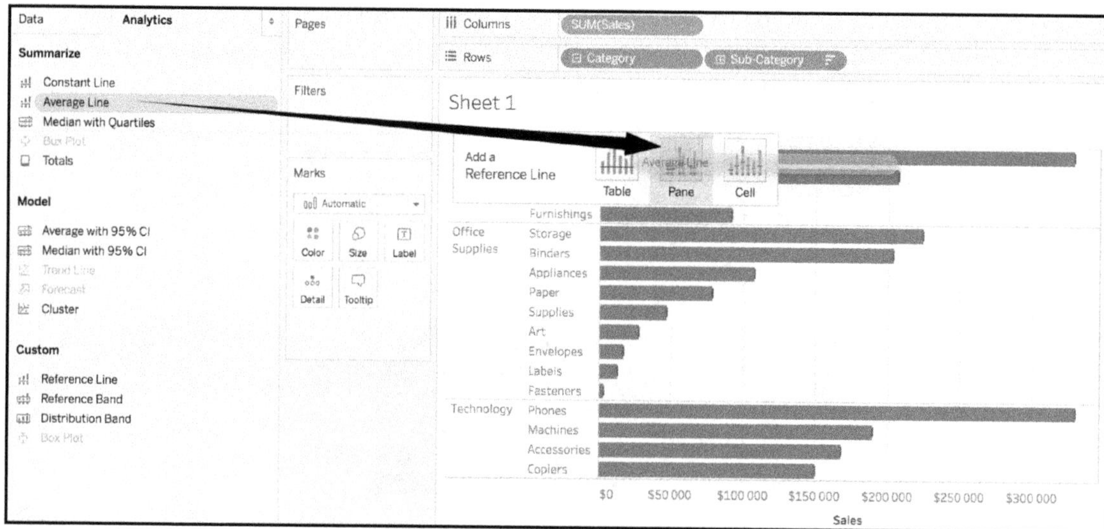

The icons help you understand the difference between the three options:

- **Table**: Tableau draws a unique line that is the average of all the **Marks**
- **Pane**: Tableau draws as many lines as there are intersections between the Dimensions (in the preceding example, three lines)
- **Cell**: Tableau draws a line for each different Dimension combinations (so it's usually not very useful when using averages)

When you click on an Average Line, you can edit the default aggregation, average, to a median, or sum for example. If you click on **Edit**, Tableau opens a menu where you can customize the Average Line. Here's the screenshot of the menu:

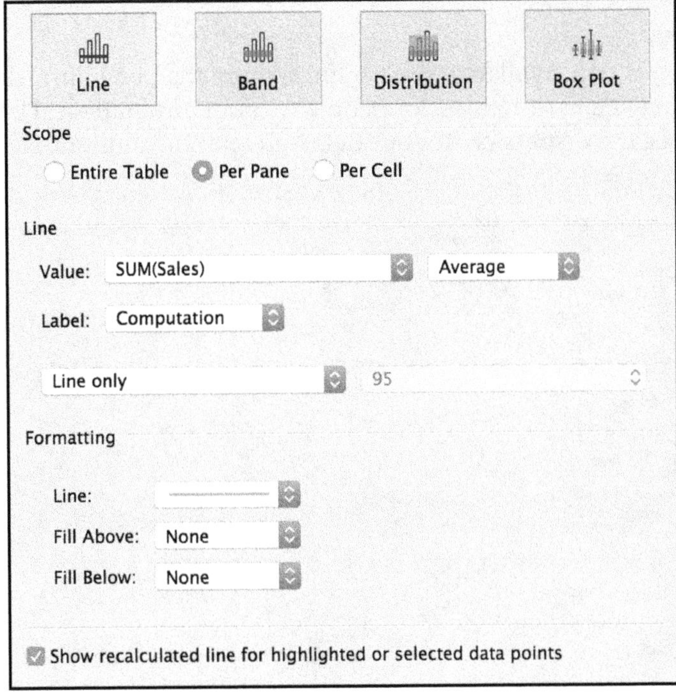

In this menu, you can change the Scope (Table, Pane, or Cell), the value used for the average, the aggregation, the label, the format, and many other formatting options. If you want to change anything regarding your line, you can find it here.

The next option combines a Reference Line and Distribution Band.

Median with Quartiles

This option creates a **Median with Quartiles** and a Distribution Band with upper and lower quartiles. As for the Average Line, you can create a Median with Quartiles on the Table, Pane, or Cell.

After adding it, if you right-click on the axis and go to **Edit Reference Line**, you can see that you can configure the **Median Line** and the **Quartiles Distribution** separately. You can also configure them with a click on the line or at the border of the quartiles.

The next option, the Box Plot, only works under certain conditions.

Box Plot

The **Box Plot** option is only available when there is more than one unstacked Mark per cell. The Box Plot may be hard to read for people without any statistical background, but it's a great tool to see the dispersion in your data and spot the outliers. Here's an example of a Box Plot:

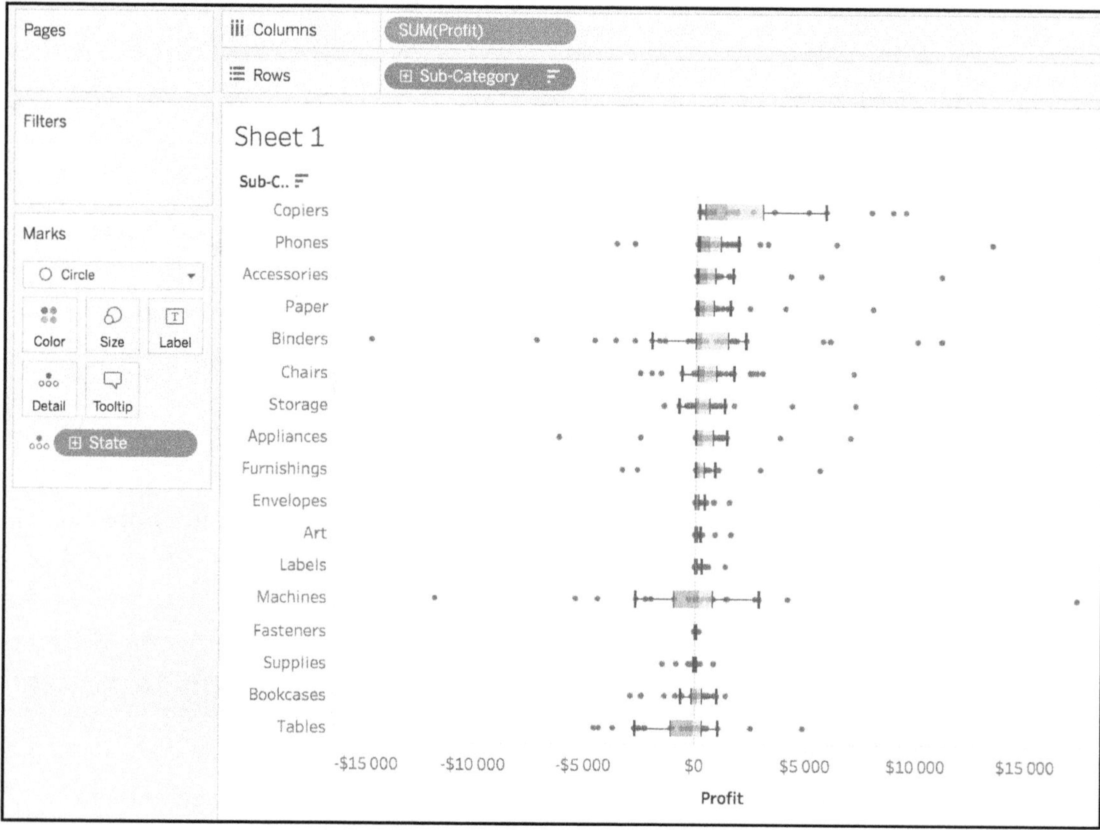

This example shows the profit made by each Sub-Category with one circle per State. As you can see, you can easily spot the outliers negative state in **Binders** or **Machines**.

The last Summarize option is a classic option called **Totals**.

Totals

When you start to drag **Totals** into the View, Tableau displays a new menu where you can specify whether you want to add the subtotals or the grand totals for **Rows** or **Columns**. Drop the option on the desired box to add Totals. Tableau uses the default property **Total using** of the Measure to choose the aggregation.

Here's an example of subtotals and grand totals:

Now, let's explore a new set of options, Model.

The Model tab

The options under **Model** don't just add a new aggregation to summarize your data, but add new statistical models like **Cluster**, **Trend Line**, or **Forecast**. Using them is as simple as in the previous section; drag and drop them in the View.

Average or median with a confidence interval

The first two options are similar to an Average Line or Median Line. The only difference is the addition of a confidence interval of 95%.

The next option is, this time, very different than what you've seen before.

Trend Line

You can only add a **Trend Line** when you have two continuous fields on opposing axes (one on Rows, one on Columns). The Trend Line can be used to see the trend of a Measure over time or the correlation between two Measures.

To add a **Trend Line**, drag and drop the option on the View. By default, the Trend Model used is **Linear**. You can specify the Trend Model to use when you drag and drop the option.

It's also possible to add a **Trend Line** with a right-click on the View, among the options available.

Here's an example of the usage of Trend Lines:

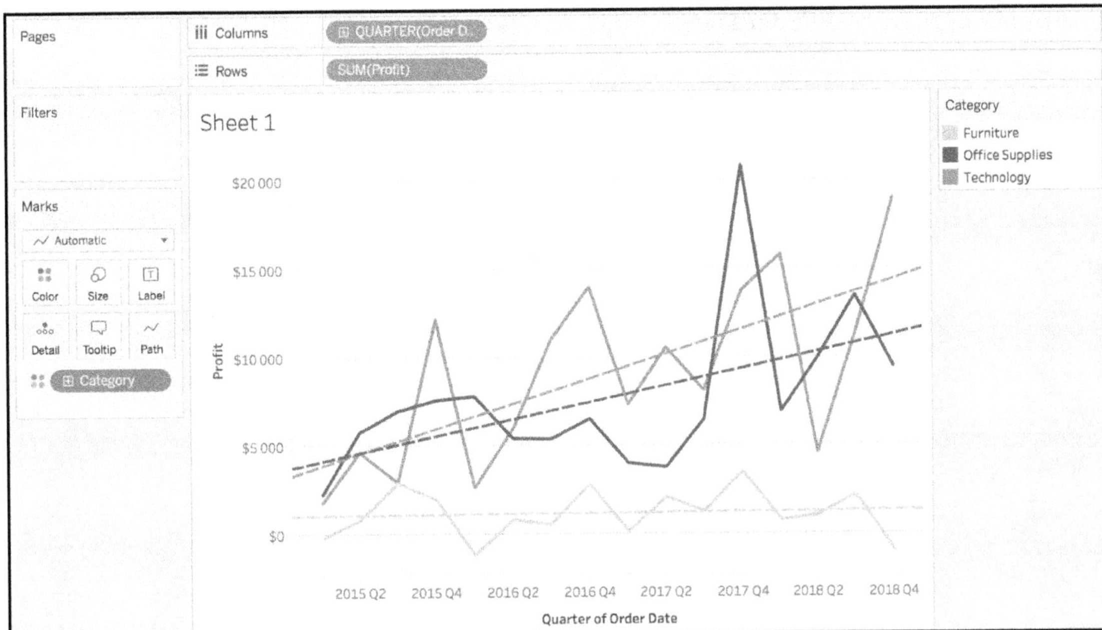

As you can see, it's easy to see that the profits are growing for **Office Supplies** and **Technology**, but stagnating for the **Furniture**.

When you hover over a Trend Line, you can see some information about the Trend Model. If you right-click on the Trend Line, you can open an advanced description of the Trend Line and the Trend Model or open the **Edit Trend Lines...** window where you can change the Trend Model and customize it.

For the next option, a Date is mandatory.

Forecast

Forecast is a great option when you have Date fields in your Data Source. You can only add a Forecast when you're displaying a Measure through a continuous date. Tableau calculates the forecast based on the existing data points. To add a **Forecast**, drag and drop the option in the View or select **Show Forecast** among the right-click options.

When you add a Forecast, the Measure is replaced by a Forecast Measure, and **Forecast Indicator** is added in **Color**. Here's an example of the Forecast of the Profit by **Continuous Quarter** of **Order Date**:

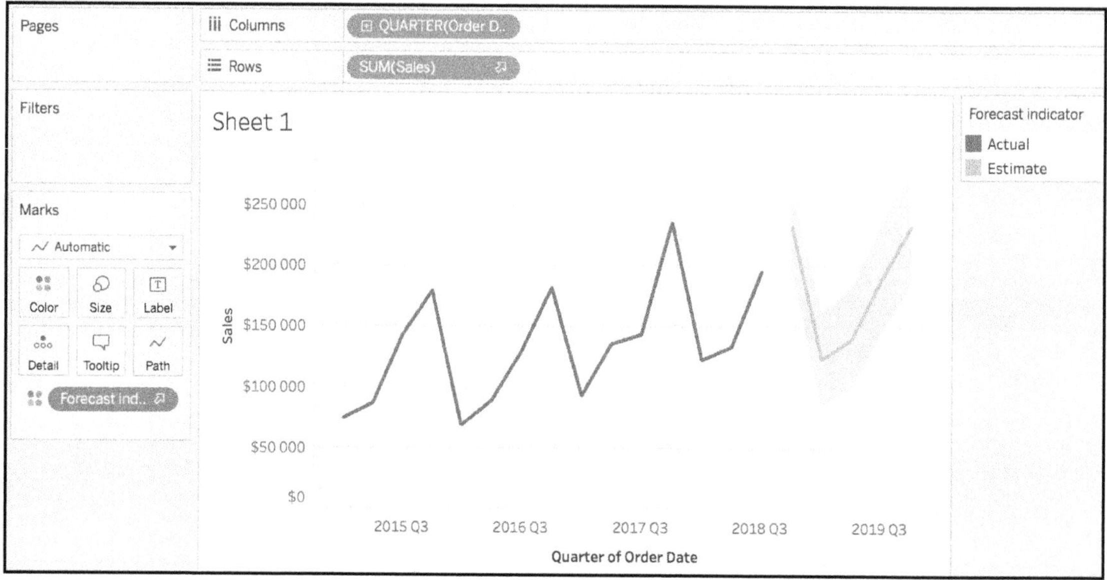

When you right-click on the View, if you hover over **Forecast**, you can find a description of the **Forecast Model** and some options configure the Forecast.

Last but not least is Cluster.

Cluster

To add a Cluster, you need to have a least one Measure and one Dimension in the View. To add a **Cluster**, double-click on the option or drag and drop it on the View.

When you add a Cluster, Tableau opens a window where you can add or remove variables (Measure or Dimension) and define the number of Clusters. Then, Tableau adds a new generated pill, **Clusters**, on **Color**. You can use this generated pill wherever you want in the View (to another property or in filters for example) or drag and drop it among the fields in your Data Source to add as a new field.

Here's an example of four clusters on the sub-categories by **Sales** and **Profit**:

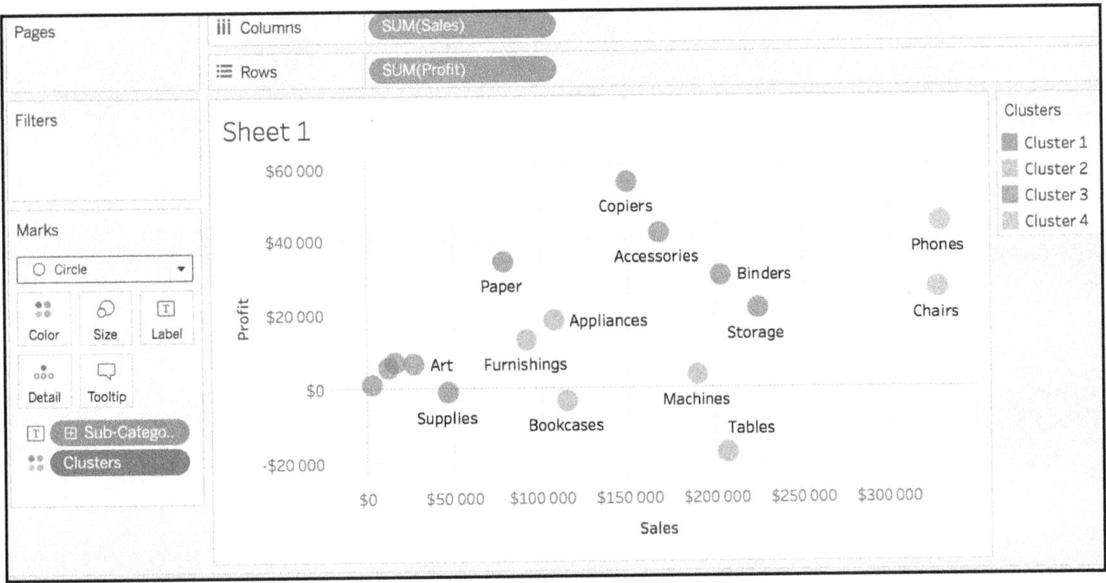

As with the other Model options, you can right-click on the **Clusters** pill to edit it or see the model description.

To finish with this section, let's see the Custom analytics options. Be careful; this will be fast!

The Custom tab

The **Summarize** options are just shortcuts or pre-configured **Custom** options such as Reference Line, Band, or Distribution.

When using a Custom option, Tableau automatically opens a window to configure it. In this window, you can set the scope, the value, change the format, the aggregation, and configure many other options. Here's an example of the **Add Reference Line, Band, or Box** menu:

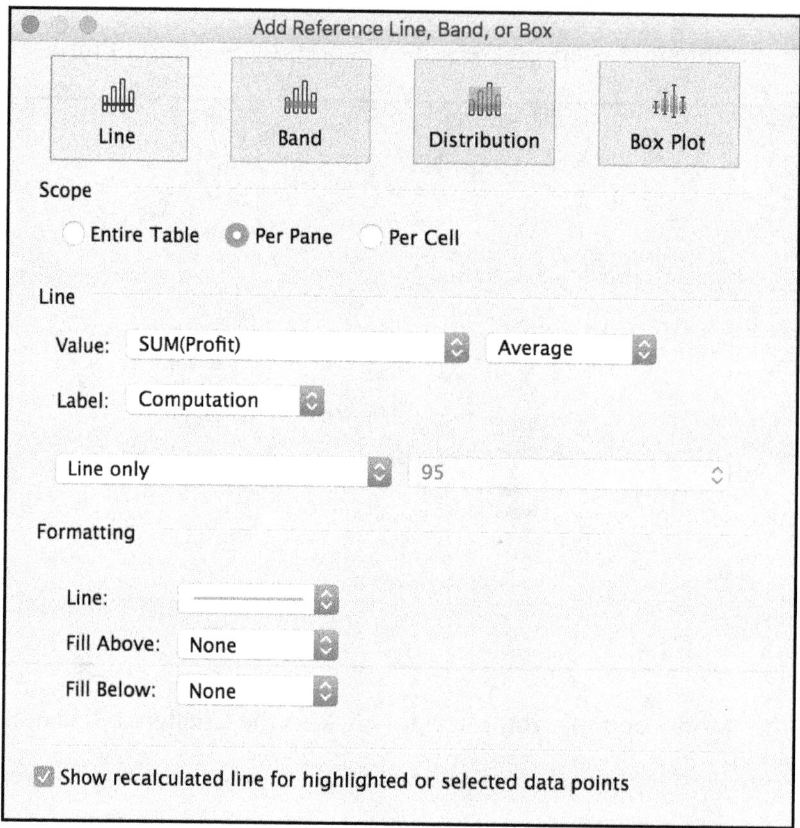

Another way to open this menu is with a right-click on an Axis and selecting **Add Reference Line**.

Custom options are not pre-configured, giving you the liberty to choose precisely what you want to display. The available values when editing a Reference Line, Band, or Box are the pills in the View and the Parameters. You will not find all the Measures in the Data Source. If you want to build a Reference Line, Band, or Box with a specific Measure, you need to add it somewhere in the View (usually in the *Detail Mark Property*, as it doesn't alter the visualization).

In this chapter, the last section, *Create a year-on-year comparator*, includes a concrete usage of a Custom Reference Line. But before that, we need to take a look at the last Tableau element, Parameters.

How to work with Parameters

Parameters are a particular element in Tableau, as with Dimensions, Measures, and Sets. They can be Continuous or Discrete depending on the data type in use. The three major aspects of Parameters are:

- They are not linked to the Data Source (they don't rely on any field)
- They only return one value at a time
- They are, by default, static, so there is no built-in way to refresh the values automatically

For the last point, you can use external Extensions, to create dynamic Parameters.

Let's start with how to create a Parameter.

Creating a Parameter

To create a Parameter, you can use the small arrow next to **Dimensions** as highlighted in the following screenshot:

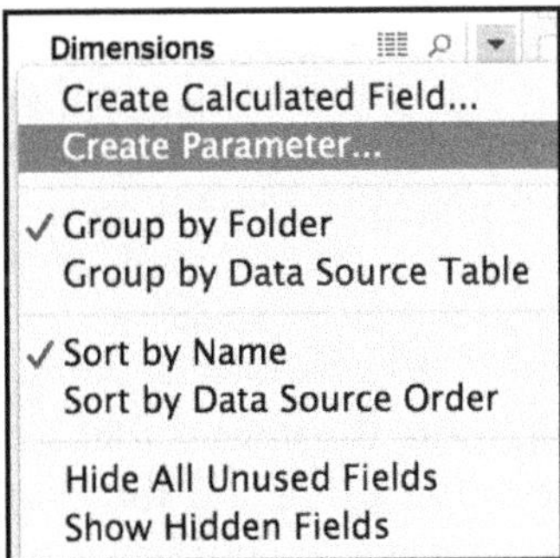

When you create a Parameter, Tableau automatically opens the **Edit Parameter** window, as illustrated in the following screenshot:

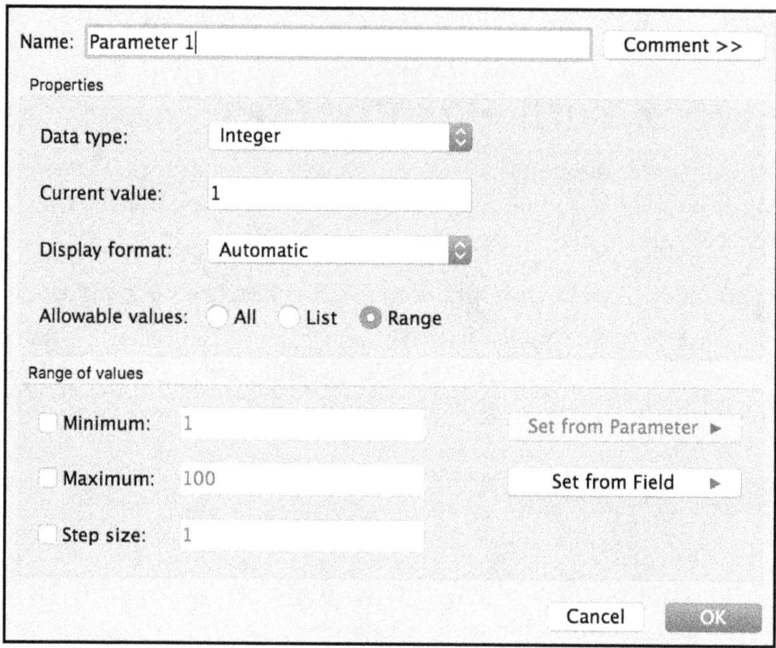

This window is the only place where you can change or configure a Parameter. On the top, you can specify its **Name** and add a **Comment** (visible when you hover over it). You can also change the Parameter properties by defining the **Data Type** and the **Current value** (the value that the Parameter will have when you finish its creation). For some data types, you can also change the default **Display format**.

The last option, **Allowable values**, is a core element of a Parameter. As you know, a Parameter is not related to the dataset and can thereby take any possible value. With the **Allowable values** option, you can, however, limit the possibilities of what the users can enter. Let's spend some time learning a bit more about the three **Allowable values** options:

- The first option, **All**, allows all possible values to be entered.
- The second option, **List**, limits the values that a user can choose from a list. For each item, you can specify the value and the alias (in the **Display As** column). You can also add all the values from a field or paste copied values from your clipboard (from an Excel file for example). Here's an example of the usage of List:

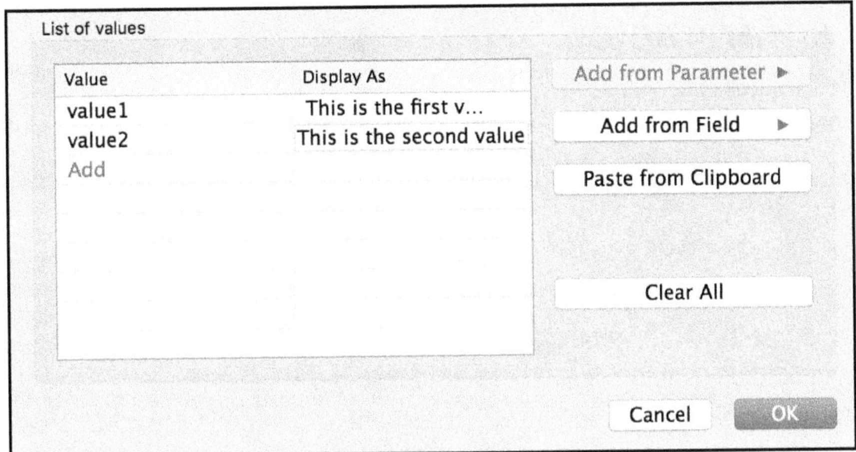

If you want to add the values from a field quickly, you can also create a Parameter with the **Create** option when you right-click on a field.

- The last option **Range**, is available for Date, Date and Time, Integer, and Float. With Range, you can set a minimum, a maximum, and a step size. The user will only be able to choose a value from that range. Here's an example of the usage of Range:

If you create a Boolean Parameter, you can't use those options, and you'll be limited to True and False, but you can change the aliases.

Click on **OK**, and your Parameter is ready! How to use it? Continue reading!

Using a Parameter

Usually, a Parameter is displayed in a Worksheet or a Dashboard. To display a Parameter in a Worksheet, right-click on it and select the option **Show Parameter Control**. On a Dashboard, you can add a Parameter from the options when you select a Worksheet or from the **Analysis** menu at the top.

Depending on the data type and the allowable value specified, the Parameter can be displayed:

- As a free Type In textbox where the users can enter any values they want
- As a Slider (usually associated with a Ranged Parameter)
- As a Compact or Single Value List (usually associated with a List Parameter)

Using the small arrow next to the **Parameter Card**, you can change the display mode and find other options to customize it as you can see in the following screenshot:

For the moment, you've only learned how to create, configure, and display a Parameter. Displaying a Parameter and selecting a value has no impact. To use a Parameter, you need to put it in a Calculated Field.

The next section is a step-by-step tutorial where you'll see the potential of Parameters and how to use them to create great analysis.

Creating a year-on-year comparator

To create a year-on-year comparator, you need to combine everything that we saw previously: **Calculated Field**, **Reference Line**, and **Parameter**.

Your mission (*if you accept it*) is to build a visualization where you can see the Sales by Sub-Categories of a selected year compared to the previous year with a **Reference Line**. **Color** also helps you to quickly spot the sub-categories where the sales are lower than the past year. Here's the final result:

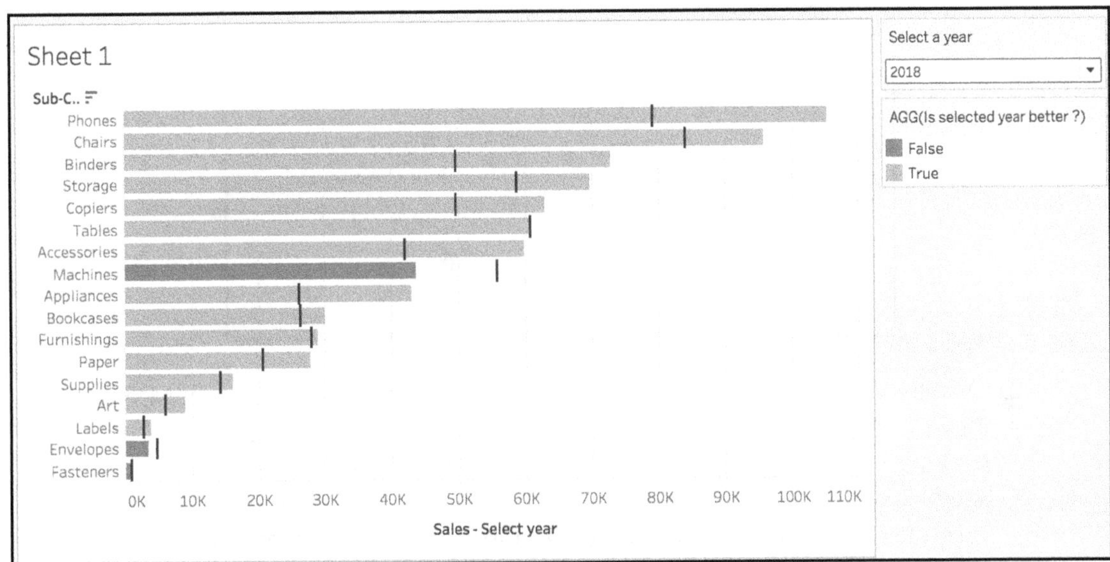

Quite impressive, isn't it? Let's build it! Follow the tutorial:

1. Create a Parameter to choose the year. Configure it as an **Integer** with a **List** of allowable values. The list is composed of four values: `2015`, `2016`, `2017`, and `2018`. You can, if you want to make it perfect, change the display of the values to remove the thousand separators (by modifying the display format or editing the **Display As** column). Name it `Select a year`, and choose **2018** as the current value.

Your Parameter configuration window should look like this:

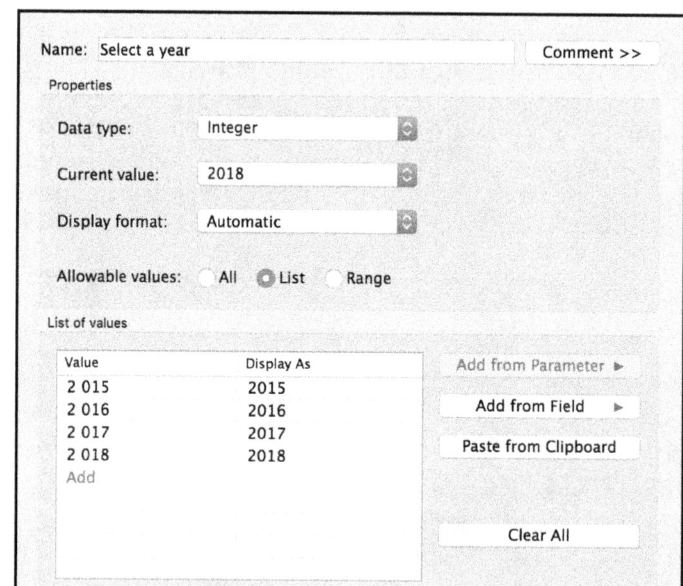

2. Display your Parameter (right-click on it and select **Show Parameter Control**).
3. Create a **Calculated Field** that will return the sales of the selected year. Name it `Sales - Selected year` and write the following formula inside: `if YEAR([Order Date]) = [Select a year] then [Sales] END`. This formula returns the Sales if the Year of Order Date is the same as the value of the Parameter.
4. Create a second Calculated Field, name it `Sales - Previous year` and write the following formula: `if YEAR([Order Date]) = [Select a year]-1 then [Sales] END`. This formula returns the Sales if the Year of Order Date is the value of the Parameter minus one (so if you select 2018 in the Parameter, the formula returns the Sales value of 2017).

For each Calculated Field make sure that the calculation is valid.

5. Build the visualization: put **Sales - Selected year** in **Columns**, **Sub-Category** in **Rows** and Sort them from highest to lowest. You can now play with the Parameter to show the Sales of the selected year.

6. Put **Sales - Previous year** in the **Detail** property. Your Worksheet should look as follows:

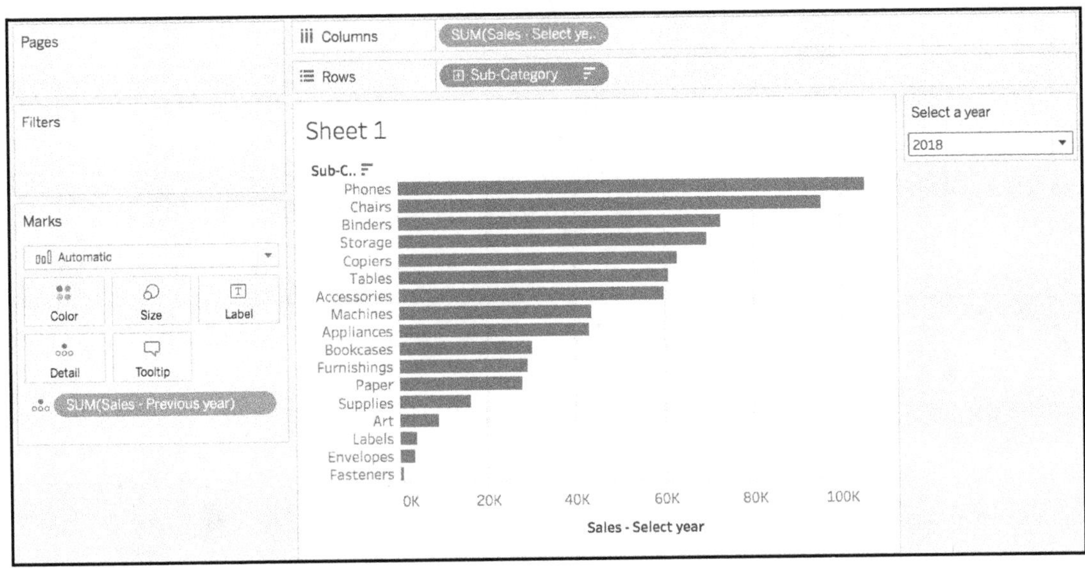

7. Go to the **Analytics** pane and add a **Custom Reference Line** on each cell. For the value of the **Reference Line**, select **Sales - Previous year** (the aggregation doesn't matter as we are on the cell level). In the Formatting part, you can make the line a bit bigger and darker. Here's how your **Reference Line** should be configured:

Line
Band
Distribution
Box Plot
Scope
Entire Table
Per Pane
Per Cell
Line
Value: SUM(Sales - Previous year)
Average
Label: None
Line only
95
Formatting
Line:
Fill Above: None
Fill Below: None

8. Visually, you should be able the see the difference between the selected year and the previous year, thanks to the Reference Line.
9. To add the final touch, create a new Calculated Field, name it `Is selected year better ?` and write the following formula: `SUM([Sales - Selected year ]) >= SUM([Sales - Previous year])`. This Calculated Field is a Boolean that returns True if the sales of the selected year are higher than the sales of the previous year and False if not.
10. Finally, put the new Calculated Field, **Is selected year better ?**, in **Color**. If you want, you can modify the Colors. In the end, your Worksheet should look as follows:

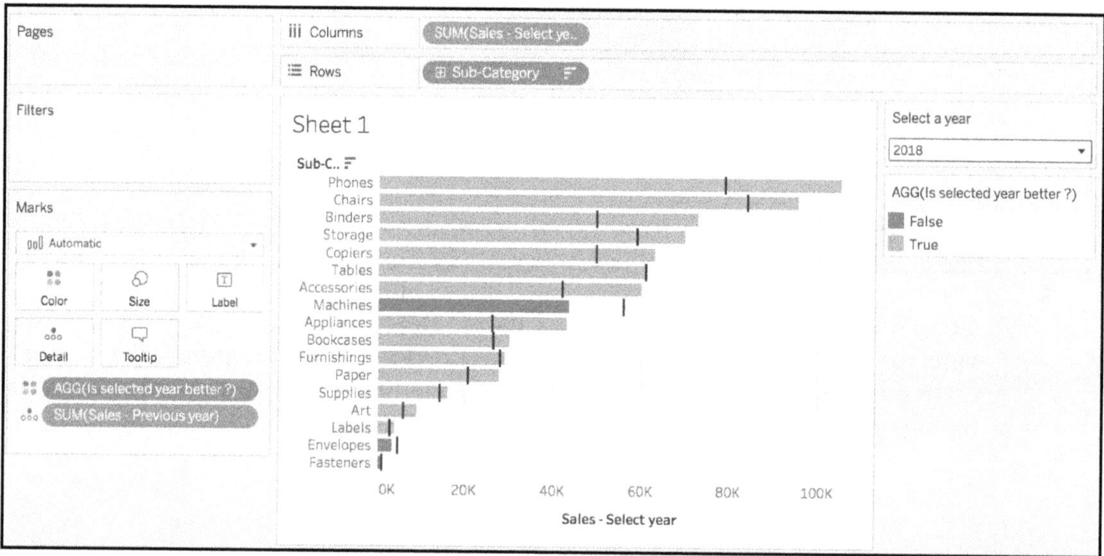

You can play with the Parameter to change the year, and you'll directly spot the problematic sub-categories. This visualization is a good exercise because it makes you practice a lot of Tableau features and it's also a great way of comparing two different years.

Summary

This chapter focused on two ways of enhancing your visualization. With the Analytics tools, you can use Models such as Trend Line, Cluster, or Forecast, but also all sorts of Reference Lines, Bands, and Distribution. You can use all these options to add new ways to visualize your data and get a deeper understanding of it. With Parameters, you can create any input to interact with the visualization. The last section of this chapter summed up what you saw during this chapter with a real use-case using Parameters and a Reference Line.

In the next chapter, we'll talk about the Data Source again. You'll discover how to connect to a Spatial file, how to work with multiple Data Sources, and how to create advanced Unions.

12
Advanced Data Connections

In a Workbook, you can add as many data sources as you want. In a Worksheet, you can see which Data Source is used thanks to the tick mark (✓) next to its icon, as you can see in the following screenshot:

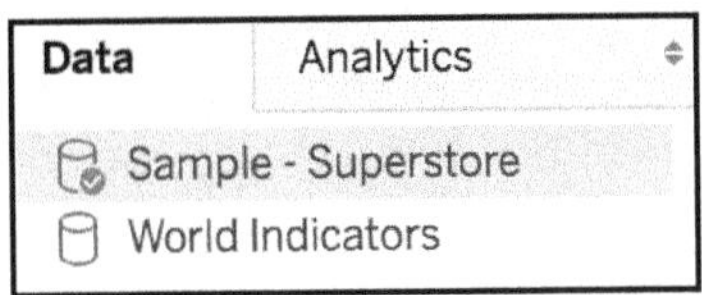

You can create different Worksheets based on different data sources and assemble them in a Dashboard. But what if you need more than that? What if you want to create a visualization using two different data sources or create a unique data source based on a different type of connection? You can do all of that, too.

In this chapter about advanced data connections, we'll see how to work with multiple datasets as well as some other new features for unions. The three sections of this chapter focus on the following:

- Cross-database Join
- Data-blending
- Wildcard union

The different examples require a specific dataset or file to be reproduced.

Let's start this chapter with a way of combining multiple datasets in one Data Source.

Cross-database Join

In `Chapter 1`, *Catching Up with Tableau 2018*, about data connection, you saw how to create joins between different Tables of the same dataset. With cross-database Joins, you can create joins between different tables from different connections of different types. It's a great way to add new dimensions to your analysis.

You can't use all the different types of connections in a cross-database Join. A published Data Source, for example, can't be joined.

As an example, let's create a join between Sample-Superstore and another Excel File, `Reimbursement`, containing the reimbursed orders.

To reproduce the following example, you need to download the `Reimbursement` Excel file available on the website, `book.ladataviz.com`, in the *Chapter 12* section, or use this link: `https://ladataviz.com/wp-content/uploads/2018/09/Reimbursement.xlsx`.

Here's what the `Reimbursement` table contains:

Order ID	Reimbursed	Reason
CA-2015-115812	y	Defect
CA-2017-152156	y	Defect
CA-2017-111682	y	Defect
CA-2017-145583	y	Delay
CA-2017-130162	n	New address
US-2017-123470	y	Wrong product

Here's how to create a cross-database Join between those two files:

1. Open Tableau, and click on the saved Data Source, **Sample - Superstore**.
2. Click on **Data Source** at the bottom-left of the window to open the Data Source workplace.

3. Next to **Connections**, click on **Add** to connect to another File or Server, as highlighted in the following screenshot:

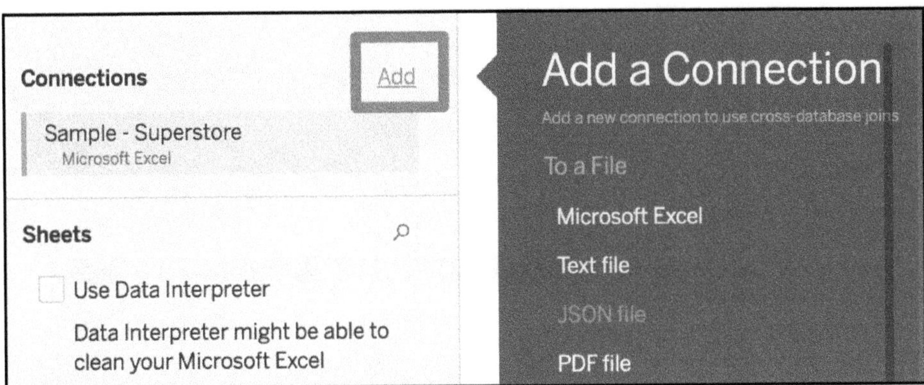

4. Search and select the **Reimbursement** Excel File. Tableau automatically opens it in the same Data Source page, underneath **Sample - Superstore.**
5. Add the **Reimbursement** table as a usual left Join:

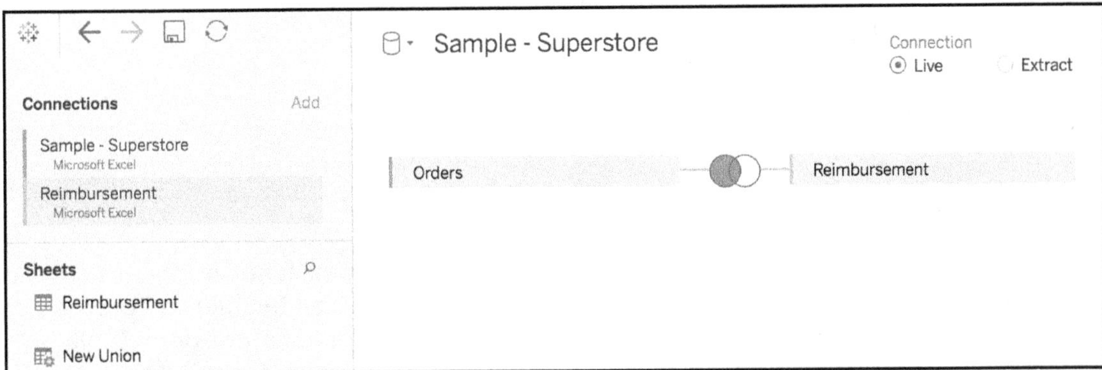

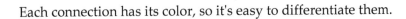

Each connection has its color, so it's easy to differentiate them.

6. Create, in a new Worksheet, a visualization that combines the sales and the reason for reimbursement using a single data source:

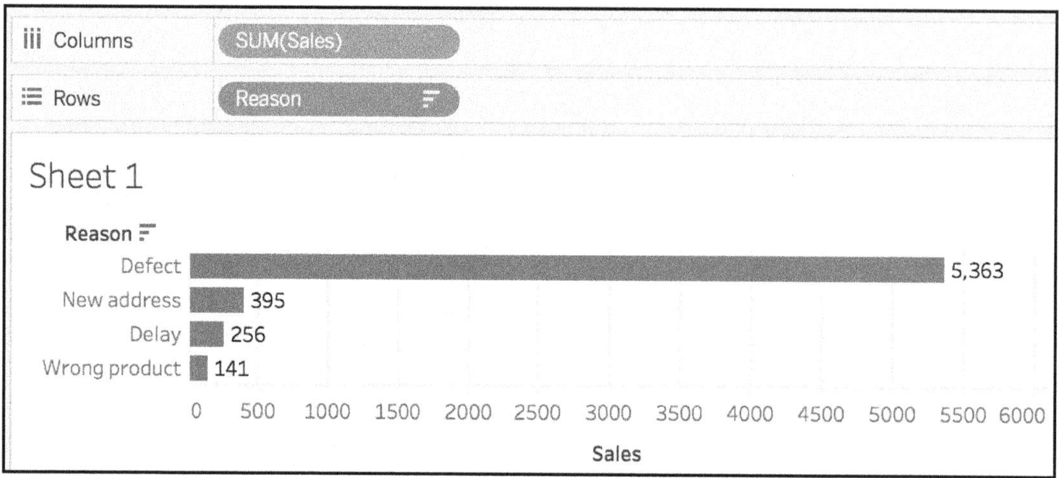

A cross-database Join has the same disadvantage as a standard join: it can duplicate the data. However, it's a great feature that allows you to combine multiple datasets of different types in a unique Data Source.

The next section presents another way of combining two datasets.

Data-blending

Data-blending is a way of using different fields from different Data Sources in one Worksheet. There is always a primary data source (the tick icon in blue) and one or multiple secondary data sources (the tick mark in orange). As for joins, one or multiple common fields are needed to create the relationships between the data sources.

Unlike joins, data-blending is often used to add new Measures. Fields coming from the secondary data sources are always aggregated. However, they are only aggregated using the common fields, so there is no data duplication. Finally, data-blending can rapidly have a negative impact on performance.

The more different values there are in the common Fields, the bigger the impact on performance.

Fields with the same name can automatically be used to create the relationship. In the secondary data sources, you can recognize the fields that can be used for the relationship with the small link icon next to their name. You can click on the link icon to enable or disable them. For example, in the following screenshot, both **Order Date** and **Order Number** can be used as links, but only **Order Date** is selected and thus, used by Tableau:

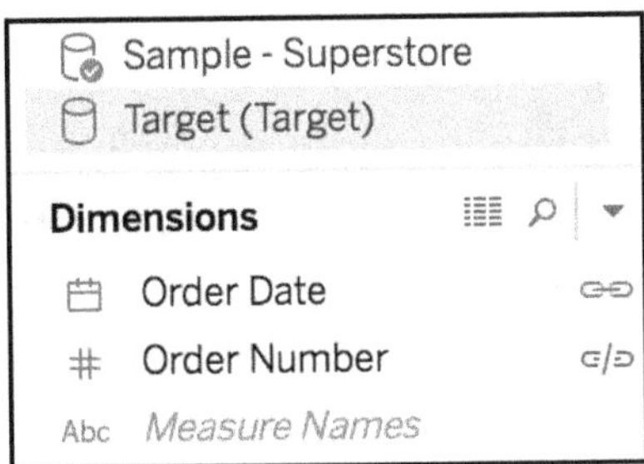

If no fields have the same name, you can use **Edit Relationships...** from the **Data** menu at the top. A new window opens to configure the relationships and, with the custom option, you select the common fields manually.

If no fields are common, you can create a Calculated Field to build the relationship.

To illustrate data-blending, we'll add a target to the Sample-Superstore.

To reproduce the following example, you need to download the `Target` Excel file available on the website, `book.ladataviz.com`, in the **Chapter 12** section, or use this link: `https://ladataviz.com/wp-content/uploads/2018/09/Target.xlsx`.

Targets are in a simple Excel file with the **Year** and the value of the **Target**, as you can see here:

Year	Target
2015	500000
2016	500000
2017	500000
2018	700000

Go through the following steps to add a target to the sales:

1. Open Tableau Desktop and select the **Sample-Superstore** saved Data Source.
2. Click on the **New Data Source** icon in the toolbar: .
3. Search and select the **Target** Excel file. Tableau should have automatically put the **Target** table in the Data Source.
4. Click on **Sheet 1**; you should now have two different data sources, as shown in the following screenshot:

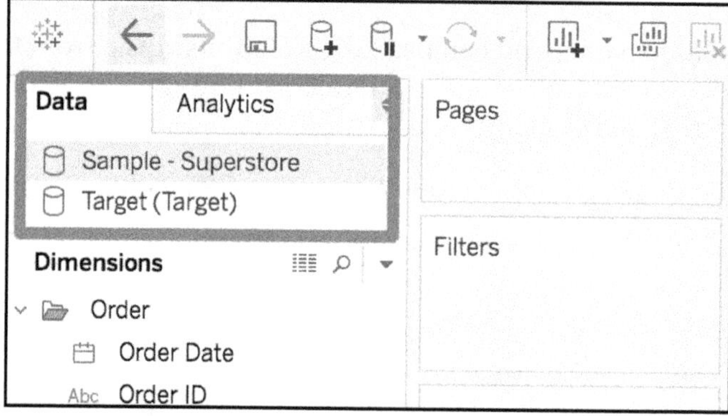

5. Create a Bar chart with the year of the **Order Date** in **Columns** and the **Sales** in **Rows**.
6. Add the **Target** Measure from the **Target** Data Source in **Detail**. A warning opens because Tableau isn't able to find a relationship between the two data sources. You current visualization should look as follows:

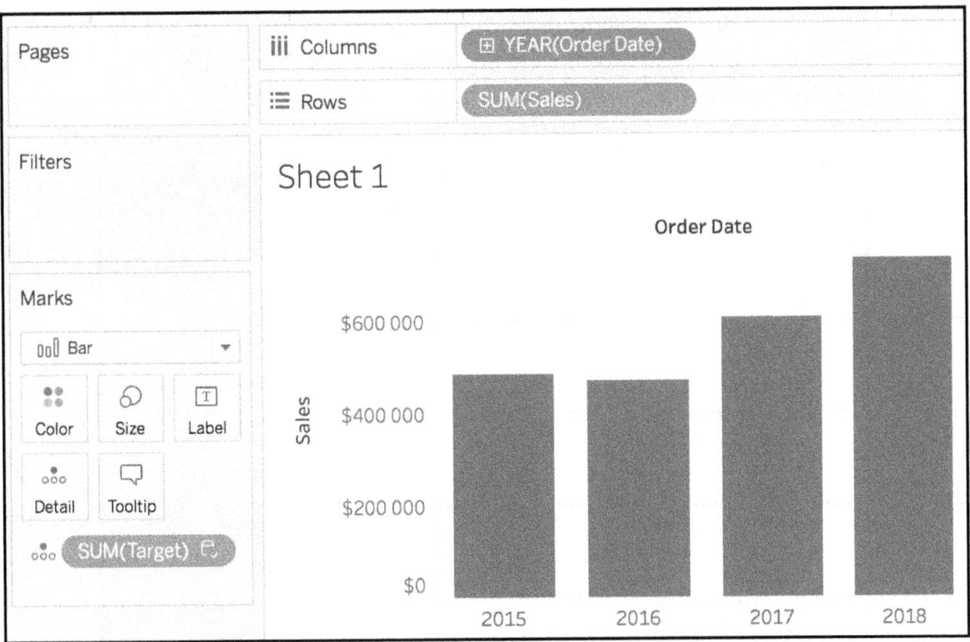

7. Open the **Data** menu at the top and click on **Edit Relationships....**
8. Choose **Sample - Superstore** as the **Primary data source** and **Target** as the secondary, then select **Custom**. The configuration window should look as follows:

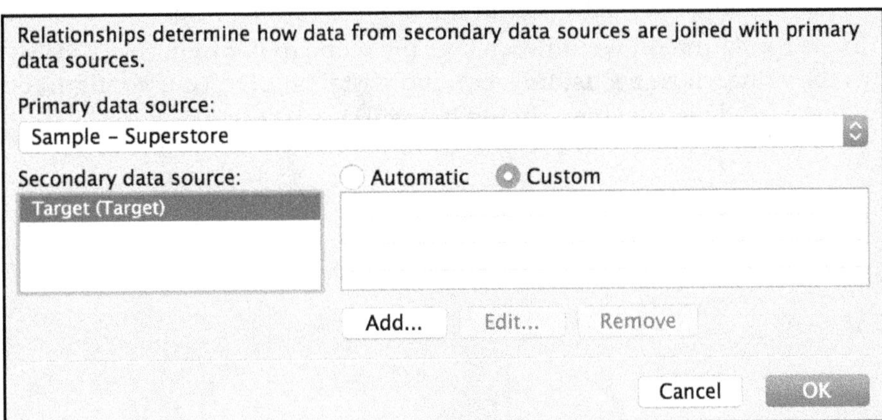

9. Click on the **Add...** button and, in the window that opens, select the **Year(Order Date)** field from the **Primary data source field** and **Year** from the Secondary, as highlighted in the following screenshot, then click on **OK**:

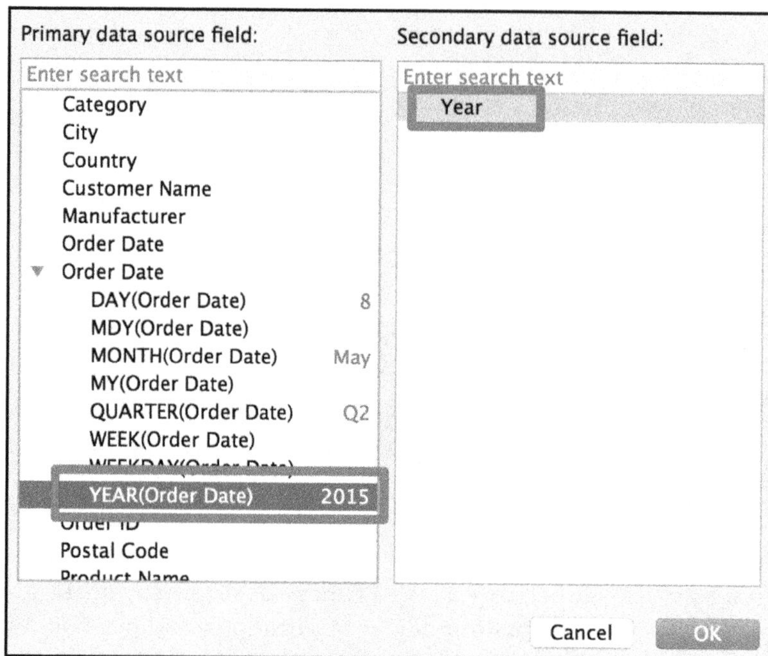

10. In the visualization, right-click on the axis then select **Add Reference Line**.
11. In the configuration window, change the scope to **Per Cell**, select **SUM(Target)** as the value, chose a **Custom** label, and write `Target`. Your configuration window and visualization should be similar to this screenshot:

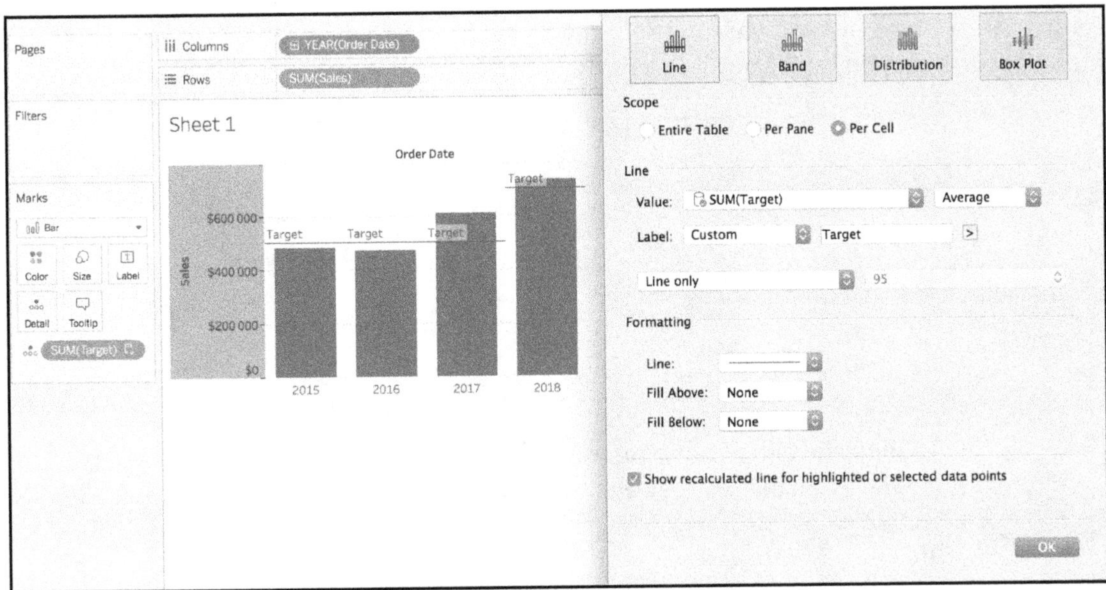

Adding the targets with a normal Join will duplicate the values. Thanks to data-blending, it's both easy and practical to add new Measures with different aggregations coming from different Data Sources. However, there are some limitations, such as you can't use the count distinct or median aggregation, and level-of-detail calculations are not allowed.

In the next section, Unions are back!

Wildcard Union

The first time you saw how to create Unions, you had to select the different tables of the same dataset. Wildcard Unions allow you to create more powerful Unions that automatically add all the files and all the tables that match a specific pattern. This kind of Union is convenient as you don't have to add the new Tables manually, you only need to refresh the Data Source.

As an example for Wildcard Union, I split the `Sample-Superstore` Excel file into four files, one for each year, and I put it in a folder named `Sales` as displayed here:

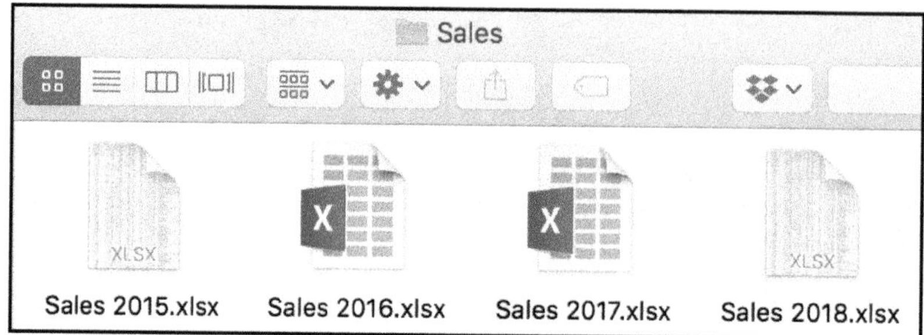

To reproduce the following example, you need to download the `Sales` zip file available on the website, `book.ladataviz.com`, in the **Chapter 12** section or use this link: `https://ladataviz.com/wp-content/uploads/2018/09/Sales.zip`.

Let's Union those files:

1. Open Tableau Desktop and chose Microsoft Excel from the list of connectors.
2. Select the **Sales 2015.xlsx** file.
3. Replace **Sheet1** with **New Union**:

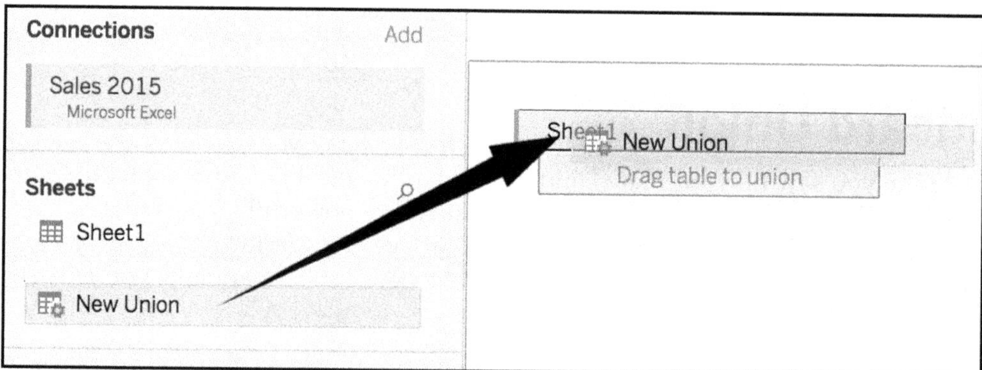

4. Select the second tab, **Wildcard**, and configure it to include all the sheets named `Sheet1`, and all the Excel Workbooks starting with *Sales* by writing `Sales *.xlsx` (use the `*` symbol to represent any other characters). Your configuration window should look like this:

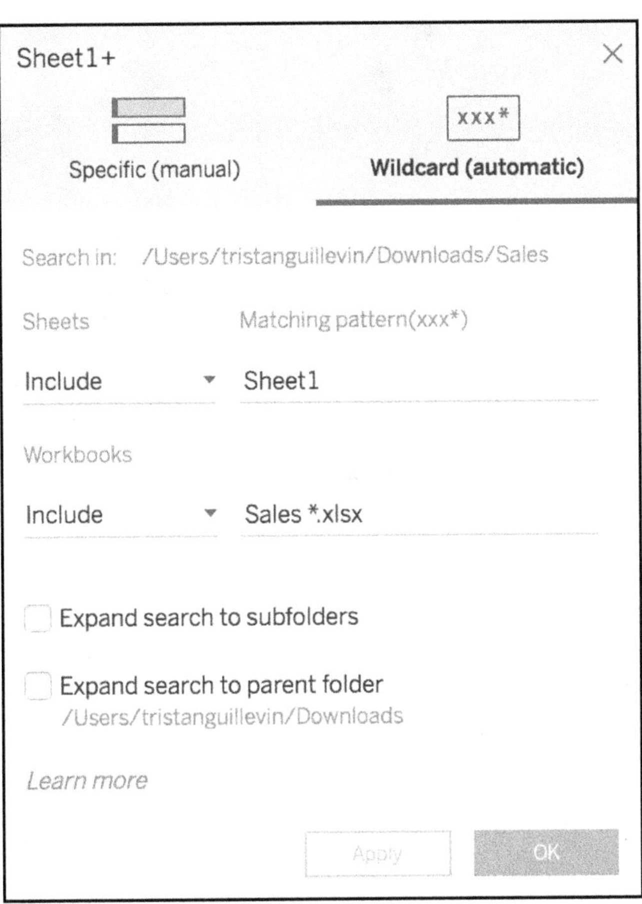

As you can see, you can also expand the search to the subfolders or parent folders.

5. That's it! To test the Wildcard Union, you can create a new visualization that displays the Year of **Order Date** and the **Sales**, with the **Path** of the different files:

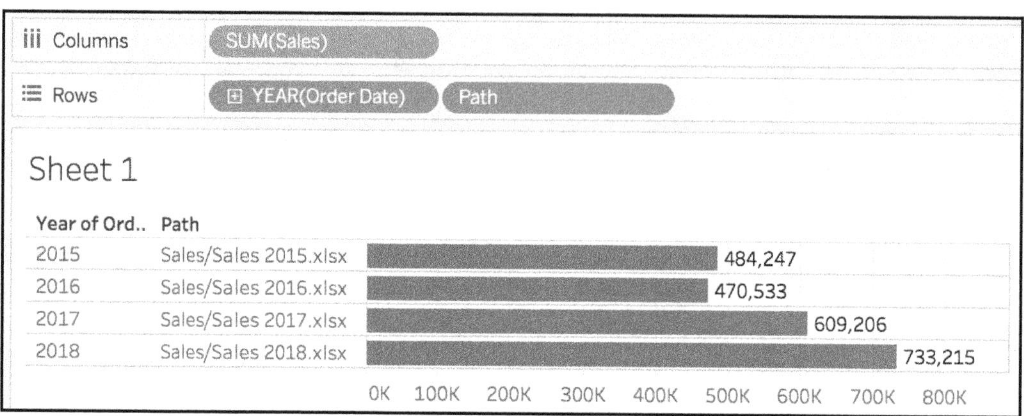

Wildcard Unions are very practical. Use them as often as you can! The only rule is to be careful with the patterns, so you don't include things you don't want!

Summary

This chapter was short but the three new features presented will undoubtedly be useful for you! With cross-database Join, you can create a unique Data Source that combines multiple different connections. With data-blending, you can create a relationship between multiple Data Sources to use their fields in the same Worksheet. Finally, you learned how to give superpowers to Unions thanks to Wildcard Unions, a feature that automatically adds files and tables based on a pattern.

We have one last technical chapter to go, and it's not a trivial one, as we'll talk about security. You will see how to secure your data on Tableau Server and in Tableau Desktop, thanks to three different layers of protection. What are you waiting for? You're almost at the end!

13
Deal with Security

In this last advanced chapter, we'll speak about security, an essential aspect of working with data. To add protection, you need to have Tableau Server. In this chapter, we'll focus on three ways of dealing with security:

- Tableau Server security
- User filters
- Row-level filters

To manage the security on Tableau Server, you need to have sufficient privilege on it. To add the user filter and build the row-level security filter, you need at least one access to Tableau Server. Let's start with the most straightforward way of securing your data on Tableau Server.

Tableau Server security

To protect your Tableau Server contents, you can click on the three dots **...** on any element (**Project**, **Workbooks**, **Views**, or **Data Sources**) to show the options and select **Permissions**. When you click on **Permissions**, Tableau opens a new window where you can specify many security options.

Here's the **Permissions** menu:

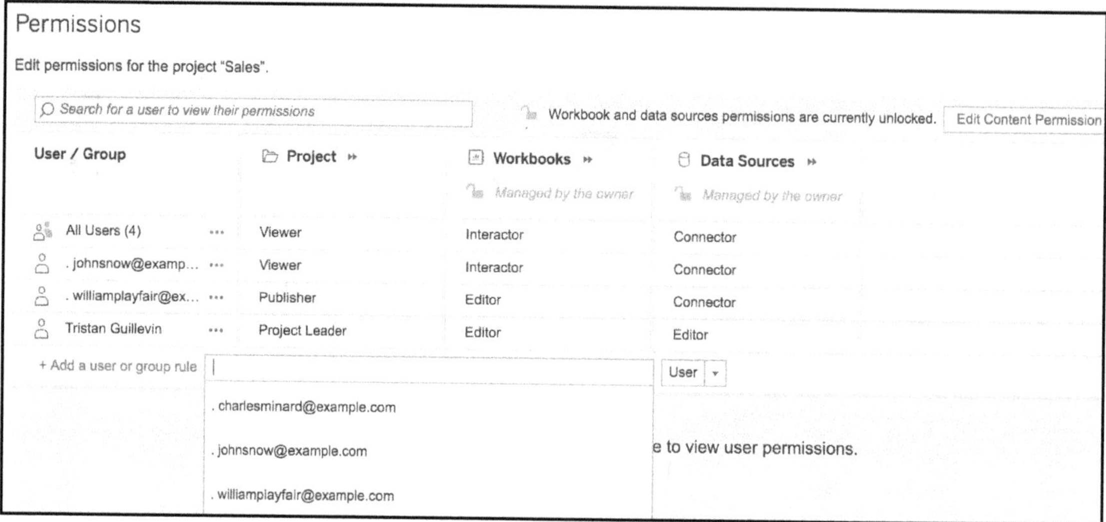

On this menu, you'll always see the **All Users** permissions. You can click on the dots to edit them. You can also click on **Add a user or group rule** to specify new permissions for specific Users or Group. When you edit the permissions, you can see, for each element, a list of pre-configured roles.

If you click on the arrows next to an element (Project, Workbooks, or Data Sources), you get more detail and the possibility to edit each permission individually. Each Permission can be allowed (green), denied (red), or unspecified (grey). To edit an individual Permission, click on its box.

Here's an example of a Permissions edition with a detailed view for Workbooks:

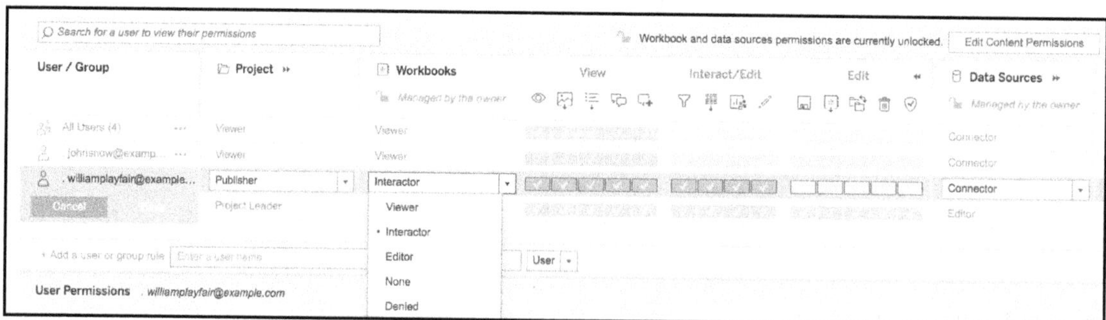

Know that all options are not available for all elements. Here's the complete list of Permissions, grouped by elements where they appear:

- **Global permissions**:
    - **View** : Specifies whether a user can see the element
    - **Save** : Overwrites the existing element on the server
- **Project permissions**:
    - **Project leader** : Someone with a project leader Permission has all Permissions on that project
- **Workbook and Data Sources Permissions**:
    - **Download** / : Downloads the Data Source or the Workbook
    - **Delete** : Removes the element from the server
    - **Set Permissions** : Gives us the ability to change and define the Permissions
- **Workbook Permissions**:
    - **Download image** : Downloads an image of the visualization
    - **Download summary data** : Downloads a summary of the data in a visualization
    - **View comments** : Sees the comments posted under a visualization
    - **Add comments** : Adds comments under a visualization
    - **Filter** : Uses the Filters available and the **Keep Only** and **Exclude** features
    - **Download full data** : Downloads the complete data used in a visualization, with all the rows and columns
    - **Share customized** : Gives us the ability to create and share a customized view
    - **Web edit** : Opens the Tableau Server edition window where a user can modify the visualization or create new ones
    - **Move** : Changes the Project of a Workbook

- **Data Sources Permissions**:
    - **Connect** : Gives us the ability to connect to the Data Sources to create further analysis on Tableau Server or Tableau Desktop

With those Permissions, you can control who has access to what on Tableau Server. You can, for example, allow only a few users to access your Workbook. But what if you want to control what those users can see? Let's say that, based on the Sample-Superstore Data Source, you want to control the Region that the users can see. To do that, you need to set a User Filter.

User Filters

User Filters are among Sets on Tableau Desktop and are based on a Dimension. Depending on who is the current logged-in user on Tableau Server, you can what data the user sees:

1. To add a User Filter, click on **Server** in the top menu, go to **Create a User Filter**, and choose the Field to secure. The following screenshot illustrates the creation of a User Filter on **Region...**:

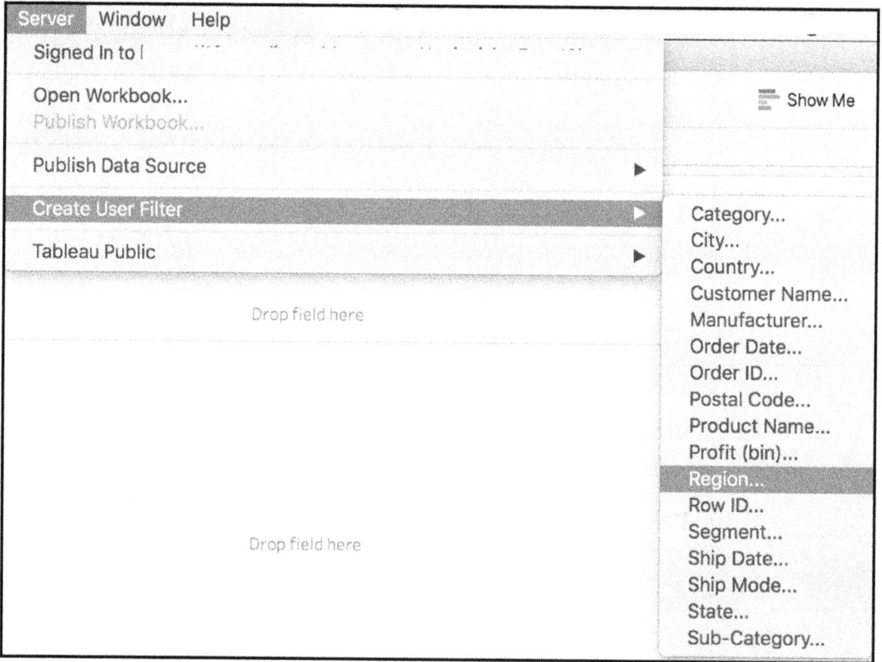

2. Tableau opens a new window where you can select, on the left, a User or a Group and select the values of the field that the User or Group can see.
3. Once you've created the User Filter, you'll see a new set in your Data Source.
4. To use a User Filter, add the corresponding set to the Filter shelf or, better, as a Data Source filter (with **Use all** option).

The reason it's better to add a User Filter on the Data Source filters rather than the Filter shelf is to increase the security. If you put a User Filter in the Filter shelf, and if a User can download or edit the Workbook, they can remove the User Filter from the Filters shelf, and they'll have access to all the data. Also, if someone starts a new analysis based on this Data Source, they'll also have access to all the data. Always put the User Filter on the Data Source Filters to make sure that no one can access data they're not supposed to see.

Now, to illustrate the usage of a User Filter, let's see an example with the Sample-Superstore Data Source. For this example, I created five Groups on Tableau Server: *Central*, *South*, *West*, *East*, and *Top Management*.

It's not a problem if you can't create the same groups as me to replicate this example. Just use existing Groups or Users on your Tableau Server, you can't break anything.

Let's start:

1. Create a new **User Filter** on **Region** and name it `Region Filter`.
2. In the User Filter configuration window, for each Group, select the members of the field that they are allowed to see. For example, for the **West** group, select the **West** value. For the **Top Management** group, select all members, and for **All Users**, select none.

Here's an example of the configuration for the **West** group:

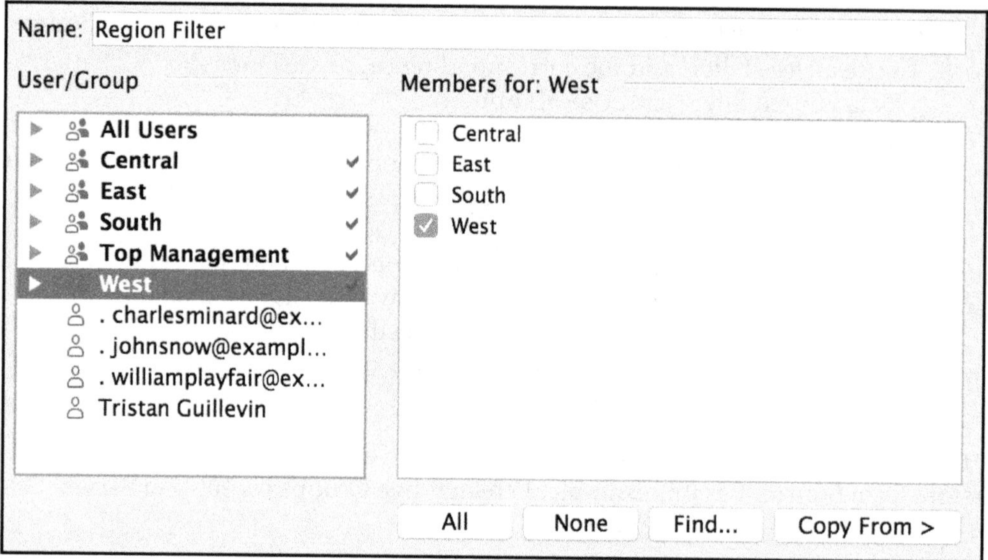

3. Build a simple visualization: double click on **State**, then add **Sales** on **Color**.
4. Put the **Region Filter Set** in the Filter shelf to test it. If you're not inside one of the Groups where we define access, you should not see anything.

5. At the very bottom of the Tableau window, you can see the current logged-in User in Tableau Server, as framed in the following screenshot:

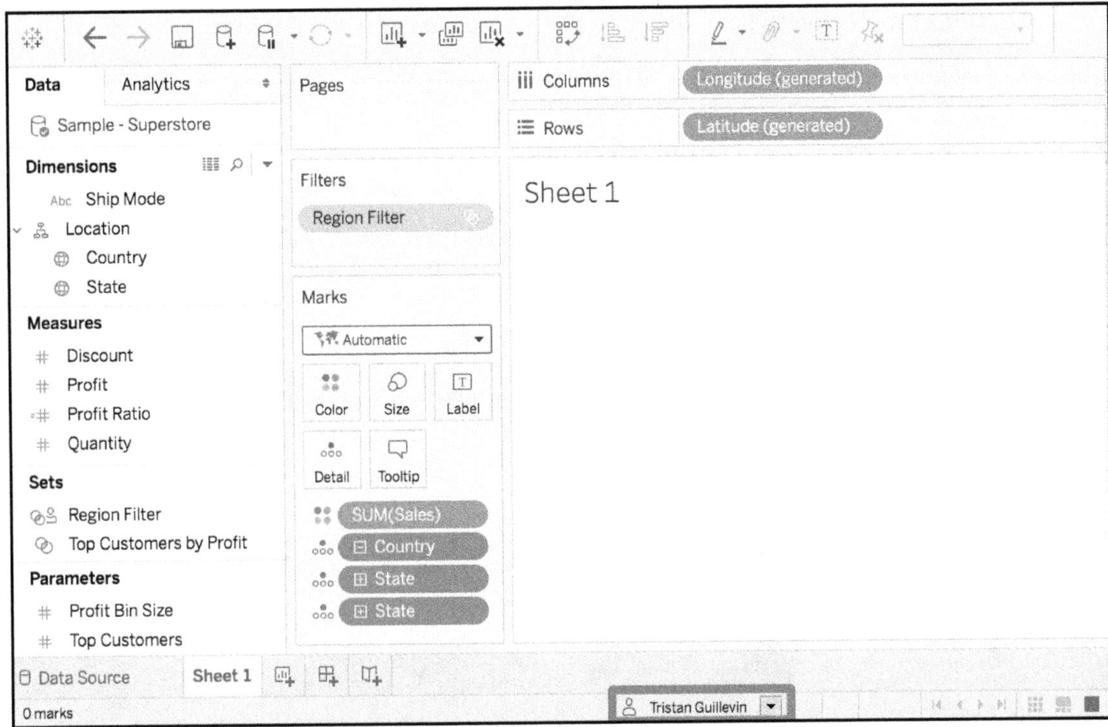

6. Beside the name of the logged-in User, you can click on the arrow to select another User or Group.
7. With this option, choose the **West** group and the User Filter will automatically filter the Region to keep only the **West** value, as you can see here:

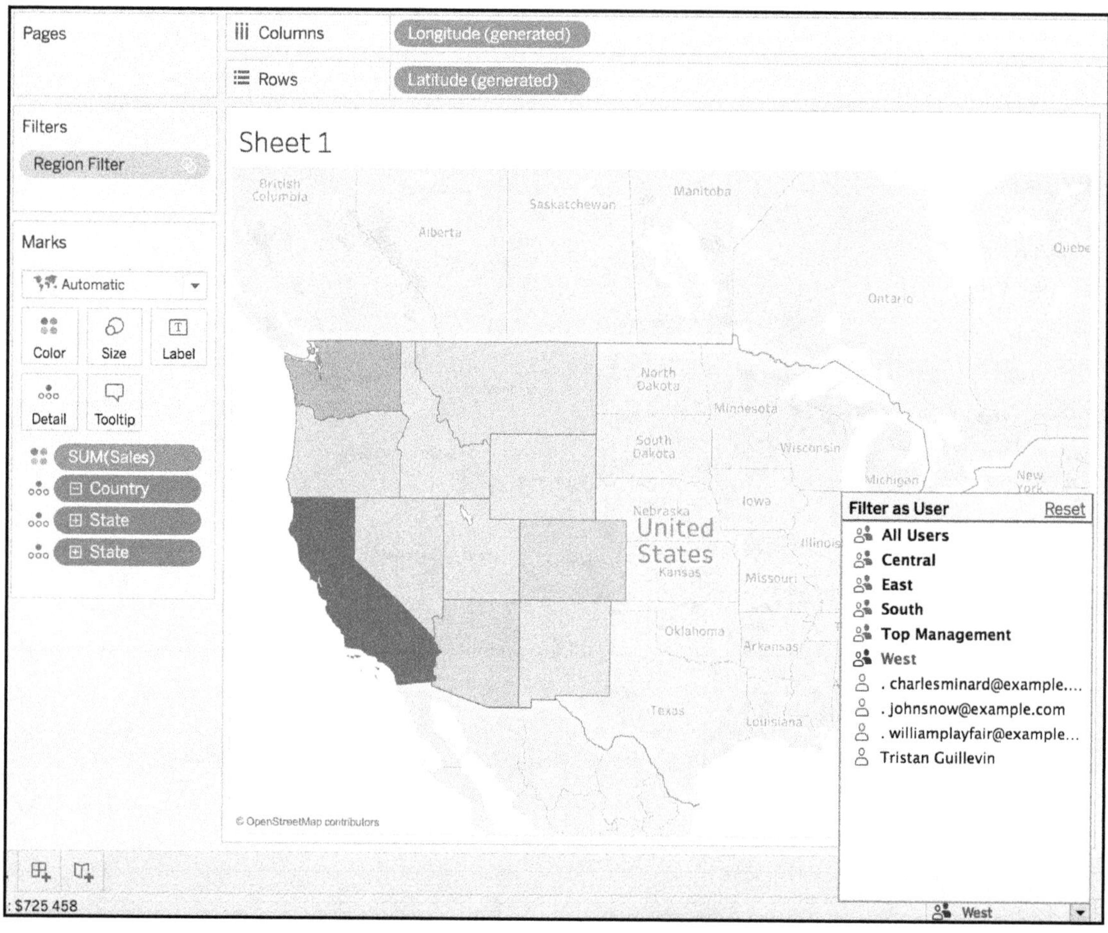

8. You can test the same with **Top Management**—all the regions will be displayed:

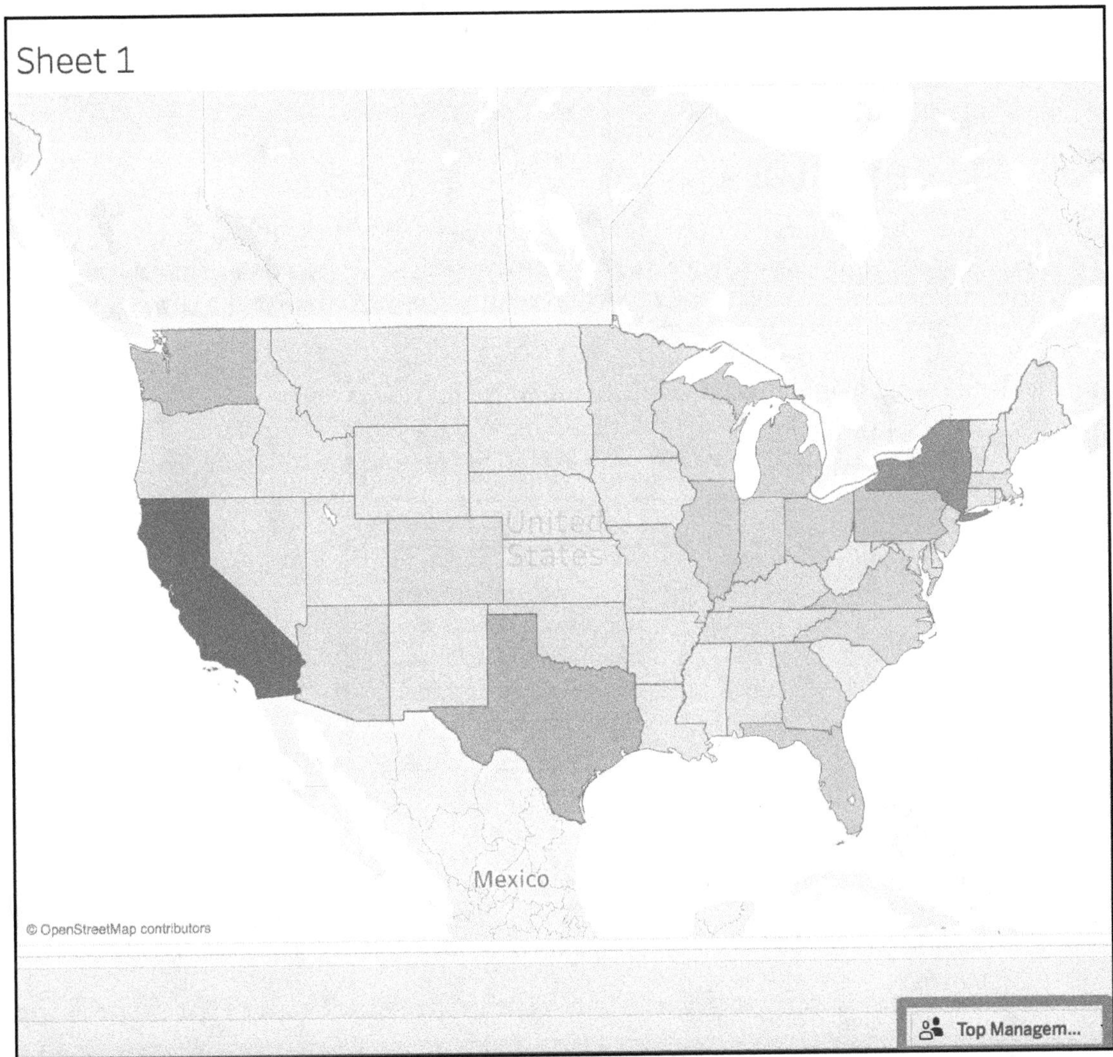

9. When you're confident that the User Filter works fine, you can remove it from the Filters shelf.
10. Right-click on the Data Source and select **Edit Data Source Filters**.
11. Click on the **Add** button, and select the **Region** Filter.
12. Select the **Use all** option, and click on **OK**. The User Filter is applied on all the data source, thereby enhancing the security of your data.

This is the first way of securing your data. As you may have guessed, if you have hundreds of Users to give access to and hundreds of different values in a Field, the User Filter will be extremely long to create and impossible to maintain. In those cases, we create a Row-level filter.

Row-level filters

To create a Row-lever filter, your Data Source must contain a field with the name of the User. It is a great solution when access is already defined in your data. This option uses a Tableau function: `USERNAME()`. This function returns the username of the current logged-in User.

Again, the best way to understand it is with an example. You can reproduce the tutorial with the Users and Groups in your Tableau Server and the Sample-Superstore Data Source. For this tutorial, I've created three Users in Tableau Server and the following Excel File, which I named `User Access`:

Region	User
Central	johnsnow@example.com
West	johnsnow@example.com
East	johnsnow@example.com
South	johnsnow@example.com
West	williamplayfair@example.com
Central	charlesminard@example.com

In the **Excel File**, we specified that:

- *John Snow* has access to all the Regions *(do not confuse John Snow, a famous epidemiologist who discovered, in 1854, that Cholera deaths were clustered around the water pumps in London thanks to data visualization, with Jon Snow, who knows nothing)*
- *William Playfair* only has access to *West*
- *Charles Minard* only has access to *Central*

Here's the step-by-step guide of how to create a Row-level filter between the data and Tableau Server:

1. Open Tableau and connect to the **Sample-Superstore** Excel File.
2. Add a new Excel connection to the **User Access** file.
3. Create a cross-database join between **Orders** and **User Access** on the common **Region** field:

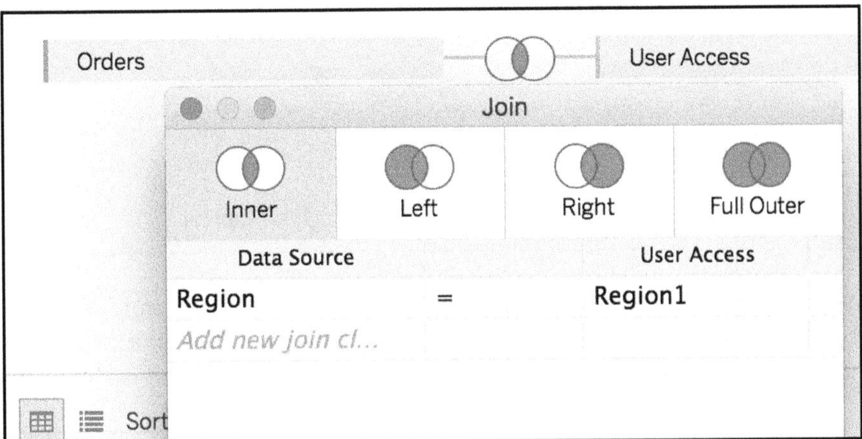

This join duplicates the data by the number of Users, but as you never show multiple users at the same time, it's not a problem.

4. On a Worksheet, create a new Calculated Field, name it `User has access`, and write the `USERNAME()=[User]` calculation. This calculation returns `True` if the current logged-in User is the same as the **User** field in the Data Source.

5. Create a new Data Source filter, add the **User has access** Calculated Field, and keep only the **True** value. The Data Source filter should look as follows:

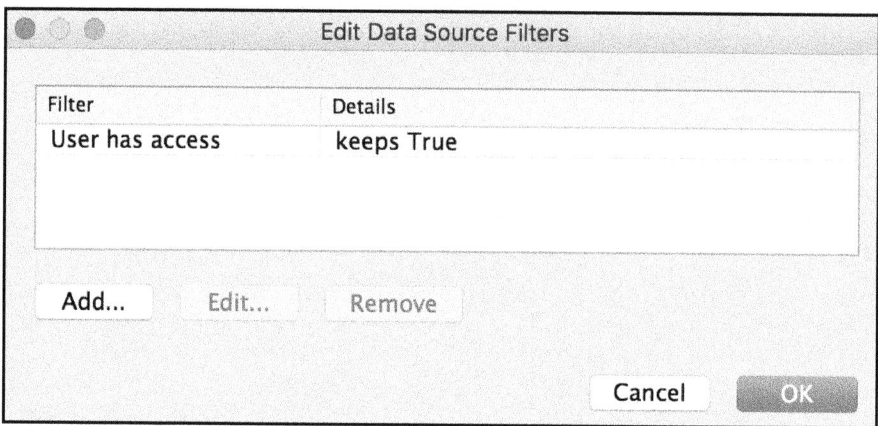

6. You can test the Filter by selecting different Users on Tableau Server with the bottom menu. Here are two examples with the user *John Snow*, who has access to all regions, and *Charles Minard*, who only has access to the *Central* region:

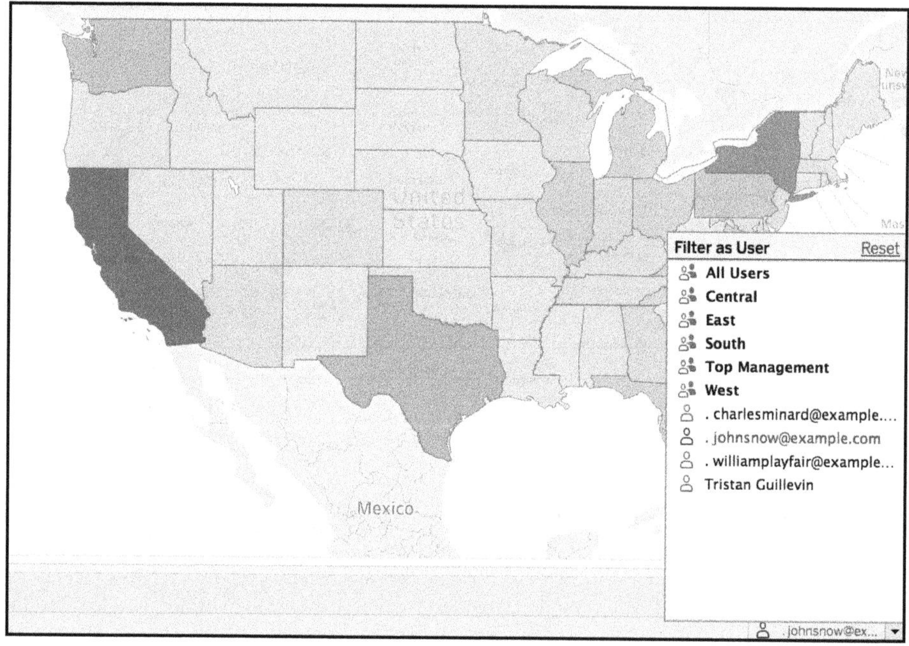

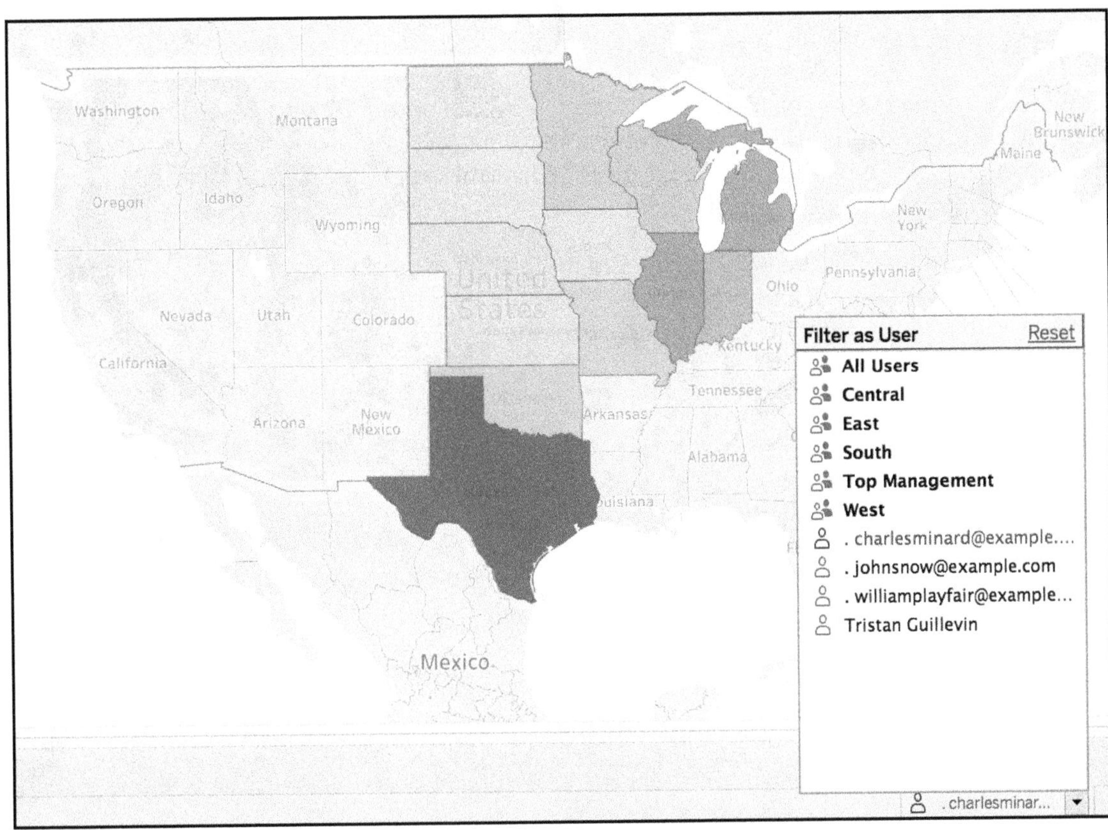

With this solution, you let the data control the security. It's a great way to handle complex situations because you can create Row-level filters based on multiple fields.

Before Tableau 2018.3, the only drawback was the data duplication: when using an extract, all the duplicated lines must be generated, which makes the Extract gigantic. Since Tableau 2018.3, you can use the multiple table schema when creating an Extract with joins. It drastically decreases the Extract size when using a Row-Level filter.

Summary

In this last technical chapter, you learned how to secure your data and content on Tableau Server. The Permissions allow you to control who can see your work and what power they have over it (download, save, edit, and more). On Tableau Desktop, with User Filters and Row-Level filters, you can control what the users can see in your data.

This book is almost finished. We've covered all the technical aspects of Tableau. The last chapter is an invitation to join the Tableau Community with tips on how to get better and better each day with different Community Projects.

14
How to Keep Growing Your Skills

That's it! You are now all set to use Tableau in a professional environment. Starting with connecting to your data, building your data source, then your first visualizations and Dashboards to publish all your work in a secure and online environment. But there is still a lot to discover and many ways to become better at using Tableau.

In this short chapter, we'll speak about:

- The Tableau Community
- Tableau Public
- Community projects
- Ambassadors, Zen Masters, and Iron Viz

Let's start with the reason Tableau is the best tool for data visualization: the Community.

The Tableau Community

Tableau is an excellent tool for many reasons. But there are a lot of great tools for data visualization. If you ask me why Tableau is better than the others, my answer would be, *the Community*.

When I started using Tableau, the Tableau Community Forums helped me a lot. No questions are left unanswered, and you'll find a lot of people eager to help you. Don't hesitate to ask any questions here: `https://community.tableau.com/community/forums`.

The Community is all about sharing. There are many events where the Tableau Community gather to share. The **Tableau User Group** (**TUG**) is a regional event (check whether there's one near your area!) where senior users meet new users and discuss new features, tips, use cases, and more. It's also a great place to share pizzas and beers!

Don't be sad if there is no TUG near you; there are many online events, such as the Fringe Festival, organized by the Tableau Community: `http://www.thefringefestival.rocks/`.

Of course, there are also two major official events: the Tableau Conference in the US and the European Tableau Conference in Europe. It is the biggest Tableau event and the best place to meet people, discover all the new features to be released and cheer on your favorite competitor at the Iron Viz event.

You'll find all the events, groups, forums, links, and webinars here: `https://www.tableau.com/community`.

The other great way to learn is on Tableau Public.

Tableau Public

Tableau Public is software, similar to Tableau Desktop, that you can download and use for free with some limitations: you need to publish your work online in a public environment, and you don't have access to all the connectors available in Tableau Desktop.

Tableau Public is, in fact, much more than that.

Tableau Public is like a social network, but while people are sharing pictures of their cats and kids on Facebook, you can only find the best visualizations available in Tableau Public. As we are data lovers, here are some figures: 250,000 Tableau Public users have published more than 1,000,000 Workbooks, generating more than 1,000,000,000 views.

On the Tableau Public website, you can find a **Viz Of The Day** section on the homepage (every day, a new Workbook is promoted by Tableau: `https://public.tableau.com/en-us/s/`), and many Featured visualizations in different categories (Greatest Hits, Sports, Social Goof, and so on). You can find a list of the current Featured Authors, a blog, and many resources to keep learning. You can also search for any author or interest. But wait, the best is yet to come.

At the bottom of every visualization published in Tableau Public, there are some buttons to open the visualization in fullscreen, share, and the best: download. When you click on the download button, you can get an image, the data, a crosstab, a PDF, and – *are you ready?* – the Workbook itself! Even the most beautiful Workbooks can usually be downloaded (it's the author's choice). It is one of the greatest ways to learn. I discover a lot by downloading the Workbooks and figuring out how the authors built them.

Creating a Tableau Public account is very simple. Once you have an account, you can start to follow authors you like and publish Workbooks. If you post a visualization, you can make it featured, delete it, or hide it with the icons you see here:

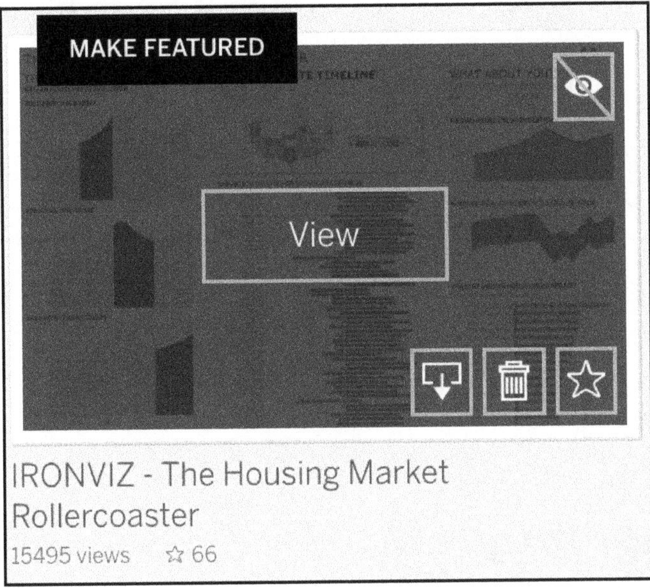

Finally, for all your published visualizations, you can edit the description and specify whether you'll allow the Workbook and its data to be downloaded. It may be against the philosophy of Tableau Public to refuse it to be downloaded, but some companies use Tableau Public as a communication tool, and they can't share all their data.

Here's what you can edit on your published Workbooks:

Title

IRONVIZ - The Housing Market Rollercoaster

Make sure your viz has a good title so people don't pass it by when they're browsing Tableau Public.

Permalink

Add URL

Plan on embedding your viz? This is an excellent way to drive traffic to your site.

Description

This workbook was created in 20 minutes, live, in front of 10,000 people during the IronViz competition in Las Vegas.

A great description can really improve your search results ranking.

Toolbar Settings

- [x] Show view controls *Undo, Redo, Revert*
- [x] Show author profile link
- [x] Allow workbook and its data to be downloaded by others

Other Settings

- [x] Show workbook sheets as tabs

The main reason why people don't share Workbooks in Tableau Public is that they don't know what data to share. The next section resolves that problem.

Community projects

This section is all about growing your Tableau skills. There are many projects created by the Community for the Community. Participating in those projects doesn't engage you in anything, you can only learn and become better. For the majority of those projects, people interact through Twitter, so I advise you to create an account to follow those projects.

Here are some Community projects:

- **Viz For Social Good – #VizForSocialGood** by *Chloe Tseng*: This project gives you the opportunity to work for non-profit organizations such as UNICEF and the United Nations. There is a new project almost every month, with a deadline to respect. You can register as a volunteer to be informed of new projects. At the end of every project, the non-profit organization chooses one visualization to feature on its communication channels. As Chloe says:

We help mission-driven organizations to promote social good and understand their own data through beautiful and informative data visualization.

Viz For Social Good was awarded a Silver for Community at the 2017 Information is Beautiful Awards. All the information that is required to join is mentioned here: `https://www.vizforsocialgood.com`.

- **Make Over Monday – *#MakeOverMonday***—by *Eva Murray* and *Andy Kriebel*: Probably the most-followed project and the best way to practice your creativity in Tableau. Every Sunday they share a new dataset to visualize in Tableau. On Wednesday, there is a webinar where Eva and Andy review some visualizations (*#MMVizReview*) and, during the weekend, they publish a blog post with all the lessons learned and the favorite makeovers. The best definition is on their website:

Makeover Monday is your weekly learning and development appointment with yourself and hundreds of passionate data people. For free!

You'll find all the information, data sets, and links here: `https://www.makeovermonday.co.uk/`.

- **Workout Wednesday – *#WorkOutWednesday***—currently run by Rody Zachovich, Ann Jackson, Luke Stanke, Curtis Harris, and guests: The most challenging Community project. Every Wednesday, they share a new visualization and the Dataset required to reproduce it. The goal is to rebuild the same visualization. Of course, it's more difficult than you think. If **Make Over Monday** helps you practice the creativity, **Workout Wednesday** is all about technical challenges. As you can read on their website:

Workout Wednesday is a set of weekly challenges [...] designed to test your knowledge of Tableau and help you kick on in your development.

Find all the challenges at `http://www.workout-wednesday.com/weekly-overview/`.

There are other projects such as **Data For a Cause** *#DataForACause* (`www.olgatsubiks.com/data-for-a-cause`) by Olga Tsubiks, and **Sports Viz Sunday** *#SportsVizSunday* (`https://data.world/sportsvizsunday`) by Simon Beaumont and Spencer Baucke, that I invite you to follow.

As you can see, there are many ways to learn and become better at using Tableau. Maybe, after some time, you'll compete as an Iron Viz contestant, or you'll be recognized as one of the Ambassadors or Zen Masters. Don't know what I'm talking about? The next – and last – section explains everything.

Ambassadors, Zen Masters, and Iron Viz

When you start in the Tableau Community, it may be hard to know whom to follow. Tableau has decided to help you by recognizing the investment and spirit of some people in the Community.

Ambassadors

The first set of amazing people are the **Ambassadors**. They are split into four groups:

- **Forums Ambassadors**: They are there to your questions in the Forum
- **Social Media Ambassadors**: They are the social network gurus, follow them to get all the news
- **User Group Leader Ambassadors**: They help the Community meet in real life by organizing the Tableau User Groups
- **Tableau Public Ambassadors**: Check their Tableau Public profiles and be ready to be blown away

Find all the current **Ambassadors** here: `https://www.tableau.com/tableau-ambassadors`.

Zen Masters

The second set of amazing people is the **Zen Masters**. They are the faces of Tableau Community. They passionately dedicate a huge amount of time to help everyone excel in Tableau. They not only create great visualizations, but they also share their knowledge as much as they can. Everyone in the Tableau Community has learned at least one thing from a **Zen Master**.

Discover who the **Zen Masters** are and what they are doing at `https://www.tableau.com/zen-masters`.

Iron Viz

As you enhance your skills, you may want to try to compete against other people in the Community. For that, you have the Iron Viz. The competition is divided into two parts: three qualification contests, the Feeders, and one Final. For the Feeders, only the theme is imposed, and the contestants have approximately one month to find the data and create the best possible visualization. There is one winner per Feeder.

The three winners of the Feeders battle during the Iron Viz Final at the annual Tableau Conference. There is no way to prepare for the Final: build a Workbook from the start, in 20 minutes, live, in front of thousands of screaming people. A jury, composed of four peoples, and the public, vote on Twitter to determine the annual Iron Viz champion. Since 2017, they have also started a European Iron Viz competition.

I advise you to participate. Not for the purpose of winning, but to push yourself further than you've ever gone in Tableau. You cannot lose; either you win, or you learn.

Summary

This chapter, even though it's not technical, is really important. This chapter is the key to continuing your journey with Tableau. This chapter is also my tribute to the Community who kept pushing me higher and higher over the last three years since I started using Tableau.

Even if you don't plan on sharing a lot or getting involved (which is understandable), keep in mind that the Community Forum is the first place to go if you have any questions regarding Tableau. Even though I tried my best to explain all the concepts in this book, no books or training sessions can cover every use case you will encounter in real life. Also, if you're searching for resources, blogs, inspiration, or webinars, you'll find it on Tableau Public or through the Community Projects.

Thanks for purchasing and reading this book. I truly hope that you've learned a lot and that you'll use Tableau with the same passion I do.

Other Books You May Enjoy

If you enjoyed this book, you may be interested in these other books by Packt:

Advanced Analytics with R and Tableau
Jen Stirrup

ISBN: 9781786460110

- Integrate Tableau's analytics with the industry-standard, statistical prowess of R.
- Make R function calls in Tableau, and visualize R functions with Tableau using RServe.
- Use the CRISP-DM methodology to create a roadmap for analytics investigations.
- Implement various supervised and unsupervised learning algorithms in R to return values to Tableau.
- Make quick, cogent, and data-driven decisions for your business using advanced analytical techniques such as forecasting, predictions, association rules, clustering, classification, and other advanced Tableau/R calculated field functions.

Mastering Tableau
David Baldwin

ISBN: 9781784397692

- Create a worksheet that can display the current balance for any given period in time
- Recreate a star schema from in a data warehouse in Tableau
- Combine level of detail calculations with table calculations, sets, and parameters
- Create custom polygons to build filled maps for area codes in the USA
- Visualize data using a set of analytical and advanced charting techniques
- Know when to use Tableau instead of PowerPoint
- Build a dashboard and export it to PowerPoint

Leave a review - let other readers know what you think

Please share your thoughts on this book with others by leaving a review on the site that you bought it from. If you purchased the book from Amazon, please leave us an honest review on this book's Amazon page. This is vital so that other potential readers can see and use your unbiased opinion to make purchasing decisions, we can understand what our customers think about our products, and our authors can see your feedback on the title that they have worked with Packt to create. It will only take a few minutes of your time, but is valuable to other potential customers, our authors, and Packt. Thank you!

Index

E

F

U

V

W

Y

Z

CPSIA information can be obtained
at www.ICGtesting.com
Printed in the USA
FFHW011559261218
49989096-54690FF

9 781788 838689